INSTRUCTION

§

Chandler Publications in

EDUCATIONAL PSYCHOLOGY

DAVID G. RYANS, *Editor*

INSTRUCTION

Some Contemporary Viewpoints

EDITED BY

LAURENCE SIEGEL

Louisiana State University

ഗ

CHANDLER PUBLISHING COMPANY
124 Spear Street
San Francisco, California 94105

ഗ

Library of Congress Catalog Card No. 67–10174
Copyright © 1967 by Chandler Publishing Company
PRINTED IN THE UNITED STATES OF AMERICA

Contents

ℰ

Preface

☙

IT FALLS UPON ME, AS MIDWIFE FOR THIS ENDEAVOR, TO MAKE SOME remarks about the purposes and history of this book. In view of the diversities of opinion comprising its substance, it is a little hazardous for an editor to attempt to write even a preface with which all contributors will agree.

Several factors conspire to make evident the need for a book presenting contemporary theories about instruction:

First, of course, there are the well-documented enrollment statistics. Both the population of school-age youngsters and the percentage of secondary school graduates seeking a higher education are increasing. Second, educational technology has been developing rapidly. Instructional television and programed instruction, for example, are no longer novelties; and computers are increasing the efficiency of educational administration, classroom management, and access to library resources. Third, society's demands upon the educational enterprise are changing. These changes entail not only the provision of increased opportunities for formal education to all segments of the society, but altered conceptions about the purposes of education in response to changing patterns of work. There is no point to vocational training for jobs that are becoming increasingly automated. Finally, as the behavioral sciences matured, it was inevitable that scholars in these fields would direct more of their attention to classroom teaching and learning. They have been materially aided in this endeavor during recent years by the availability of substantial funds from philanthropic foundations and from the federal government for studying and implementing educational change.

Out of all of this has come an interest in educational innovation directed toward two ends not mutually exclusive: quantitative and qualitative improvement. From a quantitative standpoint, schools are big business. The United States Office of Education has projected a national expenditure of about $43 billion for all elementary and secondary day schools and higher education in 1969–1970. This is an increase from about $26 billion for the same purposes a decade earlier. Even so, it is certain that we will experience significant shortages of teachers and academic facilities.

Qualitatively, the "pursuit of excellence" has become a household phrase. It is not enough merely to accommodate students in school buildings or on campuses. What we do to them has taken on a special kind of meaning that, if not unique to our era, at least has about it an air of urgency.

There is no shortage of questions about practices, curriculum, administration, and learning that may be asked in an attempt to effect the desired quantitative and qualitative improvements. There is likewise no shortage of answers. The educational enterprise has been studied for a long, long time. Recently, two books in particular, Sanford's *The American College* and Gage's *Handbook of Research on Teaching*, have compiled significant blocks of current knowledge about teaching and learning.

From this imposing mass of empirical findings grows the conviction that formal education is relatively long on practice and short on theory. Current practices often reflect, on the one hand, considerable inertia and, on the other, an almost frantic search for innovation to alleviate currently pressing problems. Although it is true that educational innovations are usually assessed, the yardstick for the assessment tends to be whatever technique we have used in the past (that is, "conventional" instruction), and the disturbing conclusion tends often to be that it apparently makes little difference *how* students are taught.

This book is committed to the idea that it *does* make a difference, but that this difference has been obscured by the relative lack of adequate theory. A sound theoretical base can (1) suggest better educational practices than are now prevalent; (2) permit predictions about the likely effectiveness or ineffectiveness of contemplated innovations, thereby offering educational administrators a highly practical basis for making judgments; and (3) guide future research efforts in systematic rather than fragmented directions.

Thus the purpose of this book is to present a sample of contemporary theoretical formulations each written by the person responsible for that formulation. The sample is not comprehensive from the standpoint of the disciplinary orientations of the contributors. They are all psychologists who have considered instructional problems with their own particular orientations toward explaining human behavior. This disciplinary bias was deliberate. In selecting contributors, they and I attempted to provide a representative spread of theoretical positions. Thus, although not all currently active educational theorists from the behavioral sciences have written for this book, those that have written cover a broad theoretical spectrum.

The intended organization of the book into clusters of formulations emphasizing (1) teaching, (2) learning, and (3) both teaching and learning was one of the determining factors in selecting contributors. The instructions to each were simply to summarize his own present theoretical position concerning instructional matters. The resultant papers were all specifically written for inclusion in this book.

It is not entirely correct to describe what emerged as either a symposium or a collection of papers. Although writing styles differ, the papers fit together with an internal logic and integrity. Thus the book does, in fact, display the range of theoretical positions concerning instruction now held by psychologists. And this display is arranged so the reader can identify the major theoretical issues and arguments.

We hope the book will serve both reference and text objectives. As a source book, it is addressed to those of our colleagues in psychology, sociology, education, and other fields who are professionally concerned with the course and facilitation of human learning in formal instructional settings. Although the book is not specifically written for educational administrators, they might well wish to examine their present and contemplated practices in the light of the formulations herein presented.

As a text, the book is intended for graduate students in certain areas of psychology and in education. It is particularly pertinent to the interests of students of instructional research, educational psychology, learning theory, curriculum, and educational administration.

On behalf of all of the chapter authors as well as myself, I acknowledge our grateful appreciation to Mrs. Mary Kay Grimes who either typed or supervised the typing of the manuscript, and handled all of the clerical matters associated with its preparation in her usual capable fashion.

In addition I am singly indebted to my wife, Dr. Lila Corkland Siegel, for her professional criticisms and personal support while the book was being assembled.

LAURENCE SIEGEL

Miami University
Oxford, Ohio
May 1965

INSTRUCTION

PART·I·

INTRODUCTION

∽

During the past two decades education has become the subject of research and thinking by behavioral scientists in a new and exciting way. The reasons for the resurgence of professional attention to educational problems by representatives of these allied disciplines are diverse. They include such factors as international competition for technological superiority; enrollment pressures generated both by population increases and societal demands; financial assistance for research on education from funds, foundations, and the federal government; improvements in behavioral-science methodologies appropriate to educational investigations; and the inclinations of behavioral scientists to help shape the future development of formal education as a significant social institution.

Even before the recent revival of interest in allied disciplines, however, the voluminous literature considering educational problems both philosophically and empirically documents the tremendous amount of continuing activity in this field. Hilgard's *Theories of Learning and Instruction*[1] and Gage's *Handbook of Research on Teaching*[2] are heroic attempts to bring order to much of this literature. At least two things are impressive when the massive body of educational research is considered as a whole. First, as Ericksen observed in his review of the *Handbook*,[3]

[1] E. R. Hilgard, ed., *op. cit.* (Nat. Soc. Stud. Educ., 63rd Yearb., Part I; Chicago: University of Chicago Press, 1964).

[2] N. L. Gage, ed., *op. cit.* (Amer. Educ. Res. Assn.; Chicago: Rand McNally, 1963).

[3] S. C. Ericksen, Review of *Handbook of research on teaching*, *Contemp. Psychol.*, 1964, *9*, 49–50.

educational studies are relatively long on empiricism and relatively short on theory. Second, the yield from educational studies seems to have been relatively low; nonsignificant differences are reported with monotonous regularity.

In preparing this book, the writers have sought specifically to contribute to the theoretical underpinnings of the instructional enterprise. By presenting several theoretical positions and methodological models, the authors hope further to organize what is now known about instruction and to suggest some future directions for empirical study.

The two chapters in Part I introduce the substantive presentations comprising the remainder of the book. Chapter 1 examines the dominant concerns of writers about educational problems prior to the recent rapid development of knowledge and technique in the behavioral sciences. This chapter provides a contextual background for comparing and assessing more contemporary theories. Chapter 2 begins by considering certain methodological impediments to testing instructional theories and ends by describing the organization of the remainder of the book.

1

An Overview
of Historical Formulations

JAMES M. HEDEGARD

University of Michigan

∽

HISTORICALLY, THEORIES OF INSTRUCTION HAVE BEEN BASED ON A COMBINA-
tion of observation and conjecture about epistemological, metaphysical, and other philosophical problems. The "good intentions" of these
theorists were often coupled with strong doctrinal religious viewpoints
interfering with thorough explorations of the problems addressed by
their theories. These factors limit the applicability of early theories to
contemporary instructional settings. In addition, methodological refinements in techniques of observation and logical analysis have inevitably led to the rejection of certain early theoretical positions. Nevertheless, many of the early theorists showed great insight in setting out
problems or their solutions in ways quite new to their own times.

 This chapter catalogues the central concerns of a number of the
early theories of instruction. Thus, it provides a historical context for
contemporary theoretical approaches. All but two of the theories
represented here deal with times between the Hellenistic civilization
and about 1920. The exceptions, Neill (1960) and Ashton-Warner
(1963), are included because they offer rather original solutions to
central problems of instruction. Theoretical positions from the Near
and Far East are not considered even though their exclusion limits the
range of subjects encompassed by the chapter.

 The theories are analyzed phenotypically; that is, the explicit statement of the theory limits the discussion, with one major exception. Because morality has been from time to time a subject in the curriculum, theories that did not explicitly address themselves to moral aspects of education are examined for implicit assumptions.

Philosophical Presuppositions

Theories of instruction state how a teacher is to teach something to a student. Their aim is for the student to come to know something. Therefore, they must assume some definition of what it means "to know," as well as some resolution of questions concerning (1) the relation between knowing and doing, and (2) the structure of knowledge. These are epistemological questions. Thus, theories of instruction presuppose epistemological positions.[1] Theories of instruction need not *be* epistemological theories since they may theorize only about the *technique* of instruction.

In a very real sense, certain metaphysical issues must be resolved prior to setting out a theory of instruction. Theories of instruction invariably prescribe certain kinds of "essential" knowledge—essential not only in the sense of "It is essential to learn X before learning Y" but also in the sense of "Knowledge of X is essential to the conduct of life." In the former sense, the selection of X, given the desirability of knowing Y, is usually justified on epistemological grounds. In the latter sense, it would seem the selection of X must be justified on metaphysical (or, in certain cases, ethical or aesthetic) grounds, especially when X is selected following a search for "the true," "the real," and so on.

In the past much more so than in the present, theories of instruction have also been theories of the curriculum, presenting the range of the content of instruction as well as its form(s). Ethical and aesthetic presuppositions underlie such selection. What the student is to read, to sing, to draw, or to look at are partly selected by the teacher or the theorist, according to the latter's aesthetic judgment of what, for the

[1] One deficiency of a study of theories of instruction which does not consider Hindu or Buddhist writings is a neglect of the issue of quality of experience. The discussion of *kinds* of consciousness is unusual in Western educational thought; an exception is Dewey (1958 [1934]).

student, is worth reading, singing, drawing, or looking at. Likewise, there is strong evidence that some of the material the child is told (or "permitted") to read in school contains strong moral pronouncements (Child, Potter, and Levine, 1946). There is a danger in neglecting moral and aesthetic tone when the curriculum is established. Such neglect imposes great responsibility on the good will of the teacher and on the general dissemination of the "central moral and aesthetic values of Western culture."

Thus, this chapter consists of an inventory of dimensions relevant to instruction and a description of the poles defining these dimensions, followed by brief descriptions of some of the major issues raised by these theories—issues somewhat neglected and certainly unresolved.

DIMENSIONS CENTRAL TO HISTORICAL THEORIES OF INSTRUCTION

I have attempted to condense the variation among a number of early theories of instruction into the nine more or less separate dimensions shown in Table 1-1. The poles of each of these dimensions are also displayed in the table. The remainder of the chapter is given to a discussion of these nine dimensions, explaining in greater detail my perceptions of the poles and the various nuances of intermediate placement on these dimensions.

1. Structure of the Learning Process

Montessori (1948 [1909]) exemplified well the view that learning involves the development of relatively independent faculties. She regarded the prime task of educating the young child (3–6 years) as developing the senses and the capacities for discrimination among the various objects in the environment. Each sense and each dimension of discrimination within a sense was to be developed separately. The discriminations sought proceeded from coarse to fine, first involving stimuli varying in only one dimension, then involving stimuli varying among several dimensions.

Dewey (1916) exemplified the "unitary-process pole" of this dimension. In *Experience and Education*, he attacked faculty theories and emphasized the coherence of behavior, suggesting that education

TABLE 1–1. DIMENSIONS CENTRAL TO HISTORICAL THEORIES OF INSTRUCTION.

	Dimension	Poles of the Dimension
1	Structure of the learning process	A unitary process vs. A set of relatively independent faculties, skills, and so on
2	Modeling and identification	Necessary prerequisites for learning vs. Irrelevancies for learning
3	Learner behavior vis-à-vis the teacher	Active vs. Reactive and passive
4	Reward and punishment	Determinants of instructional effectiveness vs. Irrelevancies for instructional effectiveness
5	Moral development	Central objective of instruction vs. Irrelevancy for objectives of instruction
6	Learner motives and emotions	Importance in structuring educational experiences vs. Irrelevancy for structuring educational experiences
7	Relationship between school and home	Provision for interrelated experiences vs. Provision for separate, unrelated experiences
8	Adaptability as an instructional outcome	Capacity for change as primary goal of education vs. Development of circumscribed behaviors as primary goal of education
9	Ego development as an instructional outcome	Goal of instruction vs. Irrelevancy for instruction

functioned best when the student has a real problem to solve, when his motives are articulated, and when complex behavior is demanded for a solution.

Whereas both Montessori and Dewey regarded "intrinsic interest" as essential to learning, they differed in their views of how such interest is to be stimulated. Dewey contended that a "real" situation is required to generate this interest, thereby keeping a student working at a task to solution. Furthermore, he maintained that real situations are complex, and therefore could not be abstracted and simplified for the learning situation. Montessori, on the other hand, saw great interest as necessary for motivating the student to carry out a long series of discrete discrimination tasks with a set of stimulus objects. She argued that if the teacher cannot arouse the student's interest with a particular set of objects, he must try another set until he finds one that captures and holds the student's attention.

In William James's thinking (1922 [1899]), the unit of learning was more like Dewey's than Montessori's. James spoke of "learning behaviors," instead of "solving problems" or "developing capacities for discriminating stimuli." He argued that generalization sums over a smaller range of stimuli than is often realized and, therefore, that learning must be fairly specific. For example, in examining the utility of "faculty development," James argued that the ability to memorize cannot be developed—only the ability to memorize a certain kind of thing. Therefore, James suggested that students be presented with diverse classroom experiences.

The Hellenic Greeks saw language learning at least as the development of a great variety of independent skills (Marrou, 1956). They so denied the existence of generalizable elements of language learning that every conceivable element of spoken and written language was memorized by the pupil. Even if a particular construction of letters existed only in combination with others (or not at all), it was presented as an isolated language element with a unique spelling and pronunciation to be learned.

2. Modeling and Identification

A striking example of the encouragement of modeling after a specific adult figure is found in Homeric Greece. The noble youth were given mentors to teach them the arts of war, the conduct of state, and so on. The youth's respect, awe, and desire to emulate—plus the mentor's desire to be respected, held in awe, and emulated—often led to great affection, to love, and many times to a physical homosexual relationship. Although the latter was *officially* condemned and punishable, it was usually tolerated and (unofficially) even encouraged to ensure the successful training of the youth by the great warrior or orator.

In later times and places, students were often encouraged to regard the teacher as a *partial* model in a less personal and certainly less emotionally involving way. Herbart (1898 [1830–1833]), for example, stated that the history teacher should exemplify what was being taught and should be a direct link to history.

Sometimes, instead of setting the tutor himself as model, educators proposed one or a small set of adult "constructions" as models. Later Greek educators set such a model of the orator. The Jesuits tended to establish the priest or, more generally, the virtuous adult as a model (Schwickerath, 1903). It is noteworthy that theories advocating these relatively fixed adult constructions tended to emphasize close, exacting teaching of specific content as well as character development. Such theories also tended, of necessity, to make morality a central topic of education.

Although abstract, the Jesuit model was embodied by the teacher. The *Ratio Studiorum* (Fitzpatrick, 1933 [Loyola, 1547–1599]) advised that the teacher could attain authority by gaining the students' esteem and affection and by generating fear. These affective responses resulted from the teacher's "manliness," that is, his gravity, firmness, and prudent consistency. That the teacher was to keep himself distant from the student and thus be a somewhat depersonalized and partial model is evident from the rule forbidding him from talking with his students outside of class except in an open place, and then only for the "greater edification" of the student.

Related to the issue of encouraging and utilizing conscious modeling or identification in the learning process is the question of the advisability of one or many teachers for the pupil at any one time. Comenius (1957 [1623–1657]) argued that each pupil should have only one teacher, in the early school years at least, so that differences in teaching styles among teachers would not compound the difficulties inherent in learning different kinds of materials. Perhaps this was what Dewey had in mind in advocating that younger pupils have one teacher for several years. Other things being equal, the more teachers a pupil has, the less likely is he to model after or identify with any one.

3. Learner Behavior vis-à-vis the Teacher

At least four criteria of activity in the instructional setting have been used to classify theories with regard to this dimension:

1. Whether the student selects the material for study (active) or the teacher makes the selection (reactive).
2. Whether the student selects the study activity (active) or the teacher makes the selection (reactive).
3. Whether the student studies real things (active) or the symbols for things (reactive).
4. Whether the student's thought processes are presumed to involve organizational principles (active) or are considered passive connections of impressions (reactive).

The first three criteria deal with activity in the role permitted the child by the teacher. The fourth deals with the nature of cognitive processes. (There is at least a fifth aspect of activity, not related to the instructional setting: self-awareness. This is discussed below as relevant to Dimension 9, ego development as a goal of education.)

Defining the poles of the dimension in terms of theorists shows that Dewey represented the "active" pole. He wished the child to select the material and the activity and to study real things. By rejecting "faculty" theories and emphasizing the dependency of reflective thinking upon attitudes, Dewey made clear his view that thinking and problem solving are complex processes. They involve more than merely storing pieces of information in racks and files to be tapped when some correspondence occurs between a stimulus "outside" and a stimulus "on file."

Neill (1960) also emphasized the freedom of the student at the school. Summerhill students are free to decide *when* to study the formal subject-matter part of their education. However, there is no evidence that this "freedom" extends into the classroom. For all the reader of *Summerhill* can tell, the formal education in the classroom may well follow a strict regimen, if the teacher desires.

In the method of both Montessori (1948 [1909]) and Ashton-Warner (1963), the student is somewhat more passive, in that the class activities are preselected by the teacher. The Montessori method allows the child to choose from a set of preselected activities and materials; whereas Ashton-Warner, preselecting the activity, allows the pupil to select the material (from his own experience) to which the activity is applied.

Greek education epitomized passivity. For example, in oratory, which the Hellenic Greeks regarded as the highest attainment of the adult male, the training consisted of memorizing great orations by paramount historical figures. For long periods of the individual's early education, he was prohibited from inventing, creating, or even combining separate materials in his orations.

Nearly all theories which leave the selection of material and task to the child assume that he will choose something relevant to the classroom. In this spirit, Neill allows the selection process months and even years to be completed and even acknowledges the passage through Summerhill of students who decided to avoid the classroom entirely, choosing none of the materials and activities offered.

Theories emphasizing students' activity tend to have no fixed models of the "ideal" adult toward which the educational process aims the student. Often some vague model of the "self-actualized" adult exists, but this is about as definite as the model gets.

Also worth noting is the relationship between this dimension and Dimensions 6 and 8 below. Theories emphasizing the activity of the child tend also to emphasize the relevance of the child's existing motives and emotional responses to the classroom situations. As opposed to these theories, those postulating a reactive child tend to encourage specific, definable behaviors.

Educational theories based upon a detailed theory of human development may vary widely with respect to the activity of the child permitted vis-à-vis the teacher. One theory may "treat each student as an individual"; another may be actuated as a procrustean bed, each student trimmed to fit the description of some developmental level (for example, Johnny can't read because he is only four).

4. *Reward and Punishment*

This dimension really combines several somewhat distinct reward-relevant variants: (1) the relevance of reward and punishment to what is being learned; (2) love and indifference as reward and punishment versus more directly physical responses; and (3) the immediacy of feedback of results as an aid to learning.

The first of these is often labeled the extrinsic-intrinsic reward distinction. The intrinsic pole of this distinction is, ideally, the "satisfaction the student gets from doing the task correctly"—the correctness of the solution being directly determinable by the student. When, however, "correctness" requires a psychologically proximal intervention by the teacher, the reward may mean little more than that the solution pleases the teacher. Partly for this reason, some theorists have advocated letting the student select the task.

It is worth noting here that few theorists have advocated making an attempt to establish motives unique to the classroom. In general, the motives to be rewarded and (seldom) punished are those of "real" life —the ones "brought from home."

The use of love as a reward and indifference as a punishment was strongly advocated by Locke (Adamson, 1912 [Locke, 1693–1706]). Locke's argument hinged on the impermanence of physical punishment and on its tendency to evoke anger and hostility rather than remorse and/or guilt. Thomas Arnold (Fitch, 1897), a relatively recent advocate of physical punishment, was unconcerned with producing an argument for the effectiveness of physical punishment. He simply cited its appropriateness, maintaining that boys are intellectually and morally inferior to men. Neill and Montessori condemned both physical and emotional punishment.

Along with an increased emphasis upon the pupil's motives in the classroom, a notable trend in instructional theorizing has been the increasing importance attached to immediate feedback in the learning process. A precursor of this development was the Jesuits' *Ratio Studiorum*, which acknowledged the virtues of immediate feedback to the student and established an elaborate structure of progressively cumulative review sessions and disputations. These forced the student to relate his knowledge to others, peers and teachers, allowing them to question and correct him.

Montessori and Dewey integrated immediate feedback into the techniques of instruction peculiar to their systems. In Montessori's method, the materials of study are themselves designed to reveal a pupil's mistakes. A circle is not for long confused with a square because it doesn't fit into the square depression in the formboard. There is no necessity for a delay while the teacher checks whether the pupil is right or wrong. The material for feedback is directly in the hands of the pupil.

In Dewey's system, the ideal learning situation is provided by a real problem to solve. In working toward the solution, the learner is provided with continual feedback. A problem which is involved and lengthy and which permits no feedback until the preferred solution is complete would not be a good learning task.

Another form of reward (which none of the theories discussed in this chapter included) is "the release from work." Some educators have held that mental and physical exertion are prerequisites for learning. When the effort of an arduous task is followed by relaxation, the learning is reinforced. Related to this form of reward, and an insidious corruptor of the student, is the demarkation of a segment of pleasurable human experiences as "reward" experiences. (Because of grade- and high-school experiences, I still regard a novel as a reward—as something to be read after all my work is done.)

5. Moral Development

Morality has often been considered a formal subject to be isolated and specifically taught. As mentioned earlier, the Hellenistic Greeks supplied their sons with constant companions whose function was moral tuition. Much more recently, the Arnolds stressed the more explicit concern with moral development as a necessary reform of English public-school education. Teaching in religious schools has always bound both moral and theological teachings to nearly all formal subjects.

Friedrich Froebel (1903 [1826]) was very much concerned with teaching Christian religion. Whereas an attitude toward life was to be taught, no specific moral teaching was advocated. Herbart centered his educational theory on morality, carefully defining "the good" and developing a scheme conceptualizing other moral concepts. Yet this theory was never translated to the instructional setting. For both these men, abstracted discussion of theology and morality, combined with extremely detailed implementation of certain instructional goals, seem almost deliberately aimed at avoiding specific discussion of the teaching of morality. Froebel wrote, "Christian theology is to be taught all students"; and Herbart wrote, "The whole problem of education may be comprised in a single concept—morality." Neither had anything to say about the achievement of these objectives.

Over the last fifty years or so, philosophers have written voluminously about the definitions of such words as *good* and *ought*. Most educational theorists have been directly concerned with morality as defined by at least some of these philosophers. For example, Firth (1952) proposed that the statement "*X* is better than *Y*" means "If anyone were, in respect of *X* and *Y*, fully informed and vividly imaginative, impartial in a calm frame of mind and otherwise normal, he would prefer *X* to *Y*." In a related vein, I am sure Dewey would have argued that if a person has a problem to solve, such as building a bridge across a chasm, he would prefer *X*, the experimental method, to *Y*, some other technique of problem solving. In teaching the experimental method, Dewey could certainly be considered, by Firth anyway, engaged in the teaching of ethics. Firth's definition and subsequent argument wouldn't satisfy everyone. Several of the paths toward definition, in the ethical domain, get no further than his toward separating out that morality pertaining to right and wrong from other kinds of decision making.

Many feel that when conversation includes sex and aggression, honesty and fidelity, it has greater "ethical" content or implication than when it concerns stacking blocks or building a bridge. The words *moral* and *morality* are more apt to be used with reference to the former. In this sense of moral, the psychoanalytic theorists and such theorists as Ashton-Warner and Neill have been more concerned with morality in their educational writings than have writers like Montessori, James, and Dewey.

It might be asked why a dimension on the teaching of morality is included, while a dimension on the development of physical skills and strength is not. First, aside from the physical concomitants of perceptual development, physical development has not often been a central issue in instructional theories.[2] Second, as noted above, the philosophers' attempts to define moral behavior have often resulted in such breadth of definition as to make most classroom activity morally relevant. This cannot be said for physical development.

6. Learner Motives and Emotions

There are at least two questions differentiating theories along this dimension:

1. Are the student's existing motives acknowledged, supported, and utilized in the classroom, or are they discouraged, perhaps even punished, and a set of motives uniquely relevant to the classroom encouraged and rewarded?

2. Are emotions besides those most useful in creating order and docility among the students tolerated and encouraged, or are they punished and rejected?

Theories which appear superficially to disregard motives and emotions really seek to limit the behavior in the classroom to (1) motives sought by the teacher and somewhat specific to the classroom, such as seeking to please the teacher and competing with and exceeding fellow students, and (2) emotions considered most relevant to maximal learning, such as pride in work well done, shame for mistakes, and guilt about failing to do homework or losing the classroom contest for "the team." At times, group motives and emotions have been encouraged (for example, a pupil takes no pride in his own work, only in his team's success).

Theories at the other pole open the door to motives relevant to extraclassroom situations and to more personal responses. With respect to motives, this often means two things:

1. Activity patterns and goal objects which have rewarded the child outside of class are utilized in the classroom as parts of learning situations.

2. Sources of personal satisfaction within the students are sought, expanded, and even generated, so that the student is not dependent upon outsiders for satisfaction with his own works.

[2] It must be noted that rather fundamental Protestant religious views of education have generated theories of education seeking character development mediated by the linking of a healthy mind and a healthy body.

Theories at this pole of the dimension allow expression of more personal emotions (such as those associated with sexual and aggressive motives) than those indicated above for the other pole. Feelings of love and affection for the teacher and the other students as well as hate and disgust concerning activities suggested by the teacher can be tolerated, considered legitimate, and need not be suppressed as rapidly as possible. Dewey, for example, acknowledged emotional responses (and stimuli) as central to the learning process at times.

On even cursory examination, this dimension seems strongly related to the other conceptual dimensions central to theories of instruction. Sanford's (1955) attempt to clarify the concept of identification links its conscious utilization in the learning process to a close but largely unconscious emotional relationship between the "identifier" and the "identificand."

As I have discussed, the activity of the student in the learning process has been closely tied to the expansion of the realm of motives and emotions relevant to the classroom. Moral development has been equivocal with respect to this dimension, except that theories which seek character development usually demand specific behaviors and therefore restrict the range of behaviors which can be exhibited in the classroom.

Herbart was a paradox with respect to his regard for the learner's affective state. He acknowledged a great variety of student responses to instruction. However, all variations were considered deviations from an ideal, and the teaching process was aimed at instructing students "despite their idiosyncrasies."

7. Relationship between School and Home

I suppose one pole of this dimension would be the complete domination of the home by the educational process, the other pole being the complete domination of the school. The midpoint is, then, the merging of the two into a single educational enterprise.

It has probably been hundreds of years since a major educational theorist advocated education solely in the home and placed this notion within a developed educational theory. In contrast, one classical Chinese view of education placed the entire burden of the educational process on the school. The parents provided the teacher not only with the child but with a switch (often brilliantly decorated). If the child was dropped from school, the family was humiliated.

Theorists like Neill, and many before him in the English public-school tradition, have advocated sending the child away to school. Most often such schooling is presumed to insure proper superego development. Neill, on the other hand, seems more concerned about the ego. At Summerhill, the superego apparently fends for itself—with the help of a few clouts by one's peers and by Neill himself if sufficiently provoked.

A merger between home and school was perhaps most completely developed by Pestalozzi (Anderson, 1931 [Pestalozzi, 1780–1826]). Ideally, according to Pestalozzi, educating should be done in the home. The existing emotional relations between parents and their children, the importance to the child of the objects in the home, and the history of infant learning in the home would all facilitate the educational process. However, Pestalozzi recognized two other aspects of instruction militating against this ideal arrangement: (1) the organization of the content of instruction; and (2) the special materials and techniques necessary to teach content requiring learning situations that are not already part of the home environment. This organization and the materials and techniques it requires must be learned by the effective teacher. Parents often either will not or cannot learn them and put them into practice. Therefore, instruction must take place in a specially established school, but the emotional environment of the school is to be as much like that of the home as possible. In Pestalozzi's view, the teacher was to be like the parent and the students like siblings. Interpersonal relations should be like those in the family.

It could be argued that Dewey's position merged the home and the school by bringing the stimuli from the home into the school and by legitimatizing the motives the child brings with him into the classroom. The inclusion of domestic activities in the curriculum, as advocated by Montessori and others, also has the effect of attempting to bridge this home-school gap for the child.

One more subtle way in which home and school are linked in the learning process is the utilization in the school setting of motives important to the child outside of school. Dewey was one of the strongest advocates of capitalizing upon the strong motives brought by the pupil into the classroom. These were tapped in constructing problems to present to the pupil.

Motives unique to the school can be found only if motives are considered quite specific. Historically, demands for obedience and control of behavior in the classroom (unsparingly criticized by Montessori) often far exceeded those of the home, in both amount and intensity of punishment. What is usually meant by creating motives unique to the classroom is either that certain reactions of the teacher or the other students become the primary goals of an existing motive or else that a cluster of behaviors becomes workable only in the instructional setting or in settings generalized from the classroom.

8. *Adaptability as an Instructional Outcome*

This, again, is a dimension difficult to separate from several of the others, especially since theories stressing adaptability as a goal of education tend to view learning as a unitary process (for example, Dewey).

Faculty theories emphasize the development of a set of capacities. The goal of these theories is usually not to stamp in a set of behaviors, but rather to develop the capacity to respond to situations with appropriate discriminations among stimuli and behaviors. Outstanding examples of the development of a set of circumscribed, definable behaviors are learning a particular job or role and learning mannerly behavior.

The approaches to education most clearly emphasizing specific sets of behaviors were the attempt of the Greeks to develop orator-statesmen and of the Jesuits to develop priests. However, the specificity of the *Ratio Studiorum* need not, in practice, have been what it appears in print. Schwickerath (1903) stated that Jesuit teaching in fact emphasizes developing the capacities and skills of the mind. In his view, "Facts are merely dumbbells."

William James ostensibly came close to this pole when he severely limited the amount of generalization which could be expected from certain learning experiences. James would have argued, however, that to oppose "adaptability" to the learning of a large set of behaviors is to create an artificial distinction. If by adaptability is meant the ability of a person to face a new situation and succeed in it (as Dewey seemed to mean), James would have argued that adaptability implies two characteristics: (1) knowledge about a sequence of behaviors for successfully coping with a situation; and (2) the ability to select this sequence of behaviors from the individual's repertoire. Although only the latter is commonly regarded as adaptability, such selection implies prerequisite knowledge. This pole, therefore, must really be reserved for those theories advocating specific stimulus-behavior relationships.

Dewey represented the other pole of the dimension. At least the second of the two aspects of adaptability noted above was a major thrust of his theory: The student should learn a way of contending with the vast array of situations of differing familiarity with which adults are faced. Dewey set out the experimental approach as the most valuable approach to solving problems in general. The first step of this approach is to analyze the problem and to marshal relevant information. Dewey readily admitted the value of having the maximal amount of relevant information. For situations likely to arise often, the individual should, if possible, have this information readily available in his memory. Therefore, Dewey would have argued that information of this type should be taught to the individual, as it is an essential part of formal education.

9. Ego Development as an Instructional Outcome

An individual with a well-developed ego has impulse control (the ability to delay gratification) and is aware of his motives, appropriate goals, and ways of achieving these goals.

All educational theories have been concerned with learning the means of attaining a certain set of goals. Usually, a set of appropriate motives are acknowledged in the instructional setting. Instruction attempts to attach appropriate behaviors and/or goals to these motives. Other motives are either to be ignored or punished when manifested in the classroom.

Montessori was quite unusual when she said that no behavior which appears purposeful should be stopped by the teacher. However, she did not actively seek to elicit such behavior. I cannot think of any instance of a theorist allowing the child to express all the behaviors within his repertoire and using the formal instructional setting only to shape behavior.

Both James and Froebel advocated *initially* giving full reign to the behavior repertoire of the child, in order to get to know him by understanding his stimulus-response connections, his character, and his perception of himself and of the world.

Although Neill's Summerhill is certainly an unrestrictive learning environment, apparently nothing constructive is done with the motives expressed. The new arrival, encountering the "free" older students, must feel as if he is playing to an empty house every time he lets an inhibition drop. The attachment of motive, goal, and means to goal seems neglected. Without these paths, the motive is frustrated. If the frustration is persistent, the motive may be suppressed, repressed, or made more intense.

Dewey sought motives brought to the classroom by the pupil to trigger a search for the solution to a problem. Learning consisted of applying a technique to the materials of past and present experience in order to reach the goal of satisfying the motive. This type is motive-relevant learning. The motive is not something created in the classroom to enable the learning to take place, and there is no attempt to recruit motives. There is the hope that the motives of the pupil are rational and appropriate to the classroom.

The further back in time one looks, the greater the theoretical emphasis on impulse-control aspects of education. The Christian concept of original sin appears increasingly important as one moves back in time toward the *Ratio Studiorum*. According to these theorists, there is little to education except "chaining the passions." The term "character development" has traditionally meant little more than this.

In general, theorists emphasizing adaptability also emphasize the motive-satisfaction aspect of ego development (for example, Ashton-Warner and Dewey). The closer one comes to atomistic learning or to the emulation of a specific adult model, the more emphasis is placed on superego functioning and on the gratification-delay aspect of ego development.

IMPLICATIONS FOR CONTEMPORARY INSTRUCTION

Throughout the preceding discussion, it has been evident that most early theories of instruction treated only two or three central dimensions systematically and treated several other dimensions in less detailed fashion. Three second-order dimensions (incorporating a good deal of the variation found among the nine dimensions) suggest the modal concerns embodied in these theories. They emphasize (1) the attempt to encourage the individuality of the student, (2) the nature of the learning process, and (3) the development of the "evaluative" capacities of the student. These dimensions may be described as follows:

1. *The pupil as an active agent in the classroom.* This dimension is, of course, defined most closely by Dimension 3 (Learner Behavior vis-à-vis the Teacher). Dimensions 6 (Learner Motives and Emotions), 8 (Adaptability as an Instructional Outcome), and 9 (Ego Development as an Instructional Outcome) very nearly collapse into Dimension 3.

2. *Learning as a unitary phenomenon.* This dimension is defined most closely by Dimension 1 (Structure of the Learning Process). Dimension 4 (Reward and Punishment) also loads highly on this dimension.

3. *Relevance of moral development to education.* This is most closely represented by Dimension 5 (Moral Development). When the school becomes the center for all education, it also acquires the task of moral development. Dimension 2 (Modeling and Identification) and one aspect of Dimension 9 (gratification-delay aspect of ego development) also seem closely related to this dimension.

Of what use is an inventory of past theories aside from suggesting a set of dimensions possibly expanding the reader's views of the central concerns of instructional theories? Certain instructional techniques and procedures of education presented in these theories depended for their utility on content and goals no longer applicable, or at least very much out of fashion. For example, the Homeric warrior-statesman and even the Athenian "citizen of the polis" do not provide viable models for the contemporary child. Other theories presented points of view regarding technique and procedure which, given their content and goals, have yet to be demonstrated relevant. There is yet to be found stable data regarding the relationships among characteristics of formal education and (1) the organization of, and procedures for the acquisition of, knowledge and the solution of problems by the adult, and (2) adult moral character (studies relating "national character" to the forms of formal education have not been too enlightening). Theories of instruction have always had a great deal of "face" validity in this regard, but the smile on the face appears more and more seductive.

In coherent combination with recently developed techniques and procedures, certain components of the earlier theories are currently being debated or put to experimental test. However, only parts of the essential combination of postulates which made up the original theory are apt to be studied or adopted. For example, many theorists have incorporated Dewey's stress on utilizing the motives of the child in instruction, while neglecting his concomitant stress on meaningful and challenging problems as the material of learning.

Probably the most important value of this way of viewing early theories of instruction is that it helps clarify the issues, procedures, and techniques meriting further exploration. These include the following:

1. What functions can negative (for example, fear-provoking) stimuli, aside from the threat of punishment, serve in education? Ashton-Warner argued that these stimuli greatly enhance learning to read, spell, and write because of their importance to the child. Can negative stimuli be induced by the teacher in a nondisabling fashion? Or must they (and the ways in which they are to be used) be brought into the learning situation by the individual student?

2. Of what value is the school as the entire environment for the student during the school years? This question seems long to have been the subject of heated debate and discussion in England, but most of the disseminated output of the debate has been in the form of polemic.

3. Of what value is the laborious development, during the early years, of the student's discriminating powers (Montessori)? Is the thus-developed child more adaptive, enriched, or only more perceptive? Would Dewey be substantially correct in arguing (as I surmise he would) that the early years are better spent working on "real" problems and more "live" situations?

4. Of what value is limiting the younger school-age child to one teacher? What are the implications for team teaching extended into these early years? Would it be desirable to maintain a single teacher-student relationship over a period of years, or alternatively a team of teachers for a student over a period of years—this team staying constant? Is the constancy of teacher-controlled procedures and the added

knowledge about the student carried through the years by the teacher(s) by this approach sufficient to offset (1) the stamping-in of erroneous impressions or (2) the stereotyped approach used by the constant teacher, or the diversity of training available in different teachers, each handling the student for a more limited period of time?

5. Into what realms of learning can be carried the creation of materials which readily reveal mistakes in their handling? Are problems created by extending into more advanced subject matters the principle of immediate feedback? Or are the techniques of problem solving currently sought (as were those sought by Dewey) those which provide constant feedback relevant to the path toward solutions, encouraging development of behavior sequences involving "chaining of responses"?

6. What can be the net effects of identification and modeling in the learning process? Are there ways of inducing modeling of some general characteristics of the teacher, like rationality, without running the risk of more specific and perhaps unconscious characterological copying? Related to identification is the question: To what extent should the teacher act like a parent?

7. The preceding question suggests another concerning moral teaching in the schools. Consider the contention that the schools do not teach values, except for the consensual values of our society. Are not those who advance it really allowing much moral teaching, perhaps specific to the teacher, to occur in the schools? It could be argued that an educational theory which at least examines the moral implications of all educational content and techniques might be more apt to produce techniques which control the moral aspects of education. The moral implications of the theoretical and practical emphasis on ego development in selecting content and technique is only beginning to be unraveled by philosophically inclined psychologists.

8. What are the full implications of Comenius's contention that substance should be taught before form? It is usually assumed that the preschool years have taught the child sufficient substance to be worked with in school. However, the proliferation of nursery schools indicates that the assumption is questionable. Should substantive learning be extended into the formal school years, prior to learning of form? If so, what substance? And in what forms to insure its acquisition? Ashton-

Warner, by the use of negative stimuli in the learning of form, essentially expanded the substance from early childhood and infancy to be utilized in the classroom. Preceding all these problems is, of course, the question of whether a meaningful distinction can be made between substance and form.

2

An Overview

of Contemporary Formulations

LAURENCE SIEGEL

ℐ

THE PRECEDING CHAPTER CONSIDERED SOME OF THE HISTORICAL ANTECED-
ents of contemporary theories of instruction. In the process of examining these early formulations, Hedegard analyzed their content by
making a subjective cluster analysis. This analysis clarified the central
concerns evident, to a greater or lesser degree, in virtually all of the
earlier positions.

In contrast with the holistic nature of early theories, most of the
recent attempts to theorize about instruction treat only some selected
aspect of the process. Instructional theory characteristically is inferred
from theoretical formulations in such areas as learning, motivation, and
communication. Obviously, a useful theory of learning can contribute
to an understanding of learning principles in a wide variety of situations and circumstances, including those I subsequently classify as
"instruction." Likewise, viewed as a social interaction, the understanding of what transpires in the classroom is enhanced by contributions
from sociological and social psychological theory.

This approach to developing instructional theories has been questioned by Gage (1963). He argues that to the extent that the instructional process is unique, integrated theories pertaining to its totality
cannot be assembled merely by collating subtheories relevant to selected aspects of the process. Thus he conceives of instructional theories as developing alongside of, rather than solely by inference from,
theories in more limited areas of the behavioral sciences.

Although both approaches described in the preceding paragraphs have merit, the latter has been generally neglected of late. Clearly, this neglect does not reflect a paucity of experimentation in instructional settings. There is an already huge and still growing literature of empirical studies on educational problems. However, this long history of educational research has not been an especially fertile spawning ground for theory.

Of the several factors contributing to this state of affairs, this chapter examines two that seem to be particularly powerful impediments to instructional theorizing. First, the methodology for investigating the instructional process too often neglects the complexity of the process, thereby increasing the likelihood of pedestrian findings and diminishing the likelihood of a substantial contribution to theory. Second, the language as it pertains to educational theory is rather loose. The distinctions among theories, models, and paradigms concerning education are often indefinite.

SOME METHODOLOGICAL INADEQUACIES

In their discussion of designs for research on teaching, Campbell and Stanley (1963) examine twelve factors jeopardizing the validity of various methodologies. The first eight of these are relevant to "internal validity": that is, they may produce uncontrolled effects confounding the effect of the independent variable(s). These include:

1. Events aside from the independent variable transpiring between the pre- and posttreatment measurement.
2. Maturation as an intervening event.
3. The effects of pretests upon posttests of the independent variable.
4. Changes in instrument calibration, observers, scores, and the like.
5. Statistical regression when groups have been selected on the basis of their extreme scores.
6. Biases resulting from differential assignment of subjects to experimental and control groups.
7. Differential loss of subjects from the compared groups.
8. Effects produced by unnoticed or unspecified interactions and erroneously attributed to the manipulated independent variable.

The four remaining factors discussed by Campbell and Stanley may act to restrict the generalizability of empirical findings. These factors include the well-known "Hawthorne effect" and various interactions among multiple experimental treatments, between selection biases and the independent variable, and between pretesting procedures and the independent variable.

Instead of retracing this ground already adequately covered elsewhere, this chapter considers in detail only two particular sources of low empirical yield in instructional research. One of these is the frequent reliance upon control-group comparisons wherein educational variables are too grossly specified. This procedure makes erroneous implicit assumptions of homogeneity and independence. The other methodological issue is that of identifying and utilizing suitable research criteria.

Control-Group Comparisons

The fundamental objective of the "instructional-comparisons strategy" is to compare some innovation in instructional procedure with older, better-established, more traditional, or "conventional" procedures for attaining the same objectives. Within the limitations imposed by measurement procedures, it is generally discovered that students learn about as much in one kind of instructional environment as they do in another. The absence of significant differences is reported with monotonous regularity. Such failures to refute the null hypothesis are often accompanied by a statement to the effect that the "Hawthorne effect" may have been a confounding variable.

This research pattern is by no means the only one used. However, there can be no quarrel with the fact that it continues to be reported with great frequency. Even recent concerted efforts to explore the effectiveness of electronic classroom aids have heavily favored the methodology of instructional comparisons (for example, Carpenter and Greenhill, 1958; Siegel, Macomber, and Adams, 1959; Macomber and Siegel, 1960).

On the assumption that subjects are properly selected for assignment to the groups, this classical method of investigation has obvious applications to a wide variety of problems. Yet in its application to *educational* problems, investigators too often make erroneous implicit assumptions of homogeneity and independence of empirical conditions. The necessity for these assumptions is self-evident. For comparisons to be made between two or more instructional procedures, each of these procedures must be sufficiently independent of the others and homogeneous within itself to permit its utilization as an independent variable. However, it is apparent that these assumptions often are untenable, even when the usual experimental controls are exerted (Hovland, Lumsdaine, and Sheffield, 1949; Lumsdaine, 1953, 1960, 1963).

Of the two design requirements, independence and homogeneity, the former is the more easily satisfied in instructional research. Nevertheless, it must be recognized that attempts to establish independent learning environments as experimental and control conditions may fail because teachers do not always share the investigator's zeal for purity of design. Teachers who discover visual devices or modes of presentation enhancing the quality of their "experimental presentations" are justifiably eager to use these in their "control sections" as well.

The requirement of homogeneity is both more difficult to satisfy and perhaps more frequently overlooked in instructional research. The investigator must assume homogeneity within each of the instructional procedures undergoing comparison in order to generalize beyond the specific samples in the investigation.

Usually, instructional procedures are superficially designated as "lecture," "televised," "independent study," or "conventional" and are treated as if they were uniform independent variables. However, such uniformity does not exist. "Conventional" classroom environments differ from one another, for example, with respect to number of students enrolled, amount and type of verbal interaction permitted or facilitated by the instructor, and the like, as well as in such obvious physical characteristics as room layout and hour at which the class is scheduled. Therefore, to designate a class as "conventional" and to use this group as a control for comparative purposes are to place reliance upon a very gross kind of descriptive designation. This criticism holds also for the gross designations applied to the various kinds of "experimental" procedures compared with the "control."

A low level of information yield must be anticipated because the gross nature of the conditions under investigation probably produces cancellation effects in group data. Instead of dealing with samples exposed to homogeneous and independent conditions, the comparisons involve samples exposed to treatments each of which is relatively heterogeneous. Thus, by collating data across samples for any treatment grossly designated as a particular kind of instructional environment, investigators may actually come close to approximating the distribution of data for the *population* of instructional treatments.

Criterion Inadequacies

Even if a valid methodology appropriate to instructional research were assumed, it is evident that criterion inadequacies alone often predestine a low empirical yield.

Gage (1963) has distinguished between "criteria-of-effectiveness paradigms" and "process paradigms" for research on teaching. The former are basically representations of the relationships between criteria of teacher effectiveness and factors presumed to correlate with these criteria. The latter focus upon the teaching process as an interpersonal relationship worthy of study in its own right.

Instructional comparisons are invariably based upon the criterion-of-effectiveness paradigm. The referent for effectiveness may be either the teacher's or the student's behavior; the assessments may be objective or subjective; the criteria may include measures-of-achievement judgments or test performance (Domas and Tiedeman, 1950). In the final analysis, *student achievement* is generally regarded as standing in a superordinate position to all other criteria (Amer. Educ. Res. Assn., 1952).

As a practical matter, the criterion of student achievement is most typically derived from course examination scores. This criterion is sometimes defended on the ground that since it satisfies the instructor as a basis for assigning grades, it reflects the attainment of educational objectives to the satisfaction of researchers. However, this defense is a weak one indeed. The process whereby an instructor is brought to the point where he is able to specify his objectives in terms amenable to evaluation is a rather laborious one (Bloom, 1956). It is unlikely that studies of relatively brief duration afford sufficient contact between instructor and researcher to permit specification and assessment of higher-level cognitive processes as dependent variables. Evaluative data in the affective domain are even more generally neglected.

Somewhat less generally recognized or made explicit is the fact that even those course examinations measuring pertinent objectives are not well suited to serve as dependent variables for educational research. Student performance on these measures reflects the operation of many variables, most of which are not controlled by the experimental design. Students, after all, operate under conditions of constraint compelling satisfactory examination performance not only in response to adequate instruction, but often in spite of inadequate instruction. They are sensitive to such external conditions as graduation requirements and pressures from parents or friends.

Finally, examination performance provides a delayed criterion for assessing instructional impact and hence is subject to considerable contamination. Certain students who never attend class and therefore never experience the independent variable under consideration may perform extremely well on course examinations by studying from comprehensive notes taken by a person who *has* attended class meetings. In such instances, the examination score reflects such variables as academic ability and motivation as well as the quality of notes taken by the one who attended class. The score may reveal what has been learned, but not necessarily what has been learned as a function of the instructional procedure under investigation. These considerations have led Bloom (1953) and Siegel *et al.* (1963) to argue for utilizing an immediately available criterion of student thinking *in situ* to supplement end-of-course measures.

SOME LINGUISTIC CONFUSIONS

Methodological inadequacies like those discussed in the foregoing section contribute to, but do not fully account for, the relative paucity of instructional theory. The language itself, and particularly the loose ways in which the designations *paradigm, model,* and *theory* are applied to instructional experimentation, is a primary contributing factor.

Paradigm

A paradigm is a general statement of presumed relationships among variables. As such, it aids research by restricting the investigator's attention to the specific variables embodied in the paradigm and by directing him to study any temporal, spatial, or other internal relationship specified by it. Thus, a paradigm is a master plan for research. It provides no explanatory concepts although it focuses research efforts by providing a context for investigation (Gage, 1963). Ultimately, of course, data accumulated in conformance with the paradigm's pattern need to be integrated and explained.

Model

A model is an aid to integrating data. Literally speaking, a model is an isomorphic representation of certain aspects of a larger and more complicated aspect of reality. Thus, a model airplane is smaller than the real thing. Because of its reduced size, a youngster can comprehend it better than he can a real airplane. He can examine it and perceive the relationships among its surfaces. The extent to which such a model contributes to his understanding of how a real airplane works depends upon the fidelity of the miniaturization with respect to both appearance and principle of operation.

The procedure whereby some known aspect of the real world is reduced to a model can be reversed. It is possible, in the absence of knowledge about the real world, to construct a hypothetical model of what this world or some object in it might be like. Testing the model to see if it "works" conveys a better understanding of that aspect of the world it is supposed to represent. This is precisely what is done, for example, when a computer is programed to represent a possible aspect of neural functioning or a set of decision-making processes. The computer program is a model of the real world presently unknown to the inquirer. The efficiency of machine operation based upon this program is a test of the representativeness or fidelity of the model, and hence of the inquirer's level of understanding from which the model was generated. Thus, as Maccia (1962) indicates, representational models of real events or objects enable investigators to *evaluate* the theory from which the model was generated.

Another form of model is the model *for* as opposed to the model *of* something. This form attempts to generalize from an area about which a good deal is known to an area about which relatively little is known. The former serves as a model for the latter. Common elements are identified in the known and speculative areas, and the laws relating these elements in the more familiar area are applied in the area of speculation. Models based upon the well-defined body of knowledge about mechanical systems are examples in point. This knowledge about mechanical inputs, controls, and outputs, and the relationships among them has provided several models for teaching-learning systems.

The usefulness of models for unfamiliar areas based upon knowledge in some other area depends upon the commonality of concepts in the two areas and the correspondence between the laws relating these concepts. Thus nothing of value can be inferred about the transmission of neural impulses by modeling this kind of transmission after the flow of water in connecting pipes.

Mathematical models can be viewed as a special case of models *for* something (that is, nonrepresentational models). Mathematical models posit a mathematical relationship as the model for a nonmathematical structure, as when a statement of mathematical probabilities is applied as a model for human decision-making behavior.

Theory

Whereas a paradigm is essentially an outline of a research plan, and a model suggests hypotheses by conceptualizing the unknown in terms of a more familiar context, a theory is constructed by relating known facts or principles to one another. By providing these relationships, theories have a threefold utility: (1) they *explain* how and why previously disparate observations are related or integrated; (2) they permit *inferences* about the operation of phenomena that cannot be investigated directly; and (3) they permit *predictions* of phenomena in advance of their occurrence.

The Nature of Contemporary Formulations

In terms of the preceding distinctions among paradigms, models, and theories, the substantive positions sampled in the remainder of the book are a mixed bag. Although each contributor takes a theoretical posture, the level of development and refinement of these postures varies. Some contributors (for example, Biddle and Adams; Siegel and Siegel) emphasize particular research paradigms and their underlying models. Their purpose is primarily to clarify a way of viewing and studying the instructional setting with the ultimate objective of generating theory. Other contributors (for example, Woodruff) elaborate a particular model by progressively integrating substantial blocks of empirically derived data. And still others (for example, Jahnke; Ausubel) present fairly rigorous theoretical positions with but slight reference to models and paradigms.

Another difference among these formulations is the particular body of theory upon which the contributors stand. The most readily classifiable in this respect are Jahnke (behavioristic learning theory) and Ausubel (cognitive learning theory). Although the other positions may rest somewhat less upon a *particular* body of theory, the chapter by Rogers evinces a psychotherapeutic emphasis, and the chapter by Biddle and Adams is derived primarily from sociological considerations.

Organization of the Book

The two foci for instructional theory about which the chapters are organized are the teacher (Part II) and the learner (Part III). Viewed through the eyes of the learner, the objective of instruction is to effect certain behavioral changes designated "learning." A theory of instruction thus becomes a variation of a theory of learning. Depending upon the theoretician's predilections, he may capitalize upon reinforcement theory, cognitive learning theory, and so on.

Instructional theories derived from learning theories implicitly assume that effective learning implies effective instruction. This assumption has been questioned by Smith (1960). As he indicates, some students learn in spite of "bad" teaching; others fail to learn in spite of "good" teaching. Thus the amount and quality of learning are neither the sole nor necessarily the most important criteria of teaching effectiveness. And valid instructional theories can be constructed about the teacher's operations as well as about the learner's operations.

Whereas Parts II and III respectively concern formulations emphasizing teacher and learner behavior, Part IV consists of two integrative formulations. Both of these come closer than any of the preceding ones to considering the total teaching-learning configuration.

This distinction among formulations emphasizing teacher behavior, learner behavior, and the teaching-learning integration is perforce an arbitrary one. Theoretical positions directed primarily to the teacher's activities must take cognizance of the impact of teaching upon learning. Similarly, theoretical positions derived primarily from concern with learner behavior must treat that behavior at least partly as a function of the teacher's operations. Thus Part V consists of a conclusion calling attention to the points of agreement and disagreement among the various positions presented in the book.

Definitions of Instruction

In approaching the task of writing about theories of instruction, each contributor has formulated a definition of the instructional process. These definitions remain intact where the writers placed them because they are critical to the arguments being presented. In spite of subtle differences among these definitions, it is appropriate at the outset to offer a concept of instruction congruent with the various definitions and ignoring the differences.

All of the chapters concern what transpires in formal educational settings. Instruction is conceived as being comprised of teaching and learning although, as will become evident, there has been a deliberate attempt to sample viewpoints emphasizing one or the other of these operations. Since the various concepts of instruction are restricted to formal educational settings, there has been a deliberate exclusion of such diverse instructional applications as propaganda, advertising, and psychotherapy.

Nevertheless, the notion of teaching-learning in formal education settings has been construed as broadly as possible. The "teacher" may be physically present (in a face-to-face setting) or absent (as in televised and programed instruction). The learner may participate in the instructional process in a classroom, laboratory, shop, residence-hall room, study carrel, or the like. The breadth of activities comprising the learner's instructional participation is similarly great, including speaking, listening, writing, reading, motor responses, and so on.

The concern with instruction transpiring in higher educational settings is made explicit. Most contributors draw their illustrations from behavior at the college and university level. However, the intent of these approaches to instructional theory is at least implicitly to embrace instruction at the lower educational levels as well.

PART·II·

FORMULATIONS EMPHASIZING
TEACHER BEHAVIOR

The three formulations comprising Part II all focus upon the teaching process, but from different perspectives. Rogers derives his propositions about teaching from psychotherapeutic theory; Woodruff, from cognitive theory; and Biddle and Adams, from social-interaction theory. Considered as statements of how teachers "should" behave, the positions advanced in Chapters 3 and 4 are more highly developed than that in Chapter 5. The latter calls particular attention to a heretofore relatively neglected component of theories of instruction: the network of teacher-student and student-student interactions.

Although Rogers and Woodruff begin from quite different vantage points, there are several noteworthy points of contact between their positions. Their views about the significance of various educational objectives are essentially similar and, in consequence, they share certain dissatisfactions with current educational practices.

Rogers states that the aim of education is to develop trust in the process by which knowledge is acquired rather than simply to communicate knowledge accumulated in the past. He writes: "Learning how to learn, involvement in a process of change— these become the primary aims of an education fit for the present world." Thus, Rogers questions several assumptions underlying much current educational practice, including the implications that students cannot be trusted to pursue their own learning and that passive learners develop into creative citizens.

Although Woodruff places a heavier stress upon the role of education in communicating substantive content, he likewise believes that formal education generally fails to affect the learner's subsequent adjustmental behavior. This failure reflects the inappropriateness of education for helping the learner acquire meaningful concepts and for making him learn and think independently. Specifically, Woodruff regards formal education as too often confining its influence largely to the perception and thinking phases of the learning-behaving cycle, without providing opportunities for decision making and trial. In this regard, he says: "Concepts may be potential acts, but they do not become used acts until the individual employs them in a situation which makes a real or truly simulated demand on him for an adjustmental action. Even less can they become part of his motivational pattern, thereby influencing him beyond the period of formal education."

Both Rogers and Woodruff regard the teacher as central to the attainment of the desired educational goals. Although they are concerned both with what the teacher does and with the climate he creates, Woodruff's emphasis is upon the former and Rogers's is upon the latter. Thus, Woodruff calls attention particularly to the need of the teacher to place real referents before the students, to provide students with appropriate behavioral experiences, and to tailor his interactions with students in ways calculated to prevent "fumbling" with their minds. Rogers uniquely emphasizes the importance of teacher attitudes, including "realness or genuineness," "acceptance" of the student, and "empathic understanding" of him.

Biddle and Adams maintain that suggestions about how new classrooms can be structured in order to provide a desired social (and perhaps intellectual) climate are somewhat premature. They argue that the relationship between the classroom's social properties and the behavior of individual participants has yet to be established. Consequently, they suggest a plan for investigating teacher behavior as a function of the total classroom context (that is, pupil behavior, the social environment, and the physical environment). Their formulation is pretheoretical and adds another dimension, the classroom milieu, to the consideration of the teaching process.

3

The Facilitation
of Significant Learning

CARL R. ROGERS *

Western Behavioral Sciences Institute

ᔈ

IN THIS CHAPTER, I WOULD LIKE TO DESCRIBE TWO TYPES OF LEARNING, two possible aims for education, and two sets of assumptions upon which the educational process can be based. It will be clear that for me the second member of each of these pairs seems more suitable for today's world. I shall then try to indicate some of the ways in which this second view might be implemented.

TWO TYPES OF LEARNING

Cognitive Learning

Some learning appears to be primarily cognitive, primarily the fixing of certain associations. A child can learn his letters and numbers in this fashion; at a later date he may learn to "rattle off" the multiplication table; at a still later date he may learn the rules for solving a binomial equation or the irregular verbs in French. Only very imperceptibly do any of these learnings change *him*. They are like the nonsense syllables which the psychologist asks him to learn as a participant in an experiment. They are learned as part of a task set before him, part of a "body of knowledge" which he is to acquire. Such learning is often painfully difficult and also often quickly forgotten.

* I am indebted to Miss Ann Dreyfuss for her assistance in various aspects of this chapter.

Experiential Learning

The other type of learning is primarily experiential, or significant or meaningful. The student says, "I am discovering—drawing in from the outside and making that which is drawn in a real part of *me*." The adolescent who devours everything he can read or hear about gasoline engines in order to make his hot rod faster and more efficient exemplifies this type of learning. The child who is trying to draw a realistic house reads or hears a few simple rules of perspective. He reaches out to grasp this material, make it his, use it. This is another instance of meaningful learning. Still another is the child who goes to books and the library to satisfy his curiosity about earthworms or the hydrogen bomb or sex. The feeling in regard to any experiential learning is, "Now I'm grasping what I *need* and *want*."

I shall define a bit more precisely the elements which are involved in such significant or experiential learning.

1. *It has a quality of personal involvement.* The whole person in both his feeling and cognitive aspects is involved in the learning event.

2. *It is self-initiated.* Even when the impetus or stimulus comes from outside, the sense of discovery, of reaching out, of grasping and comprehending, comes from within.

3. *It is pervasive.* It makes a difference in the behavior, the attitudes, perhaps even the personality of the learner.

4. *It is evaluated by the learner.* "This is not quite what I want— doesn't go far enough—ah, this is better, this *is* what I want to know." The locus of evaluation may be said to reside definitely in the learner.

5. *Its essence is meaning.* When such learning takes place, the element of meaning to the learner is built into the whole experience.

TWO POSSIBLE AIMS FOR EDUCATION

To Transmit Stored Knowledge

For the most part, the current educational system is geared to the aim of inculcating in the young the stored knowledge already accumulated, together with the values which have guided men in the past. Its natural product is the informed, essentially passive conformist.

Historically, there has been much to be said for this point of view. Because of a recent visit in Australia, I have been reading and hearing about the Australian aborigine. For twenty thousand years he and his kind have survived in a most inhospitable environment in which modern man would die. He has survived by passing on every bit of knowledge and skill he has acquired about a relatively unchanging world and frowning upon or tabooing any new ways of meeting the relatively unchanging problems. This has been the description of American educational goals as well.

To Nurture the Process of Discovery

But modern man is face to face with a situation which has never before existed in history. The world—of science, of communication, of social relationships—is changing at such a pace that knowledge stored up in the past is not enough. The physicist cannot live by the stored knowledge of his science. His confidence, his basic trust, is in the *process* by which new knowledge is acquired. In like fashion, if society is to be able to meet the challenges of a more and more rapidly changing world—if civilization is to survive—people must be able increasingly to live in a process manner. The public, like the physicist, will have to put their trust in the *process* by which new problems are met, not in the *answers* to problems of the past.

This need implies a new goal for education. Learning how to learn, involvement in a process of change—these become the primary aims of an education fit for the present world. There must evolve individuals who are capable of intelligent, informed, discriminating, adaptive, effective involvement in a process of change. Such involvement develops only in the individual who has discovered that significant learning is, though threatening, even more deeply rewarding; who has recognized that it is satisfying to take the risk of being open to his experience, both of his feelings and reactions within and of the evidence his senses bring him about the world without. Such an individual is in process of change, is continually learning, is constructively meeting the perplexities of a world in which problems are always spawning much faster than their answers. He has learned that the process of change is something in which he can live more comfortably than in rigidity, that the ability to face the new appropriately is more important than being able to repeat the old. This is a new type of aim for education.

Two Sets of Assumptions in Education

Assumptions Implicit in Current Education

From an observation of educational institutions at all levels (first grade through graduate study), I have attempted to abstract from the behavior of the educators those assumptions or principles upon which they act. It should be clear that these six assumptions are implicit, rather than explicit—that they are drawn from what teachers *do*, rather than from what they *say*.

1. *The student cannot be trusted to pursue his own learning.* The attitude of most teachers and faculty members tends to be one of mistrustful guidance. They look suspiciously on the student's aims and desires and devote their energies to guiding him along the pathway he "should" follow. I believe it is extremely rare that students have the feeling that they are being set free to learn, on their own.

2. *Presentation equals learning.* This assumption is evident in every curriculum, every lesson plan. It is especially clear if one observes a faculty committee trying to decide what topics a course shall "cover." It is clear that what is presented or covered is what is learned. Anyone who has used any method which taps the actual experience of students in a class knows that this assumption could not be further from the truth; yet it persists.

3. *The aim of education is to accumulate brick upon brick of factual knowledge.* There must be a "foundation of knowledge." These clearly defined building blocks must be assimilated before the student can proceed to learn on his own. Though this assumption flies in the face of everything known about the curve of forgetting, it remains an unquestioned assumption.

4. *The truth is known.* In almost every textbook, knowledge is presented as a closed book. "These are the facts"—about chemistry or history or literature. The student has almost no opportunity to realize that in every field it is the *search* for knowledge which is important and that the "knowledge" already gained is only the best working

hypothesis that can be formulated at the moment. Only in recent years, in such developments as the teaching of the "new mathematics" has there been the slightest dent in this assumption.

5. *Constructive and creative citizens develop from passive learners.* There seems to be great unanimity in the verbalized aim of producing good citizens, able to act constructively, with an independence and originality adequate to the complex problems of today. Yet it is equally evident that the main virtue encouraged in classrooms at all levels is that of passively learning material which is presented by the instructor, which in turn has been selected by some educational group as being important for the student to learn. This is clearly the way in which it is assumed that an independent citizenry is developed.

6. *Evaluation is education, and education is evaluation.* Taking examinations and preparing for the next set of exams is a way of life for students. There is little or no thought of intrinsic goals, since the extrinsic have become all-important. Rarely does the student ask himself, "What aspect of this subject or this book interests me?" or "How could I find out about this particular aspect of life?" The sole question is, "What will be asked on the examination?" It has gradually come to be assumed by teachers, students, and parents that report cards and grades *constitute* education. When a faculty member asked a student what he got out of a certain course, the student's response was what one would expect in this system: "I got a B."

Assumptions Relevant to Significant Experiential Learning

It is my belief that in the next few decades there is likely to be a revolution in education which will deeply challenge the foregoing assumptions. My reason for believing that such a revolution will occur is that I question whether our culture can afford to permit its citizens to develop under such an educational system. It cannot afford to develop citizens who are passive, whose knowledge is settled and closed, whose ways of thinking are rigid, who have no feeling for the *process* of discovering new knowledge and new answers.

The question for this newer approach to education will be, "How can the incorporation of the *process* of learning and changing be made the deepest purpose of the educational experience?" In endeavoring to answer this, I list below a new set of assumptions which, I believe, will replace the present principles.

1. *Human beings have a natural potentiality for learning.* They are curious about their world, they are eager to develop and learn, and they have the capacity for making constructive discriminations between learning opportunities. This potentiality for learning, for discovery, can be released under suitable conditions (which I discuss below). In short, the student's desire to learn can be trusted.

2. *Significant learning takes place when the subject matter is perceived by the student as having relevance for his own purposes.* When an individual has a goal he wishes to achieve and when he sees the material available to him as relevant to achieving that goal, learning takes place with great rapidity. How long does it take an adolescent to learn to drive a car? A very reasonable hypothesis is that the time for learning various subjects would be cut to a small fraction of the time currently allotted if the material were perceived by the learner as related to his own purposes. The evidence from various sources indicates that in many instances one-third to one-fifth of the present time allotment would be sufficient.

3. *Much significant learning is acquired through doing.* When a student is attempting to cope with a problem which is directly confronting him, effective learning is likely to occur. The brief, intensive courses for teachers, doctors, farmers—individuals facing immediate problems—provide ample evidence of learning through doing. The class group which becomes involved in a dramatic production—selecting the play and the cast, designing and making the scenery and costumes, coaching the actors, selling tickets—provides similar evidence.

4. *Learning is facilitated when the student participates responsibly in the learning process.* This assumption is closely related to the preceding. When he chooses his own directions, helps to discover his own learning resources, formulates his own problems, decides his own course of action, and lives with the consequences of each of these choices, then significant learning is maximized. There is evidence from industry as well as from the field of education that participative learning is much more effective than is passive learning.

5. *Self-initiated learning, involving the whole person of the*

learner—feelings as well as intellect—is the most pervasive and lasting.
This hypothesis has been discovered in psychotherapy, where it is the
totally involved learning of oneself by oneself which is most effective.
This is not learning which takes place "only from the neck up." It is a
"gut-level" type of learning—profound and pervasive. It can also occur
in the tentative discovery of a new self-generated idea, in the learning
of a difficult skill, or in the act of artistic creation—painting, poetry,
sculpture. One of the most important aspects is that in these situations
the learner knows it is his own learning, and thus can hold to it or
relinquish it in the face of a more profound learning, without having to
turn to some authority for corroboration of his judgment.

6. *Creativity in learning is best facilitated when self-criticism and
self-evaluation are primary, and evaluation by others is of secondary
importance.* Creativity blossoms in an atmosphere of freedom. The best
research organizations, in industry as well as in the academic world,
have learned that external evaluation is largely fruitless if the goal is
creative work. The individual must be permitted to make his own
evaluation of his own efforts.

7. *The most socially useful learning in the modern world is the
learning of the process of learning, a continuing openness to experience, an incorporation into oneself of the process of change.* I have
already discussed this assumption in speaking of the second aim in
education.

CONDITIONS FACILITATING EXPERIENTIAL LEARNING

If significant experiential learning is the preferred type, if the goal
for education is to facilitate an openness to the process of change, if the
educational approach is to be based on the assumptions or hypotheses
stated in the preceding section, how may these purposes be implemented? Fortunately, much has been discovered (particularly in the
field of psychotherapy) about the conditions which make for significant or experiential learning by the whole person. I would like to
summarize these conditions as I understand them, as they apply not
only to the climate created by the teacher in his classroom, but to the
faculty of the teacher-training institution and to administrators of
schools at all levels.

Confronting a Problem

There is no doubt that experiential learning takes place most effectively when the individual is face to face with a problem which is meaningful to him, a problem to which he desires a solution. It is perhaps not impossible to promote significant learning in the absence of such a confrontation with a problem but it is much more difficult. The current tendency to insulate the elementary- and high-school pupil from any of the real problems of life constitutes a difficulty for the teacher at these levels.

Teacher education is more fortunate in this respect. The prospective teacher can readily be given some experience in the classroom—observing, helping, being responsible for portions of the teaching—so that he becomes sharply and vividly aware of the difficult problems he will soon be facing on his own responsibility; hence, he is well motivated toward significant learning.

It is not quite so clear whether the teacher-training institution is aware of the problems it confronts. To the extent, however, that the faculty and administration of such an institution are aware of the intense critical public interest in education, to the extent that they are aware of the acute problems posed by a sharp increase in student population, to the extent that they realize the ineffectiveness of most professional education as carried on today—to this degree they will recognize the profound problems with which they are confronted and will also be in a mood for self-initiated learning.

Developing Certain Attitudes

Once the individual or the institution is clearly aware of a problem, there seems to be evidence that certain attitudinal sets in the facilitator of learning increase the likelihood that experiential learning will take place. I will endeavor to describe three of these attitudes in somewhat general terms so that the principles apply to the facilitation of learning, whether in administrators and faculty members of the teacher-training institution, in the prospective teacher, in a classroom teacher taking further training on the job, or in the pupil in the classroom.

Perhaps the most basic of these essential attitudes is realness or genuineness. When the facilitator is a real person, being what he really is and entering into a relationship with the learner without presenting a front or a façade, he is likely to be effective. To be real in this sense means that the feelings which he is experiencing are available to him, available to his awareness, that he is able to live these feelings and able to communicate them if appropriate. It means that he comes into a direct personal encounter with the learner, meeting him on a person-to-person basis. It means that he is being himself, not denying himself.

With this attitude, the teacher can be a real person in his relationship with his students. He can be enthusiastic, he can be bored, he can be interested in students, he can be angry, he can be sensitive and sympathetic. Because he accepts these feelings as his own, he has no need to impose them on his students. He can dislike a student product without implying that it is objectively bad or that the student is bad. He is simply expressing a feeling of dislike for the product, a feeling which exists within himself. Thus, he is a *person* to his students, not a faceless embodiment of a curricular requirement or a sterile tube through which knowledge is passed from one generation to the next.

It is obvious that this attitudinal set, found to be effective in psychotherapy, is in sharp contrast with the tendency of most teachers to show themselves to their pupils simply in their teaching "role." It is quite customary for teachers rather consciously to put on the mask, the role, the façade, of being a teacher and to wear this façade all day, removing it only when they have left the school.

ACCEPTANCE

Another attitude which stands out in the work of those who have been successful in promoting experiential learning is acceptance, a prizing of the student, a prizing of his feelings and his opinions. When the facilitator values the individual learner as having worth and when this prizing extends to every facet of this individual, then the likelihood that experiential learning will take place is greatly increased. A teacher who has such an attitude can be fully acceptant of the fear and hesitation of the student as he approaches a new problem as well as of the satisfaction he feels in achievement. Such a teacher can accept the student's occasional apathy, his desire to explore byroads of knowledge, as well as his disciplined efforts to achieve major goals. If he can accept personal feelings which both disturb and promote learning—rivalry with a sibling, hatred of authority, concern about personal adequacy—then he is certainly such a teacher. What I am describing is a prizing of the learner as an imperfect human being with many feelings, many potentialities. It means that the facilitator cares for the learner in a nonpossessive way; he is willing for the learner to be a separate person. His prizing or acceptance of the learner is an operational expression of his essential confidence in the capacity of the human organism.

EMPATHIC UNDERSTANDING

A further element which establishes a climate for experiential learning is empathic understanding. When the teacher has the ability to understand the student's reactions from the inside, has a sensitive awareness of how the process of education and learning appears to the student, then again the likelihood of personally meaningful learning is increased.

This kind of understanding is sharply different from the usual evaluative understanding which follows the pattern of, "I understand what is wrong with you." When there is a sensitive empathy, however, the reaction in the learner follows something of this pattern: "At last someone understands how it feels and seems to be me without wanting to analyze me or judge me. Now I can blossom and grow and learn."

SUMMARY

There is an increasing number of studies which lend confirmation to the view that when these three attitudes exist in the therapeutic relationship, they bring about constructive learning and change in the individual (Barrett-Lennard, 1962; Rogers, 1957, 1967). There is at least one pilot study indicating that teachers who are regarded by their superiors as outstanding show these attitudinal qualities in much higher degree than teachers who are rated as less effective (Barrett-Lennard, 1960). Since the aim of education, like the aim of therapy, is to produce creative and adaptive individuals, well informed about themselves and their world, it does not seem too great a leap to suggest that these attitudes are as basic to the facilitation of learning in education as they are to the facilitation of learning in psychotherapy.

Providing Resources

In addition to the learner's face-to-face confrontation with a problem and the facilitator's evincing the attitudes described above, there must be resources for learning. It is usually the responsibility of the facilitator to see that all types of resources are made available. These may be material resources, tools, laboratory equipment, supplies, and the like. They may be opportunities for observation—visiting a classroom, listening to tape recordings, going to a children's hospital. They may be written resources presenting the stored experiences of others—books, articles, reprints, student papers and reports. They may be personal resources—contact with individuals whose work or experience can contribute to the learning. Certainly, much of the effectiveness of the facilitator depends upon his imaginative organization of resources and his ability to make these resources easily and psychologically available to the learner.

SOME PRACTICAL WAYS OF ENCOURAGING EXPERIENTIAL LEARNING

Keeping in mind the conditions which have been described, I turn now to some of the newer developments in education, practical approaches which may be used to facilitate a more experiential type of learning and which may be used to implement the hypotheses basic to the second educational goal. I have selected three examples which apply specifically to classroom instruction, and one which applies both to the classroom and to the training and supervision of the instructor himself.

The Conduct of Inquiry

A specialized type of participative and experiential learning which has been receiving increasing emphasis in the last few years has been developing in science. Various individuals and national groups have been working toward a goal of helping students to become inquirers, working in a fluid way toward discovery in the scientific realm.

The impetus for this movement has grown out of an urgent need to have science experienced as a changing field, as it is in the modern world, rather than as a closed book of already discovered facts. The possession of a body of knowledge about science is not an adequate qualification for the teacher today. Hence the aim is to get the teacher away from the misleading image of science as absolute, complete, and permanent (Schwab, 1960). Suchman (1961, 1962) is one of those who have given rather specific details regarding the implementation of this aim. In trying to strengthen the autonomous processes within the learner, Suchman advocates a new approach in which special training is necessary for teachers of science. The teacher sets the stage of inquiry by posing the problems, creating an environment responsive to the learner, and giving assistance to the student in his investigative operations. This climate makes it possible for pupils to achieve autonomous discoveries and to engage in self-directed learning. They become scientists *themselves*, on a simple level, seeking answers to real questions, discovering for themselves the pitfalls and the joys of the scientist's search. They may not learn as many scientific "facts," but they develop a real appreciation of science as a never-ending search, a recognition that there is no closure in science.

It is obvious that if prospective teachers are to stimulate the spirit of inquiry among their pupils, they must have experienced it themselves. Therefore, courses in the teacher-training institution must be taught in the same fashion as Suchman describes if teachers themselves are to experience the satisfaction of self-initiated discovery in the scientific realm. This new development in the area of science constitutes a deep challenge to present concepts of teaching. According to the evidence, current educational practice tends to make children less autonomous and less empirical in their search for knowledge and understanding as they move through the elementary grades. This tendency is strictly at variance with the aim of those who focus on inquiry. When children are permitted to think their way through to new understandings, the concepts they derive in the process have greater depth, meaning, and durability. The children have become more autonomous and more solidly based in an empirical approach.

Simulation

The trend toward a more experiential type of learning shows up in the increasing use of simulation in the classroom. The essence of this procedure is that a complex situation is simulated—the relationships among several nations (Solomon, 1963; Guetzkow, 1963), a historical situation, a social conflict, a problem in interpersonal relationships— and the students take the parts of those participating in the event. Though there is no conclusive research as yet indicating the outcome of this type of learning as compared with more conventional procedures, it is already being successfully used in half a dozen universities and a number of high schools. Since it is a relatively new type of approach, I shall outline a hypothetical example.

A social studies or civics course might well simulate a problem in community policy regarding education. Different pupils might be assigned respectively to be the mayor, the head of the board of education, the members of the board of education, the superintendent of schools, the president of the PTA, the head of the taxpayers' league. Now the problem is posed to them—from their own community or from any other community where the facts are available to them—that members of the board of education want a new bond issue to expand the building plant and hire new teachers. They prepare to take their parts in the simulated situation.

What are the types of learning that would follow upon this simulation? First, each student would turn to the factual resources in order to develop his own stance on the issue and to justify his point of view. There would be a degree of self-discipline involved in searching for this factual material. The student would find it necessary to make a personal decision based on his own informed stand. He would be involved in the handling of interpersonal relationships with those who hold different points of view. He would find himself bearing the responsibility for the consequences of his own decisions and actions. Throughout the experience, there would be necessary a disciplined commitment to learning, decision, action. Such an experience would appear to develop a positive type of learning rather than a negative, critical type of thinking. Current education often develops individuals who can readily criticize any proposal or idea but cannot make a positive plan or decision regarding constructive action.

Another interesting example of the use of a type of simulation is described by Ronald Lippitt (1962). A fifth-grade class was concerned about youngsters who were know-it-alls. The whole class participated either as actors or observers in dealing with the problem. As they did so, the pupils developed a real understanding of why know-it-alls behave as they do; the class came to recognize the insecurity which so often underlies such behavior. Gradually, an attitude evolved of working *with* the problem rather than *at* it. In the process, individual students showed significant personal development, and the class as a group showed increased freedom of communication, which encouraged and supported greater individuality of participation. It was a living experience in behavioral science.

Programed Instruction

As educators well know, there has been a vast and explosive development in programed instruction (Skinner, 1961; Fry, 1963; Gage, 1963; Pressey, 1963). This is not the place to review these developments or the theory of operant conditioning upon which this work is based. It is appropriate, however, to point out that programed instruction may be used in a variety of ways. Programing can be seen as potentially providing for all learning, or it may be seen as one new and very useful tool in the facilitation of learning. As Skinner has pointed out, "To acquire behavior the student must engage in behavior" (1961, p. 389).

It is of particular interest to note that in the development of programed instruction there is a tendency toward shorter, "plug-in" programs, rather than toward the development of whole courses covering a total field of knowledge. To me, the development of these shorter programs suggests the more fruitful way in which the student may be involved in the use of so-called teaching machines. When learning is facilitated in line with the second set of assumptions presented, the student frequently comes upon gaps in his knowledge, tools which he lacks, information which he needs to solve the problem he is confronting. Here the flexibility of programed instruction is invaluable. A pupil who needs to know how to use a microscope can find a program covering this knowledge. The student who is planning to spend three months in France can utilize programed instruction in conversational

French. The pupil who needs algebra, whether for the solution of problems of interest to him or simply to get into college, can work on a program of instruction in algebra.

Used in these ways, a competently developed program undoubtedly gives the student immediate experiences of satisfaction, enables him to learn a body of knowledge when he needs it, gives him the feeling that any content is learnable, and fosters a recognition that the process of education is an intelligible and comprehensible one. He can work at his own rate and finds that the carefully designed program presents him with coherent, interrelated steps. Its stress on immediate reinforcement and reward rather than on punitive or evaluative measures is another factor in its favor. If programed learning is used flexibly, it can constitute a large forward step in meeting the massive needs for functional learning of subject matter as the number of pupils grows sharply.

Programed learning is developing in new and unexpected fields. Berlin and Wyckoff (1963) are developing programs for the improvement of interpersonal relationships in which two people work together at mutual tasks assigned by the programed text, not only learning some of the cognitive concepts in regard to interpersonal relationships but also gradually experiencing deeper and deeper communication with each other. Both industry and educational institutions have begun to make use of this developing series of programs, impressed by the fact that the learnings involve both feelings and intellect and that they have significant personal meaning for the learner.

It should be obvious that programed learning has great potential risks if it is unwisely used. If it becomes a substitute for thinking in larger patterns and gestalts, if it becomes a way of stressing factual knowledge more than creativity, then real damage may be done. But if it is perceived as an instrument which can be used by educators to achieve flexibility in education, then it is one of the most powerful tools which psychology has as yet contributed to the field.

"Sensitivity Training"

The final example of a new development which fosters a climate for experiential or significant learning is so-called sensitivity training. This is an approach which is of help in educating administrators and teachers for the newer goals in education. It also has relevance to the classroom situation.

Though not widely used as yet in educational institutions, there has been a burgeoning use of the intensive group experience in the development of business executives and government administrators. Under a variety of labels—the T-Group, the Laboratory Group, the Sensitivity Training Course, the intensive Workshop in Human Relations, the Basic Encounter Group—this approach has become an important part of the training function.

It is difficult to describe briefly the nature of such a group experience, especially since it varies greatly from group to group and from leader to leader. (See Wechsler and Reisel, 1959, for one description.) Essentially, the group begins with little imposed structure, so that the situation and the purposes are ambiguous and up to the group members to decide. The leader's function is to facilitate expression and to clarify or point up the dynamic pattern of the group's struggle to work toward a meaningful experience. In such a group, after an initial "milling around," personal expressiveness tends to increase and involves an increasingly free, direct, and spontaneous communication among members of the group. Façades become less necessary, defenses are lowered, basic encounters occur as individuals reveal hitherto hidden feelings and aspects of themselves and receive spontaneous feedback— both negative and positive—from group members. Some or many individuals become much more facilitative in relationships to others, making possible greater freedom of expression.

In general, when the experience is a fruitful one, it is deeply personal, resulting in more direct person-to-person communication, sharply increased self-understanding, more realness and independence in the individual, and an increased understanding and acceptance of others. While much still remains to be learned about the intensive group experience in all its forms, it is already clear that it helps to create in most members of the group attitudes which, among other things, are highly conducive to experiential learning.

Perhaps a few examples will convey a more meaningful picture of what is already being done. The National Training Laboratory has begun to conduct "college labs" at Bethel, Maine (Bradford, Gibb, and Benne, 1964, p. 109). Each of the T-Groups in these laboratories contains several students and several faculty members from the same college. As they share in the exploration of their interpersonal attitudes and relationships and of their work goals, their learnings have often been highly significant. There are reports that at least one department of English has been revolutionized by its experience in this college lab.

Various leaders in the group-dynamics field (Gibb, Herold, Zander, and Coffey) have transformed courses for teachers into T-Groups. So meaningful have been the learnings that in some of these institutions the demand for such groups, involving learning based on direct personal encounter, has grown beyond all expectations.

One elementary-school system in a Western city has made it possible for most of its principals and teachers to have experience in a sensitivity-training group. Likewise, when there is a difficult classroom situation, a member of the guidance department serves as leader of a "problem-solving group" in the classroom, the group including the teacher(s) as well as the pupils involved. Out of these experiences have come much more responsible behavior on the part of pupils, much improved communication in the classroom, and an administrative structure in which faculty-administrator interaction is much more free and real than is ordinarily achieved. In other words, there has been movement toward the establishment of a psychological climate in which pupils, teachers, and administrators can learn, in a self-initiated fashion, in regard to both the interpersonal problems which they face and the factual problems which they face in the world outside.

It appears highly likely that this particular development will become much more widespread in the educational world.

Conclusion

In this chapter, I have tried to present something of what would be involved if a new aim for education were adopted, that of achieving openness to change, and if focus were on that type of learning in which the whole person is involved, a meaningful experience of emotional as well as cognitive learning.

It is clear, I believe, that if this aim were selected, the basic reliance of the teacher would be upon the tendency toward fulfillment, toward actualization, in his students. The teacher would be basing his work on the hypothesis that students who are in real contact with life problems wish to learn, want to grow, seek to discover, endeavor to master, desire to create. The teacher would attempt to develop a quality of climate in the classroom and a quality of personal relationship with his students which would permit these natural tendencies to come to fruition.

The teacher or facilitator of learning who is desirous of creating the conditions for this self-fulfilling type of learning finds that there are a number of new methods already at hand which are congenial to this approach. The conduct-of-inquiry approach in science develops self-initiated learners in that field. The use of simulation techniques makes for responsible learning and decision making. The teaching machine, especially in the form of brief, specific programs, can provide the flexibility which enables the student to learn material when he most needs it. The utilization of sensitivity training for both facilitators and learners not only increases the freedom and depth of communication but also helps the individual to become more independent in his stance toward learning and toward life. These specific approaches suggest, but do not exhaust, the many ways in which the goals of the new education may be implemented.

As for the learner, the result of such self-initiated learning, such development in meeting and mastering new problems, is a more complete openness to all aspects of his experience, both the outer stimuli and his own internal reactions. He would thus be more fully and adaptively present in confronting a new problem. Martin Buber (1955 edition, p. 14) described this situation well: ". . . In spite of all similarities, every living situation has, like a newborn child, a new face that has never been before and will never come again. It demands of you a reaction which cannot be prepared beforehand. It demands nothing of what is past. It demands presence, responsibility; it demands you."

It is in this spirit that the learner would be able to deal creatively with an ever changing world.

4

Cognitive Models
of Learning and Instruction

ASAHEL D. WOODRUFF

University of Utah

✌

THE FORMULATION OF INSTRUCTIONAL PROGRAMS IN THE PAST HAS
suffered from the absence of valid underlying concepts of human
behavior and learning. Both logical and sociological theory have served
as the basis for programs without adequate psychological moorings,
and they have been disappointing.

When psychological ideas have been used, there have been two
general approaches. The more dominant has been the formulation of a
set of instructional practices based on the acceptance of some general
concept about human development, such as the "child-development
concept," or the idea that the desired behavior can be cultivated by
having students practice it in school, or the idea that children can use
knowledge in natural situations only if it is given to them in an
integrated form, as in core programs. The proposed sets of instructional practices have generally been internally consistent, but have
developed independently of systematic and validated concepts of human behavior and learning (Horowitz, 1959; Richardson and Smitter,
1959; Smallenburg and Newcomber, 1959; Bellack, 1956; Robinson,
1961; Goodlad, 1959; Woodring, 1957, Chap. 3).

The other approach begins with some data about human learning
and moves to logically implied educational practices (Buswell, 1959;
Lindgren, 1959; Thomas, 1959; Gagné and Bolles, 1959). There have

55

been relatively few such attempts, and they have had the disadvantage generally of a paucity of relevant and vital psychological data for human educational purposes. Nevertheless, I assume this approach to be the only productive one. Instruction is effective when it facilitates learning, and by learning I mean alteration of behavior. Instructional practices should be reciprocal to the behavioral processes, with special attention to the manner in which behavior changes. Furthermore, emphasis should be on decision-making behavior, rather than on the more obviously motor and reflex behavior.

Direct approaches from learning *theory* to teaching have not been helpful. On the other hand, there should be a close relationship between the actual *processes* of human behavior (and change in behavior) and the processes of teaching. This chapter uses models to portray processes; it does not reach the level of theory. It is argued, then, that a workable set of instructional practices can be developed from models of behavior, and perhaps in no other way. Hence, attention must go first to behavior and then to instruction.

A CASE FOR COGNITIVE THEORY

Two attractive descriptions of human behavior are dominant today. Operant conditioning is the S-R (Stimulus-Response) approach to environmental control of behavior. It assumes that the S controls the R and that there is an identifiable S for every R that occurs. It is the hope of exponents of this theory that even such a complex behavior as reading can be explained and developed by it (Resnick, 1963; Dale, 1962).

Cognitive theory is an S-O-R (Stimulus-Organism-Response) approach to the study of variables that develop within the organism as a stored residue of experience and that subsequently take on mediating or directive influence over behavior. The "concept" is the major mediating variable for decision-making behavior (Hebb, 1949, 1958; Harvey, Hunt, and Schroder, 1961; Levine, 1959, 1963; Pubols, 1962; Sherif, 1950; Cornwell, 1963).

Cognitive theory assumes that concepts have flexibility of combination and elaboration, giving them multiple-threat power in producing variations of responses (Cornwell, 1963; Levine, 1959, 1963; Pubols,

1962). Thus the infinite variety of behavior an individual exhibits can be produced by a much smaller number of more or less generalized concepts working in various combinations and permutations than the operant-conditioning approach would require in specific stimuli.

Both of these theories are psychologically feasible and empirically sound. The choice between them must rest on other than purely psychological grounds. For human education, cognitive theory is the only feasible choice for two reasons. First, cognitive theory provides a workable relationship between behavioral objectives and subject matter, and thus is feasible for the extremely complex problems involved in human education. The possibility of planning a curriculum for environmental control of all behaviors by means of conditioning may be hypothetically possible, but is so staggering in its complexity as to be practically impossible. It is like trying to explain organismic behavior in the formulas of biophysics or biochemistry (Alexander, 1963; Resnick, 1963).

The schools could never conduct a program based on conditioning procedures. Teachers could not manage it. It is not feasible to provide a complete dossier of all the behaviors that would have to be conditioned and the controlled treatments to produce them. Moreover, the essential controlled conditions could not be established or maintained in a school situation. Curriculum can never be other than a body of knowledge, and educational processes must be those that can lead students to a mastery of that knowledge.

Second, there is an identification between the nature of a concept and the nature of subject matter making cognitive data immediately usable in curriculum planning (Bellack, 1961; Broudy, 1954; Foshay, 1961; Klotsche, 1961; Schwab, 1961). To be sure, subject matter must be reexamined in the light of current insights into the nature of knowledge, and this reexamination implies a profound change in curriculum content and teaching practices (G. H. Henry, 1956).

Medley and Mitzel (1963) say that "the ultimate criterion of teacher effectiveness must be based on change in pupils" and that "intermediate criteria must be shown to be correlated with the ultimate criterion." If pupil behavior is the ultimate criterion, then measurement might be of either the R components of S-R theory or the O components of S-O-R theory. Although the use of O variables assumes that concepts are relevant to adjustmental behavior, it is also appropriate to consider performance on a concept test as overt behavior. There remains only the requirement that a relationship between concepts and adjustmental behavior be established, and this requirement has already been met.

The possibility of formulating useful models of instruction has improved significantly with certain recent developments. One of them is the understanding of the role of value in human behavior (Woodruff, 1952), followed closely by the recognition of concepts as mediating variables in behavior. Another development is in the field of communications. It consists of the differentiation of the verbal process from the cognitive process. Hoban (1961) says that it is a fundamental error to assume that "communication is the transmission of meaning." Whereas meaningful sets of symbols can be transmitted, meanings cannot. On the assumption that this position is valid (and there is considerable justification for such an assumption), it becomes necessary to reexamine the relationship between verbal behavior and cognitive learning. An integral part of this reexamination is a new way of looking at subject matter, of which so-called modern physics is one example (Little, 1959) and modern mathematics is another (Keedy, 1959; Beberman, 1959). This way consists primarily of translating subject matter from the realm of verbalism to conceptual form. It consists of making visible to the student the phenomena from which a knowledge finder derived a verbal statement about those phenomena and of presenting the phenomena themselves to the student for his perception and conceptualization. This development has provided a link between knowledge and behavior which has been missing in the past. It seems to provide a way of explaining the educational failure to affect behavior and of describing educative procedures which can succeed.

These two developments are in a sense two sides of the same coin. Both of them focus attention on concepts and suggest that the concept is the central figure around which it is possible to erect a structure bringing learning, behaving, and teaching comfortably together (Bellack, 1961).

The position here reported has been formulated for the primary purpose of making research data meaningful in the curriculum market. Therefore, this chapter emphasizes knowledge and seeks to show its conceptual and insightful nature in both subject matter and decision-making processes. It also assumes that motor behavior serves the purpose primarily of carrying out a person's decisions, and therefore might be treated as a secondary problem after the cognitive problem is solved. Problems of individual differences and of maladjustment are also temporarily deemphasized because both of them will be more easily handled after an adequate concept of the cognitive processes is evolved.

Assumptions Relevant to Behavior and Learning

The models in this chapter rest on some assumptions which may not be immediately evident. The reader may not agree with the assumptions, but knowing what they are is helpful in understanding the models. The models, in turn, furnish a source of hypotheses against which existing relevant data can be laid and which can be subjected to empirical tests. Thus the assumptions made explicit in the following paragraphs can eventually be evaluated through the models.

1. *Human behavior is characterized by the qualities of a cybernetic system.* There is referential input (input from real objects and processes, not from symbols which represent them); storage and internal manipulation of the input; the possibility of response during the manipulation to a communication input which has the sole possibility of guiding the attention of the subject; purposive output; and feedback from the output action into the perceptual channels. All of the models subsequently presented serve either to portray the basic structure or to elaborate some part of it.

2. *The referential input is the sole source of percepts which become concepts.* Communication input cannot perform the task of referential input. Referential input consists of literal sense perception of real objects and processes, as illustrated by an infant undergoing cuddling, a boy examining and trying a tool, or an adult having his first taste of caviar. Communication input consists of a verbal description of any of these sense perceptions. Lecture and discussion are communication inputs.

There may be serious objections to the notion that only referential input can be the source of percepts and that concepts are fully dependent on this kind of input. Some brief elaborations are needed at this point.

Referential input is generally acceded to be heaviest in infancy and early childhood. Concepts brought to maturity in later years are often the product of reflection, rather than additional referential input. This is a developmental explanation of conceptual maturity, but it is not adequate as an explanation of all learning in adult years. Referential input becomes dominant whenever a person is placed in a new environment for which he has no existing cognitive background; for example, when a boy takes his first look into the interior of an engine or into the chemical processes of nature, and when a philosophy student needs to see the structure of the concept of major and minor premises or the essential elements of the process of analysis. The need for referential input occurs over and over again in school, even in graduate school. The general failure to recognize this need has much to do with the difficulties of comprehension which generally plague students in the less exact subjects.

It would be trivial to emphasize the role of perception in this chapter if perception were not seriously disregarded at almost all levels of teaching. Verbal input can lead to concept maturation only when the essential bits of perceptual meaning are present. When they are not present, referential input is necessary regardless of school level. Furthermore, the skillful use of diagrammatic portrayals of many complex concepts in such advanced subjects as political science and philosophy could greatly reduce the time and labor of students.

3. *Internal manipulation and storage has some dimensions.* The following list is probably not exhaustive.

a. It may be either subconscious or recognized in various degrees (Kubie, 1959; Bruner, 1960).
b. It varies from the vagueness of first impressions to the clarity of mature concepts (Northrop and Morgenau, 1950).
c. It varies from subjectivity to objectivity.
d. It varies from no verbalization to complete verbalization.
e. It ranges from concreteness to "constructness," that is, from mental images of concrete referents to extensive mental constructs in three directions: categorization based on recognition of similarities of structure (generalization); integration based on recognition of processes and consequences (principles); and the discovery of *qualities* of either structures or processes, which are then abstracted and treated as reals.

f. Related to Dimension *e* is another variation which appears in the role of concepts in the decision-making process. This variation comprises a hierarchy from recognition of referents, through a level characterized by following procedures in familiar situations, through a higher level characterized by using concepts to reach conclusions, to problem solving in unfamiliar situations by means of transfer through the use of principles.

g. It varies in degree of inventiveness and also in the quantity and quality of artistic originality.

4. *Recognition of the instrumental value of processes, structural referents, and qualities is part of the internal-manipulation process.* Through feedback from vicarious or actual trial of a person's concepts about ways of behaving, the empirically substantiated value becomes part of the concept and gives rise to motives (Peak, 1960; Rhine, 1958; Woodruff, 1961, Chap. 5; Broudy, 1954, Chap. 10; Geiger, 1950; Frank, 1959). Feelings are the internal responses to the satisfying or annoying dimensions of the trial phase of behavior. This part of the response is the source of value judgment.

5. *Symbolization, or verbalization of meanings, is part of the internal-manipulation process, and verbal communication is the external manifestation of the symbolization.* Verbal communication is intimately related to cognitive patterns, but operates somewhat as a constant verbal wash over them, rather than as a part of the conceptualizing process itself. What has come to be known as the teacher-pupil interaction process is a special use of verbal communication to stimulate validity, maturity, and verbalization of concepts, discovery of principles, and originality in the internal-manipulation process of the student.

6. *Behavioral output is mediated by concepts in ways which are purposive to the reduction of stimuli, the satisfaction of underlying needs, and the attainment of goals.* The operation of this behavior is independent of conscious awareness of what is going on. That is how perceptual meaning is acquired, concepts are formed, and decisions are made with and without awareness. Awareness does not change the basic processes, but permits the intrusion of objectivity through the use of learned criteria and safeguards.

A RUDIMENTARY MODEL OF BEHAVIOR AND LEARNING

I have already maintained that the processes of instruction should be reciprocal to the processes of behavior with special emphasis upon learning. Therefore, it is to the nature of behavior that I turn first.

A rather widely accepted concept of behavior may be represented by the scheme shown in Figure 4–1. *Search* and *Selection* are compa-

Need ——▶ Energy ——▶ Search ——▶ Selection ——▶ Action

Figure 4–1. Behavior Flow Line.

rable to the O in the S-O-R paradigm; *Action* is comparable to the R. *Need* and *Energy* are the dynamics underlying the behavior.

Need is defined as a state of imbalance or deprivation in an element so essential to the maintenance of the "life" of the organism as to throw the organism into a state of excitability and keep it there until the need is met. *Energy* is defined as the presence in the system of muscular agitation requiring motor activity to drain off the energy. *Search* is defined as any mental or motor response which serves to identify a line of action appropriate to the need. Search is dominantly mental. It seems to consist of a scanning of the existing repertoire of possible responses which are in any significant way related to the felt need. *Selection* is defined as a decision, intuitive or examined, recognized or unrecognized, which terminates the searching and precipitates an adjustive act. *Action* is an adjustive move implementing search and selection.

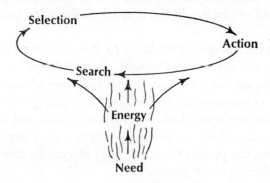

Figure 4–2. Dynamic and Adjustive Elements of the Behavior Flow Line.

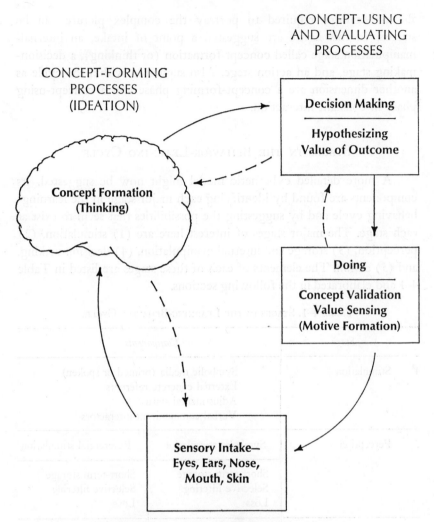

CONCEPT-FORMING
PROCESSES
(IDEATION)

Decision Making

**Hypothesizing
Value of Outcome**

**Concept Formation
(Thinking)**

Doing

**Concept Validation
Value Sensing
(Motive Formation)**

**Sensory Intake—
Eyes, Ears, Nose,
Mouth, Skin**

Figure 4–3. The Behaving and Learning Cycle.

Need and energy are continuing dynamic conditions which supply the fuel that keeps a purposive and adjustive cycle of search, selection, and action operating, as in Figure 4–2. To narrow the present task, I shall assume the constant presence of need and energy as the source of drive and turn to an examination of the search-selection-action cycle, within which there is input, internal manipulation, output, and feedback. The cycle might be redrawn as in Figure 4–3, so that the elaborations required to portray the complex picture can be started. In this figure are suggested a point of intake, an internal-manipulation stage called concept formation (or thinking), a decision-making stage, and an action stage. Also suggested within the cycle as another dimension are a concept-forming phase and a concept-using phase in constant interaction.

STAGES IN THE BEHAVIOR-LEARNING CYCLE

A more detailed cybernetic model might now be suggested. Its components are found by identifying each major stage in the learning-behaving cycle and by suggesting the possibilities that seem to exist at each stage. The major stages of interest here are (1) stimulation, (2) perception, (3) storage and internal manipulation, (4) decision making, and (5) action. The elements of each of these stages are listed in Table 4–1 and elaborated in the following sections.

TABLE 4–1. STAGES IN THE LEARNING-BEHAVING CYCLE.

Stage	Components	
1 Stimulation	Symbolic media (printed or spoken) External concrete referents Adjustmental status Verbal communicant-interactors	
2 Perception	Symbolic stimulation	Referential stimulation
	Short-term storage Selective filtering Loss	Short-term storage Selective filtering Loss
3 Storage and internal manipulation	Symbolic memoriza-tion	Conceptual storage Construct formation
4 Decision making	To perceive again To predict outcome or value To initiate action	
5 Action	Perceptual Adjustive Communicative	

Stage 1: Stimulation

Four possible sources of stimulation are suggested:

1. *Symbolic media* of all kinds, including words, signs, and numbers.

2. *External concrete referents* comprising the environment.

3. *Adjustmental status* of the person—a rich source of stimuli in the form of feelings.

4. *Verbal communicant-interactors*, such as persons with whom one may converse or exchange notes. This source of stimulation might have been included under "symbolic media" except that it has a special capacity to interact with the individual which is not true of nonhuman media. An individual often makes a communication input to a communicant who reacts and returns a stimulus which is partly a function of the first individual himself. The communicant thus functions as an alter ego either in thinking (conversation) or in action. This affects the communicator somewhat as his own thought and action might have done.

In a classroom, the student is literally bombarded by a variety of stimuli of each of these four types. He senses symbolic media primarily by listening to the content of the lecture and seeing blackboard notations, printed material, or other symbolic visual stimuli. He may be provided with demonstrations or laboratory experiences as external concrete referents. Covert stimuli in the form of feelings of pleasure, aversion, and so on are added to the stimulus configuration by the student himself. Finally, verbal interaction with the teacher and other students provides him with feedback stimulation.

Stage 2: Perception

After Broadbent (1958), it is suggested that there is a stage in which all channels of sensation deliver their cargo to a short-term storage area. Here that cargo is selectively filtered and reduced to a limited cargo which gets through to the stage of internal manipulation and long-term storage. It is not necessary or possible to elaborate this concept in the present discussion, except to note two things. First, not all stimuli get through to the long-term storage stage; that is, not all stimuli are perceived. Second, it is helpful to give at least minimal recognition to the filtering process and loss process, both of which are being studied intensively by others at present.

The possibilities for the perception stage thus include:

1. Stimulation (symbolic or referential).
2. Short-term storage.
3. Selective filtering.
4. Loss.

Although Broadbent does not distinguish between *symbolic* stimulation and *referential* stimulation, this distinction is regarded as critical to cognitive theory and generates the two parallel sets of components of the perceptual stage shown in Table 4–1. It is suggested that failure to make the distinction in some recent research and theory (Bloom, 1956; Mayzner, 1962; Morin, 1955; Staats, 1961; Kersh, 1958, 1962) has created confusion between stimulus-discrimination processes and concept-formation processes.

This confusion would not be serious in an S-R framework, but it becomes so in a cognitive framework, as will be more apparent when the stage of long-term storage and manipulation is elaborated. *Symbolic stimuli*, which are primarily verbal in nature, must be recognized as a triggering device for stimulating recall of percepts or concepts already stored. In contrast, *referential stimuli*, from objects and events, are inputs for cognitive meaning (Penfield, 1961, pp. 15–16).

Stage 3: Storage and Internal Manipulation

The two parallel sources of perception generate parallel storages:

1. *Symbolic storage*, consisting of symbolic (words, signs, data) memorization. Examples of data are the names of persons involved in some event, the height or girth of a tree, and dates.

2. *Conceptual storage*, which is the product of referential perception. This storage consists of mental images and mental *constructs*. The conceptual content is manipulated to yield meaning, which then becomes the basis for decisions (Arieti, 1962).

Concepts begin as specific mental images of concrete reals, but are soon elaborated into mental constructs of various kinds. The verbal content usually belongs to some conceptual structure (Frank, 1959; Gibson *et al.*, 1964), but not always, and is most troublesome when it lacks this relationship. It serves behavior in two ways: as a means of

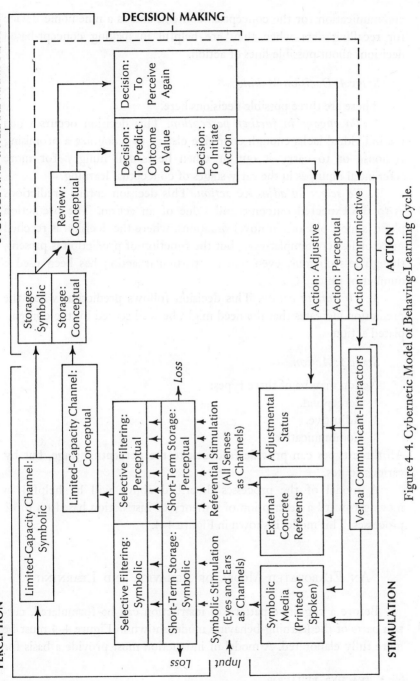

Figure 4-4. Cybernetic Model of Behaving-Learning Cycle.

communication for the conceptual content, and as a mnemonic device for recalling data when they are helpful in making concept-based decisions about possible lines of action.

Stage 4: Decision Making

There are three possible decisions here.

1. *To engage in further perception.* This decision occurs when the individual lacks enough cognitive clarity to recognize a promising response or to carry it out or when he is still hungry for more referential input, as in the early stages of conceptual learning.

2. *To select an adjustive action.* This decision entails predictions as to the expected outcome and value of an action. The prediction phase is most obvious in novel situations, where the decision is reached more or less contemplatively; but the function of prediction is present, though less obvious, even when a particular action has been used a number of times.

3. *To initiate action.* This decision follows prediction when the prediction indicates that the need might be well served by the contemplated action.

Stage 5: Action

Action may be of three types:
1. Perceptual.
2. Adjustive.
3. Communicative.

All three types can provide feedback to the perceptual stage, but by various routes.

A model of the processes described above will be helpful in moving toward a description of a theory of instruction based on those processes. This model is shown in Figure 4–4.

An Elaborated Model of Behavior and Learning

Before a cognitive pattern of instruction can be formulated, certain parts of the learning-behaving model shown in Figure 4–4 must be more fully elaborated. A model of instruction must provide a basis for two major kinds of instructional activity which are directly derived from (1) the referential-input process and subsequent conceptual elaboration and use, (2) the symbolic-input process, and (3) all of the verbal interaction activities between persons which accompany conceptual processes and purposive behavior.

Specifically, a teacher must perform these two activities:

1. Prepare and use stimuli for *referential input*, which is capable of leading to the formation of useful concepts, and prepare and use stimuli for the related symbol input of *verbal information*, which supplements the concepts with essential verbally retained data.

2. Use symbolic and verbal processes of *interaction* with students which succeed in *guiding* internal manipulation of conceptual processes, decision making, trial of learned concepts in realistic situations, and interpretation of feedback from those trials, and which cultivate higher forms of thought and useful originality.

To lead directly to a theory of instruction, it is helpful to describe in greater detail the following aspects of behavior:

1. Two closely related but motivationally distinct aspects of perception: perceiving a referent as something to learn about, and perceiving a situation which requires an adjustive action.

2. The closely related processes of concept formation and concept using, and how they affect each other.

3. The storage and manipulation stage, with particular reference to kinds of concepts that form, levels of concepts and levels of behavior, and originality processes.

4. The trial stage, with reference to concept validation or the shaping up process, the relationship between meaning and feeling, and the formation of motives.

5. The difference between empirical experience which precedes concept learning and empirical experience which follows concept learning and tests it or uses it productively; and the implications for facilitating or interfering with conceptual learning when the two are not differentiated.

Perception of Referents vs. Adjustmental Situations

Figure 4–5 contains an elaboration of two major kinds of sensory intake, both of which may be involved in a particular situation. The

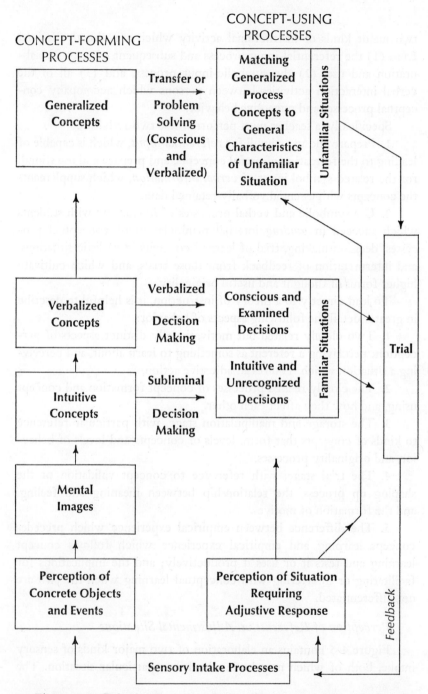

Figure 4-5. Behaving-Learning Cycle Showing Decision Making in Familiar Situations at Intuitive and Verbalized Levels, and Problem Solving in Unfamiliar Situations.

individual may perceive a situation as one which requires an adjustive response. If he does, part or all of his response is absorbed in the business of making an adjustive act. He may also perceive a situation as a set of referents without any implication for adjustmental response, but simply as things to perceive.

A mathematics presentation, for example, may be given with or without a warning that a test will follow it the next day. The warning turns a potentially interesting perceptual experience into a situation which demands an adjustive response. For some students, the threat creates more effective response to the subject matter; for others, it interferes with effective response.

It is likely that perceptual learning might flourish better when there is not too great interference from a sense of need to make an adjustive act. That the two possibilities exist side by side and may either supplement or interfere with each other seems important to a system of instruction.

It is important also to note that any realistic *trial use* of concepts is likely to occur only when the individual senses a situation to which he must make an adjustmental act and uses his newly formed concepts as the basis for that action.

Some of the best examples of this combination are found in vocational programs. In agriculture a student acquires concepts which he uses almost immediately in his farm enterprise. He makes a decision about the care of a calf, acts on the decision, and takes the consequences of his act. The feedback from this tryout has an important effect on his concept.

Concept Formation and Concept Using

The left side of Figure 4–5 represents concept-formation processes; and the right side, concept-using processes. These sets of processes are in a constant interactional relationship.

Concept formation is shown as a direct derivative of referential perception. Concept using is also shown as a direct result of perception, but of the perception of a situation requiring an adjustive response rather than typical referential perception. For example, a child might perceive another child. In one situation the perceived child is simply something to look at. In another situation he might be threatening to strike the first child. The latter situation calls for an adjustive action. Concept formation provides the mediating variables which will direct adjustive acts, and concept using provides an empirical test of those concepts and sets the stage for feedback and shaping up.

Concepts during the Storage and Manipulation Stage

The necessary elaborations for this stage are more extensive than for the preceding stages. This stage must be able to accommodate all of the complexity of human thought. At least three dimensions are required to do this: (1) substantive kinds of concepts, (2) levels of development of concepts, and (3) what Bruner (1962) and others call effective surprise, or the degree of useful originality.

KINDS OF CONCEPTS

That which is shown on the left side of Figure 4–5 as a single column of kinds of concepts is elaborated in Figure 4–6.

The physical world can be perceived in one of two major ways: as process or as structure. Ongoing events are normally seen primarily as processes. A flame of fire which is rapidly consuming a piece of paper tends to be seen as a process. Stable or static things, such as houses, boulders, and trees, tend to be seen as structures. Whether a person sees any referent as a structure or as a process is determined far more by his own set than by any property of the referent. If a referent appears before him in the role of a means, he is likely to see it at least partially, and sometimes wholly, as a process. In terms of the nature of knowledge, it is now axiomatic that if an individual is really to comprehend his environment, he must develop what has been called "a sure feel for process" (W. Johnson, 1946, p. 36).

There are processes within every structural referent, and there are more minute structures within those processes, in a continuing alternating chain from the most macroscopic objects down to the smallest elements of matter which make them up. An individual may focus his perception at any level in this chain of process-structure alternation. Objects take on a process nature when they are viewed as means or as doing something, and probably look more like structures when they are regarded as goals or just as background.

The two qualities—process and structure—become important in

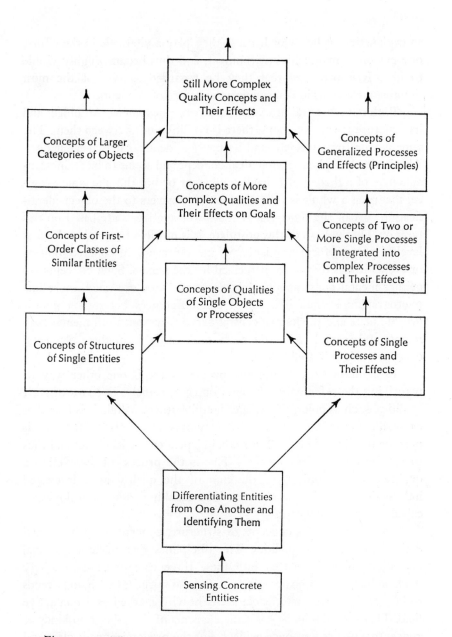

Figure 4–6. Three Kinds of Perceptual Recognition and Conceptual Organizing, in a Graduation from Simple Sensing to Conceptual Maturity.

an explanation of behavior because they play a vital role in the efforts of a person to master his environment, and thus become highly visible to him. It is proposed that they be regarded as two of the most significant elements in determining the nature of concepts.

Both structure and process are primary phenomena. An object and its structure are synonymous; there is no difference between them. The same is true for a referent and its process identity; it is what it does. This is clearly a phenomenological concept and seems to be an inescapable part of a theory of behavior, whether or not the phenomenological theory as a whole is valid. Acceptable answers to the object-identification part of the Binet test at the lower age levels are based on this position. On the basis of this postulate, it is possible to say that the first level of concept formation is that of mental images of concrete objects or events just as they were perceived by the person. Such concepts are neither mental constructs nor abstractions. They are much more like photographic images, in spite of the differences between a photographic plate and the human central nervous system. Both mental *constructs* and mental *abstractions* are soon made from these elemental concepts, as is indicated below.

In addition to structure and process, there is one other way of perceiving the referents in the environment, namely, in terms of their qualities, such as color, shape, speed, and softness. While it is true that color does not exist except as a property of some concrete referent, it is possible to think of blueness *as such*, independent of its object and thus to form a concept of a quality. This is the process of abstracting a quality from its object, of thinking of the quality as if it existed independently or in the abstract. The resulting concept is logically called an abstract concept.

Figure 4–6 shows concepts of structure, concepts of process, and derived concepts of qualities. The disciplines that make up formal education are easily sorted into these three categories: entomology tends to be largely a taxonomic or structural science; psychology tends to be largely a process science; art is heavily marked as a qualitative field. That each discipline has some elements of the other two kinds of conceptual nature is at once evident, but the predominance is clear and the practical usefulness of the three ways of categorizing concepts is also clear.

This elaboration is important because of the central role of process concepts in decision making and the overwhelming predominance of process concepts in most of the subject matter of the curriculum as a whole.

It is now necessary to note that as the brain weaves these three kinds of concepts together, the ensuing constructs move farther and farther away from concreteness and rapidly lose the nature of mental "images." Also, they become as complex as the capacity of the particular brain permits. In some people the capacity is relatively low, but in others it is fantastically high. Thus a concept such as "democracy" in anything like mature form is a mixture of structure carried to a high level of generalization, processes carried to a high level of integration, and qualities of both structure and process, at all levels of complexity.

Furthermore, integrated sets of processes become generalized or grouped together on the basis of similarities, generalized sets of structures come to be seen as means and thus as processes, and integrated with other processes. Even qualities such as "considerateness" begin to take on process aspects, and function in thinking as process concepts. There is no question as to the existence of this picture of complexity, but at its higher levels it is not yet possible to draw pictures which do justice to the complex content of a concept such as democracy, or in fact to do anything much more than marvel at it. One important thing begins to become clear, however. It is that no teacher knows how to lead a person to a mature concept of democracy, for example, and yet a bright learner can acquire or develop such a concept for himself. A lesson that must be learned is that teachers must help students perceive all of the phenomena needed for building these vital complex concepts, but in no way hinder the student from thinking deeply about their meaning and running ahead in his own comprehension. When teaching can more frequently provide a stimulating atmosphere for thinking in depth, it will be much more effective.

LEVELS OF DEVELOPMENT OF CONCEPTS

The left side of Figure 4–5 is helpful with this elaboration. Progression from the bottom to the top takes place with respect to the degree of awareness of the existence of the concept, degree of verbalization of the concept, progress in shaping up the concept or pushing it toward conformity with the world "out there" from which the stimuli come, and extent of generalization of concepts which frees them from specific situations and renders them capable of transferring to other situations, familiar or unfamiliar. The model in Figure 4–5 does not portray these three kinds of progression in detail, simply because it would become so complex as to lose its readability. The present purpose is served reasonably well by showing both concepts and adjustment in familiar and unfamiliar situations.

For familiar situations, intuitive concepts are adequate in countless instances and probably mediate a very large percentage of the actions that make up a day's behavior. Studies have frequently shown that behavior which is faithful to past experience is going on consistently while the subject is unable to verbalize his behavior satisfactorily either to himself or to someone else (Furth, 1963). This is a common phenomenon in clinical psychology.

Also in familiar situations there is behavior which is consciously selected, easily verbalized, and objectively examined. Calorie-conscious people show these qualities when they talk about their diets.

Familiar situations are marked by the use of concepts which consist of sets of procedures or clearly conceived patterns of action, such as the steps in diagnosing why a watch has stopped, in driving a car, in conducting a debate, or in carrying out an experiment and validating the findings (Gagné and Bolles, 1959, p. 19). When concepts are intuitive, they are highly subjective, often marked by error, and frequently incomplete or fragmentary; yet they mediate behavior (Bruner, 1960, p. 57). When they are brought to the level of recognition, which is usually accomplished through attempts to verbalize them, they can be subjected to objective scrutiny and can also be submitted to deliberate efforts to round them out and validate them.

Unfamiliar situations are those which are new to the individual in the particular form in which they appear. His existing concepts of processes are not adequate for unfamiliar situations. Hence, he has no learned basis for action. This is what is commonly called a problem situation. As McDonald (1959) so well describes, there are two requirements here. One consists of the ability to recognize the "general" nature of the situation, so that it can be seen as being "like" other situations with which the person has had experience. The other is the ability to "generalize" process concepts, so that they are no longer bound to specific situations, but can be related to general types of situations. Then they can be applied to a new situation, a specific trial reaction can be deduced, and behavior can be based upon the newly formed hypothesis.

For purposes of a model of instruction, the important elements here are intuitive concept formation and use, recognized and *verbalized* concept formation and use, and generalized concept formation and use. Within each of these levels, there are concepts of processes which are central in decision-making behavior and concepts of structures and of qualities, both of which contribute to the *use* of process concepts in decision-making situations.

ORIGINALITY PROCESSES

Figure 4–7 is a further elaboration of the storage and manipulation stage of the cycle of learning and behaving. It may be regarded as an additional level, above the intuitive, verbalized, and generalized processes shown in Figure 4–5.

An extensive literature is now developing from which the following concepts have been derived and reported more fully elsewhere (Woodruff, 1964). Two elements contribute to original behavior which is effective or useful. One of them is imagination (E. S. Johnson, 1961; Bruner, 1962, p. 15; Mednick, 1962; Sinnott, 1959). The other is composed of concepts of various technical processes and structures which must be used to give effective expression to original ideas or imagination. These technical concepts are part of the subject matter of such fields as harmony, composition, counterpoint, industrial chemistry, high-energy physics, and painting (Bruner, 1960). They are acquired and used in the same way as the concepts described previously.

There are differences between creative and noncreative people in these respects:

1. Preference for open perception as opposed to premature categorizing (Platt, 1961; MacKinnon, 1962).
2. Ability to follow an idea openly and freely as opposed to the ten-

dency to force an idea into a preconceived structure (Bruner, 1962).
3. Ability to live with change or even to seek it as opposed to a compulsion to maintain stability in patterns (Houston and Mednick, 1963).
4. Tendency to engage in intuitive flights as opposed to conforming easily to the force of sense perception (Mednick, 1962; MacKinnon, 1962).

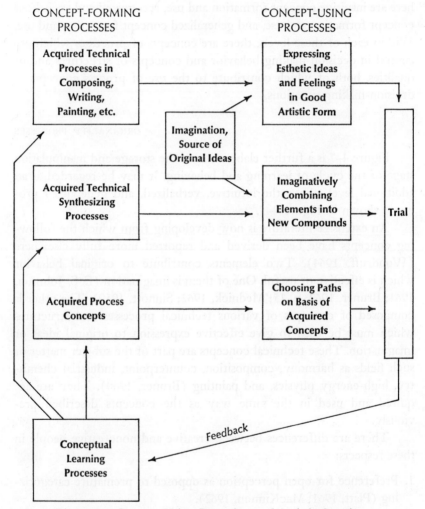

CONCEPT-FORMING
PROCESSES

CONCEPT-USING
PROCESSES

Acquired Technical
Processes in
Composing,
Writing,
Painting, etc.

Expressing
Esthetic Ideas
and Feelings
in Good
Artistic Form

Imagination,
Source of
Original Ideas

Acquired Technical
Synthesizing
Processes

Imaginatively
Combining
Elements into
New Compounds

Trial

Acquired Process
Concepts

Choosing Paths
on Basis of
Acquired
Concepts

Conceptual
Learning
Processes

Feedback

Figure 4–7. Concept Using, Invention, and Artistic Creation.

All of these differences are significant to the originality factor in creative behavior. A theory of instruction must eventually offer guidance to teachers on ways of encouraging these and other tendencies which seem to foster creativity in students. At the same time, the theory must emphasize the importance to truly useful creativity of the technical or disciplinary aspects of creative production. Otherwise, so-called creativity becomes nothing more than spontaneity with little or no lasting value.

In cognitive theory, behavior is directed by the concepts which have been produced by perception and conceptualization, the two stages described immediately preceding storage and manipulation. Decision making is an intervening process between concept formation and trial, but it was elaborated sufficiently earlier and is not discussed further here.

The Trial Stage

Two interrelated processes of significance can be identified at this point: the concept-testing process, and the motive-forming process.

CONCEPT VALIDATION, OR SHAPING UP

The term "shaping up" is useful and suggestive (Resnick, 1963). It seems to have originated in operant-conditioning theory, but aptly describes the manner in which a concept is shaped during the cyclical interaction between thinking and trying. Figure 4–3 offers a clear view of the interaction. A concept guides a response to an object, but in the response the individual perceives the object and his way of acting toward it at an empirical level, and from this perception there is feedback to the concept-forming process.

Concepts that are formed without empirical trial could take on satisfactory meaning to the person solely on the basis of the discussion of percepts acquired visually and aurally. From this discussion process, which is typical of much classroom talk, the individual can have a concept which satisfies an achievement-test question, but which may not enable him to carry out an adjustmental act in a real situation. That is, he "knows" something, but he cannot make it work when he tries to act on that knowledge. Until he tests the concept empirically, he may not discover its deficiencies. When he tests it in practice, the experience by which he discovers its deficiencies also furnishes him with new percepts, which modify the concept or shape it up in terms of the true qualities of the referent. In operant-conditioning terms, environmental control of behavior is being established and inappropriate responses are being eliminated.

School learning is generally deficient in the trial stage of learning and thus tends to have little direct transfer value. Formal education tends to emphasize discussion about concepts and to deemphasize empirical concept validation. This deficiency is probably also a prime factor in the low motivation to learn.

MOTIVE FORMATION

All behavior has both a meaning component and a feeling component. The meaning component has been adequately treated. The feeling component is a derivative of the adjustive nature of behavior. As has been extensively discussed elsewhere (Woodruff, 1961, Chap. 5; Broudy, 1954, Chap. 10; Rhine, 1958), the individual is to some degree satisfied when he has a sense of progress toward need satisfaction and is to some degree annoyed when he has a sense of failure to attain need satisfaction. The perception of the positive or negative instrumental value of an object or a process, whether that perception is intuitive or clearly conscious, furnishes an input which becomes part of the concept of that object or process. This is the origin of value, both positive and negative. Instrumental value is the foundation of motive in all of its forms: interest, sentiment, wish, major value, ideal, goal of any degree of immediacy or remoteness.

Feeling reactions, being rooted in adjustmental acts, do not occur when no adjustmental stakes are involved. They occur most regularly and most vividly at the trial stage of the learning-behaving cycle, since that is basically a stage of adjustmental action. Once established through empirical experience, feelings can be reactivated when a particular concept is recalled, and this reenacted emotional reaction often occurs when an emotionally loaded concept is being discussed. Therefore, emotions can get involved in academic discussions, but they are echoes of previous empirical experience and are not generated in the discussion. There is nothing so noticeable as the neutrality of feeling, or in other words plain apathy, which students generally feel for subject matter when their total experience consists of class presentation and class discussion (the storage and manipulation stage alone).

There seems to be some amount of vicarious identification by a learner with the feelings of others whom he observes during their trial experiences. In this manner, a hypothetical kind of feeling and value may become part of a concept simply through perception and thinking. When a decision is made involving such a concept, the empathically accepted value seems to influence the individual's prediction of what value the behavior will have for him and to prejudice him toward the action according to that value. This may give him a start toward the kind of feeling he will have through his own trial behavior, which may either substantiate it or contradict it, depending on how he interprets his experience.

Figure 4–8 suggests the relationship between meaning and feeling as it occurs in empirical experience.

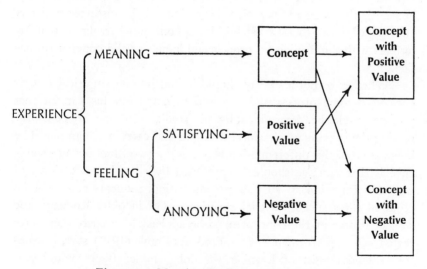

Figure 4–8. Meaning, Feeling, and Concepts.

Two Functions of Empirical Experience

At this point it is convenient to identify, within the general form of the cybernetic model, an aspect of the relationship between concept forming and concept using which is critical to the notion of the activity curriculum.

Empirical experience has been shown to have two functions with reference to concepts: a learning function, and a mediating function, followed by adjustive action.

The unexamined notion that a person learns to do by doing involves confusion between these two functions (Gagné, 1962; Woodruff, 1961, 1964; Frank, 1959; Gagné and Bolles, 1959). That confusion has frequently led to the use of student activity in so-called lifelike activities as the instructional means of teaching for the development of insight or as the attempt to influence behavior directly through formal education.

Activities carried out under simulated conditions, in which students do not already know how to act, are marked by artificiality principally because the ordinary cause-and-effect forces that normally mark those activities are circumscribed and distorted by the necessary instructional controls exercised in the situation. A common consequence is that students perceive the activity in its distorted and circumscribed form, thereby establishing a conceptual structure that interferes with the shaping-up process and impedes valid concept formation.

Whether or not a student should be put into an empirical experience with some process and required to carry out his part of that process should be determined by his readiness to use concepts for making the necessary behavioral decisions and carrying them out. The implication of this differentiation between the two functions of experience is that practice should be preceded by enough perception and concept formation to furnish the mediating concepts that will be required for a successful trial experience. Or, in older language, the subject matter of the concept must be adequately prepared and presented before performance is required. As Frank (1959) says, instruction should consist of learning *for* doing rather than *by* doing.

Since motive formation occurs during adjustive experiences and since there is a high probability of annoyance reactions when students are required to engage in activities for which they are poorly prepared, this practice can easily lead to dislike or even fear of such activities. If a sense of failure is present, it can produce loss of self-confidence and related self attitudes.

THE PURPOSE OF INSTRUCTION

The main objective of formal instruction is to have students learn about selected aspects of their world. This is accomplished under a teacher's guidance by encouraging concept formation which leads to objective behaviors.

Three assumptions are made at this point:

1. Behavior and learning are approximately as described heretofore, and the formal instructional process must take its shape from the contours of the foregoing models. It must, in effect, be the counterpart or complement of the processes of learning and behaving.

2. Instruction serves two ends: First, it produces changes in the adjustmental behavior of the learner, largely by helping him acquire concepts. Second, it makes the student think and learn independently. It should be noted that all behavior is regarded as adjustmental; that is, it is aroused by need and is an attempt to meet the need.

3. The instructor is present for the purpose of guiding and facilitating the learning process toward the achievement of certain defined goals of the educative system. The broad goals are generally set up in the form of behaviors to be attained, and curriculum content is chosen to produce the concepts which will in turn produce the desired behaviors.

BEHAVIORAL BASIS OF THE INSTRUCTIONAL PROCESS

The picture of behaving and learning presented in the elaborated model suggests that in order to accomplish the purposes of education, the teacher must be able to influence the behavioral process at the four points which were illustrated in Figure 4–3 and are further elaborated below.

Perception

At this point the task includes the clear portrayal of referents and the management of the portrayal process so that it is psychologically helpful. The task is accomplished by maintaining the conditions which facilitate concept formation. The variables include the following:

1. Use of relevant materials (Archer, 1962; Battig and Bourne, 1961).
2. Appropriate sequencing (Gagné and Paradise, 1961; Gagné *et al.*, 1962; Roe, Case, and Roe, 1962).
3. Use of informative feedback (Morin, 1955; Pishkin, 1960; Johannsen, 1962; Bourne, 1963).
4. Emphasis of essential elements of a concept and counteremphasis of nonessential or negative elements (Harris and Haber, 1963; Nies, 1962; Trabasso, 1963; Mayzner, 1962).
5. Other factors in economical concept formation (Woodruff, 1964; Burlingame, 1963; Gagné, 1962).

The process is primarily that of referential stimulation of the student's physical senses.

Thinking, Concept Formation, and Storage

At these points the task is one of cultivating the following dimensions in the conceptual structure: validity of the concepts, maturity and completeness, abstractness, generality, integration, verbalization, inventiveness, and artistic expression.[1] The process is primarily that of verbal interaction between the teacher and student and between students.

Decision Making

While decision making will go on spontaneously in all three ways (to reperceive, to predict outcome and value, or to initiate an adjustive move), an instructor can help a learner improve the quality of his decision-making behavior. As in concept formation, this instructional activity is done through the interaction process, by making students aware of the usefulness of reperceiving and by influencing their con-

---

[1] A semantic problem occurs in the use of such words as *abstraction, generalization, integration, principle,* and *concept.* There is no consensus as to their referents. In this discussion, *concept* is a generic term for any more or less organized idea in a person's mind, whether or not it is valid, mature, and shared. Such an idea may take different verbal forms, which could be called a principle, an abstraction, a definition, a conclusion, an admonition, an argument, or the like. The confusion may be compounded when some of these terms, such as *abstraction* and *generalization,* are also used to identify dimensions of concepts, but for the present there is no consensus to help dispel the confusion. This means a reader must be multilingual if he is to read various authors with any comprehension.

tinuing perception for more complete and accurate referential input, by helping them learn to make predictions consciously and to review deliberately all known pertinent information, and by helping students become aware of the factors in appropriate timing and in tactics for putting an adjustmental action into motion.

Trials of Concepts in Adjustive Actions

Trial behavior takes its pattern from a person's concepts of ways of acting. There are some practical exceptions to this derivation, such as the efforts of a child to learn to walk. There are some kinds of motor behavior which are primarily nonconceptual in pattern (Bruner, 1964). In the interest of delimitation, they are omitted from this treatment, although they have a place in a complete description of behavior of which this cognitive treatment constitutes a large part.

The acting out of a conceptually based behavior justifies assistance in shaping the act or getting it into an acceptable motor performance pattern. Introducing someone to a group is an example. A person may know the essential things to do, but require a few trials to carry them out smoothly. In such a situation the instructor acts like a coach, using a verbal interaction process and perhaps supplementing with personal examples of the action (additional referential perception).

INTERPRETATION OF EMPIRICAL FEEDBACK
FROM ADJUSTIVE ACTIONS

A person engaged in any form of behavior is also simultaneously engaged in continuous perception of the referent or the situation. Like most perceptual input, empirical feedback tends to involve subjectivity and selectivity—two limitations a competent instructor can help the student overcome. Again, the process is essentially verbal interaction, but can be supplemented by the appropriate use of sensory referents.

Interpretation of empirical feedback, already shown to involve both meaning and feeling, confronts the instructor with the problem of guarding against student misinterpretation of the experience. For example, a teacher's criticism of a student's performance may be sensed by the student as only detrimental because he is not aware of the personal advantage obtainable by constructive reaction to the criticism. Here the instructor has the problem of influencing the student's perception so that he discovers the potential for satisfaction and recognizes it as of greater weight than the discomfort involved in the criticism. There are many ways in which a learner can obtain a restricted and even invalid perceptual impression of the adjustmental effect a situation is having on him. All of these potential interpretive errors present instructional challenges to the teacher.

It is my opinion that formal education in America, except for vocational courses and a few similar performance-oriented programs, has concerned itself very little with the decision-making, trial, and feedback phases of the learning-behaving cycle. It has confined its influence largely to the perception and thinking phases. Furthermore, perception and thinking have been so poorly handled linguistically and analytically in educational research that even the provision of a perceptual base broader than that ordinarily provided in the classroom would scarcely compensate.

The omission of the decision-making and trial phases has been decisive in keeping formal education from seriously affecting adjustmental behavior. Concepts may be potential acts, but they do not become used acts until the individual employs them in a situation which makes a real or truly simulated demand on him for an adjustmental action. Even less can they become part of his motivational pattern, thereby influencing him beyond the period of formal education.

Basic Kinds of Instructional Acts

As has been indicated in the preceding section, there are three pervading contributions of the instructor. One is the preparation of subject matter for perceptual input and for conceptual organizing. The second is the guidance of student attention by means of verbal interaction during perception, concept formation, decision making, trial, and interpretation of trial. These two functions are described by Smith and Meux (undated) as "material means" and "procedural means." The third is the provision of trial situations which make realistic demands on students for adjustmental reactions, so that the concepts being learned can be subjected to trial, validation, and value formation.

Subject-Matter Preparation

It should be obvious by now that subject matter consists of the real world "out there," not of books, bodies of information, lectures, outlines, or any of the other verbal and symbolic materials that have in the past dominated the school. Putting real referents before students turns out to be a somewhat more difficult task than might be supposed at first glance. It is simple enough when real things are used directly. It is not too difficult when audiovisual media are employed for portraying real objects and events. These channels have some serious limitations, however, in such fields as English, history, and international relations. Available materials in these fields are almost entirely in verbal form. Furthermore, they are not in the form of vivid descriptions of the natural phenomena which were observed by the knowledge finders in these fields. If they were, the verbal process might be reasonably successful with many students because of the extent of their previous direct observation of human behavior.

The learning and behavior cycle offers a clue to what has happened to the knowledge first acquired by a knowledge finder. He perceived it from reality. In so doing, he employed some techniques which helped him to incorporate wide time periods by telescoping them so their trends could actually be seen, and in other similar ways to bring the natural events into a visible pattern. On the basis of what he perceived, he formed concepts of those phenomena. These concepts became instruments for decision making on his part, from which he formed various kinds of conclusions. Any conclusion is the forerunner of an act, so it is a tentative move into the phases of decision making and trial. These conclusions take various forms, such as value judgments ("truth is beauty," "overgrazing is wasteful") or admonitions ("we should preserve our forests").

In addition to acquiring concepts of the objects and processes he observed, the knowledge finder also gathered much information. He recorded most of it in symbolic form, organized into some kind of taxonomy or outline. Furthermore, the knowledge finder constructed topical outlines for storing or "filing" his concepts. The topics are like items in an index; they refer to knowledge but do not convey it.

Textbooks have consisted for the most part of these kinds of content. They represent either accumulations of topically organized and symbolically recorded information or of written conclusions and admonitions. Neither of these is in assimilable form for students. Information can be memorized, but it does not lead to concepts and understandings. Topics can be offered for discussion; but without more explicit identification of a concept, they often lead to rambling and random sampling of the endless areas of knowledge related to the topic (Bellack and Davitz, 1963). Conclusions and admonitions can also be memorized, but they are not convincing to students because they do not reveal the natural events and forces upon which the conclusions are based. Perhaps their most serious limitation is that they provide neither perception nor recall of the actual phenomena so that students can form concepts of their own from them. Instead, they give preconceived patterns of behavior to students without comprehension as to why the patterns should be followed. Thus, students tend to become procedure followers, rather than independent decision makers.

The task of recasting information, conclusions, and admonitions into conceptualized subject matter is not impossible. It is not even obscure. It requires some technical knowledge about the nature of knowledge as such, quite good comprehension of the subject matter to be recast, some sense of logical order and sequence of ideas, and much patient work. After the recasting has been done and the subject matter has been stated in the form of concepts of objects, processes, and qualities, the work of portraying these concepts so that they can be perceived by students can begin. Briefly, this task requires replicating for the student the essential elements of the discovery experience of the knowledge finder, telescoped and condensed without losing the essence, for conservation of educational time. Then the interaction process can be added to guide the learner's attention as he perceives, thinks, forms conclusions, and makes action decisions. These are the elements of a good lesson.

The implication of this section is that the whole curriculum should be put in the form of media for *presentation*, leaving the verbal process for the teacher to use in guiding the attention of students to what they are seeing in the curriculum or what they have already seen sufficiently at some other time or place. In this frame of reference, *media* might then be defined as a facile sensory language capable of delivering the phenomena in the curriculum to students in a form which facilitates perceptual input.

Teacher-Learner Interaction Process

This process is, in simplest terms, a conversation between a teacher and learner, in which certain dimensions are observable. The conversation is about the content of the curriculum or that part of it which is being utilized at any given time. Four dimensions are suggested below.

FORM OF THE CONVERSATION

A number of ways of describing this dimension have been proposed. Smith and Meux (undated, pp. 50–51) have identified the following major conversational forms: defining, describing, designating, stating, reporting, substituting, evaluating, opining, classifying, comparing and contrasting, conditional inferring, explaining, and directing and managing the classroom. Detailed refinements are described within each of these major forms. Numerous protocols are used to show how these kinds of verbal stimulation affect the student's cognitive activities.

Bellack and Davitz (1963) offer a different set of categories for sorting the same general kinds of verbal stimulation. They begin with three major dimensions:

1. What the speaker is *doing pedagogically*, for example, structuring, soliciting, responding, reacting.

2. What he is *saying* (the content of his statement), for example, *substantive* (subject matter), *substantive-logical* (cognitive processes dealing with subject matter, such as defining, interpreting, explaining, fact-stating, opining, and justifying), *instructional* (assignments, materials, routine classroom procedures), and *instructional-logical* (didactic verbal processes, including evaluation, explaining, and directing).

3. The *feeling tone* being conveyed, including valence, potency or strength, and activity. They find a cycle operating in discourse, beginning with either a structuring or soliciting move by a teacher or pupil and going on to questioning and responding, or to responding and then evaluating, with the expected elaborations of these elements.

DISTRIBUTION OF TIME

This is a relatively simple dimension, although important. At the extremes of the distribution, the teacher may do all the talking or none of it. As long as a teacher and a learner are in some kind of interaction, however, what is going on is still in essence a conversation, even though audible words may not be the whole means of interaction. If a teacher is talking and a student is listening, or vice versa, the response is at least incipient. Whether there is any optimum amount of talking by one or the other party is a matter of conjecture at present, although the assumption is generally that teachers talk too much.

Data presented by Bellack and Davitz (1963) show that teachers occupy about three-fourths of all class time which is made up of talk and initiate three of every five moves that occur. Flanders (1963) reports that two-thirds of the time spent in classrooms is spent in talking, that two-thirds of that time is occupied by the teacher, that two-thirds of the teacher's talk consists of lecturing, giving directions, or criticizing, whereas only one-third is spent asking questions and reacting to students' ideas.

Bellack and Davitz (1963) also show that pupils learned more with active than with passive teachers and with teachers who exhibited strong emotional tone. With respect to the latter finding, the amount of pupil learning was not related to the valence or direction (unpleasant or pleasant) of the emotional tone.

It is important to note that there is no essential difference between a conversation involving two people both of whom are present and talking and a conversation involving two people of whom one is represented by something he has written and the other is reading. Reading is a verbal interaction process and must be studied with the other verbal activities in education rather than with the perceptual processes which depend on the stimulation furnished by referential materials. An exception is the text containing pictorial materials.

When the interaction involves talking, it affects the mental processes of both parties. These effects, discussed below, are probably more critical than the sheer amount of interaction.

WHAT IS EVOKED

If the model of cognitive processes is valid, then it furnishes the basis for a two-dimensional aspect of conversation.

The lateral dimension is verbalism-comprehension. Verbalism is defined as the use of nonsense syllables, or words for which the individual has no meaning. Although the extreme verbalism end of the continuum may be relatively rare, it does exist. The other end of the continuum is full and penetrating insight.

It should be noted that this is a continuum of *meaning*, not of the presence or absence of *words*. Words are involved at all points in the dimension. Verbal behavior is not to be confused with verbalism, for the degree of "verbalism," which *Webster's* defines as "an empty form of words," varies all across the behavior called "verbal" (meaning communication by symbols). Consider the following statement: "For every aspect or property of the phenomenal world of an individual who is in contact with his environment, however subtle, there is a variable of the energy flux at his receptors, however complex, with which the phenomenal property would correspond." This is a verbal statement regardless of who reads it, but it is also a pure verbalism for a person lacking psychological background.

The vertical dimension is the level of thought involved, as shown in Figures 4–5, 4–6, and 4–7. Figure 4–9 shows the ascending levels of thought, beginning with the simplest at the bottom and working up progressively to the highest in complexity and comprehensiveness.

Aschner (1963), working with the upper 5 per cent of the I.Q. population in two junior high schools and making an analysis of the verbal interaction in the classroom, developed a category system for classifying the thought processes reflected in verbal behavior in a context of group discussion. Her system is like that of Guilford and Merrifield (1960). It furnishes another way of describing what is evoked by the teaching process. It includes:

1. *Cognitive memory:* recognition, rote memory, selective recall, reproducing facts or ideas.
2. *Convergent thinking:* thought processes, both analytic and integrative, within a closely structured framework.
3. *Evaluative thinking:* value-based judgments.
4. *Divergent thinking:* elaboration, divergent association, implications, and synthesis.
5. *Routine:* typical in-class give-and-take which is of interest because of its effect on the thinking that goes on.

Other aspects of the vertical dimension contained in the structure presented in this chapter are included by Aschner in her treatment of

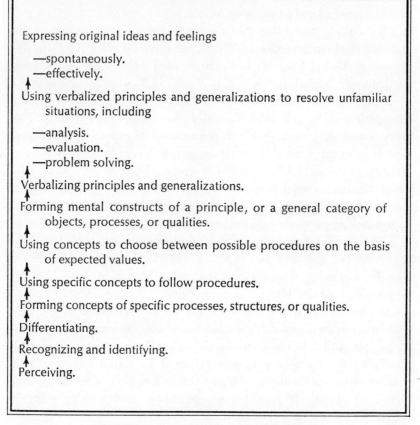

Expressing original ideas and feelings

—spontaneously.
—effectively.

Using verbalized principles and generalizations to resolve unfamiliar situations, including

—analysis.
—evaluation.
—problem solving.

Verbalizing principles and generalizations.

Forming mental constructs of a principle, or a general category of objects, processes, or qualities.

Using concepts to choose between possible procedures on the basis of expected values.

Using specific concepts to follow procedures.

Forming concepts of specific processes, structures, or qualities.

Differentiating.

Recognizing and identifying.

Perceiving.

Figure 4–9. Ascending Levels of Thinking.

content, of which she distinguishes four kinds (figural, symbolic, semantic, and behavioral), and in her treatment of measures of productive thinking, which includes ideational fluency, flexibility, originality, and penetration. Although her formulation tends to emphasize those levels particularly appropriate for students of high ability, it has sufficient range to permit application to all students.

The responses being evoked in the listener (teacher or learner) by an interaction depend upon both the lateral and the vertical dimensions of that interaction. These responses vary in meaningfulness from pure verbalism to clear comprehension and vary in depth from the first meaningful perception to the most penetrating thought and to effective creativity.

Since at least five stages have already been identified in learning and behaving (perception, concept formation, decision making, trial, and feedback), it follows that conversation between teacher and learner may profitably occur at any one or all of the stages. The teacher's objective varies somewhat from one stage to the next, as suggested by what is going on in the learner's cognitive activities. Presumably, the teacher uses the interaction process to facilitate perceiving, thinking, choosing, doing, or interpreting one's experience in doing; and his purpose has something to do with the other three dimensions of the interaction process. The verbal process may then be seen as a wash of symbolic communication across the internal cognitive processes of the learner.

Two ideas deserve emphasis at this point. First, the interaction process cannot accomplish the goals of education alone, as some current exponents seem to believe. Interaction with little conceptual content is barren. Second, the interaction process is more than a generalized instructional device. It must be specifically fitted to each of the phases of learning and behaving in order to yield its real potential. The detail in the scheme presented by Smith and Meux (undated) makes quite evident the complexity operating in conversation whether the teacher is aware of it and using it well or unaware of it and fumbling with a student's mind.

Provision of Trial Situations

Behavioral experiences have been an extraclassroom part of formal school work for many years, but only now and then have they been regarded as integral parts of the curriculum. They have been regarded as valuable for relieving tension, creating interests, or cultivating interpersonal relationships.

Most of these goals can be achieved by the kinds of activities that also furnish trial experiences for concepts formed in classes. There are innumerable ways in which students can actually use concepts formed in courses in government, social structures and cultures, speech and discourse of various kinds, journalism, English, and health. This use of activities as part of the learning process has been discussed by Wegener (1957) in his concept of a school within a school.

Recently, much attention has been given to the broad instructional objective of cultivating individual potential. This objective entails three kinds of goals: making the student an independent and self-stimulated learner, making him an independent and critical thinker, and stimulating him to use his creative capacities extensively.

In terms of a cognitive theory of behavior and learning, the creativity goal can best be described in the elaboration of the storage and concept-formation stage of the learning-behaving cycle. I have already discussed this goal extensively.

The other two goals are the products of acquiring certain kinds of concepts by means of which the learner can deliberately guide his own learning and productive activities. Four of those special kinds which can be distinguished are concepts of (1) how to learn under self-direction, (2) how to dissect natural wholes so that their more atomistic structures and functions can be perceived (analysis), (3) how to determine objectively the value of something (evaluation), and (4) how to find solutions to unfamiliar situations deliberately and systematically (problem solving or transfer).

Learning How to Learn

Building on some earlier work by Harlow (1949), Harlow and Warren (1952), Meyer (1951), Riopelle (1953, 1955a, 1955b), and Warren (1954), Restle (1958) has formulated a descriptive theory of the formation of learning-set, which consists of learning how to learn. In cognitive language, subjects (monkeys) that have gone through several learning experiments seem to acquire "Type A cues," which might be called concepts of how to learn. These concepts transcend any one learning experiment and are common to all, so that the monkey may be said to learn how to conduct himself in a learning experiment.

Human students obviously do this too. Unfortunately, since formal education is so heavily dominated by verbal learning or memorization, students learn how to conduct themselves in *verbal* learning situations, but do not learn how to acquire *concepts* independently.

If the experimental evidence as to how concepts are acquired is accepted, the process could be described phenomenally and taught to students. It is feasible to put much of the curriculum in the form of do-it-yourself packets of conceptualized subject matter, with directions by which the student can conduct himself through the perception, concept-organizing, decision-making, and trial phases of the cycle. Work in experimental centers such as the Laboratory School of Brigham Young University has already demonstrated the practicality of this approach. Students do part of their work by following study guides individually. The work is done largely in carrels, but the student uses a dial system to bring him auditory aids or goes to a laboratory to see phenomena and calls on the teacher for individual help when he wants something he cannot find for himself or wants to discuss the ideas he is forming. From this kind of curriculum, students can be led to develop the same kind of Type *A* cues that monkeys have already demonstrated, but in the cognitive realm rather than in verbal cramming and certainly on a more autonomous level. Specifically, it would appear that the student should become familiar with the perception–concept organization–trial cycle pattern, with ways of testing his concepts for validity, and with ways of deriving principles and generalizations from his perceptual experiences.

Concepts of How to Analyze

Semantic difficulties are present when the terms *analysis, generalization,* and *integration* are used because they are used somewhat interchangeably and with reference to similar but not identical aspects of higher mental processes. Nevertheless, the terms cannot be avoided. The concepts referred to in this paragraph concern the technique of dissecting any whole object, process, or idea so as to expose its component parts to perception. The process applies to any field of inquiry, but the technical processes are specific to each field. Examples are zoological dissection, analytical chemistry, internal criticism in literature, motion studies in industry, and microscopy in bacteriology. Knowledge of how to do these things exists in the form of specialized concepts which are adjuncts to the ordinary learning process. Students need first to learn consciously that analysis is an aid to deeper perception and then to learn how to carry out analytical procedures. A complete theory of instruction must include analysis as one of its elements; and if students are to become self-instructors, they need this knowledge as one of their learning tools.

Concepts of How to Evaluate

Intuitive evaluation is a constant part of cognitive activity. Because it is intuitive, it is subject to several kinds of error. Instruction is concerned with developing conscious and objective evaluation. To be objective, evaluation must be based on consciously recognized criteria, with which something is compared quantitatively.

To engage in such evaluation, an individual must have certain concepts: (1) of evaluation per se and particularly of the difference between objective and subjective evaluation; (2) of standards; (3) of processes for comparing phenomena to criteria, including the modes of comparison (for example, subjective or objective), and concepts of quantification (for example, approximation and estimate, or measurement); and (4) of ways of interpreting comparative data and making the final value judgment.

Concepts of How to Solve Problems

Buswell (1956), Osler and Weiss (1962), and others have provided evidence that problem-solving behavior depends on a knowledge of how to do it, rather than on native intelligence. Self-discovery of the processes does not seem to occur regularly enough to rely on chance. Instruction for the cultivation of problem-solving behavior apparently includes such concepts as how to generalize the characteristics of an unfamiliar situation, how to go about matching known principles to the generalized situation, how to deduce specific behaviors that are appropriate to the unfamiliar situation, and how to test behaviors in action (McDonald, 1959).

CONCLUSION

I have described an approach to cognitive instruction. Although the discussion did not include motor instruction or the disciplinary problems of a teacher, these can be described within this structure. Figure 4–10 is an attempt to put into a flow plan all of the elements of

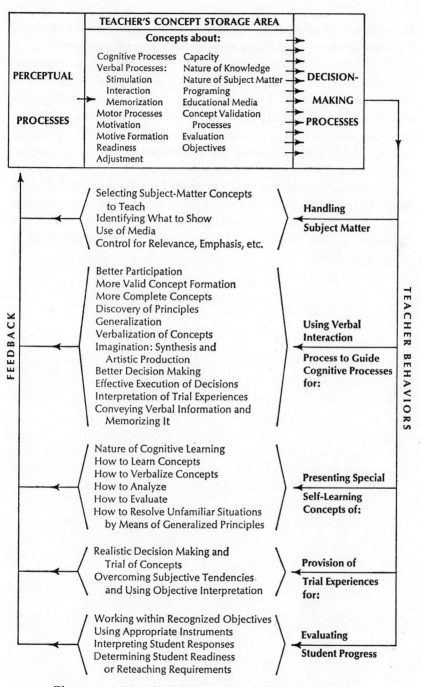

Figure 4–10. Model of Components of Teaching Behavior.

instructional behavior, from the factors which enter into the teacher's decisions to the kinds of acts which might appropriately emerge.

The proposed structure has three advantages: (1) It is consistent with research findings now available. (2) It is internally consistent and seems to be sufficiently broad to accommodate all aspects of formal education. (3) It is directly applicable to planning curricula and teaching procedures which are feasible in the context of the American school system. Its implications for teacher-preparation programs are also fairly clear.

Much research is now under way on both the content side (the nature of concepts and the nature of knowledge) and the process side (student-teacher interaction) of this approach. The findings should encourage further refinement of the structure and examination of its many propositions.

5

Teacher Behavior
in the Classroom Context

BRUCE J. BIDDLE AND
RAYMOND S. ADAMS *

University of Missouri

∽

THE PURPOSE OF THIS CHAPTER IS TO DISCUSS THE RELATIONSHIPS BE-
tween teacher behavior and the classroom context in which it is
embedded. To facilitate this discussion, we present a model comprised
of four major classes of observable phenomena and characteristics:
teacher behavior, pupil behavior, the social environment, and the physical environment. Previous studies in each of these four areas are
reviewed, and implications of the model for both conducting classroom
research and conceptualizing educative processes are discussed. Finally,
we describe the methods and concepts we are presently using in our
research on teacher behavior and the social environment.

This chapter is unique in two respects. In the first place, our
concern is not so much with the processes of instruction per se as with
the characteristics of the classroom as a social system. Teacher behavior
is discussed as one portion of a complex environment that includes the
behaviors of various pupils and the social and physical characteristics of
the classroom. In short, we are concerned with the relationships be-

* In this chapter we have used, without reference notations, materials para-
phrased from two previous publications (Biddle et al., 1965; Adams, 1965). An
earlier version of the model presented here may also be found in Biddle, 1964.
Portions of the research reported were supported at the University of Missouri
by the Educational Media Branch, U.S. Office of Education, Department of
Health, Education and Welfare, and the Office of Naval Research (Group
Psychology Branch).

tween teacher behavior and other observable conditions of the classroom, whether teacher behavior is seen to affect these others or vice
versa. From this perspective, classrooms may be said to exist as interesting social systems regardless of whether or not instruction occurs in
them.

Second, we conceptualize the social environment of the classroom
as an independently observable phenomenon. The usual way in which
social phenomena are handled in classroom studies is to conceptualize
"classroom climates" resulting from teacher behavior, pupil behavior,
or teacher-pupil interaction, and to base observational studies upon
these latter phenomena. However, we take the position that many
social properties of the classroom are directly observable in and of
themselves and that the relationships between these properties and the
behaviors of individual participants in the classroom have yet to be well
established.

The Model and Its Implications

A rudimentary model is introduced by considering clusters of
observable classroom characteristics and the relationships among them.
There follows a discussion of pertinent unobservable classroom characteristics, and the rudimentary model is elaborated accordingly.

Observable Characteristics of the Classroom

The model presented in this chapter was constructed by analytically partitioning observable classroom phenomena and characteristics
into four variable classes: teacher behavior, pupil behavior, the social
environment, and the physical environment.

TEACHER BEHAVIOR

By teacher behavior we mean all those observable characteristics
which may be said to differentiate either one teacher from another or a
teacher at a given moment in time from the same teacher at some other
moment in time. Thus, teacher behavior includes two subclasses of
phenomena: features and performances.

The teacher's *features* are relatively permanent, changing slowly,
if at all, and for the most part beyond voluntary control. Examples of

features are age, sex, general body build, states of infirmity, voice quality, and the like. His *performances* are relatively transitory behaviors that appear to be organized both with respect to the environment and with respect to his personality. Examples of performances are lecturing, the use of colloquialisms, the tone of address to a child, and loss of temper.

Theoretically, performances may vary over a wide range within any given situation; indeed, it is the potential variability of performances that distinguishes them from features. Teachers might, for instance, take off their clothes, swing from light fixtures, or recite risqué limericks. In actual fact, however, teachers do *not* normally exhibit these performances in the classroom; thus teachers may be said to be more alike in their classroom performances than are people chosen at random. Moreover, individual teachers also tend to exhibit greater homogeneity of performance from time to time than does a randomly chosen set of teachers. The individual teacher, for instance, often has a "style," a characteristic "mode of address," a "manner of presentation" or "accent." We shall term such patterns of relatively unchanging performance *traits*.

PUPIL BEHAVIOR

The general observations made about the behavior of the teacher may also be made about the behaviors of pupils in the classroom. Pupils are characterized by certain unchanging features, by performances that may be described according to action or manner, and by traits that typify them from one moment to another. In the long run, a common system of concepts should explicate the behavior of both pupils and teachers.

In most classrooms, teachers exhibit a wider behavioral repertoire than do pupils. Teachers' behaviors are also characteristically distinct from pupils' behaviors. Teachers, for instance, are more likely to lecture, lead, admonish, and instigate; while pupils are more likely to sit quietly, respond, and deviate from explicit directions given by the teacher.

The fact that differences between teacher and pupil behaviors are prescribed by educational tasks and ideology should not obscure the fact that occasionally individual pupils assume the behavior of the teacher and vice versa. It is possible, for instance, to observe a classroom in which a pupil gives a lecture while the teacher sits at the back of the room. As discussed below, some previous schemes for observing pupil behavior assume that pupils are normally in an audiential role. Such systems falter because of the variety of observable pupil behaviors in the modern classroom.

THE SOCIAL ENVIRONMENT

The social environment consists of the joint properties of social interaction that may be observed to take place at any given moment in time or characteristically over a period of time in the classroom. For instance, classrooms are characterized by common patterns of traffic movement, by rates of interaction, by physical and social groupings of actors, and by modes of usage of physical equipment. Some characteristics of the social environment are stable while others change rapidly both within a lesson and throughout the day.

Stable patterns, or *customs*, may be observed, for example, in the number of persons who normally participate in the classroom lesson, the role relationships observable within a group of pupils, the prevalence of the "lecture" form in some classrooms, and the rate of communication flow. Other aspects of the social environment are more likely to vary, particularly the exact subject matter being discussed and the moment-to-moment pattern of communication. Some classrooms have rigidly fixed customs while others, particularly at the lower grade levels, tend to exhibit greater variability.

It should be emphasized that concepts applying to the social environment are defined independently of concepts applying to the behaviors of teacher or pupils. A lecture, for instance, may be observed as a form of behavior regardless of who lectures or who is in the audience. In order to study communicating groups, it is necessary to observe the joint activities of more than one person. This does not rule out, of course, the possibility that individuals may affect, or be affected by, social environments. On the contrary, certain actor behaviors may not only touch off but be necessary for the persistence of some social environments and vice versa.

THE PHYSICAL ENVIRONMENT

The physical environment consists simply of the physical characteristics of the classroom. Some of these pervade the entire classroom:

for example, temperature, humidity, light, and sound level. In addition, most classrooms have doors, windows, and other openings at various points in the walls. They have desks, chairs, file cases, or other equipment which constrains patterns of possible social relations to a certain extent. Classrooms also have various media equipment, such as blackboards, books, pencils, television sets, and teaching machines, as well as a number of noninstructional objects, such as wastebaskets and coat racks.

As in each of the other variable classes, some aspects of the physical environment are stable (the size of the room, its flooring, its heavier furniture) while other aspects may be moved, improved, created.

A Model of Observable Characteristics

The four classes of observable phenomena and classroom characteristics discussed above are shown schematically in Figure 5–1. The rectangle in this figure represents the classroom. The arrows indicate the possible relationships between the four clusters of variables. The solid-line arrows are drawn between teacher and pupil behaviors to suggest that most research done to date has focused on these two classes of phenomena. It is quite possible, however, for pupil or teacher behaviors to reflect environmental conditions, for environments to reflect the behaviors of individuals, for the physical and social environments to interact, or for relationships between two variable classes to be affected by conditions in a third (or fourth). Since relationships of these latter kinds are probably less familiar to the reader, a few illustrations are provided in the paragraphs below.

DETERMINANTS OF PUPIL BEHAVIOR

Those who plan the physical environment of the classroom often make assumptions about its impact on pupil behavior. Pupils' desks are planned, for instance, to facilitate seatwork (the ease with which pupils can move in and out of their desks) and physical rearrangement within the classroom. Other equipment, such as the television, may have a soporific effect on pupil behavior. Some objects in the classroom context, in fact, have such prepotent effect as to constitute "seductive props"; the introduction of a snake or frog into the elementary classroom normally transcends all other stimuli.

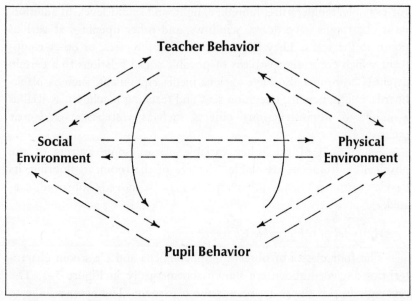

Figure 5–1. The Classes of Observable Phenomena in the Classroom and Their Possible Relationships.

The social environment is equally important. The teacher who separates two troublemakers recognizes the importance of the immediate social environment. Discussion groups may be used for increasing the degree to which individuals may verbalize their understandings or concerns. The classroom that is noisy, cheery, or sullen exerts striking effects on the behavior of individual pupils; and individual pupils may be seduced or coerced into playing certain roles in classroom interactions. Kowatrakul (1959) discovered that pupil behavior varied systematically as a function of the subgroup activities of the classroom; for instance, deviant behavior is more likely in discussion groups than in other communicative relationships.

DETERMINANTS OF TEACHER BEHAVIOR

Teacher behavior, too, may vary as a function of the physical and social environments. Classrooms that are dull and drab, noisy, or crowded make the teacher's job far more difficult. Educational media facilitate presentations by the trained teacher and often free him to devote more of his energy to counseling and other noninstructional tasks. The good teacher also responds to the cues of the social environment, watching his audience for reactions and responding to cues of puzzlement, enthusiasm, and fatigue.

To teach well, the teacher must set up and control social environments. Classroom management is, in fact, a major concern of beginning teachers, who are overwhelmed with the tasks of keeping order, managing discipline, separating combatants, maintaining a cheerful atmosphere, and suppressing the noise level. Even inadvertent teacher behavior may affect the social environment. Kounin and Gump (1958) have demonstrated the "ripple effect" of varying deviancy-control techniques on those pupils who merely look on.

The pupil also affects the environment. A sarcastic comment at the beginning of a lesson, for instance, can set a mood or tone; behavioral contagion can spread from one deviant to others (see Lippitt, Polansky, and Rosen, 1952); and the presence of one or two serious students can set a high standard of achievement and enthusiasm.

Even the physical surroundings can affect a social environment, particularly when light is low, noise level is high, conditions are crowded, or classroom equipment is inadequate or inappropriate.

DETERMINANTS OF THE PHYSICAL ENVIRONMENT

It is common to assume that the physical environment operates primarily as an independent variable in the classroom, affecting both the social environment and individual behavior. However, the physical environment may also be regarded as a dependent variable when, for instance, the art productions of a class are hung for public display. Teachers may also rearrange the equipment in the room—changing the desks from a line-and-row plan to a circular one, for instance—both to stimulate desired behavior and in response to instructional requirements.

INTERACTION IN THE SOCIAL ENVIRONMENT

As an example of the mediation of relationships between two variable classes and a third, we now consider the effects of the social environment on teacher-pupil interaction. It is normally assumed that the warm and supportive teacher has a happier and more compliant classroom than the firm or dominating teacher. But this need not be the case when the class contains a pupil who is challenging the rules. Kounin and Gump (1958) have shown that the "firm" teacher not only exacts compliance from the deviant pupil but also has positive effects on onlookers while the "rough" teacher succeeds mainly in disrupting behavior. These findings are probably unique to the "deviancy control incident."

In another example, teachers covering identical subject matter in several classes are often aware of differential success depending on the characteristics of the pupil group. In one class, it may be difficult to get pupils interested or to maintain discipline. In another class, interest may be so high that much of the learning occurs by self-instruction on the part of pupils. Not only are teacher and pupil behaviors distinct in such contrasting environments, but the same teacher behavior that is successful in one situation may be unsuccessful in the other.

Sensitive teachers are usually conscious of the need to adjust their communications to the social positions or roles of the particular pupils. Some pupils need encouragement; others, firmness; and still others, to be jollied along. The teacher who is skilled in environmental manipulation (for example, by making appropriate use of small groups and physical props) has a totally different pattern of interaction with pupils than the teacher who relies on lecturing only.

An Elaborated Model

It is also useful to conceptualize a number of other phenomena that are tied to the observable properties of the classroom, despite the fact that these phenomena may not be observed directly. These additional properties are conceptualized both to account for the persistence of classrooms as common social phenomena and to explain the apparent regularities of behavior of those persons who enter classrooms. They also help in dealing with the learning model found not only in educational ideology but also in most studies of educational outcomes.

INDIVIDUAL PROPERTIES

Consider first the model for the psychology of the classroom actor as presented in Figure 5–2. In contrast with Figure 5–1, portions of

Figure 5–2 lie outside the observable classroom—characterized, once again, by a rectangle. The actor, whether teacher or pupil, is presumed to come to the classroom with certain unobservable actor *properties.* These properties are the complements of such psychological factors as his perceptual apparatus, motives, attitudes, beliefs, cognitive structure, and so on.

It is assumed that the properties evidenced by the actor are a function of *background experiences,* including his initial socialization, the social class and home environment in which he grew up, and the

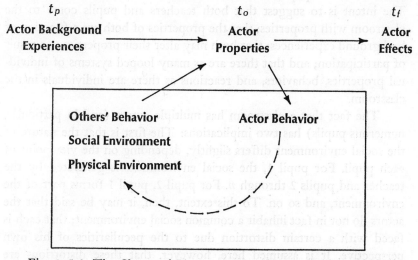

Figure 5–2. The Classes of Phenomena Involved in the Psychology of the Classroom Actor.

types of schooling he has had. It is also reasonable to assume that through the interaction between the actor and his environment certain *effects* will be produced in the future. These effects will, in fact, be various types of actor properties and behaviors that are to occur at a later time. Furthermore, such future effects reflect not only educational experiences in the classroom but also other actor experiences in his school, family, and elsewhere.

To examine the relationship between the properties of the actor and his behavior, it must be assumed that behavior reflects not only these properties but also the perceptions the actor has of others in the classroom, social environment, and physical environment. Thus, the properties of the individual actor, his behavior, and the overt characteristics of the environment arrange themselves in a looplike structure in which the actor behaves as a function of his properties, actor behavior in turn influences others, and the behavior of others in turn stimulates the actor to future behavior.

MULTIPLE CLASSROOM ACTORS

It should be noted that Figure 5–2 may be applied either to the teacher or to the pupil, both of whom are actors in the classroom arena. The intent is to suggest that both teachers and pupils come to the classroom with properties; that the properties of both are a function of background experiences; that both may alter their properties as a result of participation; and that there are as many looped systems of individual properties, behaviors, and reactions as there are individuals in the classroom.

The fact that a classroom has multiple actors (and in particular, numerous pupils) has two implications: The first is that the nature of the social environment differs slightly, depending on the viewpoint of each pupil. For pupil 1, the social environment is generated by the teacher and pupils 2 through n. For pupil 2, pupil 1 forms part of the environment, and so on. To this extent, then, it may be said that the actors do not in fact inhabit a common social environment; that each is faced with a certain distortion due to the peculiarities of his own perspective. It is assumed here, however, that these distortions are minimal and that it is useful to conceptualize a common social environment in which all actors are members. This assumption necessitates restricting the concept of social environment to "public" aspects—to events that are presumably observable and audible to all participants. Although a whispered interaction among three persons may constitute a social environment for the participants, this environment (at least its communicative content) cannot form part of the shared environment of others in the classroom.

The second implication is that the environment changes as the teacher shifts attention from one pupil to another. At the moment in time that the teacher is interacting with one pupil, this interaction may be referred to as the *microenvironment*, whereas the environment involving *all* persons in the classroom is the *macroenvironment*. As used here, the microenvironment is but one type of communication group that may exist in the classroom. It may never occur in some classrooms, though such situations are unlikely—where the teacher is completely quiet or always addresses pupils in audiential groups. Nevertheless, the microenvironment is frequently encountered in classrooms and is presumed to have great potency by some investigators.

SOCIAL PROPERTIES

Quite apart from the properties characterizing the individual actors of the classroom, certain unobservable social properties also underlie the social environment of the classroom. Classrooms are structured for specific task purposes which are embodied in the goals of community members who set up and pay for a school system. Certain kinds of regulations and rules are imposed on the classroom by administrative arrangement. Normally, for instance, the class is given a grade and/or subject-matter assignment. Moreover, the classroom exists in a social context that has informal properties stemming both from the school itself and from its embedding community. The teacher is a member of various cliques and organizations, pupils represent various social classes and castes, and members often bring to the classroom the knowledge of these unobservable characteristics which "everyone knows" about each individual. (To appreciate the extent to which informal social properties may dominate educative processes, see Gordon, 1957.)

Stable Characteristics of the Classroom

While the major concern in this chapter is with those characteristics of the classroom that change during the course of the lesson, many of the above concepts may also be used to characterize stable or structural characteristics of the classroom.

For instance, teachers may be differentiated from one another in terms of their physical features: age, sex, race, physique, voice quality, stature, or handicaps. In fact, some school systems make it a practice to assign teachers on the basis of age, sex, race, and the like and to deny certain jobs to teachers with the "wrong" characteristics regardless of other, excellent qualifications. It is more common, however, to hear teachers characterized in terms of their traits or properties. Teachers are often thought to be competent or incompetent, warm or cold, pupil-centered or subject-oriented, trained or untrained, and to possess or lack certain skills.

Pupils, too, may be characterized by such unchanging features, traits, or properties as race and physique. Some teachers are especially concerned with the youngest or oldest child in the class, with the child who (alone) represents racial characteristics differing from those of the other children, or with a handicapped or maladjusted child.

The social environment and its properties may also evidence stable or traitlike characteristics. The number of students and the student-teacher ratio tends to be constant. Traffic patterns, subgroups, and role structure may also be stable, as may status relations among pupils and norms defining appropriate behavior. Grade, subject matter specified, and the nature of the educational task are almost certain to remain constant.

Finally, the physical environment also exhibits stable characteristics over which classroom participants have no control. The size, shape, building materials, and major artifacts are usually a "given" for the classroom. (On the other hand, knowing that physical features are present in the classroom does not mean knowing how they are used. A motion-picture projector assigned to a classroom is usually located on a shelf gathering dust.)

Pupil Learning as a Function of Teacher Behavior

One way of summarizing some of the implications of our model is to apply it to the usual paradigm of pupil learning. For purposes of this discussion, it will be assumed that most educators accept a paradigm in which teacher classroom behavior leads to learning on the part of the pupil. Thus, the normal pattern of educational investigation is to examine the influence of various forms of teacher behavior (for instance, forms of instruction, teacher mannerisms, or disciplinary techniques) upon pupil behavior (achievement on standard academic tests, attitude, or social adjustment).

This simple paradigm has a number of shortcomings in terms of the model presented in this chapter. In the first place, the classroom is *not* a Skinner Box. Although learning theory presents some sophisticated and well-supported theorems relating patterns of stimulus variables to patterns of learning, it is not known what kinds of stimulus variables characterize the average classroom. The teacher, of course, is one of these variables. So are the pupil actors plus the physical and social environments. These latter factors are only partially under the control of the teacher and may either vitiate the teacher's efforts or provide additional, unintended educative experiences.

Obviously, a pupil cannot fully attend to the teacher while he is being tormented by the pupil sitting next to him. Again, the physical environment may interfere with educational attainment: the classroom may be noisy, too hot or cold, or poorly illuminated. It is also possible that the pupil may learn more from the "reinterpretation" of the teacher's message provided by his neighbor than from the teacher, or it may turn out that some pupils are inordinately sensitive to classroom "atmosphere" and the collective opinions of others.

Another difficulty with the usual learning paradigm is that the pupil plays two roles in the instructional situation: an active, responding role as a member of the microenvironment; and a passive, audiential role when watching the teacher interact with others. In the simple learning paradigm, the pupil is treated as a direct respondent to teacher behavior. Unfortunately, one teacher typically faces thirty or more pupils. Thus, *most* of the time pupils are in audiential roles and therefore cannot verbalize their doubts or trial answers for direct feedback. This suggests that the teacher is not an ideal "stimulus device" for the typical pupil. Rather, most pupils are either bored by the repetition of material they already know or confused by the overrapid presentation of things they do not understand—or perhaps both bored and confused in alternation.

Third, and perhaps of greatest importance, there are many possible routes aside from the direct one by which the teacher can influence learning. Teachers may, for instance, contact pupils with regard to helping others with their homework; or the teacher may manipulate the physical environment in some way as to affect pupil learning (such as the use of educational media); or the teacher may set up social environments that are conducive to high pupil motivation and involvement. Gump (1964) suggests, for instance, that teachers have their greatest impact on pupils not as "stimulus devices" but as environment manipulators, and that there is more variation in pupil behavior (and learning) as a function of variations in the social environment than of variations in teacher behavior. If Gump's suggestion is valid, much if not more time should go into studying the relationships between teacher behavior and social environments, on the one hand, and social environments and pupil learning, on the other, as is spent studying the direct effects of teacher behavior on pupil learning.

Beyond this point, to conduct studies of classrooms making the assumption that only one cause (teacher behavior) leads to only one outcome (pupil learning) is to beg the issue. It is perfectly possible, as has been suggested, for the classroom to have other outcomes. The teacher may change as a result of classroom participation: may learn and grow, or become sour and embittered. Social environments created in one classroom may be applied in other situations: friendships, dominance relationships, or norms of interaction may be taken from the classroom into other school and nonschool settings. Even the physical environment of the classroom may occasionally be viewed as an effect. Concern with these broader outcomes suggests a far wider range of questions about classroom phenomena, in turn affecting the forms of conceptualization used for studying the observable phenomena within the classroom.

Previous Research Using Observation

We turn now to a review of previous research on the observable characteristics of classroom phenomena. This review is brief; an excellent comprehensive review of classroom research methods is presented in Medley and Mitzel (1964). After discussing methodology, we consider the concepts used for each class of observable phenomena in the classroom.

Methods of Study

Most studies of classroom characteristics have used one or more behavioral observers stationed in the classroom. These observers code behavior in predetermined categories. Examples may be found of studies which coded:

1. Only pupil behavior (Urban, 1943; Jersild *et al.*, 1939).
2. Only teacher behavior (Harrington, 1955; Wispé, 1951).
3. Both pupil and teacher behavior (Anderson and H. Brewer, 1945; Anderson and J. E. Brewer, 1946; Anderson, J. E. Brewer, and Reed, 1946; Medley and Mitzel, 1955, 1958, 1959).
4. Characteristics of the physical environment (Barr, 1929; Medley and Mitzel, 1955, 1958, 1959; Cornell, Lindvall, and Saupe, 1952).
5. Characteristics of the social environment (Cornell, Lindvall, and Saupe, 1952; Damrin, 1959; Kowatrakul, 1959; Smith, 1960; Meux and Smith, 1964; Gallagher and Aschner, 1963).

In no studies reviewed by the authors have the physical and social environments of the classroom been studied by themselves. We have also discovered no studies concerned with the effects of the physical environment on teacher or pupil behavior.

As pointed out by Medley and Mitzel (1964), there are several types of coding systems that have been used for achieving reliable observations. In their terms, a *sign system* is one in which the observer uses a checklist to tally his observations. For instance, Morsh (1956) asks observers to check off observations that pupils "doodle," "slump," "yawn," and the like. In contrast, a *category system* is one in which the items given to the coder are mutually exclusive, are presumed to exhaust behavioral alternatives, and are to be rated throughout the occurrence of behavior. For example, in the Withall system (1949, 1951), observers are asked to make a judgment for each act by the teacher; while in the Flanders system (1959, 1960a, 1960b, 1964), judgments are made about the behavior of the teacher or pupils every three seconds. A third type of system, here termed a *rating system*, may also be found in such studies as that of Ryans (1960), in which the observer is asked to delay judgments until after the classroom session and then to rate behaviors in terms of over-all judgments. Following Medley and Mitzel (1964), we exclude rating systems from this analysis on grounds of inadequate face validity for observational purposes.

A few observational systems were developed for use with audio-tape recordings of classroom interaction (for instance, Withall, 1949, 1951; Smith, 1960; Meux and Smith, 1964). One investigator is presently working with sound motion pictures of actual classrooms

(Kounin, unpublished), while a number of investigators (including the authors) are presently working with videotapes of classroom sessions. However, observations mediated by mechanical aids are still relatively rare.

Methodological Problems

Certain methodological problems are inherent in the nature of the phenomena under study, whereas others result from the nature of the observational task itself.

With respect to the phenomena, it is clear not only that classrooms vary enormously from one another in terms of style of teaching, constituent groups, physical equipment, and social processes, but also that the behavior patterns characterizing a classroom are remarkably unstable and come at a very rapid pace. Not only are classrooms complex, but they are also evanescent. As suggested by Medley and Mitzel (1964), most previous studies have focused upon only a minute fraction of the total number of variables observable within the classroom and have taken only a small sample of classrooms on which to validate instruments.

The fact that most studies to date have used only one observer in the "live" classroom has posed additional difficulties. To simplify the task of the overloaded observer, many investigators have not distinguished concepts applying separately to the teacher, the pupils, and the social system. Furthermore, of necessity, the observer has concentrated on only a minute portion of the total web of interaction: the microenvironment, for instance, or a single pupil. Thus, little information has been gathered about the wider effects of significant instructional acts. These two sources of low yield have been magnified by a third source: whereas frequencies of occurrence of classroom behavior are tabulated, the behavior *sequences* are usually ignored (see, however, the contrasting studies of Flanders, 1960b; and Smith, 1960).

Another problem mentioned by many investigators is teacher sensitivity to observation and the general feeling that it is "immoral" to observe in the classroom. Teachers are accustomed to operating in isolation from other adults and resist attempts to observe them whether by the principal, performance rater, or research investigator. The presence of an observer in the classroom may make a considerable difference in the pattern of interaction taking place. Classroom participants are often "on their best behavior" when the visitor enters.

Finally, the fact that much pupil learning is presumed to be covert suggests that in this vital respect the processes of education are not observable at all. For this reason, some investigators of the classroom have despaired of measuring meaningful pupil behavior and have attempted, rather, to relate observed teacher behavior to pupil properties that are measured at the end of the lesson or school year.

This does not mean that pupil behavior cannot be observed or is not meaningful. It does suggest, however, that there may be a more subtle relationship between pupil behavior and pupil properties than is generally assumed for the teacher. It also suggests that to be truly useful for educational purposes, learning theory must address itself to the formation of covert properties in the pupil, such as the learning of norms, values, or cognitive information.

Some of the comments above may be summarized by assuming that behavioral-observation methods involve a four-step process. First, there is the step of freezing the data. *Freezing* occurs when the complex, effervescent, rapidly shifting pattern of behaviors characteristic of the classroom are stopped and recorded in some convenient form so that they may later be analyzed. A photograph of the classroom exemplifies such freezing. Obviously, many characteristics of the situation may be observed from a photograph, including the physical equipment present, the spatial relationships among the bodies of the actors, gestures, and the like.

Frozen information is not in an appropriate form for statistical analysis. It must therefore go through a second process, conversion. *Conversion* is the translation of the raw information of the frozen behavioral record into measurements, counts, scores, or other quantifiable units which can be analyzed. It is possible, for instance, to measure on a photograph the dimensions of the classroom or the distances between people, to count the persons present, and to "score" each individual on paying attention to others.

In the third step of behavioral-observation methodology, converted records are put to *analysis*. They are tabulated; statistics are computed for them; and they are presented in the form of charts, graphs, or conclusions of some sort. Finally, in the last step, results are subjected to *interpretation*.

It is our opinion that for serious research on the classroom each of the four steps—freezing, converting, analyzing, and interpreting—should be carried on independently and, to the greatest extent possible, should be mechanized. In the majority of research projects on classroom interaction, the steps of freezing and converting are combined by requiring the observer both to integrate the material he has just seen and to tabulate or score his observations. This contamination of observational steps contributes to the over-all unreliability of observation methods.

Freezing and conversion need not be carried on simultaneously by a single person, of course. In the specimen-record methodology (see Barker and Wright, 1955), an observer is responsible for recording in written form everything the actor does and for noting, again in written form, all stimuli to which the actor is responding. A specimen record is thus a frozen analogue of actual behavior. It provides raw information that may be converted in various ways. But even the specimen-record technique has its shortcomings. On the one hand, the observer is responsible for translating into symbolic form activities that were either symbolic or nonsymbolic in their original state. On the other hand, no observer can possibly pick up all the detail involved in even a single actor's environment, let alone record in comprehensible form the complex characteristics of the thirty or more people who make up the typical classroom.

With modern devices, freezing can be accomplished with visual and audio mechanical records. Visual-audio records, such as those made by sound motion pictures or videotapes, are impartial, as detailed as the investigator wishes to make them, and utterly reliable. They may thereafter be converted at the investigator's leisure, and during the conversion process they may be played back over and over until reliability of the conversion process is assured.

At present, the conversion process itself cannot be mechanized. The investigator is still responsible for conceptualizing, and coders for coding, the processes of interaction that occur in the classroom and are recorded in the frozen record. Thus, the processes of conversion are subject to unavoidable questions about reliability.

The other two steps of the observational process, analysis and interpretation, are more familiar. For the most part, modern methods of analysis are mechanized through the use of statistics and error-free computer programs. This does not mean that interpretation has been mechanized. On the contrary, the interpretation of tabulated results and statistical significances is still very much an "art," and many an interesting finding has been "lost" due to inept presentation by its discoverer.

Concepts for Observing Teacher Behavior

It is difficult to make any reasonably restricted summary of the conceptual underpinnings of observations of teacher behavior. First, we will review the major orientations of these studies and then comment upon both the breadth of concepts used to date and some related problems.

ISOLATED ASPECTS OF TEACHER BEHAVIOR

A number of investigations have focused on deliberately restricted or isolated characteristics of the teacher. Thus, Johnson (1935) and Kounin and Gump (1958; see also Kounin, Gump, and Ryan, 1961; Alden, 1959) have studied teachers' disciplinary techniques. Smith (1960; see also Meux and Smith, 1964), Aschner (1958), and Wright and Proctor (1961) have investigated the logic of teacher presentations; while Harrington (1955) has investigated teacher smiles(!)

PUPIL-CENTEREDNESS

Although the style of pupil treatment is technically another aspect of teacher behavior, many studies have concentrated on it. Referring to the teacher's approach variously as "dominative" (versus "integrative"), "teacher-centered" (versus "learner-centered"), or "direct" (versus "indirect"), these studies have focused on the degree of authoritarianism and have attempted to relate this dimension to pupil morale, learning, and other dependent variables. Studies in this group include those of Anderson and J. E. Brewer (1946); Anderson, J. E. Brewer, and Reed (1946); Withall (1949, 1951; see also Polansky, 1954), Mitzel and Rabinowitz (1953); Wispé (1951); Hughes (1959); Calvin, Hoffman, and Harden (1957); and Flanders (1959, 1960a, 1960b, 1964). The energy with which this particular dimension of teacher behavior has been pursued has appeared to reflect not only the common training of many of these investigators but also the coincidence of (1) demonstrations in small groups that autocratic and democratic leadership styles could be discriminated and had differential effects (see Lewin, Lippitt, and White, 1939) with (2) the pupil-centered ideology of progressive education.

In another approach, teacher behavior is observed in terms of the pedagogical techniques employed. Thus, teacher behavior is coded as "summarizing," "lecturing," "encouraging," "assigning," "explaining," "demonstrating," and so on by such investigators as Barr (1929); Morsh (1956); Wrightstone (1934); and Cornell, Lindvall, and Saupe (1952).

Still other investigators have used concepts that appear to represent a wider variety of interest fields, for instance, pedagogical *and* social activities. Typical extended studies have been those of Medley and Mitzel (1955, 1958, 1959; see also Morrison, 1961; Wilk *et al.*, 1960; Bowers and Soar, 1961; Soar, 1962); Solomon (1962); and Spaulding (1963). These studies have attempted to correlate various dimensions of teacher behavior in order to establish patterns of joint occurrence.

Finally, whereas most studies have conceptualized teacher behavior in absolutist terms, a few have conceptualized teacher behavior as dependent upon preexisting conditions—particularly upon certain types of pupil behavior. Thus, Kounin and Gump (1958) have studied teacher response to pupil deviancy, while Smith (1960) and Wright and Proctor (1961) have viewed the teacher within a complex conceptualization of the microenvironment, in which the responses of both teachers and pupils were jointly analyzed for logical content.

One way of integrating the coverage of studies of teacher behavior is to examine the broad fields from which their concepts appear to have been taken or into which results have been incorporated. We have attempted to make such a summary in Table 5–1, which details cover-

TABLE 5–1. FIELDS OF COVERAGE IN STUDIES OF OBSERVED TEACHER BEHAVIOR.

	Instruction				Teacher-Pupil Interaction			Teacher Traits			
	Pedagogical style	Logic of presentation	Verbal energy	Subject-matter orientation	Response to pupils	Small-group encouragement	Management techniques	Warmth and humor	Supportiveness	Directiveness	Hostile or autocratic dominative
Barr (1929)				✓			✓				
Johnson (1935)								✓	✓		
Morsh (1956)									✓		✓
Anderson and Brewer (1945)				✓					✓	✓	✓
Withall (1949)				✓					✓	✓	✓
Hughes (1959)				✓					✓	✓	✓
Flanders (1960a, 1960b)				✓					✓	✓	✓
Wispé (1951)										✓	
Calvin et al. (1957)	✓									✓	
Medley and Mitzel (1955)	✓		✓		✓	✓					✓
Harrington (1955)								✓			
Wrightstone (1934)					✓						
Spaulding (1963)		✓	✓		✓	✓		✓	✓		
Kounin and Gump (1958)					✓		✓				
Smith (1960)			✓	✓	✓						
Wright and Proctor (1961)				✓		✓					
Cogan (1956, 1958)	✓						✓				
Solomon (1962)			✓	✓	✓						

age under the headings Instruction, Teacher-Pupil Interaction, and Teacher Traits.

It is evident from this table that although considerable attention has been given to teacher-pupil interaction, there has been little concern with the instructional process and particularly with the instructional content. Similarly, few of these studies drew their concepts from such psychological constructs as motives, beliefs, or attitudes. Also underrepresented are concepts drawn from management exigencies—from the necessities of maintaining discipline and from the physical properties of the classroom.

Finally, in examining this table, the authors were surprised by the degree to which teachers have been conceptualized as "purveyors" whereas popular educational philosophy has long stressed other aspects of the teacher's role. For example, the California Teachers Association (1952) describes the teacher as (1) a director of learning, (2) a counselor and guider, (3) a mediator of culture, (4) a member of the school community, (5) a liaison between school and community, and (6) a member of a profession. Even though a number of these roles are performed in settings other than the classroom, it may reasonably be asked why so little attention has been paid in observational studies to counseling and guidance and mediating culture.

Concepts for Observing Pupil Behavior

Many of the generalizations about teacher-behavior studies are appropriate also to reported observations of pupil behaviors. Again, various instruments representing a variety of theoretical orientations have been used. However, as suggested earlier, the fact that educational ideology suggests *covert* learning processes in a *nonresponsive* pupil has appeared to put a number of investigators off their stride. Thus, there are fewer observational studies of pupil behavior than of teacher behavior, and those that have been published exhibit both a narrower range of concepts and fewer fields from which concepts have been drawn. Flanders (1960b), for instance, uses seven categories for categorizing teacher behavior (accepts feeling, praises or encourages, accepts or uses ideas of student, asks questions, lectures, gives directions, criticizes or justifies authority) and only two for pupil behavior (student talk—response, student talk—initiation).

As with teacher behavior, a number of studies have recorded isolated aspects of pupil behavior. Thus, Horn (1914) and Pucket (1928) studied hand-raising; Olson (1931), the act of whispering; and Urban (1943), health-related acts.

It is interesting that most of the studies reporting observation of teachers for pupil-centeredness do not also report observations of pupil behavior. However, Zander and van Egmond (1958) have attempted to study pupil attempts to influence other pupils.

A rather large number of investigators have attempted to observe pupil behavior conceptualized in pedagogical terms, such as "paid close attention," "was slow to respond," "leaves seat," "holds up hand," or "tells experience." Frequently, these observations are part of studies that also used pedagogical terms for describing teacher behavior, for example, Barr (1929); Morsh (1956); Wrightstone (1934); and Cornell, Lindvall, and Saupe (1952). Other studies also using pedagogical concepts include Anderson and J. E. Brewer (1946); Jersild et al. (1939); and Thorndike, Loftus, and Goldman (1941).

Several recent studies have appeared in which a wider range of concepts has been used to deal with pupil behavior, including those of Kowatrakul (1959); Bonney and Powell (1953); and Solomon (1962).

Except incidentally (for instance, in the determination of whether a pupil responded to the teacher or initiated interaction on his own), studies conceptualizing pupil behavior in terms of a preexisting stimulus have not been encountered.

Concepts for Observing Social Environments

It should be stated at the outset that we are aware of no studies in which the social environment has been given as much independent status as a variable class as is done in this chapter. Thus, our comments about previous studies conceptualizing social environments are based upon a recoding of procedures that may not have been designed originally for the explicit study of environments.

The problem of summarizing previous treatments of the social environment is further complicated by two problems. The first is the relative paucity of terms in English that refer unambiguously to social events. It is fairly certain that such terms as "cohesiveness," "group size," and "role structure" refer to social processes. But is "pupil enthusiasm" a description of a social environment or of the behavior of several individuals? The second problem stems from the tendency to confuse states of the social environment with acts that determine them or vice versa. We have already encountered this tendency in certain previous studies wherein the behavior of the teacher is converted to "social climate" when findings are interpreted.

STUDIES OF THE MACROENVIRONMENT

Studies of the macroenvironment have emphasized the social groups that may occur in the classroom—their size, membership, and duration (see Thomas *et al.*, 1929; Cornell, Lindvall, and Saupe, 1952; Medley and Mitzel, 1955, 1958, 1959). Damrin (1959) has gone further, suggesting that classroom groups go through phases of planning and operations and that group types may be observed: for example, "semi-controlled," "disinterested," or "rollicking." In another type of conceptualization, Kowatrakul (1959) has conceptualized forms of total classroom activities, while Hughes (1959) has viewed the assigned subject matter of the classroom as a social environment. Finally, Withall (1956) has demonstrated the feasibility of measuring aspects of the social environment (teacher-pupil distances) by photographic means.

STUDIES OF THE MICROENVIRONMENT

At least three groups of studies are now reported in which the microenvironment is conceptualized. Smith (1960; see also Meux and Smith, 1964; Aschner, 1958) is concerned with the logic of teacher-pupil interactions, using such concepts as "explanation" and "valuation." Wright (1959) and Wright and Proctor (1961) are more specifically concerned with teacher-pupil interaction; they use a complex code which differentiates content, process, and attitude. Gallagher and Aschner (1963) are concerned with "cognitive memory," "convergent thinking," "divergent thinking," "evaluative thinking," and "routine" in the microenvironment.

Concepts for Observing the Physical Environment

To the best of our knowledge, there have been no reports of systematic observations of the physical environment as related to teacher behavior, pupil behavior, or social environment. This does not mean that educators are uninterested in the physical environment. On the contrary, vast numbers of studies have examined pupil learning, attitudes, or adjustment as a function of various educational media. In addition, teachers have strong opinions about the effects of light, heat, movable furniture, colorful decorations, and the like on classroom interaction.

Occasional studies of particular physical features of the classroom environment have been reported. Thus, Barr (1929); Medley and Mitzel (1955, 1958, 1959); and Cornell, Lindvall, and Saupe (1952) provide occasional references to the use of training aids, blackboards, textbooks, and the like by teachers (and, less often, by pupils). But it should be emphasized that the presence of environmental factors and their use are two quite distinct concepts. Although a teacher cannot behave with regard to a blackboard unless one is present, once it is there a blackboard may be used for transmitting information, for practice and drill, for punishment, or as an object to be cleaned. It also has distinctive visual, tactile, and even auditory (chalk squeeks) properties that condition classroom interaction.

Ideological Problems

In addition to the methodological problems which have plagued studies of the classroom to date, a number of ideological problems have also affected the methods and concepts chosen. The first of these ideological problems has already been mentioned several times: the focus upon relationships between the teacher and the pupil rather than a broader focus in which the classroom is seen as a comprehensive social system.

Another problem stems from the understandable desire to apply research findings in solving problems of the educational world. This laudable aim has sufficiently dominated classroom research that certain investigators have chosen methods not for their conceptual sophistication but rather because they could be easily applied in the classroom, taught to relatively untrained observers, or used immediately in retraining teachers. (In this connection, see especially Flanders, 1960b.) In our opinion, research on the classroom should not be confused with the application of findings in order to ameliorate specific problems—although the latter may be an ultimate aim.

A third ideological bias has been that of progressive education. It may be true that the practitioners and consumers of American education are overwhelmingly concerned with teacher-pupil relationships and with socializing for "adjustment" rather than for "achievement" (see Biddle, Rosencranz, and Rankin, 1961). This concern does not, however, excuse such biases on the part of classroom investigators. We find it difficult to believe that the "ultimate and only" dimension along which classrooms may be viewed is that of democracy-autocracy; indeed, we find it hard to conceptualize an environment containing one enormously powerful teacher and thirty-odd egregiously powerless pupils in terms of "democracy."

Finally, it is significant that the majority of research on classroom processes has been performed by *educational* researchers, whose vocabulary has reflected pedagogical concerns of the day. Thus, the words used for describing teacher and pupil behaviors have been drawn extensively from the repertoires of educational psychology and educational philosophy and, to a far lesser extent, from the concepts of psychology and sociology proper and their related disciplines.

In many ways, research on the classroom to date resembles research on leadership of perhaps two decades ago. Prior to World War II, leadership studies unsuccessfully searched for the universal "traits" characterizing the successful leader. With the development of group dynamics as a discipline, leadership was nearly abandoned as a field of inquiry in favor of examining the various roles people might play in groups (some of which roles might be called "leadership") and how these roles related to group functioning and outcomes. Today it is possible to provide a set of predictive relationships between personality factors and group behavior (Mann, 1959; Borg, 1960; Petrullo and Bass,

1961). Our contention is that such a sharp advance in knowledge about the classroom is possible only if ideological commitments are abandoned in favor of a serious look at actual classroom processes.

CONCEPTUAL PROPOSALS

About three years ago, we began a study of classroom interaction using methods and concepts designed to reflect the model and to handle the problems discussed in this chapter. Approximately 100 classroom sessions have been recorded on videotape to date. In the section immediately following, we briefly describe the equipment and techniques being used. (For a fuller description, see Biddle and Johns, unpublished.)

Instruments and Design

The system used is designed to make videotape records of various types of social interaction in both field and laboratory conditions, including classrooms. It consists of two remotely controlled video cameras with zoom lenses (usually mounted in boxes with half-silvered mirrors to prevent observation of the cameras by classroom personnel); several types of microphones, including a small broadcasting microphone that may be hung around the neck; a control console capable of accepting and blending two video images and handling two separate sound circuits; control, video, and sound cables permitting operation up to 500 feet from the source; a panel truck from which the system can be operated and for transportation; a trailer for cable storage and field generator; a portable tape recorder capable of storing one video track and two audio tracks; and playback facilities.

We place the two camera boxes in the classroom several days ahead of time to minimize equipment effects. One box is placed at the front of the classroom to record the faces of pupils. The other camera is placed at the rear and follows the teacher. The two video images are then blended at the control console to make a composite image showing all faces, and this composite is recorded.

Both cameras are controlled from the console, which is generally left in the panel truck. The teacher wears a lavaliere microphone, and

4–6 microphones are hung at strategic locations within the classroom. Generally, we record the teacher's microphone on one audio channel and blend the outputs from the other microphones for recording on the other channel. The system tolerates great variations in light (we have never had to use other than actual classroom illumination), but the ambient noise level of the average classroom is so high that we find we cannot understand all of the verbal communications no matter how carefully we place microphones. (We are convinced that similar difficulties are, in fact, encountered by teacher and pupils alike.)

To date, our pilot studies have used a factorial design in which five structural variables have been examined for their effects on classroom processes. These are (1) age (young versus old teacher), (2) sex (male versus female teacher), (3) grade level (first versus sixth versus eleventh grade), (4) subject assigned (mathematics versus social studies), and (5) teaching style (pupil-centered versus subject-centered). Style is rated by the school principal and, as it turns out, is unreliably assessed.

Teachers in the pilot study were volunteers and appeared to represent the upper two-thirds of the total range of teaching ability. Classrooms chosen for study were located in St. Louis County and Jefferson City, Missouri, and all represented a range of socioeconomic status, with middle-class pupils predominating. Data from this initial pilot study are still in analysis, although initial results will shortly be forthcoming.

Given the records of classroom processes described here, it is possible not only to go back over a certain behavioral sequence again and again, but also to design far more complex systems of concepts for data interpretation than have heretofore been used. In the following section, we present proposals for coding the social environment. A section proposing concepts for teacher behavior follows.

Concepts for the Social Environment

According to common usage in sociology, it may be observed that the social environment exhibits both structural and functional properties. *Structure* means an order that is observed to persist among the communicating actors of the system. Examples of structure are number of persons, their spatial locations, and patterned ways in which they address one another. *Function* refers to what goes on within the system; that is, to those properties that are exchanged or communicated. Thus, whereas structure refers to the size and composition of a group, function refers to what the group is doing.

Various structural characteristics of the classroom may be observed. We have found it convenient to separate two aspects of structure: *communication structure*, referring to the patterns of symbolic exchange among actors in the classroom; and *spatial structure*, referring to their physical locations with regard to one another. We also differentiate two components of function: *content*, that about which actors are communicating; and *manner*, the joint style with which they are interacting. Each of these components is discussed separately below.

One of the properties of the classroom is that it does not always constitute a single interacting group. In fact, the number of occasions when all members of the classroom are attending to a given stimulus may be in the minority. Often classrooms may be observed in which one or more individuals are gazing elsewhere or whispering to their neighbors, in which the microenvironment has ceased to hold the attention of others, or in which independent groups have been created for various purposes. Therefore, we treat the numbers and sizes of communicating groups as observable properties of classrooms constituting their *communication-system structures*.

In addition, it is also possible to note the characteristic roles played within the communication process and the allocation of individuals to these roles. For all practical purposes, we find it convenient to differentiate three communicating roles for classroom groups: *initiator*, *target*, and *audience*. The initiator is the person engaged in transmitting information; the target is the person to whom the initiator addresses himself; the audience is comprised of those persons who witness the transmission of information.

Not all communication groups evidence three roles, of course. A class that is sitting and watching a television program, for example, is a one-role group. Two-role groups occur primarily in two forms: the initiator-target group, in which two persons are in private exchange (and in which the roles of initiator and target generally switch from one person to the other); and the lecture group, in which the teacher (or pupil) verbalizes and others listen. A typical three-role group occurs when the teacher and a pupil are in interaction and are watched by others. We do not claim that these three role types exhaust the variability of observable roles in the classroom, but they seem adequately to characterize most classroom groups.

Positions are also observable in the classroom. Minimally, there is a vast positional distinction between the powerful, adult teacher and the less powerful, immature pupils. But additional pupil positions are often distinguishable, such as sex, race, "the picked on," "the deviant," and the like. Each communicating group can be characterized in terms of the positions of those who are involved in it. Whereas one group, for example, may involve only female pupils, another may include the teacher as a member. It is convenient for coding purposes to consider position members as they display the roles which are also observable within communication groups. We shall thus speak of the *role allocation* of the classroom as the unique assignment of persons—identified in terms of their positions—to the roles structured for classroom groups at any given moment. Role allocations may be analyzed either for the complement of positions assigned to designated roles or the complement of roles entered into by designated position members.

SPATIAL STRUCTURE

Classrooms are also characterized by various physical relationships between persons and by fixed and semifixed features of the physical environment. Several characteristics of spatial structure may be noted; for example, physical groupings of persons, their bodily orientations, their facial orientations, and their proximity to desks, blackboard, and other equipment. Moreover, spatial structure interacts with communication structure, for individuals who are in interaction are usually closer together and look at one another more continuously than those who are not in interaction.

The complexities of these possible relationships require a decision about research priorities. We have chosen in our own research to examine in detail only two aspects of spatial structure: the locations of role performers within communication-system structure, and the locations of position members. In effect, then, we are currently coding the spatial positions of identified initiators, targets, and audiences; we are also noting the spatial locations of the teacher and other identified position members.

The problem of locating classroom actors can be fairly difficult. If all classrooms were characterized by a column-and-row arrangement of pupils' desks with the teacher's desk, the blackboard, and the flag at the front of the room, it would be simple to devise a locational code to express spatial structure unambiguously. Unfortunately, the classrooms we have observed show wide variation in spatial arrangement. In some, the pupils' desks are arranged in one or more circles; in others, there are no desks at all, only three large tables; in still others, pupils face one another in Quaker-meeting style. How can spatial generalizations be made among environments that are this disparate?

Our tentative solution to this problem is to define vertical and horizontal scales in sufficiently vague terms that they may be applied to any classroom arrangement. These scales are:

Vertical Dimension	*Horizontal Dimension*
Diffuse	Diffuse
Front	Right side
Forward	Right
Middle	Middle
Rear	Left
Back	Left side

With the exception of the first category (diffuse), each scale provides an ordered set of alternatives for locating a person or a group, and supplementary instructions are provided defining each category for all encountered forms of classroom layout. The first category, diffuse, is included to handle cases for which a large pupil group needs to be referenced or where rapid, oscillatory behavior is observed for a single actor.

CONTENT

Communicating groups exchange information, and gross or fine distinctions may be made about that which is exchanged. We are presently using a four-category scheme for coding content. Given a knowledge of the subject assigned to the classroom lesson (algebra), it is easy to distinguish between two kinds of subject matter: *Intrinsic* subject matter is content that pertains to the assigned task (communications concerned with definitions, with algebraic proof, with mathematical symbols, even with the history or application of algebra). Other types of subject matter (such as American history, democratic values, the location of the public library, or a trip to Mexico last summer) are referred to as *extrinsic*.

The other two forms of communication concern events of the classroom itself. *Sociation* is coded whenever the communicating group concerns itself with the states of individuals (comfort to an injured party, exhortations to be good citizens, inquiries after health, statements of positive or negative effect). *Organization* is coded whenever the group concerns itself with the administration of the classroom (collecting milk money, setting up turns). It is here presumed that these four categories exhaust the universe of content with which communicating groups in the classroom may deal, even though more molecular content distinctions could be made.

MANNER

Communicating groups also evidence observable styles of interaction. Such terms as "discussion" and "lecture" refer to manneristic distinctions which have appeared frequently in pedagogical literature and which were first considered by the investigators as potential ways of describing group activities. However, we concluded that these words did not adequately describe observable manners for classroom groups, particularly at the primary level. Instead, we are now using three manneristic distinctions that are also presumed to be mutually exclusive and exhaustive of the universe of manner:

1. *Operation* refers to the limiting case in which groups are not really exchanging information but are performing nonsymbolic acts (group singing, making aeroplanes, recitation and drill).

2. *Information dissemination* refers to all communication exchanges devoted to conveying information ("answers" given to a question, "dates" in a history lesson). Statements coded under information dissemination are concerned with (a) facts—provision or clarification; (b) comments, questions, or assertions; and (c) illustrations or demonstrations performed for the express purposes of soliciting, exhibiting, or substantiating evidence.

3. *Intellectualization* refers to all exchanges devoted to reasoning, considering, deductive and inductive thought, opinion giving, judgment making, assessing and evaluating, and interpreting. Whereas the emphasis in information dissemination is upon facts, the emphasis in intellectualization is on understanding. It is also presumed that operation, information dissemination, and intellectualization nest. *All* manners are operations; in some of these, symbols are disseminated, a few of which emphasize understanding.

Given any conceptually independent dimension of a phenomenon occurring over time, an *episode* is defined as the period of time during which a given category of that dimension is coded. For instance, for some measurable period of time, the classroom may have but a single communicating group (episode 1); at a later time, it breaks apart into two groups (episode 2); and still later, into two groups and an isolated person (episode 3).

We consider now the problem of episode boundaries. Is it necessarily true that when communication-system structure changes, there is also a change in the spatial locations of persons or in content or manner? This chain reaction is certainly not implied by the concepts for understanding the social environment. Although it may be true that functional and structural episode boundaries tend to coincide, whether they do or not is a matter for discovery and not for judgment a priori. Thus, we cannot assume a "unitary" character for the operations of the social environment, as is done in structuring episodes for the individual (see Barker and Wright, 1955). Instead, it is necessary to note *any* change of a dimension of the social environment as a boundary and then to investigate the coincidence of episode boundaries among other phenomena. Thus, counts and sequences of "communication-system episodes" will have different properties from counts and sequences of "content episodes."

Concepts for Teacher Behavior

One of the most obvious characteristics of the proposals for conceptualizing social environments is their molecular character. Therefore, we have designed concepts that may be sequentially recorded and that have the potential for generating a large number of secondary, molar characteristics for any given classroom.

Given the frozen records of classroom interaction on videotape, it is also possible to construct molecular concepts for observing teacher behavior. In fact, it is likely that the individual acts of teachers (and their pupils) will be found to be the units which, in sequence, make up the grosser episodes of the social environment. Our intent, then, is to design a system of concepts for expressing teacher behavior that may be either analyzed sequentially or summated to generate a wide variety of molar dimensions applying to a given teacher.

What is an act? In common with other investigators of teacher behavior, we use the term "act" to refer to the irreducibly minimal form in which human behavior may be understood. Acts may be "symbolic," in which case information is transmitted, or "nonsymbolic" (for example, doodling).

Following the terminological usage suggested by Thomas and Biddle (1966), we describe the minimal symbolic act as a *transitor*. A transitor is any form of behavior which references a phenomenon; thus, whenever a person speaks, uses symbols, or expresses meanings, his behavior is transitive in form. Transitors are characterized by two realms of meaning: the act of reference, and the referenced material.

The act of referencing may appear in any of several modalities. Individuals may *report* ("tomorrow is Tuesday"), *demand* ("Johnny, you must eat your peas"), *question* ("What is the name of that fish?"), *evaluate* ("I don't like spinach"). Sometimes the transitive modality is clear, as in the above examples; at other times, it is ambiguous. For instance, is the sentence "I expect you to eat your fish" a report, a demand, or an evaluation? Despite such occasional ambiguities, *transitive modality* represents one of the basic dimensions of observable symbolic acts.

That which is referenced in a transitor (its content) is also a primitive quality of the communicative act. Transitors may reference behavior ("Johnny, you should eat your potatoes"), persons ("I like Mary"), nonhuman subjects ("I like dogs"), physical equipment and its use ("turn on the television please"), impersonal events ("Constantinople fell in 1453"), and nonobservable phenomena ("I don't believe in ghosts"). Some reference forms may be simple, as in the above examples; others may be complex and filled with contingencies ("returning residents are granted a $100 exemption after a stay abroad of at least 48 hours, except in the case of residents returning from Mexico or the Virgin Islands of the United States"); still others may be unclear in all or portions of their content ("I have a vague feeling of discomfort, doctor"). However, all transitive acts have discriminable references as well as modalities. A shift in either modality or reference marks the act boundary.

Modality and reference are not the only two observable dimensions of the act. Indeed, acts may be judged for numerous qualities in addition to those of the dimensions defining them. They may be delivered, for instance, with enthusiasm or timidity, with various accents, with stammering, and with various emotional overtones. Each of these is an additional, codable quality of acts; the qualities do not define the act, although they may so circumscribe the act gestalt as to constrain or even reverse the apparent meaning of the referent. For example, the words "I hate you" delivered with a grin or tender expression may mean quite the opposite of its apparent content to the target person. Or, the discussion of an algebraic theory may be delivered in such a manner as to convince the target that he is despised, loved, or ignored by the speaker.

TRANSITIVE SEQUENCES

Most teacher behavior consists of elaborate sequences of transitors that are tied together, rather than of isolated transitors occasionally emitted in response to pupil questions or other environmental stimuli. We now consider two forms of transitive sequences.

The first form encountered in teacher behavior is the *extended transitor*. When the teacher says, "I presume that Jane is not thinking about the lesson," he is referencing not Jane's action but a transitive process presumed to be taking place in Jane's mind. Transitive sequences may be covert, as in the example above, or completely overt ("John tells me that Mary hit Richard") and either may be short, two-step affairs or may involve a vast number of transitive forms strung together. Extended transitive sequences may appear with one or with several modalities reflected in their various transitive components ("John, what did Mary tell you about Suzy's dislike of spinach?").

Another form of sequence is *causative*. Transitors are often strung together in such a way as to imply a causal link among them. For instance, teachers may accompany a demand made of the pupil with a threat of punishment for refusal to comply. Or the teacher may warn a pupil about the danger of crossing the street without looking both ways. Or a mathematical proof may be demonstrated in such a way that *A* leads to *B* leads to *C*. Causative sequences may sometimes be recognized by their apposition of component transitors; indeed, sometimes parts of the sequence are left out (when, for instance, the teacher merely signals a deviancy or references a threat without actually spelling out what the child is presumed to be doing wrong). More often, however, causative sequences are signaled by recognized connecting phrases ("if . . . , then," "therefore").

Causative sequences should not be confused with *transitor logic*. Causative sequences may or may not be logical, but so may other forms of transitive sequence, including sequences of exchange between two or more actors. Thus, the analysis of logic in transitive sequences is a field of inquiry (see Smith, 1960; Meux and Smith, 1964) rather than a specific form of sequence. And other properties of acts (such as the manner of their delivery) may affect the form of subsequent transitors in interaction quite as much as the logic of their contents.

NONSYMBOLIC BEHAVIOR

The difficulty in coding nonsymbolic acts is that we do not know the appropriate level of abstraction with which to describe them. An actor may think of (and it may be meaningful to code) acts in terms of muscle movements, the discriminable sequence of actlets that make up the whole, the physical effects intended, or the larger goal that is served. In symbolic acts the speaker himself provides a frame of reference in the form of modality and reference material chosen. However, it is only when he *discusses* nonsymbolic behavior that we are given a concrete peg with which to describe observed nonsymbolic acts.

For instance, if the teacher references the act of a pupil ("John, do not chew that gum; throw it away"), it is meaningful thereafter to observe the pupil (and perhaps other pupils) to see what effect this act has had on gum-chewing behavior. Again, if a symbolic act references a previously occurring nonsymbolic act (the teacher says, "For heavens' sake, John, stop pulling Mary's hair and pay attention"), it is reasonable to back up in examining the record and find out whether John was in fact pulling Mary's hair immediately prior to this transitor. In this way, some of the nonsymbolic acts occurring in the classroom may be identified and coded.

The vast majority of nonsymbolic acts are *not* symbolized in other act-transitors. Should these be ignored? Given the high proportion of symbolic acts emitted by most teachers, other behavioral forms are often ignored, but pupils often react to the classroom situation with enthusiasm, hand-raising, general noise, inadvertent display of emotion, and other nonsymbolic performances that never evoke comments by the teacher or others. Our general position is that these latter act forms should be coded with the same dimensions of meaning that are used to provide additional information for symbolic acts, such as *implied effect, use of instruments,* and *mode of delivery.* These codes must be arbitrarily given to units of behavior that are not determined primarily by observing pupils but rather by considering pupils as reactors to other events.

There are two basic ways, then, in which nonsymbolic behavior may be coded. First, certain acts may be coded as "zero-order" transitors because their contents are referenced by actors, and we are interested in finding relationships between symbolic acts and those phenomena they reference. Second, behavior (especially pupil behavior) may be coded in noncontent and nonmode terms provided only that actlike boundaries are established for coding purposes by reference to other boundaries in the system.

BIAS

The restriction of concepts for teacher behavior to those enunciated in symbolic acts may offend some investigators who are concerned with the "other-directedness," "authoritarianism," or "responsiveness" of the teacher. These concepts are inadequately mapped in the vocabulary of the average teacher. Should the possibility be ignored of observing the teacher in terms that are analytically conceptualized by the investigator?

Our answer is, temporarily, *yes*. There are at least three reasons for this position. First, many of the more sophisticated concepts for describing teacher behavior (for instance, "responsiveness") may be directly defined in terms of relationships between teacher acts, pupil acts, and other classroom phenomena. It is also likely that a much larger vocabulary describing the teacher will be developed when act records are available in convenient form. Second, until act records have been examined in some detail, there is probably little reason to choose one set of analytic concepts over another; the act record is too rich, and too little is known about act sequences to judge. Finally, there has to be a start somewhere, and the development of non-act-related concepts would require a separate identification of coding units. Actually, our presumption is that the vast majority of concepts already used for rating teaching behavior holistically may be developed with far greater reliability from sequences of act scores and that many additional concepts will be developed during the analysis.

Conclusion

The reader may have detected a penchant for the field study in the proposals advanced here. In effect, we have said that what is known today about the processes of the classroom is insufficient to suggest the present utility of experimental studies. Indeed, concepts presently available for describing teacher behavior in the classroom context may be said to describe only a small portion of what transpires.

That little is known about the stimulus characteristics of the instructional environment does not mean these characteristics are unknowable. Rather, for the first time it is possible to contemplate a theory of instruction that does justice to the immense complexity and sophistication of the master teacher at work—and to back it up with evidence.

PART·III·

FORMULATIONS EMPHASIZING

LEARNER BEHAVIOR

The chapters in Part III develop theories of instruction from the standpoint of how a student learns. Theories of *teaching* are here regarded as special derivatives of school learning theory. The three writers take the position that learning theory is basic to understanding the instructional process and that effective teaching entails the appropriate application of principles derived from learning theory. As Jahnke indicates, this application entails two primary functions performed by the teacher: arranging the optimal environment for learning to take place; and helping the learner learn to learn.

Using learning theory as their base for developing theories of instruction, these writers are concerned with all aspects of the instructional setting that enhance or interfere with learning. Because of certain unique properties, summarized in Ericksen's statement, the teacher is regarded as one very important component of this setting: "There are many sources of inputs into any thinking-student system, but the classroom teacher is especially important. As with a good book, a good teacher at any grade level is well programed and he is interesting; he is also sensitive to feedback cues from his students." But Ericksen himself is quick to point out that the teacher is only a means to the end of enhancing the learning process; and despite the importance of the teacher's role, he is but one of several available means.

Given the pervasive concern with facilitating school learning, there are subtle differences among these writers in their conceptions about *what* is to be learned, and some more obvious differences in their perceptions about the *conditions* encouraging learning.

On the matter of what is to be learned, Ericksen is unequivocally committed to the attainment of "higher-order" cognitive objectives. He writes about "the student who is trying to acquire conceptual knowledge, not to blow glass, to roll the French *r*, or to memorize the names of things. Furthermore, matters pertaining to his character, his mental discipline, his social status, his personal adjustment, and his interests, attitudes, and values are considered only in terms of their supporting or distracting influence on the process of acquiring knowledge."

Ausubel takes a related view in distinguishing between rotely and meaningfully learned materials. The latter are less vulnerable to forgetting and, in Ausubel's view, facilitate the course of subsequent learning. Without necessarily making a judgment about the relative value of various educational objectives to society, Ausubel emphasizes the development of concepts on tactical grounds: these anchor subsequent learning.

Jahnke comes to grips less than Ericksen or Ausubel with the issue of what is to be learned. In Jahnke's terms, instruction is effective when it prepares the individual to observe his environment and the consequences of alternative responses to the environment. He provides a taxonomy of learning tasks encompassing both generalized and highly restricted response patterns.

The differences among these writers become most evident when they consider *how* learning occurs and, in consequence, how the instructional setting should be arranged.

Jahnke and Ausubel write from two classically polar positions. According to Jahnke, learning is predicated upon developing and embellishing stimulus-response bonds. It may entail (1) enlarging the repertoire of responses evoked by a stimulus, (2) elaborating the range of stimuli sufficient to evoke a particular response, (3) bringing certain responses now in the learner's repertoire under the control of a new stimulus, or (4) restricting the stimuli presently effective for evoking a particular response. A critical determinant of learning efficiency is reinforcement. Hence, a critical factor in instructional efficiency is the mediation of reinforcement.

Ausubel feels that it is precisely this view that has largely impeded progress in making a useful transition from empirical studies to classroom applications. Whereas Jahnke speaks of the accretion of knowledge by progressive elaboration and differentiation of stimulus-response bonds, Ausubel speaks of the psychological organization and accretion of knowledge through subsumption. In Ausubel's view, the critical determinant of instructional efficiency is the use of appropriately relevant and inclusive introductory materials (that is, organizers) to provide the "ideational scaffolding" necessary for subsumption to occur.

Ericksen stands outside of this disagreement. He makes his camp with the student as an idiosyncratic learner who can be little assisted by nomothetic theories. Instead, he views instruction as relating to the idiographic process of learning. Since student-centered variables (particularly memory, meaningfulness, and motivation) are the most important determinants of learning, the most effective instructional setting is the one that provides appropriately for individual differences among learners.

6

The Zigzag Curve
of Learning

STANFORD C. ERICKSEN [*]

University of Michigan

ℒ

THE TEACHER IS AN OMNIBUS MAN WHO IS EXPECTED TO MEDIATE ALL good things between society and children—the accumulated knowledge as well as social norms and desired traits of character. Clearly, it is necessary to sharpen the job description of a teacher, to mark out the denotative reference to the behavior bounded by a theory of instruction.

Ideally, the initiative for clarifying his instructional role should come from the teacher himself. Teachers, however, like everyone else, selectively perceive themselves to appear to their best advantage. Therefore, when a teacher writes a theory of instruction, some degree of protective self-interest might be suspected in his otherwise rational statements. Perhaps for this reason the teacher is inclined to talk about the teaching process with greater emphasis and detail than he gives to his analysis of the learning process.

In principle, at least, a learning theorist should be a better teacher than someone who is less knowledgeable about the conditions that control behavior change. However, it is interesting to note how infrequently teaching procedures reflect what psychologists are sup-

---

[*] Throughout the chapter, I repeat or paraphrase material, but without reference notation, from an earlier publication of mine: The place of thinking in an ideal university, *Amer. Psychol.*, 1962, *17*, 763–771.

posed to know about how humans learn, remember, and generalize. There are many reasons and possible explanations for this state of affairs, but I am inclined to pass it off as a type of Jost Law effect: teaching traditions are older and stronger than is the dependence on learning research. This means that the social pressures dominating working environments tend to maintain the well-established norms of how a teacher teaches. A frontal attack by a professor of psychology on his university colleagues about ways to improve their teaching would be shunted aside with dispatch and strong feelings. This chapter is essentially an account of how a learning theorist might define his job as a teacher, and how he might utilize that segment of information being reported by his behavioral-science colleagues that seems to have relevance for understanding human learning in the natural setting.

To What Does a Theory of Instruction Refer?

If teachers want the authority to define their job, they must accept the responsibility for drawing sensible boundaries and for being concerned with verifiable events. Otherwise, they will simply be talking about the teaching weather, with no action indicated; they must not hide behind the mystique of teaching or the ego-enhancing platitudes.

A theory of instruction, like any good theory, should be parsimonious in the sense of reducing the number of concepts needed to account for multiple events. Such a theory can focus on events within the context of any one of several aspects of education: a small or a large school system, a given grade, curricular matters, educational technology, teacher training, and so on. A theory of instruction might also be directed to the way a student learns—and this is where my soapbox stands.

I should state outright that I am writing about the student who is trying to acquire conceptual knowledge, not to blow glass, to roll the French *r*, or to memorize the names of things. Furthermore, matters pertaining to his character, his mental discipline, his social status, his personal adjustment, and his interests, attitudes, and values are considered only in terms of their supporting or distracting influence on the process of acquiring knowledge. Questions about how and what students learn are sometimes masked when teachers and administrators become heavily involved with problems of student morale, morality, and motivation. These are important problems and someone must do the appropriate amount of worrying and decision making, but a theory of instruction should bypass these intermediate issues and make its impact on the classroom (broadly defined) as a place where students learn and think.

Books, audiovisual aids, and specific teaching assignments come and go, but students remain. The individual learner is the final and unique component in all instructional arrangements. The student is the necessary antecedent for the existence of the teacher, and the evaluation of any aspect of teaching must ultimately represent changes in the behavior of the student. The slope and height of the learning curve are more a function of what the student himself contributes than of any other single set of variables.

In essence, then, a theory of instruction is really a statement about the procedures that enhance the learning process; it provides a rationale for the way a teacher functions as the director of this process. Many writers sound this theme but with varying degrees of specificity. For some, it is a preamble pronouncement (Gage, 1963, Preface and Chap. 3) to a broad survey of instructional categories and procedures. Other authors and source books stay within the more conventional boundaries of learning research and theory (Bigge, 1964; Bugelski, 1964; Meierhenry, 1961; Hilgard, 1964; Travers, 1963). This emphasis on *learning* needs to be repeated at intervals; otherwise, teachers soon drift in the direction of their professional bias and concern themselves with teaching per se. Teachers, like other professionals, have a weakness for separating the means from the ends. The frequently used phrase "the teaching-learning process" suggests the changing orientation of teachers toward viewing the student as a learner rather than as a listener.

A Definition of Instruction

Instruction is a multimedia implementing process between two anchoring points: the student and a body of knowledge. The teacher is the monitor as well as a participant in this information-processing system. As every sandlot player knows, ground rules are particularly necessary when some of the players are also referees. However, ground rules are not the same as theories, and definitions have still a different function. I would propose, as a definition of instruction, a statement which summarizes in capsule form the interaction among the teacher, the student, and the subject matter: *Instruction is an idiosyncratic man-machine information-processing system in which the teacher is the monitor.*

Normally, I resist condensed and tightly worded definitions like this one; they smack too much of phrase making and linguistic labeling. Murphy, in his *Personality* (1947), avoids the fault of using a mere phrase to define a complex phenomenon. Witness his index entry: "Personality defined, 1 ff." The "ff." is the 999 pages in the book. The combination of words in my definition of instruction was selected to bypass the response sets that are elicited in anyone scanning the familiar language of teaching, curricula, students, and instructional materials. I am quite willing to trade off initial meaningfulness to gain entry into a different universe of discourse which might be used to represent a new and better pattern for conducting the educational enterprise.

To preview the argument that follows:

Monitor: The teacher functions as the director of the learning process.

Idiosyncratic: The enterprise of instruction requires explicit recognition of and adaptation to the individuality of students—the prime responsibility of education in a democratic society.

Man-machine: The student interacts with books, lecture notes, homework, audiovisual aids, computers—any and all kinds of people and devices used in instruction.

Information-processing: By the various man-machine interactions, the student is presented with information, stores it, transforms it according to his needs, and retrieves it. His acquisition of knowledge, by reducing uncertainties, reinforces and motivates further learning.

System: This word alludes to systems theory, which may be a passing fad. But in passing or until it passes, it provides a major contribution—an integrating set of principles between the individual student and a succession of supersystems (the class, school, community, and society).

If teaching is viewed as a special form of group behavior, it might be in order to develop a social subtheory about the nature of the interaction between the teacher and his group of students. However, if attention is focused on the individual student moving upward on his own idiographic curve of learning, little help is given by generating a new set of nomothetic theories—social, cognitive, S-R, or other. There are already a number of conceptual arrangements and formal theories about learning and also about individual differences. What the educational psychologist does need is a definitive set of guiding principles to help make the transformation from laboratory-based learning theory to human learning in the classroom.

My purpose, therefore, is not to develop a formal theory of instruction but to describe those changes that are taking place in education and in psychology that encourage, if not require, considering the individual student as the primary element in the educational process. The preceding definition is as close as I will come to a formal statement. The meat of this chapter is intended to be in the successive sections which support the thesis that instruction is related to the idiographic process of learning.

THE SHIFTING EMPHASIS FROM DISCIPLINE TO CONTENT TO METHODOLOGY

Students go to school with different objectives than were dominant a generation ago—not altogether different reasons, but the center of gravity has shifted. Education is moving away from purposes of mental and personal discipline and toward a more open and straightforward emphasis on learning and on the ability to transfer and utilize the facts, concepts, procedures, attitudes, and values acquired in a course of study.

As the growth rate of new knowledge continues to accelerate, it becomes even more critical than in former years that theories of instruction focus on how and what the student learns. Teachers at all levels must begin to take active measures to reduce the curricular lag between what is "nice to know" in contrast to what the present student generation "needs to know." The slow-to-change teacher might unknowingly actually hinder the student's educational efforts to protect himself from informational obsolescence. From the medical school faculty, for example, I have heard expressions like: "Half of what we teach will be outdated ten years from now, and half of what the physician will need to know in ten years has not yet been discovered."

Diekhoff (1964, p. 188) summarized quite well the instructional implications resulting from our rapidly changing curricula:

As the high school comes closer to doing the job professors imagine for it, professors will be forced to imagine an appropriate new job for the college. If so, we must first learn that the American educational system is sequential, that changes in one level of education require changes in others, that the task is shared by all teachers in all schools. We shall find ourselves engaged in re-examination and revision of our own programs, undergraduate and graduate. Starting late, the university must as usual scramble to catch up, to keep up, and finally to get far enough ahead to exercise its function of leadership by example as well as by precept.

How will teachers and students adapt to the rapid outpouring of new knowledge and the curricular revisions that are in process? Textbooks and instructors are the established information-givers, but the role of the teacher in many subject areas is moving away from the comfortable function of transmitting pat answers to familiar questions. James G. Miller has developed the concept of information input overload in relation to information-processing systems. These adjustment processes can be generalized to apply to teachers and students at all levels (1961, pp. 121–122):

So also is the problem of the average college student. At least since Aristotle, no man has been able to process all the available information about the world. In modern times facts have increased with speedy acceleration. The student must select among many alternative courses to take in the brief time available to him. More than four courses a semester are ordinarily considered to exceed his channel capacity. He has available the various adjustment processes. Some are rewarded by his environment and others are punished. For example, when he takes true-false tests, *omissions* are punished . . . *Filtering*, electing certain courses and omitting all the rest . . . *Approximation*, giving vague answers on essay examinations, is disapproved when recognized. *Multiple channels*—getting help from others

—is punished by expulsion for plagiarism. And *escape* from the overload, leaving school in midsemester, results in suspension.

The geometrical increase in new knowledge requires that teachers reassess their familiar patterns of instruction. It seems inevitable, for instance, that better use must be made of the student's ability for independent learning by transferring to him more responsibility for acquiring factual and descriptive information. The teacher must raise the conceptual level of classroom instruction ("chunking" is another way of adjusting to information input overload); he must emphasize the meaning of the Table of Contents while, on his own, the student acquires the information given in the Index. In his paper "The Acquisition of Knowledge" (1962a) and in Chapter 10 of this book, Gagné suggests the instructional procedures that should increase the transfer of conceptual material in contrast to more familiar classroom teaching methods that emphasize rote-level original learning.

Considerably more is known about substantive teaching, whether for facts or taxonomic concepts, than about the teaching of research procedures. It is easier for the chemist to teach laboratory techniques (and the answers given by his research) than to teach the abstract and complex methods of research. Despite this difficulty, teaching in the future will need to place far more emphasis on methodological matters, such as the problem-solving skills and concepts related to investigating and evaluating procedures—heuristic searching, logical inference, validity, confounding variables, and so on. Unfortunately, there is not too much agreement about how to define "the problem-solving skills."

The fundamental teaching problems for contemporary education thus become (1) how to teach abstract concepts without divorcing the student from the experience, logic, and scientific data that support these constructs in their sequential development through the curriculum; and (2) how to help the student utilize this conceptual knowledge outside the classroom in concrete problem-solving or decision-making settings. These two base-line requirements apply all the way from primary grades to postgraduate training and help to define the curricular substance and the instructional objectives of the teaching process.

In summary, a systematic treatment of instruction points to the way a teacher helps the individual student learn. Such a statement should focus on matters of conceptual learning, especially on concepts that relate to how new knowledge is created and, in turn, modified or discarded; how society and individuals must also change and adapt to new information about the real world, society, and man himself. The 3 R's are only prerequisite acquisitions to the kind of information processing that is important in education today.

THE HIGH RELEVANCE OF LEARNING THEORY

Learning theory is the best source of supply for general statements which can give logic and meaning to the instructional process. The principles of learning provide a foundation to stabilize the educational process in those places where the sands are shifting, for example, new instructional procedures and radical changes in the curriculum. Insofar as there is confidence in an underlying invariance in the way humans learn, there is no alternative but to establish some degree of conceptual linkage between these invariant processes—the laws of learning—and the patterns of classroom teaching.

The analysis made by Xhignesse and Osgood (1963) highlights the differential dependencies between basic learning research and educational psychology. On the basis of the larger network of 20 journals, the authors summarized the flow of traffic relating to *The Journal of Educational Psychology* and *The Journal of Experimental Psychology* (pp. 29–30):

JEdP produced a relatively small number of articles and made a correspondingly small number of citations; a relatively small proportion (32%) of its citations were to other journals in the network and it contributed little to the network's total traffic. However, it displays a high degree of congruence with other journals by tending to cite those journals which cite it, but it cites twice as much as it is cited; it thus maintains a relatively good balance among sources (more so than among destinations) and functions more as a condenser of information than a filterer.

[In contrast], *JExP* cites other journals in proportion to their citing it, but it is cited almost twice as often as it cites, and it is highly selective in citing others. It functions as a filterer of information into the network and displays a relatively short time perspective.

This analysis of a communication net is a refreshingly different type of evidence with respect to the responsibility of the education researcher to draw information from basic and theoretical studies and then to "condense" and "filter" these findings for classroom utilization.

The Movement away from Classical Theory

For many years, those teachers who have been interested in the experimental and theoretical approach to human learning and thinking have successfully bypassed the suggestion that they, or other teachers, must practice what they preach. They have developed a type of scientific immunity which protects them from the responsibility of validating findings and theories in the natural learning setting. Kimble (1953, p. 19) illustrated this isolationism quite well when he stated that future scientific research on learning should "be prosecuted relatively unhampered by any alleged responsibility to education or by the free play of the market place." In a similar vein, Spence (1959, pp. 84–85) said:

> . . . the phenomena that the experimental psychologist . . . of learning has taken as the object of his studies, and about which he has attempted to formulate his theories, have little or nothing to do with learning in real life situations, including even the kinds of learning that are supposed to go on in the schoolroom. . . . [We] have not been interested in the practical aspects of learning for many years.

I accept the need for protecting the basic researcher's freedom of inquiry, but this disclaimer should not be interpreted as a mandate to resist the extension of learning research into settings beyond the traditional laboratory. The use of the white rat, the stylus maze, nonsense syllables, and the memory drum was dictated by (1) the restricted availability of other subjects and substance for research on learning, and (2) the apprenticeship limitations in knowing how to adapt empirical methods to studying human variables. Learning research has now moved ahead on both counts. The all-encompassing theories of gestalt psychology, behaviorism, and the systematic formulations associated with the names of Clark Hull and Edward Tolman still have high relevance to the educational process. However, the conceptual distance from these broad hypotheses and postulates to the concrete learning site is usually too great, with few intermediate checkpoints so far as the teacher is concerned.

As Gagné (1962b, p. 90) points out, the movement from theory to practice is not a unidirectional process:

If I were faced with the problem of improving training, I should not look for much help from the well-known learning principles like reinforcement, distribution of practice, response familiarity, and so on. I should look instead at the technique of task analysis, and at the principles of component task achievement, intratask transfer, and the sequencing of subtask learning to find those ideas of greatest usefulness in the design of effective training. Someday, I hope, even the laboratory learning psychologist will know more about these principles.

Historically, research analysis of the learning process was closely tied to practical problems facing the classroom teacher. The pragmatic orientation of American functional psychology provided the conceptual bridge between the new biological conceptions of behavior and their educational application. Names like James, Dewey, Thorndike, Woodworth, Angell, and Judd are cross-referenced in the history of both psychology and education. However, the separating drift became more distinct as education began to model itself more and more in the pattern of a profession, and psychology moved closer to its preferred identification as a scientific discipline and was thereby released from becoming primarily the teachers' technical aide. The task of trying to understand perception, learning, motivation, and personality extends far beyond the limits of the schoolhouse, and psychology moved on to develop a broad and systematic treatment of the full range of behavioral events.

Contemporary experimental psychologists are directing their research to particular aspects of the learning process. As Amsel (1961, p. 34) said: "We seem now to be in a different theoretical atmosphere in psychology . . . in which theory is made in smaller pieces than before and is quickly reduced to experimental operations. It is an era of tighter, more data-bound generalizations." Also, Marx and Hillix (1963, p. 57) indicated: "There is a growing tendency to replace the traditional system with a more limited type of theory; to use models as well as theories; and to demand far more precision, logical development, and explicitness of the more limited statements."

These changes are characterized by an interest in particular behavioral categories, such as verbal learning, memory, transfer of learning, concept formation, problem solving, and the like. Even so, the results and generalizations should not be expected to provide neat, off-the-shelf solutions to problems of teaching. They do offer sets of basic principles that are both adequate and appropriate to serve as the first approximation for a particular pattern of instruction.

Carroll has given us an excellent example of a transitional report, that is, an analysis directed at the gray area between basic research and its application in the natural setting. His special attention is on concept learning, but he must report that "one searches the literature in vain for any comprehensive treatment of concept teaching. One is reassured that there are gaps to be filled" (1964, p. 178). However, a multiplication of interpretive articles and essays will never actually "fill the gap" between basic learning theory and its application to the student—and that is why, presumably, teachers are trained. The teacher must be the active mediator between the nomothetic general principles and the idiographic requirements of the individual student.

Gagné (1962b) and others (Glaser, 1962) have called upon their experience in military and industrial training to show that it would be inefficient to attempt to "doctor" the teaching process by turning to patented and prepackaged corrective measures. This is an easy temptation, but one to be avoided in favor of a more discriminating prescription which has been specifically prepared to meet particular aspects of learning as they occur in the complex variety of the schoolrooms, laboratories, and independent study programs that mark the educational process today.

Mosel (1964, pp. 485–486) is quite explicit in his analysis of the contrast between learning theory and the task of the teacher:

Psychologists probably know more about human learning than any other aspect of human behavior. The amount of research devoted to learning undoubtedly exceeds that in any other area, with the consequence that the amount of empirical information concerning human learning is so great that no one research psychologist could master it all. And the theories of learning are the most sophisticated and most highly developed of all psychological theories. But despite all this, our knowledge does not help very much when it comes to the actual tactical problems of how to teach people.

Mosel thinks that much of the difficulty results from the molecular emphasis of learning theory in contrast to the molar level of behavior with which the teacher must deal. To make this transition, it will be necessary, he believes, to replace the classical principles of learning with a set of operational rules that designate the "strategies of action in the design of learning tasks rather than empirical statements about cause and effect in learning." He defines the issue with a crisp and arresting statement (p. 485): "Thus, although we know much about how people learn, we do not know much about how to get them to learn what we want them to learn."

Stirrings of Unrest

In 1952, a symposium was held in Washington, D.C., on "Psychology of Learning Basic to Military Training Problems." Most of the participants had worked both sides of the street. They knew what they were talking about in regard to both theory and practice, and their appraisal can be accepted as a fair statement of the state of applied learning in the immediate postwar years. Table 6–1 lists the participants and the topics which defined the dimensions for this interchange.

The speakers recognized the hiatus between theory and practice, and this bothered some but not others. Hilgard's assignment was to identify the limiting characteristics of learning theory with respect to its usefulness in training. His topical outline indicates some of the detours and routes typical of the travel between theory and application in the year 1952 (1953, pp. 3–9):

1. SOME TROUBLES WITHIN THEORIES OF LEARNING
   1.1 Major theories are unnecessarily tied to outmoded "schools" of psychology.
   1.2 Some theories are too closely associated with a single standard reference experiment.
2. RELATIONSHIPS BETWEEN THEORIES OF LEARNING AND PRACTICAL PROBLEMS OF TRAINING
   2.1 Because of the preoccupation of the theorist with aspects of learning most readily quantified, the theories are the weakest at the very points at which the practical trainer asks his questions.
   2.2 Because so much of the effort of the learning theorist has gone into debate over distinctions important only in the quarrels between

theorists, the similar practical consequences of divergent theories are often overlooked.

2.3 The gap between theory and practice does not leave the practitioner entirely on his own; students of psychology have a great deal of relevant empirical knowledge not adequately represented in the precise theories of learning.

TABLE 6–1. PARTICIPANTS AND TOPICS IN THE 1952 SYMPOSIUM ON PSYCHOLOGY OF LEARNING BASIC TO MILITARY TRAINING PROBLEMS.

Speaker	Title	Discussant
Ernest R. Hilgard *Stanford University*	Theories of Human Learning and Problems of Training	Gregory A. Kimble *Duke University*
W. K. Estes *Indiana University*	Models for Learning Theory	Frederick Mosteller *Harvard University*
Don Lewis *State University of Iowa*	Motor Skills Learning	Robert M. Gagné *Human Resources Research Center, U.S.A.F.*
John L. Kennedy *Rand Corporation*	Learning for Performance in Groups	Launor Carter *HumRRO*
Neal E. Miller *Yale University*	The Role of Motivation in Learning	Richard L. Solomon *Harvard University*
I. E. Farber *State University of Iowa*	Motivational Factors in Verbal Learning	L. Starling Reid *University of Virginia*
James J. Gibson and Eleanor J. Gibson *Cornell University*	Perceptual Learning in Relation to Training	D. O. Hebb *McGill University*
Harry F. Harlow *University of Wisconsin*	Human Problem-Solving	Donald W. Taylor *Stanford University*

Hilgard closed his presentation by asking some interesting questions which might still be pondered, for they are as yet unanswered (p. 11):

Why have learning theorists withdrawn from their responsibility to education? What will learning theory be like when it incorporates all that we already know about learning, including what we know through the clinic?

Are we perhaps developing learning theory too independently of other fields of psychology, asking them to lean upon learning theory, when perhaps learning theory needs to lean upon them? Can basic research on learning be done in the context of practice? Can it be done only there?

Hilgard's views can be followed in sequence since he wrote the wrap-up chapter in the 1964 yearbook of the National Society for the Study of Education as well as the short postscript comparing the 1964 volume with the 1942 yearbook, which was concerned with similar issues. In effect, he emphasized the need for an explicit research attack on transitional problems (p. 418): "In other words, we believe that scientific psychology of learning has the obligation to go all the way from theory to practice, using criticized data in every step." This is a rather mild statement but, even so, it probably would have received a strong rebuttal if given in the 1952 Washington symposium. Several participants seemed quite defensive in protecting the freedom of "scientific psychology" from the pressure of educational utility.

Another example of a critical, but constructive, analysis of the relation between learning theory and educational practice is the careful review of audiovisual educational practices by Neal E. Miller. He underlined the need for a new and different research orientation in order to accomplish better generality from classroom studies directed at the instructional effects of audiovisual aids. Miller's main point, however, is relevant to most problems in educational research (1957, pp. 61–62):

We believe that the greatest advances in graphic communication are likely to come from basic research of a theoretical-analytical type at the pure science level. Completely empirical comparisons of different media in a given situation can yield results which are largely an artifact of unspecified characteristics of the particular representatives of the media which the experimenter happens to use. Such results tell us little about the inherent properties of different means of representation. A better theoretical analysis of how people learn from pictures and words will help us to design more discriminative experiments.

With this paragraph, Miller probably put his finger on the weakness which has been most characteristic of research on teaching.

Another bench-mark reference in the expanding reach and overlapping pattern of learning research and education is the Northwestern University symposium by Spence, Melton, and Underwood (1959). Spence maintained that learning theory is still trying to establish the footings on which the foundation, then the walls, then the roof, and finally the functional fixtures can, in some remote future, be introduced to complete the psychological understanding of schoolroom learning.

Melton was more positive in his response to the basic question. He stated (p. 96), however, that a teacher must first accept the basic assumption that he "must know how to manage the learning process in order to achieve the acquisition, retention, and readiness for use of certain knowledges, skills, and cognitive capabilities." Melton's first corollary deals with the interaction of motivation and learning, and the second recognizes the importance of individual differences. Both of these corollaries indicate the key places to look to find ideas to improve instruction theory.

The third paper in the symposium, by Underwood, comes closer to providing a specific example of a substantive tie-in between learning theory and classroom teaching. Underwood asked the question (p. 107): "Are the tasks which have been used to study verbal learning in the laboratory representative of the verbal tasks in the school curriculum?" He then proceeded to develop a rapprochement between the primary theories, represented in this instance by Thorndike, and his own work on verbal learning. The language of verbal-learning theory and the language of classroom learning will, in time, find a satisfactory degree of overlapping meanings. If they don't, it would seem that research thinking and teaching thinking have drifted into an intolerable state of pigeonhole sterility.

With a few significant exceptions, the growth of experimental psychology during the past thirty years has been parallel with that of education and each has sharpened its own image. In seeking to avoid entanglements with practical affairs, the experimental psychologists may have developed a too-conceptual world. On the other hand, educational research has been criticized for its emphasis on short-range, empirical fact finding and for showing too little concern with analytical theory and interpretive generalizations.

Both the learning theorist and the teacher must assume greater responsibility for strengthening the interchange between laboratory-based learning theory and learning as it occurs in the classroom. Psychology is a human science par excellence and cannot, in good faith, rest its case as to the nature of human learning on the evidence derived from white rats, conditioned responses, nonsense syllables, and other small bits of behavior in the contrived environment of the laboratory. However, to move this research effort out of the laboratory and into another man's classroom is not a trivial matter. In the industrial and military training settings, there are many examples of two-way advantages resulting from the joint research attack by the scientist and the practitioner (Gagné, 1962c; Glaser, 1962).

Learning = f (*Variables*)

The basic formulation for the learning psychologist is uncomplicated: Learning = f (variables). However, the universe of variables is infinite; and to make systematic progress toward establishing some degree of order, the psychologist usually arranges an arbitrary set of subcategories, namely, environment variables, task variables, and organism variables. This latter set, the variables provided by the student himself, refers to the individual-difference characteristics of the student, such as his motivation, intelligence, past experience, special aptitudes, and the like. The experimental literature indicates that organism-centered (student-centered) variables are, by far, the most important factors in determining how rapidly and how much the student will learn and be able to retrieve.

A frequent pitfall to be avoided when conducting research on teaching is the excessive involvement with variables having secondary importance for learning. Task and environment variables such as schedule changes, class size, informational input media, room environment, and teacher-training programs are relatively easy to manipulate and seem to attract a disproportionate amount of attention. The result is a monotonous repetition of reports showing insignificant differences between two methods of teaching when measured in terms of student performance (Ericksen, 1964).

A more powerful effect can be expected from those instructional changes that release and give greater freedom to individual-difference variables, such as a student's motivation, his memory, and the degree of meaningfulness he can attach to informational stimuli given by lectures, books, films, slides, demonstrations, and the like. The student-linked factors—his own capabilities for learning—are the key factors that will open up new resources for making significant changes in the quality of the educational process.

Suppes (1964, p. 80) adds considerable force to this generalization when he reports: "From our standpoint, the most significant aspect of this individual treatment is the fantastic differences in rate of learning." He goes on (p. 82):

Data of this sort, which may be multiplied tenfold by references to the literature, argue that by far the greatest improvement in subject-matter learning will result from an almost single-minded concentration on individual differences. I am sure that the optimum sequencing of curriculum materials, the analysis of the subject matter so as to present it in steps of the proper size, etc., are not nearly so important elements in learning as the single one of individual accommodation.

It is possible to identify at least three of the student-centered factors that carry heavy weight in shaping the direction and the rate of learning. Among the better things a teacher or a researcher can do to improve the course of learning is to release specific variables within these three categories: memory, meaningfulness, and motivation. A few comments about each of these factors will illustrate their central place in the instructional process.

MEMORY

A teacher must be interested in the antecedent "history" of the ideas that a student brings into the classroom which serves as the new starting point for developing the next phase in his own interlocking cognitive arrangements. The student's past experience, his memory, influences the course of learning in some unexpected ways. Underwood and Postman (1960) have demonstrated, for example, that proactive inhibition (PI) is a more powerful memory factor than most theorists had realized.

The PI phenomenon has direct implication for teaching. Many of the terms and concept labels that are presented to a student at the start of a new school year are already known and have relevant meaning. These redundant concepts would presumably be overlearned in the further course of study. However, other terms and topics carry considerable PI since the original meaning for the student must be replaced by new definitions and associations. Many instructors in undergraduate psychology, biology, and physics courses, for instance, feel that they must do considerable debunking. The question is: Are the debunked concepts (those with high PI loadings) forgotten at a different rate than the low PI and the redundant concepts? If so, what might the instructor do about it? The study by Entwisle and Huggins (1964) touches on this issue in showing negative transfer effects in classroom learning. However, the PI effects, as such, were not demonstrated since no retention measures were used.

MEANINGFULNESS

Many theorists tend to associate meaningfulness with the cognitive theories of Wertheimer (1945), Katona (1940), and the gestalt tradition. However, the work of Noble (1953) and Underwood and Schulz (1960) clearly establishes this factor as a nonpartisan variable having a strong influence on the progress of learning.

Verbal learning can be viewed as a process of giving meaning to arbitrary symbols. Furthermore, the ultimate validity of what has been learned is measured by the ability of the student to retrieve and to utilize original learning in the transfer situation. Concepts are not packaged "chunks" of information to be acquired and stored in memory like books in a library, but should be quickly available for generalized use from one classroom to another or to the world outside.

MOTIVATION

Traditional experimental research on verbal learning and concept formation is deficient in its treatment of the intrinsic motivation to learn the meaning of words and ideas. Hilgard's analysis (1963, p. 277) indicates some of the changes that are taking place and the difficulties that remain before there evolves a better basis for managing the motivating conditions that promote the breadth and depth of learning:

Our learning theories have been particularly weak in dealing with hierarchies of value, with overlapping motives (of both short-range and long-range significance), the kinds of motives that characterize the human individual with continuous memories, with capacity to bind the past through the present with the future.

Walker (1964) has helped to update the concept of motivation by reference to "psychological complexity" as a determiner of the direction and continuity of behavior. His treatment illustrates the greater degree of sophistication that is beginning to appear in the understanding of the dynamics of the learning process.

As the use of automation for information-giving purposes increases, the teacher must give greater attention to his motivating function in helping to "arouse" the student and to maintain his vigilance in learning the preprogramed information. Conventional classroom instruction is often done in an atmosphere of rather stringent motivational inflexibility, and teachers could make better use of the intrinsic motives which are released when the subject matter is fused with the student's own aspirations and values (McKeachie, 1961, 1962).

The ability to start this learning chain reaction is probably one of the defining characteristics of the master teacher. By the time a serious student goes to college, he has (acquired) an intellectual-curiosity drive, a continuing interest in searching for the abstract principles that will provide a parsimonious integration of a multiple series of events. Conceptual ordering can be exciting and, for a student, if not for a saint, knowledge can be its own reward. This will most likely happen when the teacher gives the student the intellectual freedom to seek the particular pattern of information which will reduce his own uncertainties (Berlyne, 1960; J. McV. Hunt, 1961; Koch, 1961; White, 1959).

What about information theory and the motivating effect of uncertainty? As more is learned about heuristic searching, simulated decision making, cybernetic loops, and the reduction of uncertainty (E. B. Hunt, 1962; Jones, 1961; Jones, Wilkinson, and Braden, 1961), I am certain there will be considerable reason to pay more heed to intellectual curiosity and its motivating role for academic progress.

THE IDIOGRAPHIC PRESS

The generalized, smooth functions of nomothetic learning theory can serve only as a frame of reference within which teachers direct their attention to the irregular learning progress of the individual student. Teachers soon learn to tolerate the unpredicted redirections of the zigzag curve of learning. Even so, many teaching habits have the effect of imposing a number of intellectual constraints on students. As one reminder that instruction should not stop short of individuality, the nomothetic-idiographic relationship is depicted in the masthead of the bimonthly *Memo to the Faculty* published by the Center for Research on Learning and Teaching, at the University of Michigan (see Figure 6–1).

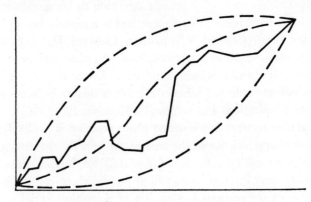

Figure 6–1. One Picture Saves . . .

The descriptive statement for this masthead diagram is, in part:

We know there is considerable competition for your attention and hope that our new "trademark" will increase our visibility. Within the two coordinates (y = amount learned; x = successive study periods), the three dotted lines represent generalized learning curves taken from the science of learning. These provide the frame of reference for the irregular learning curve of an individual student—the object of our attention. (Obviously, a good teacher took hold of this student about halfway through the semester and pulled him out of his learning doldrums.)

Psychologists and teachers do not need to read another chapter on the importance of individual differences. Nearly everyone subscribes to this undefined but treasured totem. Progressive educators and traditionalists, capitalists and communists, all fly the same phenotypical banner; for example, the Russians are revising their "teaching methods in the direction of the fullest development of the student's independence and initiative" (Bogoyavlenskii and Menchinskaya, 1959, p. 3, as quoted in Brozek, 1962, p. 543). The repetitive incantation to protect individual differences seems to have taken on a quality of self-indoctrination to a good intention—a quality reminiscent of *Brave New World*. All of this phrase making does not, however, release the researcher and the teacher from their responsibility for showing both why and how the familiar patterns of education might be reshaped to provide a more effective idiographic impact.

The Neglect of Individuality

If there are any sparkling new ideas about teaching, they should perhaps be dressed up in a different language, thus reducing the negative transfer generated by the many traditions, biases, preconceptions, fixed beliefs, and opinions that have accumulated around all aspects of the educational enterprise. The language of systems theory, intermingled with the terminology of information theory, may help to avoid some of the trite phrases and overworked sequential dependencies that interlace the habits of talking about teaching. Verbal dissimilarity is one of the best ways to break the mediational chains in the proactive-inhibition paradigm and thus gain greater freedom to remodel the place of the teacher and his instructional relations with his students.

First, I will describe the tradition-bound, conservative, liberal arts college; it will be my straw system. For many years this crusty institution seemed determined to maintain a relatively impermeable system boundary to keep out the novel and to reduce diversity and individuality—to keep things uniform, freeze the curriculum, and emphasize the controlling effects of college traditions. New knowledge, when admitted, was quickly recoded and filtered into the prevailing curriculum. The student adjusted himself to the fixed and uniform instructional pattern; his inputs and outputs were largely predetermined and were about the same as for another student. What was being learned had only a low probability of reducing a student's uncertainty about questions outside of this prescribed informational world.

The input of a new class of entering students each year made the steady state a little difficult to maintain, but after four conforming years the college graduates moved quite comfortably from the academic setting into the outside supersystem to assume their ruling-class responsibilities. What was good for aristocracy was also good for higher education, and vice versa (Stewart, 1962). Fortunately, there has been considerable progress away from this extreme-right conception of the traditional university.

In this lock-step institution, thinking—like justice, truth, and love of country—was a frequently praised ideal, although the more usual mental process was ordinary rote memorizing. Students were learning to memorize knowledge, and the memorizing process per se was apparently valued over the factual and conceptual content of what was learned. The energy resulting from the "mental discipline" would, presumably, be sufficient to keep the wheels in the black box moving for the many years ahead, and this was a neat solution for the transfer-of-learning problem.

So much for the ultratraditional college, which I view as being more of a self-conscious cultural subsystem than a psychologically sound learning and thinking environment. The students were bright, but even so, educational efficiency would not be expected where nomothetic treatment is given to what is essentially an idiographic process.

Research on Individual Differences

Contemporary psychological research provides considerable support for helping education change from lip service only to actual implementation of its instructional adaptations to the differences between students. The practical uses of learning data can now be moved farther up on the priority scale. On every hand, traditional behavior theorists are being reminded that they might now remove their clean white gloves, step out of their assumed role of detached dignity, and step into the schoolroom to observe how real people are learning to use symbols and to think about real problems, for therein lies a direct source of validating data for learning theory.

The classroom was the site of psychology's first professional contribution, and it should continue as a preferred applied outlet for the basic research done in most areas of psychology. However, educational psychology must move off the plateau of studying behavior in general (that is, a classroomful of students providing grouped data) and reshape the accumulated knowledge about human learning, thinking, and motivation to meet the instructional requirements for the individually different student. Clinical and counseling psychologists have acquired some degree of expertness in moving from the nomothetic to the idiographic, but what about the learning psychologist? A number of precedents, patterns, and models is available for showing ways to improve educational adaptations to the individual student.

INDIVIDUAL ASSESSMENT AND PREDICTION

Parents, teachers, and researchers are asking what characteristics are being screened out when more and more students are sifted through the random mesh of a general scholastic-aptitude test. Can it be said that creativity, for example, has left the land of poetry and become a measurable dimension? Despite the strong caution given by McNemar (1964), the work of Guilford (1959), Getzels and Jackson (1962), C. W. Taylor and Holland (1962), and D. W. Taylor (1963) has important implications for education. For want of operational definitions and validated predictors, education has not yet had a clear opportunity to learn how to manage, if not to educate, highly creative students. Perhaps educators should get ready. Teachers can handle fast learners, but the sudden expression of a sequence of novel, creative, or original responses by their students would leave them wondering about the meaning of their norms, standard scores, and unidimensional learning curves. How does a teacher grade creativity, originality, and the talent for serendipity?

It has been interesting to stand outside and watch the test and measurement men move their arguments back and forth concerning actuarial assessment versus the diagnostic evaluation of the individual. Meehl (1960), Murray (1956), Holtzman *et al.* (1961), Fricke (1963), and Holland (1961) are a few of the many contributors to this significant problem. Obviously, it is hard to measure individual motives, as Lindzey and his coauthors (1958) have already confirmed.

THE INDIVIDUAL PERSONALITY

"Personality Dynamics" has now become a separate category in the *Annual Review of Psychology,* and this event reflects Freud's long-term contribution in keeping psychology's feet to the motivational fire. The influence of Gordon Allport and Carl Rogers must also be given top billing when assigning credits for the better understanding of the unique personality and the dynamics of individual behavior in the setting of complex educational and social institutions.

Insofar as teachers are concerned with intervening personality variables, they must be able to recognize and to control, in an educationally relevant way, the classroom behavior of students who differ with respect to their achievement needs, anxieties, cognitive styles, and the like. Most teachers are sensitive to matters of student motivation, and contemporary research can give them a better understanding of the motivational patterns dominating the classroom pursuits, educational or otherwise, of each student (Brown, 1962).

SOCIAL CONFORMITY AND INDIVIDUALITY

Lewin had a significant influence in reorienting the structure of social psychology from a fairly static, census-taking, attitude-testing technology into a conceptual system which is making a vital contribution toward understanding individuality in a society that demands conformity. A number of research programs are investigating the interacting effects of social motives (teachers' as well as students') with the type of intellectual content the community expects its students to learn (Brown, 1962; Cartwright and Zander, 1953; Coleman, 1961; Festinger, 1957; Fox and Lippitt, 1964; Klein, 1958; Newcomb, 1962; Rokeach, 1960; Sherif and Hovland, 1962; and many others). The conflicts that inevitably appear among the interests, aspirations, and values of the student and those of the teacher and the parent (the community) could be reduced by incorporating some of the knowledge that social psychologists can offer to a theory of instruction. The neglect shown to the information coming from these research programs continues the incompatibility between the idiosyncratic needs of many students and the pressures on the educational program from the "school board" and the "Carnegie unit"—pressures that are obviously a source of considerable instructional noise and inefficiency.

"ONTOGENY RECAPITULATES PHYLOGENY"

Comparative psychology has moved a long way from the Columbia obstruction box and its use in the experimental investigation of motivation. Ethology and the several related developments in the study of animal behavior—early experience, imprinting, critical periods, and so on—have strengthened the longitudinal orientation of comparative-behavior scientists. Thanks to the careful experimental and conceptual thinking of Hebb, J. G. Miller, Mowrer, Harlow, Lindsley, Olds, Beach, Brown, and Berlyne, there is now a more specific understanding of individual motivation. Terms like "arousal" and "self-activating systems" point to what may be found upon peeking inside to see what motivation looks like.

SIMULATED THINKING

The "higher mental processes" is a standby phrase, and the prevailing vectors from a complex society are pulling toward a greater understanding of how the individual student thinks. Hebb (1960) is one who has urged better research toward this end.

With the insurance protection of operationalism and mathematical models, learning theorists are now attempting detailed descriptions of the cognitive processes. The book by Miller, Galanter, and Pribram (1960) reflects the new IBM "THINK," the new simulation psychology; they discuss the "processes" that go on inside without actually needing to know much more than how to program the inputs and utilize the feedback outputs. Decision making, artificial intelligence, communication, and information processing are further examples of the mathematically modeled approaches, the results of which are being backlogged in technical reports and journals. Investigators like Fitts (1963), Edwards (1962), Suppes (1964), Atkinson (1963), E. B. Hunt (1962), and Feigenbaum and Feldman (1963) cannot long be ignored by educational psychologists.

Science is still in the heuristic stage of the computer-based research approach to the behavioral processes. The principles that mark this new area are as yet rather broad and tentative. Interestingly enough, however, the computer can perform two important functions that are crucial in meeting the educational requirements for individual instruction: (1) programed variability, that is, the branching capability to provide the more appropriate "teaching" inputs for the different levels of comprehension and retention and different rates of learning by individual students, and (2) memory storage, that is, the computer's capacity to hold and to retrieve the responses made by each student in the learning dialogue with his computer tutor. These two computer features represent, however, two of the reasons why the software lags behind the hardware. Teachers have yet to learn how to program textbooks, lectures, slides, movies, videotapes, audiotapes, and the like for their storage and effective presentation to the student in the independent study situation. The toil and tumult in this surging area of educational technology give stark evidence of the gross instructional neglect of the idiosyncratic learning curve which is inevitably generated by the individual student in his pursuit of knowledge. In some respects, the computer has called our bluff regarding the high priorities teachers claim to give individual differences, and they should be embarrassed by the primitive state of the art of teaching the individual student.

On Teaching Students How to Think

Up to this point in the chapter, I have developed two main ideas: (1) Instructional procedures should be based on learning theory; that is, how much and how well a student learns are a function of variables, many of which are under some degree of control by the teacher. (2) The focus of instruction should be toward the individual student, rather than the class, as the functional unit for the educational enterprise. The research patterns in contemporary behavioral analyses are adding to the knowledge about individual differences and their interaction effects with the learning process.

In this third and final section, I continue my inferential analysis of those cognitive processes which are important for classroom learning. With or without a computer, investigators are continuing to pursue the basic issues of concept formation, originality, reasoning, generalizing, decision making, problem solving, and creativity. Many rigorous experimental investigators are making a strong research push against the slow-moving, culture-bound conclusions about man's mind and how it thinks.

In almost all grades and curricula, students are required to identify and form concepts, to understand principles and laws, and to make generalizations that extend beyond the specific information on hand. In some respects, the most challenging site for studying the instructional process is the mathematics classroom because its uniform abstract quality provides a homogeneous psychological task. The essence of abstract thinking is also found in any course requiring discrimination and manipulation of invariant relations leading to the formation of concepts and principles.

The rest of this chapter is, therefore, oriented toward that indestructible educational buffer: teaching students how to think. I have observed that teachers are more strongly attracted to concrete, substantive issues than to theories about how students think. As a long-time teacher of psychology, I enjoy pedagogical shoptalk as much as the next teacher; for the present, however, I intend to return to the thinking student and to examine some basic features of the abstraction process.

To be specific, the abstraction process is the means by which the individual gains some degree of freedom from the limitations of time, places, and specific things. Abstraction learning is distinguished from perception learning, but their interacting function is also noted as students acquire new concepts and retrieve these "ideas" for solving a problem or understanding an event at a later date and in a different situation.

After several years of personal research with the abstraction process, I have become quite impressed with the power of this environment-free, invisible, inferential, idiosyncratic aspect of thinking. It is no news to say that students don't all think the same way, but it would be news to say a little more about the etiology of these differences. What is there about the thinking process that *requires* an emphasis on individuality? Studies on the abstraction process suggest one answer.

Perception Learning versus Abstraction Learning

The transitional research program was intended to extend the rat-linked concepts of place and response learning to the human level (Ericksen, 1962). The animal learning model was used to sharpen the distinction between situation-bound perceptual learning and the stimulus freedom represented by the human ability to respond to abstract relations.

As an intervening variable, abstracting is defined on the input side by a series of perceptions, while a verbalized concept label provides the usual output operation. To get at the in-between process of abstracting, we needed a laboratory procedure which would permit us to magnify the abstraction process and slow it down to "observable" proportions. For this purpose we devised a human three-point walking maze, modified from the Peterson (1918) procedure. As in the case of the place- and response-learning rats, we needed a learning task in which the subject traversed a particular route but with "dual controls," that is, perception learning or abstraction learning, depending on the conditions introduced by the instructions or directly by the experimental setup.

Abstraction is best understood in contrast to perception, although this tenuous distinction is not intended to be absolute. Perception is usually considered to be situation-bound and is linked to the present stimulation of the senses; it is impossible, by definition, to perceive absent events. In contrast, the term "abstracting" refers to those responses, usually verbal or otherwise symbolic, that are consistently given to some definable relation inherent in the stimulus situation. The end product of the abstracting process is the ability to respond adaptively to certain relationships which have been recognized, delimited, and utilized as the modus operandi in generalized problem-solving activities. These abstractions can represent relatively simple conceptual dimensions, such as temporal concepts (slow-fast) or spatial dimensions (right-left), or they can embrace the more complex value dimensions which lead to esthetic, economic, or ethical concepts and principles.

The symbolic manipulations required in mathematics and formal logic represent the situation-free nature of abstraction learning. At an elemental level, the beginnings of the abstraction process can be inferred from the absolute versus relative discrimination studies done with lower animals. These transposition experiments and the relevant theories provide a meaningful linkage between the extensive knowledge about discrimination learning and the research being directed at human concept identification and attainment.

As far as the instruction process is concerned, our findings support the position that there is no inherent difference in the difficulty level, the "mental demands," imposed by these two cognitive processes. The frequent overgeneralized responses made by preverbal infants indicate some degree of abstracting ability (Carroll, 1964). However, it would be fruitless to debate the issue of the relative difficulty levels of perception and abstraction learning since these processes must be interpreted as overlapping and interacting phenomena. It can be insisted, however, that the instruction process should place its greater emphasis on abstraction learning. It is by this means that a student uses specific facts and perceptual information as the inductive starting point for attaining those concepts which have greater generality and adaptive utility.

In our usual experimental arrangement, the subject first stood on a treadle at the apex of a seven-foot equilateral triangle and faced the opposite side. His choice was to walk to one of the two treadles at the other two points in this triangle. The perception-learning subjects made their choice on the basis of spatial and environmental cues, such as "going to the treadle by the door." The abstraction-learning subjects ignored the room environment and simply learned to go "right" or "to the left." Having made the first correct choice, the subject then had to walk to one of the two other treadles, and this decision-making sequence proceeded through twelve choices for each trial. One trial followed another until the criterion was reached.

Figure 6–2 gives a schematic presentation of the contrast between perception learning and abstraction learning. The abstraction condition was introduced by blindfolding the subjects (and also by eliminating differential auditory cues) or by starting each successive trial from a different apex in the maze. In effect, this procedure rotated the maze in the room and "forced" the subject to abstract the maze track out of the room environment.

The perception-learning subjects (P) acquired a sequence of spatial cues which tied the maze pattern to the objective room environment, for example, window, door, table. In contrast, the abstraction-learning subjects (A) acquired a patterned sequence of directional cues which related the task to himself—"go right, left, and around." In abstraction learning, the individual served as a replacement for the objective, external environment, and was himself the frame of reference, the anchor against which the maze task was accomplished.

The results showed that the abstraction learners could master the original maze task as efficiently as did the perception learners. Our primary interest, however, was to observe the transfer effects. The transfer task consisted of either a different maze pattern on the walking maze or a 9-inch triangle of push-buttons located in an adjacent room.

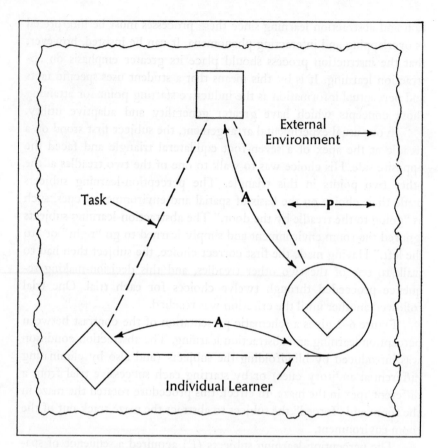

Figure 6–2. A Schematic Contrast between Perceptual Learning, *P*, and Abstraction Learning, *A*.

Under these transfer conditions, the abstraction learners demonstrated significantly better performance than did the subjects whose original learning was under the perception-learning conditions. Several variations in this basic experimental procedure gave confirming data.

In summary, abstraction learning can be viewed as a form of idiographic behavior. When a person abstracts, he is moving away from the controlling influence of stimulus factors in the external environment and is mediating, in some idiosyncratic way, a common relationship between successive perceptual samples. When the abstraction learner goes from one room to the next, he takes most of his learning with him, and this is judged to be a learning, concept-forming, or problem-solving advantage over the situation-bound, perceptual learning represented by going from one place to another.

Rote Learning versus Concept Learning

Based on our earlier research with rats and with the human walking maze reviewed above, Professor L. E. Thune and I conducted a two-phase extrapolation of these laboratory findings into both the simulated and the real classroom (Thune and Ericksen, 1960; Ericksen and Thune, 1961). In the first study we taught groups of students to perform the basic operations of adding, subtracting, and multiplying with a desk calculator. These tasks gave greater emphasis to symbolic manipulations than was required by the walking maze and thus took us one step closer to the natural learning environment of the classroom.

The primary comparison was between the rote and the concept groups; the other two groups served as controls. The rote-learning subjects were given direct practice on the Friden calculator and were tested for initial proficiency. Twenty-four hours later, retention tests were given and the subjects were then transferred to the Marchant calculator. After a brief familiarization period, they were given two tests of transfer proficiency on this second machine.

The treatment of the concept group was a projection of the abstraction-learning condition. Their initial instruction and practice were accomplished by a schematic diagram of calculators in general, but they received exactly the same series of tests as did the rote group: to solve a number of addition, subtraction, and multiplication problems directly on one calculator, followed by transfer tests with the other machine.

Both the rote and the concept groups performed significantly better on the initial proficiency tests than the instructional control group, thus showing that both types of special training exercise were effective in teaching the fundamentals of calculator operation. The rote group was somewhat superior to the concept group on the initial proficiency test but the difference was not significant. In contrast, the concept subjects showed relatively more improvement on the retention test, and this advantage continued through the transfer tests, where the concept group demonstrated 50 per cent greater positive transfer

TABLE 6–2. EXPERIMENTAL PARADIGM.

Condition [1]	Day 1 Sequence of Events				Day 2 Sequence of Events		
	Friden familiarization (18 min.)		Initial proficiency test [2] (7 min.)	Retention test [2] (7 min.)	Marchant familiarization (18 min.)	Transfer test I [2] (7 min.)	Transfer test II (6 min.)
Rote N = 6	→	Rote practical training exercise (20 min.)	→	→	→	→	→
Concept N = 6	Same	Concept practical training exercise (20 min.)	Same	Same	Same	Same	Same
Instructional control N = 6	Same	"Rest" alphabet puzzle (20 min.)	Same	Same	Same	Same	Same
Transfer control N = 6					Same	Same	Same

[1] A single replication involved four groups, one for each of the four conditions, with six subjects in each group. Four such replications were employed.

[2] Three alternate forms of the same proficiency test were used in counterbalanced order as the Initial Proficiency Test, Retention Test, and Transfer Test I, two subjects in each group of six receiving each form of the test at each of the three testing periods.

effects than did the rote-learning subjects. We judge the major finding to be the confirmation of the higher retention and transfer effects of abstraction learning as compared with perception learning.

The second study was a classroom demonstration project which was intended (1) to continue the projection of the perception-abstraction contrast from the laboratory to the field setting, and (2) to explore the disquieting research realities encountered in using a college classroom for evaluating laboratory-derived hypotheses. The statistical findings were inconclusive, but the methodological lessons were impressive. Figure 6–3 presents the schematic outline of the classroom project.

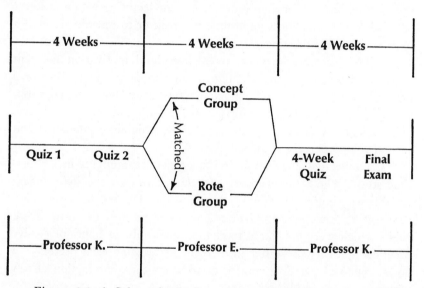

Figure 6–3. A Schematic Outline of the Procedural Sequence for the Classroom Study.

In the rote class, the instructor literally kept his finger on the page of the text; and his presentation emphasized specific, factual, technical, and taxonomic information. In the concept class, the teacher (the same person) did not refer to specific text material but used the class hour to develop one or two basic concepts which were, however, derived from the text. He also presented appropriate positive and negative instances as supplements to those given in the textbook.

All students in both sections took the same examination at the end of the four-week experimental period and at the end of the course. Half the test items were of a rote nature and half conceptual, and the two sets had been balanced for level of difficulty. Originally, we intended to test the students again six months later, but too few of the students in this summer-school course returned in the fall.

On the basis of the experience given by this pilot study, we would not encourage other investigators to use similar designs for evaluating instructional methods. Some of the procedural pitfalls can be identified:

1. It is difficult for the teacher to maintain a two-phase role. An experienced teacher inevitably develops some lecturing habits and verbal chains that are almost impossible to break or to restrain through a succession of class meetings.

2. The instructor cannot, over time, hold motivation constant apart from teaching method. The normal rapport and motivational demands of classroom teaching require too many uncontrolled variations and adjustments by the instructor. He cannot behave as a unitary, independent variable and, at the same time, maintain a consistent and natural role as perceived by the class.

3. Intellectual inertia and resistance mask the effects in a short-time study. The total exposure of each student to the independent variable was limited to eight 1½-hour sessions. During their preceding 12–13 years, these students had acquired certain how-to-go-to-school habits which were not likely to change with only 12 hours of passive practice. Students also differ in the type of teaching each prefers, but no attempt was made to control or to assess these interaction effects within our small and biased sample.

4. The textbook and the examinations have a leveling effect on different instructional methods. Apart from the lecture, all students received their formal input of information from the same textbook. Furthermore, they knew that the examinations would be primarily a reflection of textbook information. Milton (1962) and Jensen (1951) suggest that under these conditions, the contribution from the teacher himself is not a significant factor.

5. Paper-and-pencil criteria are inadequate measures of complex behavioral changes. Despite the built-in contrast between the rote and

concept test items, they still contained common factor loadings such as general intelligence, memory, reading comprehension, and the like.

Summary of the Abstraction-Learning Studies

On the basis of these laboratory, simulation, and classroom studies (together with a secret combination of data and logic), it is our position that "teaching a student how to think" means first helping him acquire the concepts representing the abstract relationships which are fundamental to the subject matter. The second step is to establish the transfer task and to measure how well the student can retrieve and utilize the abstracted information he has learned. The conventional classroom examinations are compromise measures, and more valid ways are needed to assess the levels of proficiency each student may have attained in the way *he* acquires, generalizes, and utilizes the original learning that took place in the classroom.

More simply, classroom instruction at all levels of education should be oriented around concept learning, the abstractions of which are to be clearly identified and understood, not just memorized. This last point is important, for it means that the learner must have the freedom to abstract and to do this in the only way he can—by establishing his own idiosyncratic pattern of subjective associations. A concept is an abstracted end product. As Bruner (1962, p. 96) has put it, "Material that is organized in terms of a person's own interests and cognitive structures is material that has the best chance of being accessible in memory." Carroll (1964, p. 183) makes essentially the same point: "Concepts are, after all, essentially idiosyncratic in the sense that they reside in particular individuals with particular histories of experience that lead them to classify those experiences in particular ways." Both Riley Gardner (1964) and Witkin (1964) stress the importance of individuality, of cognitive style, in the development of cognitive structures.

I have no evidence suggesting that educators back away from or soften the instructional emphasis on the attainment of concepts. Our own studies support the rationale behind the new curricular hierarchies that are receiving considerable attention and action at all levels of education. Again, mathematics can serve as an example. If abstract mathematical concepts can be moved down from college to the first grade, a corresponding adjustment can and should be made in other curricular areas. This approach can be called, quite naturally, the "new think."

DIVERSITY, INDIVIDUALITY, AND THE NEXT GENERATION OF TEACHERS

The pragmatic objective is to show how to promote the free and idiosyncratic pursuit of knowledge. Scientific probing is a good model, which, among other things, demonstrates that intellectual exploration and discovery are not always high adventure. The long periods of background preparation may be laborious and unexciting, but are valuable just the same. The student should perceive this initial phase of reading, rote learning, and review as the means of gathering together, into one head, the information resources which have a high probability of serving a prerequisite function for his own creative thinking.

Elementary schools, high schools, and colleges throughout the country are engaging in a variety of programs to "improve" instruction. More often than not, however, these modifications and innovations do not come to grips, in a direct and systematic way, with the primary event—the acquisition of knowledge by the individual student. As stated earlier, one basic goal for educational change must be to recognize the individual student rather than the class as the functional unit in the instructional process. Medicine and law are far more individualized professions than is education, despite the long tradition of respect, affection, and verbal attention given to individual differences by psychologists and teachers. One of the disturbing features of American education is the way economic considerations have been allowed to blunt instructional adaptations to the individuality of the student.

A few sentences can cut through the many trappings and the false fronts that confuse and mask the base-line contribution of educational technology. The widely publicized claim that teaching machines and programed instruction have established the educational breakthrough for adapting to individual differences is a gross overstatement. Adapting to the *rate* of learning is only one dimension, and any tutor, live or automated, must be able to respond to the other differences that mark the idiosyncratic learning progress of each student. The more significant impact of programed instruction is its clear demonstration of how learning progresses in a closed system.

Briggs (1964, p. 273) summarizes the essential contrast between the open- and closed-loop features of information-giving media:

While textbooks have the advantage that they can be reviewed, outlined, scanned, and re-read, as well as read in a straight linear fashion, they still do not represent a closed-loop system of teaching; for example, they do not in themselves require defined responses from the student, and they do not provide feedback to either the student (for confirmation or correction) or to the textbook author (for purposes of revision of the text). Films and TV in themselves suffer from many of the disadvantages of textbooks—that is, they are not closed-loop systems, either. Further, they suffer from a fixed pace. . . . The lecture, also, suffers the deficiencies of other open-loop systems, except that the lecturer may respond to cues from the students, and thus he may either change pace or change the program. . . .

In short, all the procedures named above, except programmed instruction, are open-loop systems. To make any of them function as closed-loop systems requires supplementary efforts by the teacher in the form of quizzes, review of main points, etc.

It should be quickly pointed out that although the closed-loop system is quite efficient, it is to be preferred only when there is little ambiguity about what the student should learn. Firm and stable units of knowledge represent a considerable proportion of elementary- and high-school instruction. The college or university teacher, however, has a greater obligation to meet with his students to discuss problems for which preprogramed answers are not yet available or are at least debatable. This means that the individual student, as an information-processing system, must be free to move back and forth between both closed and open systems. Entropy is the inevitable consequence of closed systems, despite their apparent short-term efficiency for learning. John Gardner's popular book, *Self Renewal* (1963), defines quite well the personal and social significance of an educational system that minimizes the indoctrination of fixed beliefs and maximizes innovation, versatility, and continuous intellectual inquiry.

Closed-circuit television, programed instruction, and high-speed computers can be expected to play an increasingly important role in the instructional process. Numerous high schools and colleges demonstrate the instructional adaptations being made of various automated information-giving procedures. However, observations of such schools make quite apparent the limitations that exist. For example, in too many instances the technological aids seem to reflect an administrative pressure to improve the economic "efficiency" of the teaching program. The path of least educational resistance seems to be to present the same information, in the same way, to larger and larger blocks of students.

Under the chapter heading, "An American Tragedy in Education," Callahan (1962, p. 246) summarized his analysis of the steadily growing influence of "business management" in education:

The tragedy itself was fourfold: that educational questions were subordinated to business considerations; that administrators were produced who were not, in any true sense, educators; that a scientific label was put on some very unscientific and dubious methods and practices; and that an anti-intellectual climate, already prevalent, was strengthened. As the business-industrial values and procedures spread into the thinking and acting of educators, countless educational decisions were made on economic or on non-educational grounds.

Instructional uniformity and educational orthodoxy represent a basic limitation in an overextended and nondiscriminating use of automated teaching. As the mass-produced, uniform, and standardized pattern of information giving becomes more generally used in our educational systems, the greater becomes the responsibility of high-school and college teachers to alert their students and to press them into *independent* learning and thinking. The teacher is far too valuable a person to spend his time giving routine lectures about relatively stable and fixed areas of knowledge. All members of the educational establishment must become increasingly sensitive to the need for intellectual diversity and must encourage a greater tolerance for uncertainty.

There are many sources of inputs into any thinking-student system, but the classroom teacher is especially important. As with a good book, a good teacher at any grade level is well programed and he is interesting; he is also sensitive to feedback cues from his students. He realizes that the teacher's first responsibility is to define the goals of instruction and to do this with a sufficient degree of behavioral clarity that the student can observe his own progress toward these goals.

As our Center works with departments and individual faculty

members throughout the University of Michigan, we repeatedly note their surprise in discovering how much effort and time are required to adapt conventional lecture material for effective use in the independent study setting. We now know that regardless of the medium used for giving information, the instructor must identify, in a far more exact way than might have been his custom, the substantive goals that students should achieve in his course. The highly skilled, professional task of making explicit the analysis of course objectives and the logical sequencing of substantive materials is, in some respects, the most critical single contribution by the teacher to the improvement of instruction.

The instructor should delegate the sequential learning of prerequisite information by the student to the "machine" and to the independent study carrel. As a teacher, he should encourage and assist his students to pursue the more complex levels of learning, thinking, and decision making. When sitting in the classroom, college students deserve the benefits of the kind of intellectual inquiry that is characteristic of a questioning and research-oriented faculty. The ideal university professor is a man who treasures dearly his tradition of academic freedom as he stands at the penumbra between the challenge of the new and the acceptance of the known. He is in the key position to integrate new findings into the body of knowledge and, as a teacher, to reinterpret the familiar dialectic.

Sir Eric Ashby (1963, p. 9) stated this broad educational issue in clear and arresting terms:

At their best, universities endow the men and women who pass through them with a characteristic intellectual equipment: it is the capacity to reconcile orthodoxy and dissent. Let me explain: the intellectual life demands a respect for what has gone before and acceptance of a rigorous discipline to a tradition of learning. To this extent universities are a point of stability in society: they anchor a society to its own past. But orthodoxy is celibate; it breeds no fresh ideas; unless tradition is continually re-examined, it becomes oppressive. So in the course of their evolution universities have learnt not only to pass on a corpus of knowledge and ideas . . . To train young people in this dialectic between orthodoxy and dissent is the unique contribution which universities make to society. Any change in the pattern of universities which endangers this function endangers the society which the university serves. It is for this reason that universities have to combine teaching with research.

7

A Behavioristic Analysis
of Instruction

JOHN C. JAHNKE
Miami University (Oxford, Ohio)

⌇

THE TITLE OF THIS CHAPTER HAS TWO COMPONENTS MERITING INITIAL elaboration: behavioristic analysis and instruction. Since this is to be a behavioristic analysis, the chapter is concerned with the learner's observable behavior and with the stimulus antecedents of that behavior in instructional settings. It is frequently helpful to express the relation between stimulus and response by the familiar notation S-R. When appropriate, the notation S-R-Reinforcement is used to indicate a behavioral sequence terminating in that state called reinforcement. In brief, reinforcers are those consequences of behavior which strengthen a particular S-R relationship.

Instruction, the process to be analyzed in these terms, is used in its most general sense to signify any environmental circumstances which establish the conditions of learning. *Learning* is defined as a relatively permanent behavioral change resulting from experience (Kimble, 1961).

VARIETIES OF INSTRUCTION

The analysis of the instructional process is a part of the analysis of the learning process. Both processes involve much the same kinds of interactions between the organism (learner) and his environment. For learning of any kind to occur, certain conditions must be satisfied. While there is not unanimous agreement as to what these conditions are, there is some evidence that certain behaviors can be acquired simply through the learner's observation of the environment. Other learned behaviors appear to require that the learner observe his environment, respond overtly to it, and then observe the effects of the response upon the environment. As noted above, the consequences of responding are thought to affect the probabilities of the learner's subsequent responses to the environment.

That kind of learning commonly said to involve instruction appears traditionally to be defined implicitly in terms of two major characteristics: the learner is presented with a formal subject matter to be mastered; and learning is mediated by a specially qualified instructor. Although such a definition may prove useful, it is unduly limited for present purposes. As identified here, the instructional process encompasses all situations involving the acquisition of behavior. Therefore, this process may sometimes be spontaneous or accidental and may involve unintentional content. Learning and instruction of some sort surely occur when a child immerses a container in water, finds that the container fills, and repeatedly engages in that activity. Similarly, learning and instruction of some sort surely occurred when Sir Arthur Fleming accidentally observed that a green mold replaced a bacterial culture, and was led to determine whether the one was the cause of the disappearance of the other.

Sometimes there is an intended subject matter or content of instruction, as in the typical classroom situation. Often, however, there is an unintentional content accompanying an intentional content. For example, a student can come to "appreciate" science at least partly because of his chemistry instructor's enthusiasm for his subject. Sometimes the instructional process is carefully rehearsed or proceeds according to some plan, as when a scientist carefully designs and executes an experiment or when a parent shows his child that a burning match is hot. Sometimes the instructional process involves only the learner and his environment; perhaps more frequently, the process is mediated by another person (an instructor) or by the person's surrogate (a textbook or a teaching machine). Sometimes the process involves a single person; sometimes, groups. Sometimes the process prepares the learner for immediate practical interaction with the environment, as when an apprentice works side by side with a master craftsman. Alternatively, the process may prepare the learner for contingencies remote in time, space, and probability, as when the etiology of a rare, exotic disease is described to the medical student. Sometimes the process requires an overt response to the stimuli presented; sometimes, not.

Because of the variety of circumstances in which instruction occurs, many specific conditions affect the ultimate probabilities of the learner's responses to his environment. But whatever the circumstances, the learning and instructional processes deal basically with the interaction of the *individual* with his environment. To the extent that instruction, even though presented to a group, prepares the individual to observe his environment and the consequences of alternative responses to the environment, it would be expected to be successful.

Formal and Informal Instruction

Many varieties of instruction could be identified in terms of the dimensions described above. For convenience, and at the risk of over-simplification, only two kinds of instruction will be identified here: formal and informal. By formal instruction is meant the type of classroom instruction typical of current educational practice and with which most analyses have been concerned. Informal instruction includes all instances of instruction occurring outside the formal classroom situation.

FORMAL INSTRUCTION

As used here, formal instruction refers to that of the typical American classroom. Only some of its more salient properties are cited here. Its primary objective is usually to communicate a particular, formalized content. The content is importantly, if not exclusively, verbal. This instruction is mediated by an instructor or his surrogate. Almost without exception, its purpose is to prepare the student for the eventualities of the more remote future.

Although these general characteristics apply to the classroom as it is known today, they do not necessarily apply to the classroom of the future. They are in need of critical examination with respect to their effectiveness in facilitating instruction. Some writers interested in instruction in particular and education in general have seen room for improvement in the classroom situation. For example, Skinner (1954) has argued that there is a notable lack of skillful programs for presenting the content of formal instruction, that the construction of a repertoire of skilled behaviors may require a carefully planned, extended series of responses with reinforcement at each step, and that the conditions required to develop such contingencies are difficult, if not impossible, to establish in today's classrooms.

It is clear that some features of classroom conduct are inconsistent with some of the best-known principles of behavioral science. In addition to the points made earlier, Skinner (for example, 1953) has also argued that the reinforcers used in the classroom, such as good grades, diplomas, and social approval, are weak and "unnatural." They are nonfunctional, or extrinsic, in the sense that they exist apart from the learning task itself and do not directly result from the confrontation of the learner with his environment. Skinner has maintained also that reinforcers are not used often and promptly enough and that classroom behavior is too frequently controlled with essentially aversive techniques. Such inefficiencies and deficiencies in instructional technique, argues Skinner (1954, p. 92), tend to subvert the aims of education: "Skills are minimized in favor of vague achievements—education for democracy, educating the whole child, educating for life, and so on." These criticisms are not without foundation, particularly in classes above the elementary grades. Skinner's proposals to remedy some of these criticisms are to be found elsewhere (1948, 1954, 1958).

INFORMAL INSTRUCTION

The content of informal instruction is idiosyncratic, in the sense that what the learner carries away from his observations of the environment cannot be readily predicted, and is frequently not communicated verbally. Informal instruction does not require the participation of a specially qualified instructor; it frequently involves an interaction only between the learner and his environment. It deals primarily with the here and now, and it appears to deal essentially with the acquisition of everyday knowledge and skill. It involves reinforcers, such as increased competence in dealing with the environment (see White, 1959), which are "natural" or intrinsic.

Self-instruction, in the sense of "learning from one's own experience," is an example of informal instruction. So also are the child's learning to talk, play, and dress in a certain way and his acquisition of simple principles of ballistics as he throws a ball. Many basic perceptual, motor, and social skills learned "informally" during infancy and early childhood are the foundations upon which formal classroom instruction builds. Hebb (1958, p. 144) makes a related point: "The learning that normally occurs during infancy . . . is prerequisite to the learning capacity with which we are familiar in the adult: that is, adult learning essentially consists, to a large extent, of transfer from the learning of infancy." In the same vein, Carroll (1960) has suggested that the parents' vocabulary and grammar condition the readiness of the child to respond to the verbal environment of the classroom.

It is probably correct to say that in the past there has been too little cognizance of the importance of informal instruction to the establishment of an adequate, basic repertoire of responses. It is probably also correct to say that there has been too little cognizance of the role of informal instruction, as here defined, in a spectrum of activities ranging from the child's play with a magnifying glass to the research worker's experiments in the laboratory. It follows that if informal, especially *early* informal, instruction is as important as it may be (Fiske and Maddi, 1961; Hebb, 1958, Chap. 6; Fowler, 1962), it may be advantageous systematically to afford opportunities for this kind of instruction.

Instruction as Dialogue

Instruction has already been characterized as a process whereby a learner and his environment, including the instructor and other learners, interact. Such interaction may be thought of as a dialogue between the learner and his environment. Instruction, especially formal instruction, is typically regarded as a dialogue involving answerable questions. The learner poses a question of the environment, and the environment offers the reply. As noted earlier, this type of dialogue is almost always mediated by an instructor. However, there are several other kinds of instructional dialogue, at least one of which would probably be categorized as an informal dialogue. Here the learner may simply probe the environment without asking a formal question. Alternatively, he may be a passive recipient of information transmitted by the environment.

An instructional dialogue will likely be most fruitful when the learner and the environment interact freely with one another and when the learner is sensitive and attentive to those stimuli that afford him a substantial gain in information. While the view usually expressed is that the educated man is one who is in better control of nature, there is much to recommend the alternative view that the educated man is one who is more sensitive to the control which nature exerts over him (see Skinner, 1953, p. 255). The careful observer is the one who pays attention to what nature is saying and who is prepared to respond to that information. What is commonly called "discovery," in particular, demands the careful observation of nature; that is, the careful searching out of its hidden facts and the studied skepticism of the obvious.

Frequently, the environment provided by an instructional dialogue does not transmit information to the learner simply and directly. In this less simple case, the learner must ask clarifying questions of the environment. The usual device for asking questions of the environment is some sort of experiment.

When the information transmitted by the environment is extensive or subtle, the dialogue can be facilitated by the mediation of an instructor or his surrogate. When such mediators participate, there are usually, but not always, specified items of information about the environment to be imparted. The instructor has already learned much from the environment and thus is able to call attention to important events and the relations between them and their antecedents. The primary function of the mediator is to arrange conditions so that the learner has an optimal opportunity for perceiving and understanding information transmitted by the environment. Secondarily, the mediator may help the learner to "learn how to learn"; that is, help to establish in the learner the ability to know what information is needed and to extract such information from the environment.

The mediator's task is not simple, for the learner's capacity to profit from the information with which he has been presented depends upon many factors. At minimum, the learner's capacity is affected by habits of attending to the environment and by the information about the environment which he brings to the dialogue. Such factors have been discussed at some length by Gagné (Chap. 10 in this book) and many others (for example, Deese, 1958; Underwood, 1949; Woodworth and Schlosberg, 1954). Such factors may be grouped into two major categories: (1) characteristics of the learner, such as his motivation and abilities; and (2) characteristics of the learning situation, such as the nature of the information to be acquired, the sequence in which the information is presented, and the nature of the response required of the learner.

A science of learning, which should greatly increase a mediator's effectiveness, is developing rapidly. However, there is yet to be constructed a sturdy bridge between the science of learning and the actual management of instructional dialogues. Some attendant difficulties, such as the immaturity of the science, the inadequacy of its present taxonomy of tasks or skills, and the confusion concerning the proper function of technology and research, have been cited by Melton (1959). If separable from these problems, another difficulty may be that the rules for applying the principles of the science of learning to the particular situation are meager. For such reasons, the management of instructional dialogues largely remains an art. Advances in the effectiveness of a dialogue between man and nature may be expected from the development of an adequate educational technology, oriented toward applying the principles of learning to the instructional dialogue. The interested reader may consult Bugelski (1964) for a direct attack upon this problem.

A Taxonomy of Learning Tasks

The classificatory scheme tentatively offered here has the advantages of being relatively brief and of affording a relatively simple conceptualization of learning tasks. It also has the advantage of being based upon an analysis of the behavior required of the learner for successful acquisition of a task. Because some tasks are complex and result in more than a single outcome and because the taxonomy has only a small number of classificatory categories, this scheme has the disadvantage of becoming somewhat unwieldy in the analysis of complex cases.

The taxonomy here proposed consists of a fourfold classification of learning tasks. Of these four classes, two are primarily concerned with the stimulus side of the S-R paradigm, and two with the response side. These outcomes, listed briefly, are (1) *expansion* of the range of *stimuli* to which a response may be made; (2) *restriction* of the range of *stimuli* to which a response may be made; (3) *expansion* of the range of *responses* which may be made to a stimulus; and (4) *restriction* of the range of *responses* which may be made to a stimulus. Each outcome is the result of specific training procedures, and all of the outcomes can be (or already have been) given descriptive names (see Figure 7–1). The established and proposed names for each class of outcome and the outcomes themselves, schematized in S-R form, are presented in Figures 7–2, 7–4, 7–5, and 7–6. Behavioral illustrations of the four classes of outcomes are presented below. An attempt was made to choose relatively simple and pure illustrations for each outcome class; however, more complicated illustrations have also been included.

While the simplest learning tasks result in only one of these outcomes, more complex tasks may produce several. Teaching a child to be cautious toward a flaming match, a task resulting in a single Class

CLASS 1: Stimulus elaboration See Figure 7-2.	**CLASS 2:** Stimulus discrimination See Figure 7-4.
CLASS 3: Response elaboration See Figure 7-5.	**CLASS 4:** Response differentiation See Figure 7-6.

Figure 7–1. Four Classes of Simple Outcomes. Schematic diagrams of the four classes are given in Figures 7–2, 7–4, 7–5, and 7–6.

1 outcome, requires only a slight addition to the range of stimuli already effectively controlling the desired response. Such a task requires only that the new stimulus (the match) come to control the avoidance response (withdrawal of the hand) already under the control of an old stimulus (such as the word *hot*).

Teaching a child to speak French fluently, a much more complex task, results in several kinds of outcomes. Among other things, such a task requires that the child increase the number of responses made to a stimulus (learn French as well as English words for objects and actions), restrict the range of stimuli to which a particular response is made (associate the French word with its appropriate referent and use it in its appropriate context), and restrict the range of responses made to a stimulus (pronounce the French word correctly and with facility). With these two illustrations as an introduction, attention is redirected to the outcomes in the figures. Each of the four classes of outcomes and the procedures used in establishing them are discussed in turn below.

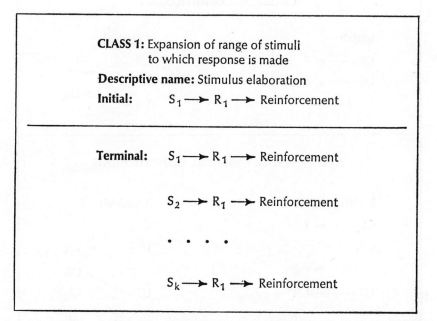

Figure 7–2. Simple Outcome, Class 1.

Class 1: Expansion of the Range of Effective Stimuli

The consequence of some training procedures is to expand the range of stimuli controlling a response (see Figure 7–2). Both classical and instrumental training procedures may be used to accomplish this outcome.

In the familiar classical, or Pavlovian, procedure, a neutral stimulus (the conditioned stimulus, CS) is paired with an adequate stimulus (the unconditioned stimulus, US). The US, of course, elicits the response (unconditioned response, UR) in question. After repeated pairings, the CS comes to elicit the response (now called a conditioned response, CR) previously elicited by the US alone (see Figure 7–3). In this manner, a response already in the learner's repertoire comes to be elicited by stimuli other than the original eliciting stimulus.

There is a variant of the procedure just described. After the previously neutral stimulus effectively controls the response following

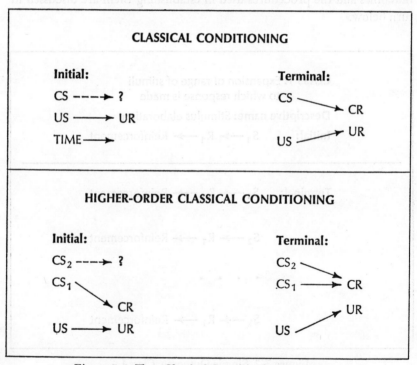

Figure 7–3. Two Classical Conditioning Paradigms.

classical conditioning, the CS can then function as a US to establish the control of yet other neutral stimuli. Such a procedure is also a classical conditioning procedure and is termed higher-order conditioning. This variant is also schematized in Figure 7–3. With both these procedures, a larger range of stimuli becomes effective in controlling a response; and with both, specific training may be given with one particular CS. However, other stimuli sharing characteristics of the CS also acquire some degree of control of the response without the benefit of special training for this purpose. Such an occurrence is called induction or, more frequently, stimulus generalization.

A famous experiment (Watson and Raynor, 1920) illustrates both simple classical conditioning and stimulus generalization. In this particular experiment, Pavlovian techniques were used to train a child to fear a white laboratory rat. Each time the rat (CS) was within view, the stimulus (US), a loud sound, adequate to produce a fear reaction (UR) was presented. With repeated pairings of the rat and the sound, the child became frightened when the rat alone was presented (CR). In addition, fear generalized to other stimuli similar to the white rat—a rabbit and a white fur muff.

Much casual evidence suggests that, although probably unwanted and often unnoticed, similar training occurs with some frequency in the classroom. Frequently, for example, a particular subject matter, say mathematics as a rather gross example of a CS, is paired with failure and disapproval, potent US's. Such circumstances may account, at least in part, for the tension and discomfort some college students feel when forced to take a course in this subject matter.

A new stimulus can also be made to control a response by instrumental conditioning procedures, so called because the organism's response is instrumental in producing reinforcement. When reinforcement is contingent upon behavior, as when a student receives an A grade on his term paper only if it meets certain standards, instrumental conditioning procedures are in effect. To increase the number of stimuli in control of an instrumental response, the response is reinforced when it is made in the presence of new stimuli. Thus, a child may have originally learned to say "thank you" only when given food, but with further training may come to give this response when receiving any courtesy.

Stimulus generalization, which operates in instrumental conditioning as in classical conditioning, also assists the spread of effective stimulus control. Suppose that a very young child has had experience with his own dog, and after repeated reinforcement, he correctly gives the verbal response "doggie" to that stimulus. If the child then sees another dog similar to his own, the response is likely generalized to the new stimulus. If the generalized response is reinforced, the tendency to emit the response becomes stronger and comes under the control of two stimuli rather than one. With continued training, the response is made to an ever larger number of specific stimuli.

In the preceding illustration, there is some possibility that the child may see an animal that looks like a dog but is not and nonetheless calls it a "doggie." If this response is undesirable, it is necessary to restrict the range of stimuli to which the response is made (a Class 2 outcome, to be described below) through differential reinforcement of responses. Reinforcement for correct responses and nonreinforcement for incorrect responses result in the child's discrimination between dogs and other animals.

This illustration points up the interesting fact that a single task, such as learning to identify dogs, may require an increase in the number of stimuli gaining control of a response at the same time that it requires a reduction in their variety. This is precisely what happens in the formal instructional situation where, for example, zoology students learn to identify "canines," and physiology students "enzymes." While such tasks (concept formation or concept-learning tasks) are extremely important, they are not simple illustrations of Class 1 outcomes and therefore are not discussed further here.

Class 2: Restriction of the Range of Effective Stimuli

Some tasks require that a response which is originally made to many stimuli come under the control of one or a single class of stimuli (see Figure 7–4). Once again, either classical or instrumental conditioning procedures may accomplish this aim. If the classical conditioning procedure is used, the technique and the result are called *differential conditioning*. If the instrumental conditioning procedure is used, the result of the technique is called *stimulus discrimination*, and the technique itself *discrimination learning*. The essential aspects of these procedures are described below.

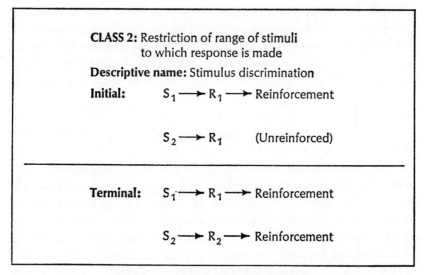

CLASS 2: Restriction of range of stimuli
to which response is made

Descriptive name: Stimulus discrimination

Initial: $S_1 \longrightarrow R_1 \longrightarrow$ Reinforcement

$S_2 \longrightarrow R_1$ (Unreinforced)

Terminal: $S_1 \longrightarrow R_1 \longrightarrow$ Reinforcement

$S_2 \longrightarrow R_2 \longrightarrow$ Reinforcement

Figure 7–4. Simple Outcome, Class 2.

DIFFERENTIAL CONDITIONING

In general, the purpose of differential conditioning is to eliminate one or more of the conditioned stimuli controlling a response. If it is the generalized response which is to be extinguished, all stimuli giving rise to the response are repeatedly presented. Only the original CS, however, is paired with the reinforcing stimulus, the US. With such a procedure, the reinforced stimulus persists in its control of the response, whereas the nonreinforced stimuli do not. If two or more conditioned stimuli have been established separately in control of the response, the principle described above also applies. Again, only the CS sought to remain in control of the response is paired with the US.

With such techniques, a dog may be conditioned to salivate to a 100-cps tone, but not to salivate to a 96-cps tone (Pavlov, 1927); and a child to salivate to the word *khorosho* ("well," "good"), but not to the word *plokho* ("poorly," "badly," "bad") (Razran, 1961, pp. 100 ff.). Similarly, it would be expected that through differential conditioning, students may generally experience one emotional state in one teacher's classroom and an entirely different emotional state in another's.

There is at least one variant of the differential conditioning procedure. In the procedure described above, the US is presented with a particular CS and is not presented with all other CS's. In the variant, a positively reinforcing US is presented with a particular CS and an aversive stimulus is presented with all other CS's. Unfortunately, there appears to be little literature on the effects of such a procedure.

DISCRIMINATION LEARNING

This is the instrumental conditioning analogue of differential conditioning. When a response occurs in the presence of a particular stimulus, it is reinforced. If that response occurs in the presence of any other stimulus, it is not rewarded, or, in a variant of the procedure, it is punished. In general, the purpose of discrimination training, as of differential conditioning, is to establish differential reactions to two or more stimuli. In its limiting case, stimulus discrimination requires the discrimination between the presence of a stimulus and its absence. Thus, simple classical and instrumental conditioning situations requiring responses when a stimulus is present and no response when it is absent involve stimulus discrimination. When, for example, a dog salivates to a tone, it clearly discriminates between the presence of the tone and its absence. If a child responds when he is called but continues playing when he is not called, he clearly discriminates between the call and its absence. If students whisper in the classroom when the teacher momentarily leaves the room but stop as soon as he returns, they clearly discriminate between the teacher's presence and his absence.

Most discrimination learnings probably require something slightly different from detecting simply the presence of the stimulus and its absence as described in the limiting case. Usually the organism is required to produce one response to one cue and another response to a different cue. This type of stimulus discrimination is illustrated by the child who comes to cross a busy intersection when the traffic signal is green, but remains standing on the curb when the signal is red. Also illustrative is the child who, when circumstances permit, eats his dessert but leaves his vegetables untouched. Stimulus discrimination is also evident in the use of plural verb forms in sentences with plural subjects and singular verb forms in sentences with singular subjects.

Each of these illustrations implies that under different stimulus conditions, quite different responses produce quite different consequences. Crossing a busy street when the traffic signal is green is generally more reinforcing than crossing when it is red. Eating dessert results in the "pleasures of sensation" (Pfaffman, 1959), while refraining from eating vegetables may be supposed to avoid unpleasantness. Agreement between subject and verb similarly may be supposed to be more uniformly reinforcing to the user of language than is nonagreement.

As implied by the examples chosen above, stimulus discriminations frequently evolve spontaneously or informally. A child soon learns from the consequences of his behavior which responses in which context are reinforcing. Cherry pies taste good; mud pies do not.

Stimulus discriminations need not depend upon the learner's *overt* responses to the stimuli involved. Thus, a child may use a simple tool correctly (although not necessarily skillfully) after he has seen the tool's use demonstrated once. At another extreme, an animal's responses during conditioning may be artificially blocked (Beck and Doty, 1957; Kellogg *et al.*, 1940; Light and Gantt, 1936); yet, after removal of the block, a differential response to stimulation may be left unimpeded. While the generalization may prove premature, it appears that outcomes of both Classes 1 and 2 do not depend upon the learner's production of *overt* differential response. Implicit, cognitive, or central nervous response may suffice.

It is probably obvious that the more difficult stimulus discriminations are those requiring that the learner respond differentially to aspects of compound stimuli and to compound stimuli whose attributes bear particular relationships to one another. For example, it is with some difficulty that a person may be trained to give one verbal response to a large, furry, long-tailed, four-legged animal that barks and another verbal response to a small, furry, long-tailed, four-legged animal that purrs. In general, the greater the number of stimuli to be differentiated, the more difficult is the process of discrimination (Garner, 1962, pp. 31 ff.).

Stimulus discrimination is also difficult if the stimuli must be produced by or within the discriminator himself. To the degree that discriminative stimuli are internal to the learner, they are typically outside the effective control of an instructor. To the degree that they are outside the instructor's control, formal instruction will prove ineffective. While learning based on internal discriminative stimuli *does* occur, it frequently occurs with difficulty and is sometimes faulty. The child can learn to say appropriately, "I am thinking," in response to internal cues; the response is learned slowly, however, because the child himself must discover the internal circumstances which are the appropriate cues for the verbal response. Since such internal cues are beyond the direct observation of an instructor, it is difficult for him to mediate the contingency between such cues and the child's response. Because the child sometimes emits the response under inappropriate circumstances, and yet the response is reinforced, prevarication or inadequate self-knowledge often results. (For a more complete discussion of these points, see Skinner, 1953, pp. 257–261.)

An instructor can play a role when responses are to be made to private events, although great effectiveness is not uniformly to be expected. His role is typically to infer the occurrence of such events from their accompanying visible manifestations and then verbally to cue the response. Such mediation would be expected to facilitate learning only to the degree that control of the response can be transferred from the instructor to the learner himself. This point also bears on the shaping of skilled behavior, a Class 4 outcome, considered in more detail on pages 198–201.

Class 3: Expansion of the Range of Responses

Some tasks require a broadening of the range of responses made to a stimulus (see Figure 7–5). Whereas both classical and instrumental procedures may accomplish this aim, instrumental procedures probably are typical of actual practice.

Even the simplest conditioning situations can result in the production and learning of more than a single response. A noxious stimulus produces a variety of autonomic and skeletal responses, many or all of which can become associated with the eliciting stimulus. In this way, the range of responses made to a stimulus is increased. To further expand the range of responses by classical procedures, the CS may be presented with a variety of unconditioned stimuli, each eliciting a different response. Proper choice of the unconditioned stimuli would insure that responses incompatible with each other were not elicited. To expand the range of response to a stimulus by an instrumental procedure, each new response made in the presence of a discriminative

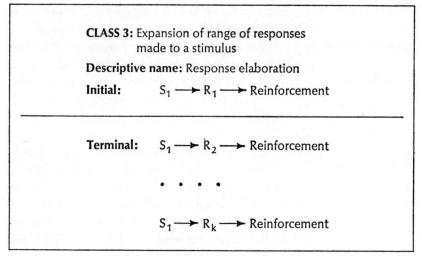

CLASS 3: Expansion of range of responses
made to a stimulus

Descriptive name: Response elaboration

Initial: $S_1 \longrightarrow R_1 \longrightarrow$ Reinforcement

---

Terminal: $S_1 \longrightarrow \dot{R}_2 \longrightarrow$ Reinforcement

• • • •

$S_1 \longrightarrow R_k \longrightarrow$ Reinforcement

Figure 7–5. Simple Outcome, Class 3.

stimulus is reinforced. (A variant of this procedure would penalize slow responses or failures to respond and would, parenthetically, also thereby result in more than a single outcome.) In this way, a response repertoire is established for a particular occasion.

By way of illustration, consider the behavior of one child in response to another who is crying and apparently unhappy. Typically the first child initiates activities directed toward the second with the apparent objective of getting him to stop crying and to "feel better." The first, for example, may make soothing verbal statements. That failing, he may put his arm about the crying youngster in an apparent attempt to comfort him. He may divert his attention by offering a toy or by playing the "clown"; he may physically attack the source of the first child's unhappiness, and so on. Since these responses are likely to be reinforced, they are likely to be called forth more easily in the future by this and other similar stimulus situations. Since these responses are also likely to be reinforced intermittently, it would be expected that once learned, they would extinguish slowly. The first child described above has acquired a repertoire of "mollifying behavior." Under suitable circumstances, the several responses of his repertoire would be called forth promptly and appropriately, and persist throughout periods of nonreinforcement.

As another example, consider the clinical behavior of the autistic child. Autism is characterized by an inability to respond effectively to the environment. Therefore, a major aim of therapy is to increase the number and variety of the patient's responses. Ferster and DeMyer (1962) report a partially successful attempt to do this. In brief, these investigators instituted training enabling the child to emit behavior that could be positively reinforced. By strongly reinforcing and by never punishing responses to the environment, they broadened the child's behavioral repertoire.

There is a parallel between this clinical example of autistic behavior and the behavior of many students. There are those students who passively receive information from their books and instructors, but who fail to act on this information or to impart new information themselves. It is possible that these students' customary ways of reacting to reading assignments and lectures can be made more variable and productive. Such students appear to need to learn to make a wider variety of responses to the classroom situation. It is possible that some simple conditions, such as the prompt, positive reinforcement of the students' queries concerning their lessons and the establishment of laboratory facilities enabling the students to answer their own questions, may help make for "active" rather than "passive" learners.

Certain circumstances demand a selective increase in appropriate responses rather than a wholesale increase in sheer number of responses. Selective increase requires that only appropriate responses be reinforced and inappropriate responses be extinguished. It results in mixed outcomes—notably those of Class 2 and Class 3 in the present terminology.

Class 4: Restriction of the Range of Responses

Certain tasks emphasize the selection of the appropriate response to a particular stimulus (see Figure 7–6). In some situations, the response in question is already within the learner's repertoire. Because the response is reinforced when it is emitted whereas other responses are not, the reinforced response is quite literally selected from the remainder of the repertoire.

In other situations, the response in question is not already within the repertoire, although other responses, from which the desired response can be generated, are. Such a training outcome has been called

CLASS 4: Restriction of range of responses
made to a stimulus

Descriptive name: Response differentiation

Initial: $S_1 \longrightarrow R_0$ (Unreinforced)

$S_1 \longrightarrow R_0^1$ (Unreinforced)

$S_1 \longrightarrow R_0^{11}$ (Unreinforced)

• • • •

Terminal: $S_1 \longrightarrow R_1 \longrightarrow$ Reinforcement

Figure 7–6. Simple Outcome, Class 4.

response differentiation. Unlike Class 1 and 2 outcomes, Class 3 and 4 outcomes place great emphasis upon the learner's production of an overt response. The outcome of Class 4 places particular stress upon the precise characteristics of the response. Many outcomes of Class 4, especially those involving chains of skilled behavior, also appear to place particular stress on self-initiated, internal cuing of behavior; to that degree, they represent mixed outcomes (Class 2 and Class 4).

The essence of response differentiation is that a progressively more appropriate response becomes attached to a particular stimulus. The responses may become qualitatively or quantitatively more appropriate to the stimulus. Many responses may have to be made before one produces a reinforcing consequence. Once made, however, that response gains in strength. The beginning typist frequently misstrikes the keys (qualitative imprecision), but gradually comes to strike the right key at the right time. The initial finger movements are carried out slowly and weakly (quantitative imprecision), but gradually become faster and stronger.

When the response to be differentiated has a low initial probability of occurrence, conditions may be arranged to make its occurrence more likely. New stimuli known to be associated with the desired response may be added to the old ones. The learner may be instructed as to the nature of the response desired. The task may be eased by simplifying the response or by reducing the number of responses from which selection is to be made. Similarly, a response approximating the desired form may be extrinsically reinforced the first few times the response appears. On subsequent occasions, reinforcement is given only when the response more and more closely approximates the desired form (the method of approximations).

Extensive repertoires requiring highly skilled movements may be established in this fashion. Whereas such acts are not customarily expected in an animal's repertoire, Pierrel and Sherman (1958) report training a laboratory rat to mount a spiral staircase to a platform, then run along to another platform by pushing down and crossing a raised drawbridge, then to climb a ladder, pull a car by hand-over-hand pull of an attached chain, pedal a car through a tunnel, climb a flight of stairs, run through a tube, step into an awaiting elevator, and raise a Columbia University flag over it. This started the elevator, and the rat then descended to the ground floor, where he pressed a lever and received a primary reinforcement of food. The example just given involves outcomes of Class 2 as well as Class 4. However, it clearly illustrates the selection of differential responses from a repertoire and the establishment of some novel ones.

Although all four classes of outcome comprising this taxonomy may evolve spontaneously and informally, informal learning appears to be particularly characteristic of Class 4 outcomes. Before the child enters school, he already has a basic repertoire of motor skills (acquired primarily by response differentiation) and perceptual-motor skills (acquired by both external stimulus discrimination and response differentiation). By age five, the child's motor behavior is typically broadly based, quite smooth, and continuously graded. He maintains and regains balance and posture readily; he can move slowly or rapidly; he can dodge and turn. He can throw objects and catch them, although facility in catching lags behind facility in throwing. He can imitate most gross and many fine movements, including those of the vocal apparatus, frequently with great élan. This list could be continued and would serve even further to demonstrate the fundamental importance of Class 4 outcomes. But most, if not all, of the skills described above arise without the benefit of formal instruction. Whatever shaping of such behavior has been accomplished by age five has resulted largely as a consequence of natural contingencies of reinforcement. A child learns to throw a ball with "good form" because these are exactly the conditions which make for throws of accuracy and distance. A child learns to speak distinctly and with appropriate intonations because these are the conditions which lead to social reinforcement.

IMPLICATIONS OF A BEHAVIORISTIC ANALYSIS

It is possible here to discuss briefly only a few of the implications of the principles presented in the previous section. These implications are presented for any heuristic value they may have.

The Role of Guidance

As used here, the term *guidance* refers to those situations wherein the instructor cues the learner's behavior. Cuing can be either direct or indirect. In direct cuing, the instructor may actually perform the movements while the learner follows his behavior more or less passively. In indirect cuing, the learner performs the movements under the control of symbolic cues (often verbal) from the instructor. The golf instructor who actually attempts to guide the swing of the beginner is cuing directly. The diving coach who describes what he wants done before the diver leaves the springboard and who then calls commands to his diver in midair is cuing indirectly.

STIMULUS DISCRIMINATION

Either direct or indirect guidance should be helpful in establishing stimulus discriminations (Class 2 outcomes) in which the stimuli, such as those of the external environment, are readily discriminated. Where cues are more difficult to discriminate, guidance would be expected to be more difficult to effect, but still should facilitate learning. Successful guidance in such cases appears to depend upon the instructor's ability to make the controlling cues apparent to the learner. There appear to

A Behavioristic Analysis / JAHNKE · 201

be some tasks for which guidance, as described above, may not facilitate the learner's apprehension of the stimuli produced by his own
movement, nor the self-initiation of movement. For these reasons,
certain instances of guidance may be expected to be relatively unsuccessful in establishing skilled repertoires cued by internal stimulation
(response differentiations, Class 4 outcomes).

RESPONSE DIFFERENTIATION

For response differentiation, the response in question is by definition not readily available at the outset of training and must be selected
from the repertoire (or added to the repertoire) by differential reinforcement. Repeated responding is often necessary to bring the response to sufficient strength so that it can be elicited promptly and
efficiently by the appropriate cues.

The refractoriness of such situations to the effects of guidance lies
in the fact that important cues guiding skilled spatial or temporal
behavior must be generated by the learner himself. Guidance of such
behavior is unsuccessful to the extent that it fails to duplicate the
pattern of stimulation (particularly proprioceptive) which in fact
guides the skilled response. A boy may *observe* hundreds of professional basketball games, in which great skill is abundantly manifest,
without any appreciable effect upon his own motor behavior. A student of languages could *listen* interminably to properly spoken French,
yet be unable to pronounce the words correctly.

Differential reinforcement of self-initiated and self-guided behavior appears crucial to the establishment of response differentiations.
Guidance would be expected to be successful in establishing response
differentiations only to the degree that externally imposed control of
the learner's behavior is transferable to the learner himself. Any instructional technique allowing the learner to apprehend more readily
the private cues controlling skilled behavior might be expected to
facilitate learning. A classic example (Lindahl, 1945) involved an instructional device which gave an immediate visual representation of the
pattern of foot movements made by the learner during the operation of
a machine, movements whose execution was ordinarily difficult to
learn.

By extension, devices for instruction like the teaching machine, which has been used to present facts and to emphasize the relations between cue and behavior, theoretically have at least the same potential for success with *discrimination* training as has the very best human instructor. Such devices would also appear to have the same deficiencies as the human instructor when the task is heavily weighted with *response differentiation,* since important cues controlling skilled behavior are produced by the learner's own responses.

The Appropriateness of Instruction

Another implication of a behavioristic analysis concerns what might be called the goodness of fit between the content of instruction and the "professed" or "intended" objectives of instruction. For example, an instructor of a graduate-level course in research methods may wish his students to become "good scientists." Frequently in the past, instructors of such courses have relied primarily upon a verbal description of the methods of scientific research. Such a procedure may in fact allow the student to *understand* the nature of good science (that is, make the appropriate stimulus discrimination). However, such a procedure probably develops only some of the skills which are actually required to *practice* good methodology. In addition to knowing what has constituted good and bad research, a student must also be sensitive to research problems; he must be familiar not only with research design, but with the kinds and operation of laboratory equipment; he must know not only what is a satisfactory report of research, but also how to write one; he must know not only what others do in the laboratory, but also how to do it himself. Instructors must continually review the content of their courses with an eye to increasing the fit between what is taught and what is to be demanded of the student when he has left the classroom.

On the Effectiveness of Instruction

The final implication considered here is that to be effective, formal instruction may require a preliminary analysis of the behaviors required by the task. Such systematic analysis may disclose that whereas one task requires that responses already in the learner's repertoire come under the control of new stimuli, another requires that a skilled response to the correct cue be made at the correct time. Thus, different educational goals may require different instructional techniques. Instruction which is primarily verbal and does not require an overt response from the student may suffice for the attainment of certain educational objectives. On the other hand, verbal instruction accompanied by active, overt responding in a variety of training situations may be necessary for the attainment of other objectives. While it is not possible to pursue such an analysis in detail here, a brief general illustration is provided by considering the task facing the instructor of Introductory Psychology.

A considerable effort is devoted in most first courses in psychology to the *acquisition* and *understanding* of psychological terminology and of basic psychological information. It is probably true that somewhat less effort is devoted to the student's *application* of terminology and information to the affairs of his daily life, although this lack may be due only to one's relative inability to instruct for this kind of behavior. Other objectives of instruction might be listed, but the three (especially the first two) listed above are probably those which in fact are measured by the examination procedures used by the instructors themselves.

The *acquisition* of psychological vocabulary and information appears largely to require the acquisition or broadening of a repertoire. According to the present analysis, such behaviors would more likely be members of Class 3 or mixed Classes 1 and 3. Responses (terms, facts) which were not in the student's repertoire at the start of the semester are there when the semester ends. Psychological terms as well as laymen's terms exist to describe events; "common sense" is supplemented, if not supplanted, by psychological fact.

The *understanding* (proper use) of vocabulary and information, on the other hand, appears largely to require the emission of a response in an appropriate context. According to the present analysis, such behaviors would be considered members of Class 2, stimulus discrimination. Not only must the terms and facts be in the student's repertoire, they must be brought forth under the appropriate conditions: words and facts must be related to the appropriate physical- and social-environmental cues.

Finally, in addition to the acquisition and understanding of terms and facts, such knowledge must also be applied to the learner's environment. The proper *application* of terms and facts appears primarily to involve stimulus discrimination (Class 2 outcome) and, less uniformly, two additional ingredients: (1) shaping skilled motor behavior (response differentiation, Class 4 outcome); and (2) increasing the range of stimuli effective in calling forth a given response (Class 1 outcome).

As a specific example, suppose that the student in Introductory Psychology is presented with the notion of *reinforcement* (defined early in this chapter). The use of this term by the instructor in the classroom, the student's frequent reading of the term, and his probable vocal rehearsal of the term increase the likelihood of the student's emission of the response. With the reinforced repetition of the response, the likelihood of its being maintained as a stable component of the repertoire is further increased. In this and other ways, the word "reinforcement" becomes available for use (Class 3 outcome). By his use of the term in different contexts, the instructor brings the notion of reinforcement under the control of a variety of discriminative stimuli. The student becomes aware that the term is emitted appropriately under certain conditions and not under others. It can be inferred that the student understands the term when he responds appropriately to these certain conditions.

One behavioral test of such understanding is to determine whether or not the student can recognize a proper usage of the term; for example, *Q:* "Are smiles reinforcers?" *A:* "Yes." Here the student's response is clearly under the control of relevant environmental stimuli and, as such, affords an example of stimulus discrimination (Class 2 outcome). Another such test might be to determine whether or not the student himself uses the term in its appropriate context. For example, when the student sees a youngster show off because of the attention he thereby attracts, the student may identify "attention" as a reinforcer. A third test might be to determine whether or not the student is able to group related terms and correctly categorize sets of facts. Such activity implies that the student really understands or has the "idea"—that what appear to be different terms or facts are indeed linked by a common defining property. A student, for example, might be said to understand the notions of primary and secondary reinforcers if he classified "food and water" as the former and "money and praise" as the latter. All such behavioral tests require that a given response (or a functionally unified set of responses) be related to appropriate stimuli. All appear to involve stimulus discrimination predominantly, if not entirely.

It is one thing to understand terms and facts, and it is another to apply them properly. To begin with, the student must have the propensity actively to operate on information he receives and to seek the relationships between such information and the environment. Such a characteristic may be described as a generalized tendency to respond (Class 3 outcome) or, perhaps more graphically, as a "learning how to try" (Skinner, 1953, pp. 248 ff.). To the extent that such behavior is missing, the student's application of terms and facts cannot occur.

In addition, it must be remembered that much of a student's training has been verbal and that skillful application of knowledge (mixed outcome) frequently requires the student to respond to the real world—the referents of the verbal statements which have comprised his training experience. It cannot be assumed that transfer from the word to the environment will be immediate and complete.

Finally, it cannot be assumed that because information has been presented to the student, the information has been encoded in such a manner that it will be available for use at all, let alone for use in the appropriate context.

The application of terms or facts to the real world is difficult for other reasons, some of which have been considered earlier in this chapter. At least some of the stimuli controlling the response must be generated by the student himself: it is one thing to recognize a confounding variable in a research design when it is pointed out, and it is another to search routinely for such errors in research reports. The task may be difficult because the attempts to apply information often are not effectively reinforced; reinforcement may come too slowly or intermittently or may be too subtle to have a strong effect. Application may also be difficult because of an instructor's (or student's) failure to train for application. While conditions are often established which reinforce a student's *particular* application, this alone is insufficient. There must be established other occasions, less and less similar to the one originally reinforced, in order to increase the likelihood of successful responses to truly novel conditions.

8

A Cognitive-Structure Theory
of School Learning

DAVID P. AUSUBEL

The Ontario Institute for Studies in Education
University of Toronto

ৡ

THIS CHAPTER DISCUSSES A THEORY OF CLASSROOM LEARNING THAT DEALS
with the meaningful acquisition and retention of subject-matter knowledge. After defending the thesis that theories of learning *can* have
relevance for the educational process, I consider, in order, the following salient components of this theory:

1. A cognitive-structure conception of meaning and meaningful learning.
2. Process differences between meaningful and rote learning.
3. The psychological organization and accretion of knowledge
   through subsumption.
4. The nature of forgetting.
5. The identity and role of the major cognitive-structure variables in
   meaningful learning and retention.
6. The manipulation of cognitive-structure variables for the purpose of
   facilitating subject-matter learning.
7. The impact of some practice and task variables on cognitive structure, with particular reference to the influence of repetition or frequency.
8. The role of motivational variables in meaningful learning and retention.

The Decline of Classroom Learning Theory

Three principal reasons account for the serious decline in knowledge and theorizing about classroom learning that has taken place over the past thirty years. First, the vast majority of studies in the field of school learning have been conducted by teachers and other nonprofessional research workers in education. These studies have been typically characterized by glaring inadequacies in conceptualization and rigor of research design and have been too narrowly oriented toward improving particular academic skills or techniques of instruction, rather than toward the discovery of more general principles affecting the improvement of classroom learning and instruction.

Second, the more rigorously conducted research in learning theory has been undertaken largely by psychologists unconnected with the educational enterprise who have investigated problems quite remote from the type of learning that goes on in the classroom. The focus has been on animal learning or on short-term, fragmentary, rote, and nonverbal human learning, rather than on the learning and retention of organized bodies of meaningful material. Experimental psychologists can hardly be criticized if laboratory studies of short-term, fragmentary, and rote learning have had little applicability to the classroom. Like all pure research efforts in the basic sciences, these studies were designed to yield only general scientific laws as ends in themselves, quite apart from any practical utility. The blame, if any is to be assigned, must certainly lie with educational psychologists. In general, they have failed to conduct the necessary applied research and have succumbed to the temptation of extrapolating the theories and findings of their experimental colleagues to problems of classroom learning.

Finally, for the past generation, educational psychologists have been preoccupied with measurement and evaluation, personality development, mental hygiene, group dynamics, and counseling. Despite the self-evident centrality of classroom learning and cognitive development for the psychological aspects of education, these areas were largely ignored in both theory and research.

Although the steady retreat of educational psychologists from problems of classroom learning was temporarily expedient, it was highly unfortunate in the long run. Rotely and meaningfully learned materials are represented and organized quite differently in cognitive structure and hence conform to quite different principles of learning and retention.

Not only are the respective learning processes very dissimilar, but the significant variables involved in the two processes are usually markedly different; and even when similar, they have very different effects. In the first place, most classroom learning tasks are potentially meaningful; that is, they are relatable on a nonarbitrary, substantive basis to a previously learned background of meaningful ideas and information. Rotely learned materials, on the other hand, are discrete and relatively isolated entities which are only relatable to cognitive structure in an arbitrary, verbatim fashion. Second, because they cannot be anchored to existing ideational systems in the learner's cognitive structure, rotely learned materials are much more vulnerable to forgetting. Thus, they manifest retention properties that are both quantitatively and qualitatively different from those characterizing meaningfully learned materials. Whereas *rote* learning and retention are influenced primarily by the interfering effects of similar rote materials learned immediately before or after the learning task, *meaningful* learning and retention are influenced primarily by the properties of the relevant subsuming ideas in cognitive structure with which they interact.

Extrapolation of rote learning theory and evidence to school learning problems therefore had many disastrous consequences. It perpetuated erroneous conceptions about the nature and conditions of classroom learning, led educational psychologists to neglect research on factors influencing meaningful learning, and hence delayed the discovery of more effective techniques of verbal exposition. As will be seen below, it also convinced some educators to question the relevance of learning theory for the educational enterprise and to formulate theories of teaching that conceptualized the nature, purposes, and effects of instruction independently of its relationship to learning. Moreover, it encouraged many teachers to perceive and present potentially meaningful materials as if they were rote in character. Finally, it persuaded others that since psychologists conceptualize all verbal learning as a rote process, meaningful learning could be achieved only through the use of nonverbal and problem-solving methods.

THEORIES OF LEARNING VERSUS THEORIES OF TEACHING

Disillusionment regarding the relevance and usefulness of learning theory for education has been responsible in part for the recent emergence of "theories of teaching." The justification for such theories has been advanced on both historical and logical grounds.

The Historical Argument

Gage (1964) cites the historical record to show that theories of learning have had very little applicability to educational practice and very little influence on it, as reflected in educational-psychology textbooks, courses devoted to teaching methods, or the day-to-day operations of classroom teaching. He argues further that theories of learning are insufficient *"in principle."* For example, he states:

> while theories of learning deal with the ways an organism learns, theories of teaching deal with the ways in which a person influences an organism to learn. . . . The goal of education—to engender learning in the most desirable and efficient ways possible—would seem to require an additional science and technology of teaching. To satisfy the practical demands of education, theories of learning must be "stood on their heads" so as to yield theories of teaching. (pp. 268–269)

Actually, however, *both* of Gage's arguments are based essentially on the historical failure of learning theory to provide a relevant basis for pedagogic practice. But this undeniable shortcoming of learning theory to date is by no means a necessary or inherent limitation in the applicability of such theory to education; it is merely characteristic of the prevailing brand of school learning theory which, for the most part, has been uncritically extrapolated from the general body of laboratory learning theory. A truly realistic and scientifically viable theory of classroom learning, on the other hand, would give a prominent place to *manipulatable* variables that influence the complex, meaningful kinds of verbal and symbolic learning occurring in school and similar learning environments. It therefore makes for a more integrated and heuristically valuable body of pedagogic theory to include the nature and effects of these latter variables under the rubric of school learning theory, rather than to formulate a separate and fragmented body of teaching theory. Of course, only general principles of deliberately facilitating school learning would be considered part of learning theory. The more detailed and applied aspects of pedagogic technology that are derived from these principles, both generally and for particular age groups and subject matters, would continue to be taught in methods courses comparable to the clinical phase of a medical student's training.

The Logical Argument

In contrast to Gage's historical argument, Smith (1960) presents a strictly logical rationale for formulating theories of teaching that are independent of theories of learning. He rests his case on the propositions that (1) learning and teaching are neither coextensive nor inextricable from each other, (2) a theory of learning cannot tell one how to teach, and (3) teaching is not the same as didactics.

RELATEDNESS OF TEACHING AND LEARNING

Smith's insistence that learning and teaching are different and separately identifiable phenomena does more than belabor the obvious. It clears up some widely prevailing semantic confusion—since, in his words, it is frequently inferred that "if the child has not learned the teacher has not taught" or has taught incompetently. Teaching and learning are not coextensive because learning is influenced by many conditions, of which teaching is only one—and neither a necessary nor a sufficient one at that. Thus, pupils can learn without being taught (that is, by teaching themselves); and even if teaching is manifestly competent, it does not necessarily lead to learning if the pupils concerned are dull, inattentive, unmotivated, or cognitively unprepared.

Nevertheless, once these unwarranted inferences about the coextensiveness and inextricability of learning and teaching are discarded, it is practically useful to focus on those aspects of teaching and learning that *are* reciprocally related to one another. These reciprocal relationships include the purpose, effects, and measurement of teaching.

Hence, although it is true that teaching is ontologically distinct from learning and can be analyzed independently of what pupils learn, what would be the practical advantage of doing so? Teaching is not an end in itself; the facilitation of learning is the only proper end of teaching. Even though the failure of pupils to learn does not necessarily indict the competence of the teacher, learning is still the only feasible measure of teaching merit. Furthermore, as pointed out below, teaching itself is only effective to the extent that it effectively manipulates those psychological variables which govern learning. By teaching is essentially meant the deliberate manipulation of learning processes by some external agency for the purpose of enhancing learning outcomes. It would seem reasonable, therefore, to suppose that the discovery of the most effective methods of manipulating learning processes would be dependent on and related to our understanding of the nature of these processes.

It could be argued, therefore, that undue emphasis on the separateness of learning and teaching generates as much semantic confusion as it dissipates. It is helpful to insist that the two concepts are not coextensive; but if after this legitimate point is made, emphasis continues to be on their separateness rather than their reciprocal relatedness in terms of purpose, effects, and measurement, the waters, in my opinion, are left in an even muddier state than they were before.

LEARNING THEORY AS A POINT OF DEPARTURE

Although a valid theory of learning per se cannot tell teachers how to teach, it offers the most feasible point of departure for discovering general laws of effective teaching formulated in terms of both mediating variables and cause-and-effect relationships. Teaching largely consists of a process of deliberately manipulating those psychological variables and conditions which influence learning in the most efficacious manner possible. Hence, it is from a theory of learning that there develop defensible notions of what factors in the learning-teaching situation need to be influenced, and in what direction. The only other possible approach is to vary teaching factors at random or to rely on intuition. The latter approach is not only more time-consuming, but yields only purely empirical laws that cannot be formulated in general terms with respect to the psychological conditions and intervening cognitive variables involved.

It is realized, of course, that an adequate theory of learning is a *necessary* but not a *sufficient* condition for the improvement of instruction. Valid principles of teaching are necessarily based on relevant principles of learning, but are not simple and direct applications of these principles. Laws of classroom learning merely provide general direction for discovering effective teaching principles; they do not themselves indicate what these principles are. The development of effective teaching principles requires additional research taking account of practical problems and new instructional variables not implicit in the learning principles. In other words, I would classify basic principles of teaching as special derivatives of school learning theory. Such principles are products of an engineering type of research based on whatever modifications of this theory are necessitated by the practical difficulties or the additional new variables involved in the task of teaching.

I would also take issue with Smith's critique of the proposition he advances to account for the origin of the notion that one can tell how to teach from knowledge of how learning occurs; namely, that if one knows the cause of a phenomenon, one can thereby control it for practical ends. It is true, for example, that medical science can treat a disease successfully without knowing its cause, and that it can know the cause of a disease without knowing how to treat it. But to rest the case at this point and to carry the analysis of this proposition no further are to repudiate practically everything learned about the research methodology of applied science over the past three hundred years.

It is true that many practical and useful discoveries are made accidentally, without any understanding of the principles and relevant variables involved. But who would advocate this as a *deliberate* research strategy? Ordinarily, scientists search for practical methods of control that can be related to general statements of relationship among the relevant variables. The superiority of this approach inheres in the fact that methods of control based on general principles are not only understandable and interpretable, but also more widely transferable to other practical problems. It could be discovered as an empirical fact that teaching method X (for example, emphasis on valid techniques of definition and explanation) facilitates learning. But the practical value of such knowledge is quite limited. Would it not be preferable to formulate the research problem so that it could be ascertained in what ways method X influences relevant psychological variables and intervening cognitive states in the course of facilitating learning, retention, or problem solving? It strikes me as extremely wasteful to search for more efficient methods of teaching that can only be described in terms of characteristics of the teaching act and cannot be related to laws of learning. Even when scientists do stumble accidentally on useful empirical laws, they immediately launch new hypothesis-oriented research to explain in more general terms the underlying basis of the particular accidental (empirical) discovery.

Further, although knowledge of causation does not imply immediate knowledge of effective control procedures, it offers a tremendous advantage in discovering such procedures. It narrows down the field and enables the trial of procedures that have proved successful in controlling related conditions. Knowing that tuberculosis was caused by a microorganism, for example, did not provide an immediate cure. But it suggested such approaches as vaccines, immune sera, antisepsis, quarantine, and chemotherapy which had been successfully used in connection with other infectious diseases. I do not agree with the opinion of Smith's scientist friend who asserted that knowledge of the cause of cancer would not help in discovering a cure. In my opinion, this assertion has little face validity in the light of the history of such applied sciences as medicine and engineering.

TEACHING AND DIDACTICS

Although it is possible, as Smith asserts, to separate the "acts of teaching" from didactics, "the science or art of teaching," I would question why anyone would want to do so as an end in itself. The teaching act per se, divorced from the way teaching ought to be conducted on psychological grounds, *does* have its own descriptive properties which can be observed and categorized. I would think, however, that this categorization would be only a preliminary procedural step prior to *qualitative* evaluation of the *content* of the different acts of teaching in terms of their influences on the psychological conditions and intervening cognitive processes involved in learning, retention, and problem solving. Mere descriptive categorization of the teaching act can only yield quantitative data about the relative frequencies of occurrence of the various categories. Such data do not identify or shed much light on the really significant attributes of the teaching act that influence learning.

Suppose, for example, a project to determine the effects of various logical operations of teaching on learning outcomes. The first step might be to categorize the component units of a given teaching sequence in terms of a category system dealing with logical operations. The next step, I think, would be to devise a scheme for appraising the quality or properties of the particular operations placed in the various categories. Would it not be the properties of a definition—its logical quality, clarity, distinctiveness, power, functional utility, and so on—that would influence learning, rather than the empirical fact that "definitions" constituted, say, 17 per cent of the teacher's total logical operations in a given teaching sequence? And finally, shouldn't these various qualitative attributes of logical operations be related to psychological variables and processes, for example, to the clarity and stability of emerging meanings in cognitive structure, to the possession of substantive rules and tools of analysis in problem situations?

Thus, for a category system based on the logical operations of the teaching act to have more than descriptive value at a superficial level of counting, the qualitative merit of the logical operations—and their relation to psychological conditions and processes of learning—must be used as the independent variable in teaching-learning studies. This approach does more than describe the teaching act as an end in itself, that is, as an independent variable completely divorced from the psychology of learning. It assumes that whatever value the logical operations of teaching have as independent variables affecting learning outcomes is derived from their effects on cognitive structure.

A Cognitive-Structure View

Since the theory of school learning that I am presenting deals exclusively with meaningful verbal learning, it is important that I be very explicit in stating what I mean by *meaning* and *meaningful learning*.

Meaning

Meaning, first of all, refers to the articulated and differentiated cognitive content evoked by a particular symbol or set of symbols. The representational character of symbols inheres in their power to elicit a cognitive content substantially equivalent to that elicited by their significates (that is, by the objects and situations they signify) or by synonymous, already meaningful symbols or groups of symbols. At the simplest level of representational symbolism, signs become meaningful when they are able to evoke images that are reasonable facsimiles of the perceptions evoked by their significates. New signs, like second-order concepts, can then acquire meaning by being related to or subsumed under established meanings in various ways (for example, as synonyms, antonyms, derivatives, elaborations, qualifiers, combinatorial products) without requiring that the learner have any direct contact with their significates. Thus, according to the cognitive-structure view, meaning is an idiosyncratic phenomenological product of a meaningful learning process in which the potential meaning inherent in symbols and sets of symbols becomes converted into differentiated cognitive content within a given individual. Potential meaning thus becomes converted into phenomenological meaning when a particular individual, employing a meaningful learning set, incorporates a *potentially* meaningful sign or proposition within his cognitive structure.

Symbolic material possesses potential or logical meaning if it can be related on a nonarbitrary, substantive basis to a hypothetical human cognitive structure exhibiting the necessary ideational background and cognitive maturity. This criterion of logical meaning applies primarily to the attributes of the learning material itself. If the material manifests the characteristics of nonarbitrariness, lucidity, and plausibility, then it is, by definition, also relatable to the aforementioned hypothetical cognitive structure. Obviously excluded, therefore, from the domain of logical meaning is the vast majority of the almost infinite number of possible relationships between concepts that can be formulated on the basis of purely random pairings. This does not mean that all propositions with logical meaning are necessarily valid or even logically correct. The issues of substantive and logical validity simply do not enter into the determination of logical meaning. Propositions based on unvalidated premises or on faulty logic may conceivably abound in logical or potential meaning.

Corresponding, therefore, to the distinction between the logical and the psychological structure of knowledge, there is an equally important distinction between logical and psychological meaning. Actual phenomenological meaning is an idiosyncratic psychological experience. Subject-matter content can at best have logical or potential meaning. It is nonarbitrary subsumability of logically meaningful propositions within a *particular* cognitive structure that creates the possibility of transforming logical into psychological meaning. Thus, the emergence of psychological meaning depends not only on the learner's possession of the requisite intellectual capacities and ideational background, but also on his *particular* ideational content. When an individual learns logically meaningful propositions, he does not learn their logical meaning per se but the meaning they have for him. Psychological meaning is always an idiosyncratic phenomenon.

The idiosyncratic nature of psychological meaning does not rule out the possibility of social or shared meanings. The various individual meanings possessed by members of a particular culture are ordinarily sufficiently similar to permit interpersonal communication and understanding. This intracultural homogeneity of shared meanings reflects both the same logical meaning inherent in potentially meaningful propositions and the interindividual commonality of ideational background.

New meanings are therefore acquired when potentially meaningful symbols, concepts, and propositions are related to and incorporated within cognitive structure on a nonarbitrary, substantive basis. Since cognitive structure itself tends to be hierarchically organized with respect to level of abstraction, generality, and inclusiveness, the emergence of most new meanings reflects the subsumption of potentially meaningful symbolic material under more inclusive ideas in existing cognitive structure. Sometimes the new material is merely illustrative of or directly derivable from an already established and more inclusive concept or proposition in cognitive structure. More typically, however, new meanings are learned by a process of correlative subsumption. The new learning material in this instance is an extension, elaboration, or qualification of previously learned concepts or propositions. In contrast, "naming" and vocabulary acquisition largely involve the establishment in cognitive structure of a relationship of representational equivalence either between first-order concepts and concrete images or between higher-order categorical concepts and their criterial attributes (various combinations and transformations of the primary concepts).

Meaningful Verbal Learning

It follows from the previous discussion that meaningful verbal learning is simply that kind of learning which takes place when potentially meaningful verbal material is substantively related to or subsumed under an individual's existing knowledge in a nonarbitrary and nonverbatim fashion so that new meanings are acquired and made more available. Meaningful learning, then, presupposes both a meaningful learning set on the part of the learner and an exposure to potentially meaningful material that can be nonarbitrarily and substantively related to his existing knowledge.

Meaningful learning is by no means the same as the learning of meaningful materials. In meaningful learning, the materials are only *potentially* meaningful. If they were already meaningful, the goal of meaningful learning (that is, the acquisition of new meanings) would be accomplished in advance. It is true, of course, that in most potentially meaningful learning tasks, the component parts of the material are already meaningful; but in these instances the task as a whole is only potentially meaningful. For example, in the learning of a new geometrical theorem, each of the component words is already meaningful, but the learning task as a whole (that is, learning the meaning of the theorem) is yet to be accomplished.

This distinction between the meaningful learning of potentially meaningful material and the learning of already meaningful material is not mere academic hairsplitting. There are many examples of nonmeaningful or rote learning of meaningful materials. In the learning of a list of paired adjectives, each adjective is already meaningful, but the learning task itself is not potentially meaningful because these arbitrary associations between adjectives cannot be related to or subsumed under existing knowledge in a nonarbitrary, nonverbatim fashion. As mentioned above, in the learning of a new geometrical theorem, each component word is already meaningful, and the learning task as a whole is also potentially meaningful. But unless the learner manifests a meaningful learning set, no meaning will emerge: he will merely learn rotely a series of words which are arbitrarily related to one another and to his structure of knowledge. Thus, it is important to distinguish between the *meaningful* learning of *potentially* meaningful material, on the one hand, and the *rote* learning of *already* meaningful materials that either do or do not constitute potentially meaningful learning tasks, on the other.

Cognitive theorists maintain that meaningful verbal learning is the human mechanism par excellence for acquiring and storing the vast quantity of ideas and information represented in any body of knowledge. The distinctively human capacity for meaningful verbal learning depends upon such cognitive capabilities as symbolic representation, abstraction, categorization, and generalization. These latter abilities make possible the acquisition of generic concepts and propositions, and hence the subsumptive emergence and retention in cognitive structure of those correlative meanings comprising the bulk of knowledge.

Two factors are largely responsible for the superiority of meaningful verbal learning for processing and storing information. First, the nonarbitrary relatability (anchorability) of potentially meaningful material to established ideas in cognitive structure enables the learner to exploit his existing knowledge as an ideational matrix for interpreting new information. Thus, he avoids the interfering effects of concurrent rote information. Second, the substantive or nonverbatim nature of this relatability circumvents the drastic limitations imposed by the short item and time spans of rote memory on the amount of information that human beings can process and remember.

Cognition versus Perception

The distinction between perceptual and cognitive processes in meaningful verbal learning is particularly difficult to delineate because the products of both processes (that is, perceptions and meanings) result from interactions between verbal-stimulus input and cognitive structure. If verbal meaning results when potentially meaningful verbal materials are incorporated within relevant subsuming concepts in existing cognitive structure, and if this process of acquiring meanings is conceded to be cognitive in nature, when and how in this sequence of events does perception play a role in meaningful verbal learning?

In addition to the general theoretical importance of distinguishing between perception and cognition in this context, two special problems exist with respect to the relationship between these two processes in meaningful verbal learning. First, how does each process contribute to the measured discrepancy between stimulus and remembered content that designates the qualitative aspect of forgetting in meaningful retention? Second, to what extent do *repeated* encounters with potentially meaningful material alter the relationship between the two processes?

PERCEPTION PRECEDES COGNITION

Obviously, information and ideas have to be perceived before they can be incorporated into cognitive structure and give rise to meanings. Meaning, in other words, results from the subsumption of *perceived* potential meanings under established concepts and propositions. Perception therefore precedes cognition in meaningful verbal learning. This implies that the product of the perceptual process is not meaning itself, but rather the immediate content of awareness that follows from the preliminary interpretation of the sensory input (visual or aural) furnished by the potentially meaningful learning task. This perceptual content of awareness is intermediate, in terms of both time and process, between primitive sensation and the actual emergence of meanings. It consists of the separate meanings of the component words comprising the learning task as well as a general appreciation of the syntactical relationships among these components, but stops short of apprehension of the meaning of the message as a whole.

SELECTIVE DISTORTION OF MEANING

It follows from this analysis that most of the discrepancy initially occurring between the presented and the remembered content of verbal prose material, reported by Bartlett (1932) and others, reflects the influence of cognitive rather than perceptual processes. Selective emphasis, omission, and distortion resulting from initial interpretation of the presented material are manifestations of the selective emergence of meaning rather than of selective perception. The emerging new meanings are consonant with the learner's cultural frames of reference (Bartlett, 1932), attitudinal biases (McKillop, 1952), and experimentally manipulated advance sets (Jones and de Charms, 1958). This consonance occurs because each individual possesses an idiosyncratic array of established and relevant concepts in his cognitive structure under which the new material may be subsumed; the resulting meanings in each learning situation are a function of the *particular* subsumptions that occur. In all learning situations, the relative weight of idiosyncratic cognitive structure in determining the content of the meanings in question, as compared to that of the stimulus material, is enhanced by the use of prose material that is relatively unfamiliar, ambiguous, cryptic, and interpretable in several alternative ways.

Selective distortion of meaning can occur much less readily on a perceptual basis, and only to the extent that the component words and syntactical structure of the message are selectively perceived or misperceived. This eventuality is more likely to occur in laboratory than in real-life learning situations, and reflects the raising and lowering of tachistoscopic thresholds by motivational variables (Postman, Bronson, and Gropper, 1953) and antecedent meaningful context (Haselrud, 1959).

REPETITION TELESCOPES PERCEPTION AND COGNITION

Repeated encounters with or exposures to potentially meaningful messages change the relationship between perception and cognition in meaningful verbal learning. During the initial encounter, the potentially meaningful message is perceived, and the perceived content is then incorporated into cognitive structure to yield a corresponding meaning. As a result of this initial emergence of meaning and the concomitant alteration of cognitive structure, the learner is sensitized to the potential meaning in the message on subsequent encounters with it. Eventually, perhaps as early as the second trial, the two processes (perception and cognition) are telescoped into one. The message *immediately* conveys actual rather than potential meaning to the learner; verbal meaning, so to speak, becomes a product of perception rather than of cognition. Partly because of this telescoping effect, repetition, as pointed out below, has a particularly consolidating effect on retention: the learner does not have to grasp meanings on later trials and can concentrate solely on trying to remember them. Similarly, because of previous encounters, the immediate apprehension of the meanings of familiar component words in unfamiliar messages is part of the perceptual process preceding cognition during initial exposure to these messages.

THE PSYCHOLOGICAL ACCRETION AND ORGANIZATION OF KNOWLEDGE

The principle of subsumption, in my opinion, provides a key to understanding the processes underlying the psychological accretion and organization of knowledge. The human nervous system as a data-processing and data-storing mechanism is so constructed that new ideas and information can be meaningfully learned and retained only to the extent that more inclusive and appropriately relevant concepts are already available in cognitive structure to serve a subsuming role or to provide ideational anchorage. Thus, subsumption accounts for accretion to the psychological structure of knowledge by determining the acquisition of new meanings, their retention or resistance to assimilation, and the forgetting process itself. Over a period of time, the nature and outcome of this accretion process, that is, the cumulative residue of what is meaningfully learned, retained, and forgotten, determines how knowledge is psychologically organized. Therefore, the subsumption process also ultimately explains why an individual's organization of the content of a particular subject-matter discipline in his own mind consists of a hierarchical structure in which the most inclusive concepts occupy a position at the apex of the structure and subsume progressively less inclusive and more highly differentiated subconcepts and factual data.

Learning

Meaningful learning occurs as potentially meaningful material enters the cognitive field and interacts with, and is appropriately subsumed under, a relevant and more inclusive conceptual system. The very fact that such material is subsumable in nonarbitrary, substantive fashion accounts for its potential meaningfulness and makes possible the emergence of phenomenological meaning. If it were not subsumable, it would form discrete and relatively isolated traces.

The initial effects of subsumption, therefore, may be described as facilitating both learning and retention. Only orienting, relational, and cataloguing operations are involved at first; hence, for a variable period of time, the recently catalogued subconcepts and informational data can be dissociated from their subsuming concepts and are reproducible as individually identifiable entities. These preliminary operations are obviously essential for meaningful learning and retention, since the hierarchical incorporation of new material into existing cognitive structure not only is the basis for the emergence of new meaning but also must necessarily conform to the prevailing principle of cognitive organization. Furthermore, subsumption of the traces of the learning task by an established ideational system provides anchorage for the new material, and thus constitutes the most orderly, efficient, and stable way of retaining it for future availability.

The foregoing account of meaningful learning makes a sharp distinction between the rote-meaningful and the reception-discovery dimensions of learning. Contrary to the traditional position of Progressive Education, autonomous discovery, as part of a problem-solving approach to learning subject matter, is *not* considered a prerequisite for meaning as long as the learner employs a meaningful learning set and studies potentially meaningful material. Nevertheless, simply because in reception (expository) learning, the content of what is to be learned is presented rather than discovered, it cannot be assumed that such learning is purely a passive phenomenon. It is still necessary for the learner to relate the new material to relevant, established ideas in his own cognitive structure; to apprehend in what ways it is similar to and different from related concepts and propositions; to translate it into a personal frame of reference consonant with his own idiosyncratic experience and vocabulary; and often to formulate what is for him a completely new idea requiring much reorganization of existing knowledge.

Retention and Forgetting

Although the stability of meaningful material is initially enhanced by anchorage to relevant conceptual foci in the learner's cognitive structure, such material is gradually subjected to the erosive influence of the reductionist trend in cognitive organization. Because it is more economical and less burdensome to retain a single inclusive concept than to remember a large number of more specific items, the import of the latter tends to be incorporated by the generalized meaning of the former. When the second, or obliterative, stage of subsumption begins, the specific items become progressively less dissociable as independent entities until they are no longer available and are said to be forgotten. Thus, the same subsumability that is necessary for meaningful reception learning somewhat paradoxically provides the basis for later forgetting.

This process of memorial reduction to the least common denominator capable of representing cumulative prior experience is very similar to the reduction process characterizing concept formation. A single abstract concept is more manipulable for cognitive purposes than are the dozen diverse instances from which commonality is abstracted to form the concept. Similarly, the memorial residue of ideational experience is also more functional for future learning and problem-solving occasions when stripped of its tangential modifiers, particularized connotations, and less clear and discriminable implications. Hence, barring repetition or some other special reason (for example, primacy, uniqueness, enhanced discriminability, or the availability of a specially relevant and stable subsumer) for the perpetuation of dissociability, specific items of meaningful experience that are supportive of or correlative to an established conceptual entity tend gradually to undergo obliterative subsumption.

Unfortunately, however, the advantages of obliterative subsumption are gained at the expense of the differentiated body of detailed propositions and specific information constituting the flesh if not the skeleton of any body of knowledge. The main problem of acquiring a firm grasp of any academic discipline, therefore, is counteracting the inevitable process of obliterative subsumption that characterizes all meaningful learning.

Learning versus Retention

In reception learning, the distinctive attribute of both learning and retention is a change in the availability of the meanings derived from the subsumed learning material. Learning refers to the process of acquiring particular meanings from the potential meanings presented in the learning material and of making them more available. It represents an increment in the availability of new meanings; that is, it is the situation that prevails when new meanings emerge or are first established or when their dissociability strength is increased by repetition or by conditions increasing discriminability. Retention, on the other hand, refers to the process of maintaining the availability of a replica of the acquired new meanings. Thus, forgetting represents a decrement in availability; it is the situation that prevails between the establishment of a meaning and its reproduction or between two presentations of the learning material. Retention, therefore, is largely a later temporal phase and a diminished aspect of the same phenomenon or functional capacity involved in learning itself. Later availability is always at least in part a function of initial availability.

Derivative versus Correlative Subsumption

It is important to distinguish between two basically different kinds of subsumption occurring in the course of meaningful learning and retention. *Derivative* subsumption takes place when the learning material constitutes a specific example of an established concept in cognitive structure or when the material supports and illustrates a previously learned general proposition. In either event, the material to be learned is directly and self-evidently derivable from or implicit in an already established and more inclusive concept or proposition in cognitive structure. Under these circumstances, the meaning of the derivative material emerges quickly and effortlessly and, unless greatly overlearned, tends to undergo obliterative subsumption very rapidly. If such data are needed, however, they can easily be synthesized or reconstructed by appropriately manipulating specific elements of past and present experience so that they exemplify the desired concept or proposition.

More typically, however, new subject matter is learned by a process of *correlative* subsumption. The new material in this process is an extension, elaboration, or qualification of previously learned propositions. It is incorporated by and interacts with relevant and more inclusive subsumers in cognitive structure, but its meaning is not implicit in, and cannot be represented by, these latter subsumers. Nevertheless, in the interests of economizing cognitive organization and reducing the burden of memory, the same trend toward obliterative subsumption occurs. But in this instance the consequences of obliterative subsumption are not as innocuous as in derivative subsumption. When correlative propositions lose their identifiability and can no longer be dissociated from their subsumers, a genuine loss of knowledge occurs. The subsumers cannot adequately represent the meaning of the propositions in question, and hence the availability of the subsumers in memory does not make possible a reconstruction of the forgotten material.

The problem of acquiring a body of knowledge, therefore, is largely concerned with counteracting the trend toward obliterative subsumption in retaining correlative materials. Bruner's exclusive emphasis on "generic learning" or on acquiring "generic coding systems" (1957, 1959, 1960) as a means of facilitating school learning is unrealistic because it focuses on derivative aspects of subsumption which are atypical both of the subsumption process in general and of most instances of incorporating new subject matter. It is true, as he asserts, that most specifics of subject-matter content can be forgotten with impunity as long as they are derivable or can be reconstructed when needed from those generic concepts or formulas which are worth remembering. But the analogous forgetting of correlative content results in a loss of knowledge that cannot be regenerated from residual generic concepts. The conceptualizing trend in memorial reduction (that is, obliterative subsumption), which is functional or at the very worst innocuous in the case of derivative material, constitutes the principal difficulty in acquiring a body of knowledge in the more typical context of learning correlative propositions. Hence, the problem of meaningful learning and retention cannot ordinarily be solved by incorporating a representation of the criterial characteristics of a situation, or a contentless depiction of the ideal case (Bruner, 1960) and then ignoring the loss of specific content that occurs. The main purpose of learning generic concepts and propositions is not so much to make possible the reconstruction of forgotten derivative instances as to provide stable anchorage for correlative material; and it is the inhibition of the rate of obliterative subsumption in relation to this material that is the major problem confronting teachers in transmitting subject-matter content.

Psychological versus Logical Organization of Knowledge

It would be instructive at this point to contrast the psychological and the logical organizations of knowledge. I have already alluded to the distinction that the former is characterized by phenomenological or psychological meaning, whereas the latter is characterized by logical or potential meaning. In addition, there are important differences in the process of organization, the arrangement of component elements, and the cognitive maturity of content.

PROCESS OF ORGANIZATION

The logical and the psychological structures of knowledge obviously differ in the kinds of processes that enter into their organization. From a process standpoint, the laws applying to the psychological organization of knowledge are the laws of meaningful learning and retention; whereas the laws governing the logical organization of knowledge are derived from the logic of classification. Nevertheless, these two sets of process laws overlap. Thus, not only do both kinds of organizational processes rely on the logic of classification, but they also employ the same principle of structuring knowledge in terms of unifying elements which manifest the greatest generality, inclusiveness, and explanatory power and which are capable of relating and integrating the widest possible array of subject matter.

The difference between the two kinds of organizational processes stems from two characteristics of the psychological but not the logical structure of knowledge:

1. The psychological structure of knowledge is subject throughout its development to systematic decrement. This decrement results from the gradual loss of the identity and availability of subsumed materials as their distinctive import is assimilated by the more general meaning of their more inclusive and established subsumers.

2. Both the learning of new ideas and their memorial resistance to the aforementioned decremental processes are largely a function of such properties of existing cognitive structure as the availability of relevant subsumers, the stability and clarity of these subsumers, and their discriminability from the new learning material.

Therefore, the psychological structure of knowledge is an organized residue of inclusive subsumers and of those elements of related subsumed materials that have managed to resist the process of memorial reduction or assimilation, plus the residual products of forgetting, namely, the original subsuming ideas which have completely assimilated their subsumed materials.

It is reasonable to assume that the psychological and the logical structures of knowledge differ with respect to the sequential placement, ordering, and arrangement of component elements. The kinds of processes involved in the psychological organization of knowledge imply a hierarchical type of structure which is progressively differentiated in terms of degree of generality and inclusiveness. This is the kind of structure which obviously results when new learning materials are subsumed under relevant, more inclusive concepts in existing cognitive structure. The logical structure of knowledge, on the other hand, although using general and inclusive ideas as organizing elements, strives for topical relatedness and homogeneity rather than progressive differentiation in the sequential arrangement of subject matter. Psychologically, however, this kind of structure is not approached until the later stages of subject-matter sophistication. Only after an individual develops mature cognitive capacities and acquires an expert, specialized knowledge of a subject can he easily reorganize the psychological structure in terms of the topically most homogeneous and systematic ordering of relationships among component facts, concepts, and propositions. This degree of parallelism between the logical and the psychological structure of knowledge does not exist during the early stages of intellectual development and subject-matter sophistication.

It is apparent that the logical structure of a subject is necessarily dependent on and a product of human cognitive processes. Only human beings who possess mature cognitive capacities and whose psychological structure of knowledge in a particular discipline is highly sophisticated can structure this field of knowledge in a logically satisfactory fashion. It is evident, therefore, that the following degree of interdependence prevails between the logical and the psychological structures of knowledge: On the one hand, the psychological structure of knowledge is a derivative of subject-matter content abstracted from the logical structure of knowledge, and psychological meaning is an idiosyncratic elaboration of logical meaning. On the other hand, the logical structure of knowledge is a topically systematized reorganization of the psychological structure of knowledge as it exists in mature scholars in a particular discipline.

COGNITIVE MATURITY OF CONTENT

Just as level of subject-matter sophistication determines the sequential arrangement of the psychological structure of knowledge, general level of intellectual maturity—particularly along the concrete-abstract dimension of intellectual functioning—determines the cognitive maturity of the content contained in this structure. The logical structure of subject matter, on the other hand, does not manifest any developmental variability in cognitive maturity of content. Whereas the level of abstraction, generality, explicitness, and precision characteristic of the logical structure of subject-matter content is invariably and necessarily high, being the product of sophisticated scholars, the same high level of maturity in these cognitive attributes of content is found in the psychological structure of knowledge only when the individual is in the advanced stages of intellectual development.

During the elementary-school period, for example, when the child is in the stage of concrete logical operations (Inhelder and Piaget, 1958), he is dependent upon current or recent concrete-empirical experience for understanding or manipulating relationships among abstractions, or ideas about ideas. When such experience is not available, he finds abstract propositions unrelatable to cognitive structure and hence devoid of meaning. This dependence upon concrete-empirical props self-evidently limits his ability meaningfully to grasp and manipulate relationships among abstractions, since he can acquire only those understandings and perform only those logical operations which do not go beyond the concrete and particularized representation of ideas implicit in his use of props. Thus, where complex abstract concepts and propositions are involved, he is largely restricted to a concrete or intuitive level of cognitive functioning—a level that falls far short of the clarity, precision, explicitness, and generality associated with the more advanced stage of intellectual development.

Beginning in the junior-high-school period, however, the child becomes increasingly less dependent upon the availability of concrete-empirical experience in meaningfully relating complex abstract propositions to cognitive structure. Eventually, after sufficient gradual change in this direction, a qualitatively new capacity emerges: the intellectually mature individual becomes capable of understanding and manipulating relationships among abstractions without any reference whatsoever to concrete, empirical reality. Instead of reasoning directly from a particular set of data, he uses indirect, second-order abstractions for structuring the data; instead of merely grouping data into classes or arranging them serially in terms of a given variable, he deals with all possible or hypothetical relations among ideas. He can now transcend the previously achieved level of intuitive thought and understanding and can formulate general laws relating general categories of variables that are divorced from the concrete-empirical data at hand. His concepts and generalizations, therefore, tend more to be second-order constructs derived from relationships among previously established abstractions already one step removed from the data.

Relative level of abstraction of subject-matter content becomes an important pedagogic consideration in determining the order in which pupils should be introduced to the different scientific disciplines. On strictly logical grounds, it might be argued that the various disciplines should be introduced in the order of their relative phenomenological complexity—that the phenomenologically more fundamental and simple laws of physics and chemistry should be mastered before the phenomenologically more complex and variable data of biology are studied. Psychologically, however, the logically simple laws of physics and chemistry are more abstract and difficult than the logically complex laws of biology, which are both more descriptive in nature and closer to everyday, concrete experience.

FACTORS INFLUENCING MEANINGFUL LEARNING AND RETENTION

It follows, from the very nature of accretion to the psychological structure of knowledge through the subsumption process, that existing cognitive structure—an individual's organization, stability, and clarity of knowledge in a particular subject-matter field at any given time—is the major factor influencing the learning and retention of meaningful new material in this same field. Since potentially meaningful material is always learned in relation to an existing background of relevant concepts, principles, and information, which provide a framework for its reception and make possible the emergence of new meanings, it is evident that the stability, clarity, and organizational properties of this background crucially affect both the accuracy and the clarity of these emerging new meanings and their immediate and long-term retrievability. If cognitive structure is stable, clear, and suitably organized, accurate and unambiguous meanings emerge and tend to retain their dissociability strength or availability. If, on the other hand, cognitive structure is unstable, ambiguous, and unorganized or chaotically organized, it tends to inhibit meaningful learning and retention. Hence, it is largely by strengthening relevant aspects of cognitive structure that new learning and retention can be facilitated. Thus, the details of a certain discipline are learned as rapidly as they can be fitted into a contextual framework consisting of a stable and appropriate body of general concepts and principles. When there is a deliberate attempt to influence cognitive structure so as to maximize meaningful learning and retention, the heart of the educative process is touched.

In my opinion, the most significant advances that have occurred in recent years in teaching such subjects as mathematics, chemistry, physics, and biology have been predicated on the assumption that efficient learning and functional retention of ideas and information are largely dependent upon the adequacy of cognitive structure. Since existing cognitive structure reflects the outcome of all previous subsumption processes, it in turn can be influenced substantively by the inclusiveness and integrative properties of the particular unifying and explanatory principles used in a particular discipline, and programmatically by methods of presenting, arranging, and ordering learning materials and practice trials.

Cognitive Structure and Transfer

I have just hypothesized that past experience influences new meaningful learning and retention by virtue of its impact on relevant properties of cognitive structure. If this is true, all meaningful learning necessarily involves transfer because it is impossible to conceive of any instance of such learning that is not affected in some way by existing cognitive structure; and this learning experience, in turn, results in new transfer by modifying cognitive structure. In meaningful learning, therefore, cognitive structure is always a relevant and crucial variable, even if it is not deliberately influenced or manipulated so as to ascertain its effect on new learning. Even a single practice trial in laboratory studies of short-term learning reflects the influence of existing cognitive structure and induces modification of that structure.

Much more saliently than in laboratory types of learning situations, school learning requires the incorporation of new concepts and information into existing and established cognitive framework with particular organizational properties. The transfer paradigm still applies here, and transfer still refers to the impact of prior experience upon current learning. But in school learning, prior experience is conceptualized as a cumulatively acquired, hierarchically organized, and established body of knowledge which is organically relatable to the new learning task, rather than a recently experienced constellation of stimulus-response connections influencing the learning of another discrete set of such connections. The relevant aspects of past experience in this type of transfer paradigm are such organizational properties of the learner's subject-matter knowledge as clarity, stability, generalizability, inclusiveness, cohesiveness, and discriminability—not degree of similarity between stimuli and responses in the two learning tasks. Recent prior experience is not regarded as influencing current learning by interacting *directly* with the stimulus-response components of the new learning task, but only insofar as it modifies significant relevant attributes of cognitive structure.

Because training and criterion tasks in laboratory studies of transfer have usually been separate and discrete, theorists have tended to think in terms of how prior task *A* influences performance on criterion task *B*. If performance has been facilitated, in comparison with that of a control group which had not been exposed to task *A*, it is said that positive transfer has occurred. Actually, however, in typical classroom situations, *A* and *B* are not discrete but continuous. Task *A* is a preparatory stage of *B* and a precursive aspect of the same learning process; *B* is not learned discretely but in relation to *A*. Hence, school learning deals not so much with transfer in the literal sense of the term as with the influence of prior knowledge on new learning in a continuous, sequential context. This latter learning context also typically involves correlative subsumption. Hence, as pointed out above, the relevant transfer effect of usual concern is not the ability to reconstruct forgotten details from generic principles or to recognize new phenomena as specific variants of these principles, but rather enhanced ability to learn and *retain* the more detailed correlative material.

Moreover, unlike Bruner's (1960, p. 16) use of the term "nonspecific transfer," the kind of transfer just described is not restricted to those instances in which "a general idea . . . can be used as a basis for recognizing subsequent problems as special cases of the ideas originally mastered." Actually, the principal effect of existing cognitive structure on new cognitive performance is on the learning and retention of newly presented materials where potential meanings are given—not on the solution of problems requiring the application and reorganization of cognitive structure to new ends. Thus, a transfer situation exists whenever existing cognitive structure influences new cognitive functioning, irrespective of whether it is in regard to reception learning or problem solving.

Principal Cognitive-Structure Variables

The learner's acquisition of a clear, stable, and organized body of knowledge constitutes more than just the major long-term objective of classroom learning activity or the principal *dependent* variable (or criterion) to be used in evaluating the impact of all factors impinging on learning and retention. This knowledge (cognitive structure), once acquired, is *also* the most significant *independent* variable influencing the learner's capacity for acquiring more new knowledge in the same field. The importance of cognitive-structure variables, however, has been generally underestimated in the past because preoccupation with noncognitive, rote, and motor kinds of learning has tended to focus attention on such situational and intrapersonal factors as practice, drive, incentive, and reinforcement variables. But in the search for knowledge about the processes underlying meaningful reception learning and retention, it is not enough to stress the importance of relevant antecedent experience that is represented in existing cognitive structure. Before fruitful experimentation can be attempted, it is necessary to specify and conceptualize those properties (variables) of cognitive structure that influence new learning and retention.

In the more general and long-term sense, cognitive-structure variables refer to significant organizational properties of the learner's *total*
knowledge in a given subject-matter field and their influence on his
future academic performance in the same area of knowledge. In the
more specific and short-term sense, cognitive-structure variables refer
to the organizational properties of only the *immediately* or proxi-
mately relevant concepts within a particular subject-matter field and
their effects on the learning and retention of small units of related
subject matter.

One important variable affecting the incorporability of new meaningful material is the *availability* in cognitive organization of relevant
subsuming concepts at an appropriate level of inclusiveness to provide
optimal anchorage. The appropriate level of inclusiveness may be defined as that level which is as proximate as possible to the degree of
conceptualization of the learning task—considered, of course, in relation to the existing degree of differentiation of the subject as a whole in
the learner's cognitive background. The more unfamiliar the learning
task, that is, the more undifferentiated the learner's background of
relevant concepts, the more inclusive or highly generalized the subsuming concepts must be in order to be proximate.

What happens if an appropriate relevant subsumer is not available
in cognitive structure when new potentially meaningful material is
presented to a learner? If some existing concept cannot be utilized for
subsuming purposes, rote learning occurs. More typically, however,
some tangentially relevant subsumer is pressed into service. This type
of subsumer obviously cannot provide very adequate or efficient anchorage; therefore, it gives rise to unclear, unstable, and ambiguous
meanings of short term. The same outcome may also result when
appropriate relevant subsumers *are* available, if their relevance is not
recognized. For both reasons, therefore, in meaningful learning situations, it is preferable to introduce suitable organizers whose relevance is
made explicit rather than to rely on the spontaneous availability of
appropriate subsumers.

A second important factor presumably affecting the retention of
potentially meaningful learning material is the extent to which the
material is *discriminable* from the established conceptual systems that
subsume it. A reasonable assumption here, borne out by preliminary

234 · LEARNER BEHAVIOR

investigation, is that if the new concepts are not originally salient and clearly discriminable from established subsuming foci, they can be adequately represented by the latter for memorial purposes, and would not persist as dissociable entities. In other words, only discriminable categorical variants of more inclusive concepts have long-term retention value.

Last, the learning and longevity of new meaningful material in memory are a function of the *stability and clarity* of its subsumers. Ambiguous and unstable subsumers not only provide weak anchorage for related new materials, but also cannot be easily discriminated from them.

IMPLICATIONS OF COGNITIVE-STRUCTURE VARIABLES FOR TEACHING

What are some of the pedagogic implications both of the foregoing model of the psychological structure of knowledge and of the factors that influence its accretion and organization? Perhaps the major implication for teaching is that since existing cognitive structure reflects the outcome of all previous meaningful learning, control over the accuracy, clarity, longevity in memory, and transferability of a given body of knowledge can be most effectively exercised by attempting to influence the crucial variables of cognitive structure.

In principle, deliberate manipulation of the relevant attributes of cognitive structure for pedagogic purposes should not meet with undue difficulty. It can be accomplished both substantively and programmatically (1) by using for organizational and integrative purposes those unifying concepts and propositions in a particular discipline that have the widest explanatory power, inclusiveness, generalizability, and relatability to the subject-matter content of that discipline; and (2) by employing suitable programmatic principles of ordering the sequence of subject matter, constructing its internal logic and organization, and arranging practice trials. Hence, transfer in school learning consists primarily of so shaping the learner's cognitive structure, by manipulating the content and arrangement of his antecedent learning experiences in a particular subject-matter area, that subsequent learning experiences are maximally facilitated.

A Cognitive-Structure Theory / AUSUBEL • 235

The principal strategy advocated in this chapter for deliberately manipulating cognitive structure so as to enhance proactive facilitation or to minimize proactive inhibition involves the use of appropriately relevant and inclusive introductory materials (that is, organizers) that are maximally clear and stable. These organizers are introduced in advance of the learning material itself and are also presented at a higher level of abstraction, generality, and inclusiveness. Since the substantive content of a series of organizers is selected on the basis of their appropriateness for explaining, integrating, and interrelating the material they precede, this strategy simultaneously satisfies the substantive as well as the programing criteria specified above for enhancing the organizational strength of cognitive structure.

In contrast to organizers, summaries and overviews are ordinarily presented at the same level of abstraction, generality, and inclusiveness as the learning material itself. They simply emphasize the salient points of the material by omitting less important information, and they largely achieve their results by repetition.

The function of the organizer is to provide ideational scaffolding for the stable incorporation and retention of the more detailed and differentiated material that follows in the learning passage, as well as to increase discriminability between the latter and related interfering concepts in cognitive structure. With completely unfamiliar material, an "expository" organizer is used to provide relevant proximate subsumers. These subsumers primarily furnish ideational anchorage in terms that are already familiar to the learner. With relatively familiar material, a "comparative" organizer is used to integrate new concepts with basically similar concepts in cognitive structure as well as to increase discriminability between new and existing ideas which are essentially different but confusable.

Progressive Differentiation of Learning Tasks

When subject matter is programed in accordance with the principle of progressive differentiation, the most general and inclusive ideas of the discipline are presented first and are then progressively differentiated in terms of detail and specificity. This order of presentation presumably corresponds to the postulated way in which knowledge is represented, organized, and stored in the human nervous system. The order also recognizes that new ideas and information can be meaningfully learned and retained only to the extent that more inclusive and appropriately relevant concepts are already available in cognitive structure to play a subsuming role or to furnish ideational anchorage.

Even though this principle seems rather self-evident, it is rarely followed in actual teaching procedures or in the organization of most textbooks. The more typical practice is to segregate topically homogeneous materials into separate chapters and to present them throughout at an undifferentiated level of conceptualization in accordance with a logical outline of subject-matter organization. This practice, although logically sound, is psychologically incongruous with the postulated process of how meaningful learning occurs, that is, with the mechanism of accretion through a process of progressive differentiation of an undifferentiated field. Thus, in most instances, students are required to learn the details of new and unfamiliar disciplines before they have acquired an adequate body of relevant subsumers at an appropriate level of inclusiveness.

As a result of this practice, students and teachers are coerced into treating meaningful materials as if they were rote in character, consequently experiencing unnecessary difficulty and little success in learning and retention. Mathematics and science teaching, for example, still rely heavily on rote learning of formulas and procedural steps, on recognition of stereotype "type problems," and on mechanical manipulation of symbols. In the absence of clear and stable concepts which can serve as anchoring points and organizing foci for the incorporation of new potentially meaningful material, students have little choice but to memorize learning tasks for examination purposes.

Progressive differentiation in programing subject matter is accomplished by using a hierarchical series of organizers (in descending order of inclusiveness), each organizer preceding its corresponding unit of detailed, differentiated material. In this way, not only is an appropriately relevant and inclusive subsumer made available to provide ideational scaffolding for each component unit of differentiated subject matter, but the various units in relation to one another are also progressively differentiated, that is, organized in descending order of inclusiveness. The initial organizers, therefore, furnish anchorage at a global level before the learner is confronted with *any* of the new material. For example, a generalized model of class relationships is first provided as a general subsumer for *all* new classes, subclasses, and species before more limited subsumers are provided for the particular subclasses or species they encompass.

Thus, when undergraduates are first exposed to organizers presenting relevant and appropriately inclusive subsuming principles, they are better able to learn and retain completely unfamiliar ideational material (Ausubel, 1960). Differential analysis in another similar study showed that the facilitating effect of organizers occurs only for those individuals who have relatively poor verbal ability and who therefore tend spontaneously to structure such material less effectively (Ausubel and Fitzgerald, 1962). The greater retention by pro-South than by pro-North students of a controversial passage presenting the Southern point of view on the Civil War can also be explained in terms of the relative availability of appropriate subsuming ideas (Fitzgerald and Ausubel, 1963). The pro-North students lack relevant subsumers to which the pro-South passage can be functionally related. The material therefore cannot be clearly and securely anchored to cognitive structure, competes with existing meanings, and is consequently ambiguous and subject to rapid forgetting. The pro-South students, on the other hand, possess relevant subsuming concepts; hence, the material can be readily anchored to cognitive structure and is less ambiguous and subject to forgetting.

In sequential school learning, knowledge of earlier material in the sequence plays much the same role as an organizer in relation to later material in the sequence: it constitutes relevant ideational scaffolding and hence a crucial limiting condition for learning the latter material. Two of the principal advantages of programed instruction are its careful sequential arrangement and gradation of difficulty, which insure that each attained increment in learning serves as an appropriate foundation and anchoring post for the learning and retention of subsequent items in the ordered sequence.

Consolidation

By insisting on consolidation or mastery of ongoing lessons before new material is introduced, the instructor makes sure of continued readiness and success in sequentially organized learning. This kind of learning presupposes, of course, that the preceding step is always clear, stable, and well organized. If it is not, the learning of all subsequent steps is jeopardized. Hence, new material in the sequence should never be introduced until all previous steps are thoroughly mastered. This principle also applies to those kinds of intratask learning in which each component task (as well as entire bodies of subject matter) tends to be compound in content and to manifest an internal organization of its own.

Abundant experimental research (for example, Duncan, 1959; Morrisett and Hovland, 1959) has confirmed the proposition that prior learnings are not transferable to new learning tasks until they are first overlearned. Overlearning, in turn, requires an adequate number of adequately spaced repetitions and reviews, sufficient intratask repetitiveness prior to intra- and intertask diversification, and opportunity for differential practice of the more difficult components of a task. Frequent testing and provision of feedback, especially with test items demanding fine discrimination among alternatives varying in degree of correctness, also enhance consolidation by confirming, clarifying, and correcting previous learnings.

The stability and clarity of existing cognitive structure are important both for the depth of anchorage they provide in related new learning tasks as well as for their effects on the discriminability of these new tasks. The discriminability of new learning material is in large measure a function of the clarity and stability of existing concepts in the learner's cognitive structure to which the new material is relatable. In learning an unfamiliar passage about Buddhism, for example, subjects with a greater knowledge of Christianity make significantly higher scores on the retention test than do subjects with less knowledge of Christianity (Ausubel and Fitzgerald, 1961; Ausubel and Youssef, 1963). This significantly positive relationship between Christianity and Buddhism scores holds up even when the effect of verbal ability is statistically controlled. When a similarly organized passage about Zen Buddhism is introduced after the Buddhism passage, knowledge of Buddhism facilitates the learning of Zen Buddhism when verbal ability is held constant.

In more directly sequential tasks, where the learning of Part II materials presupposes understanding of Part I materials, the stability and clarity of the antecedent material crucially affect the learning and retention of the later material (Ausubel and Fitzgerald, 1962). Even in the learning of controversial ideas contrary to prevailing belief (for example, the learning by Illinois students of the Southern point of view about the Civil War), the students who know more about the Civil War period are better able to learn and remember the "other-side" arguments (Fitzgerald and Ausubel, 1963), presumably because they find them more discriminable from established ideas than do less knowledgeable students. Thus, much of the effect of overlearning—both on retaining a given unit of material and on learning related new material—is probably a reflection of enhanced discriminability, which can be accomplished by increasing the clarity and stability of either the learning material itself or its subsumers.

Perhaps the most important feature of automated instruction, insofar as the facilitation of meaningful learning and retention is concerned, is not the incentive and drive-reducing effects of immediate feedback, but the extent to which such instruction influences learning by enhancing the stability and clarity of cognitive structure. By deferring the introduction of new material until prior material in the learning sequence is consolidated, automated instruction maximizes the effect of stability of cognitive structure on new learning. Moreover, by supplying immediate feedback, it rules out and corrects alternative wrong meanings, misinterpretations, ambiguities, and misconceptions before they have an opportunity to impair the clarity of cognitive structure and thereby inhibit the learning of new material.

Integrative Reconciliation

The principle of integrative reconciliation in programing instructional material can be best described as antithetical in spirit and approach to the ubiquitous practice among textbook writers of compartmentalizing and segregating particular ideas or topics within respective chapters or subchapters. Implicit in this practice is the assumption (perhaps logically valid, but certainly psychologically untenable) that pedagogic considerations are adequately served if overlapping topics are handled in self-contained fashion, so that each topic is presented in only *one* of the several possible places where treatment is relevant and warranted, that is, the assumption that all necessary cross-referencing of related ideas can be satisfactorily performed, and customarily is, by students. Hence, little serious effort is made explicitly to explore relationships among these ideas, to point out significant similarities and differences, and to reconcile real or apparent inconsistencies.

Among the undesirable consequences of this approach is that multiple terms are used to represent concepts which are intrinsically equivalent except for contextual reference. This multiplicity generates incalculable cognitive strain and confusion and encourages rote learning. Second, the erection of artificial barriers between related topics obscures their important common features. The acquisition of insights dependent upon recognition of these commonalities is thus impossible. Third, since significant differences among apparently similar concepts are not made clear and explicit, these concepts are often perceived and retained as identical. Finally, adequate use is not made of relevant, previously learned ideas as a basis for subsuming and incorporating related new information.

The principle of integrative reconciliation also applies when subject matter is organized along parallel lines, that is, when related materials are presented in serial fashion but there is no *intrinsic* sequential dependence from one topic to the next. Unlike sequentially organized subject matter, successive learning tasks are inherently independent of one another in the sense that understanding of Part II material does not presuppose understanding of Part I material. Each set of material is logically self-contained and can be adequately learned by itself without any reference to the other. Order of presentation is therefore immaterial. This situation, for example, prevails in presenting alternative theoretical positions in ethics, religion, and epistemology; opposing theories of biological evolution; and different systems of learning and personality theory.

Nevertheless, although successive learning tasks of similarly organized material are not intrinsically dependent on one another, much cognitive interaction obviously occurs among them. Elements of a parallel sequence learned earlier serve an orienting and subsuming role in relation to elements presented later. The latter are comprehended and interpreted in terms of existing understandings and paradigms provided by analogous, familiar, previously learned, and already established concepts in cognitive structure. Hence, learning the unfamiliar new ideas requires that they be adequately discriminable from the established familiar ideas. Without discriminability, the new meanings are so permeated with ambiguities, misconceptions, and confusions as to be partially or completely nonexistent as dissociable units. If, for example, the learner cannot discriminate between new idea A' and old idea A, A' does not really exist for him; it is phenomenologically the same as A. Furthermore, even if the learner can discriminate between A and A' at the moment of learning, unless the discrimination is sharp and free from ambiguity and confusion, there will be a tendency in time for A' to be remembered as A when the two ideas interact during the retention interval.

In some instances of meaningful learning and retention, the principal difficulty is not one of discriminability but of apparent contradiction between established ideas in cognitive structure and new propositions in the learning material. Under those conditions, the learner may dismiss the new propositions as invalid, may try to compartmentalize them as isolated entities apart from previously learned knowledge, or may attempt integrative reconciliation under a more inclusive subsumer. Compartmentalization, of course, may be considered a common defense against forgetting. Arbitrary isolation of concepts and information prevents interaction with and obliterative subsumption by relevant concepts in cognitive structure. This is a modified variety of rote learning, in which new learning material is allowed to interact with only certain of several potential subsumers. Through overlearning, relatively stable subsumption may be achieved, but the fabric of knowledge as a whole is unintegrated and full of internal contradictions.

Organizers may be expressly designed to further the principle of integrative reconciliation. They do this by explicitly pointing out in what ways previously learned, related concepts in cognitive structure are either basically similar to or essentially different from new ideas in the learning task. Hence, on the one hand, organizers explicitly draw upon and mobilize all available concepts in cognitive structure that are relevant for, and can play a subsuming role in relation to, the new learning material. This maneuver effects great economy of learning effort, avoids the isolation of essentially similar concepts into separate, noncommunicable compartments, and discourages the confusing proliferation of multiple terms to represent ostensibly different but essentially equivalent ideas. On the other hand, organizers increase the discriminability of genuine differences between the new learning materials and analogous but often conflicting ideas in the learner's cognitive structure. Comparative organizers, for example, have been successfully used in facilitating the meaningful learning and retention of an unfamiliar passage dealing with Buddhism (Ausubel and Fitzgerald, 1961; Ausubel and Youssef, 1963) and of a controversial passage presenting the Southern point of view about the Civil War (Fitzgerald and Ausubel, 1963).

Internal Logic of Learning Material

The internal logic of the learning task is obviously relevant for meaningful learning and retention outcomes since the existence of logical or potential meaning within the material (that is, its relatability to a hypothetical human cognitive structure with the necessary background knowledge) is a prerequisite for the emergence of psychological (phenomenological) meaning. Logical meaning, as previously pointed out, is a function of the plausibility, lucidity, and nonarbitrariness of the material rather than of its logical or substantive validity. Hence, "internal logic" is used somewhat idiosyncratically here to designate those properties of the material that enhance these latter criteria of logical meaning.

At least four aspects of the internal logic of material affect the extent to which it is endowed with potential meaning:

1. Adequacy of definition and diction, including precise, consistent, and unambiguous use of terms; the definition of all new terms prior to use; and the use of the simplest and least technical language that is compatible with conveying precise meaning.

2. Use of concrete-empirical data and of relevant analogies when developmentally warranted or otherwise helpful in the acquisition, clarification, or dramatization of meaning.

3. Encouragement of an active, critical, reflective, and analytic approach on the part of the learner by requiring him to reformulate the material in terms of his own vocabulary, experiential background, and structure of ideas.

4. Explicit delineation of the distinctive logic and philosophy of

A Cognitive-Structure Theory / AUSUBEL • 243

each subject-matter discipline—that is, its implicit epistemological assumptions; the general problems of causality, categorization, inquiry, and measurement that are specific to the discipline; and the distinctive strategy of learning how to learn the particular subject matter of the discipline.

PRACTICE AND TASK VARIABLES

Practice variables are important both because they influence the efficiency of learning and retention of the immediate task at hand and because, by virtue of such influence, they significantly affect all three cognitive-structure variables specified above and, accordingly, the learning of related new materials. Most of the knowledge about the effects of practice variables, however, pertains to rote and motor learning and to single rather than sequentially organized tasks.

Frequency

In terms of historical significance, theoretical importance, and relevance for current educational practice, few issues in educational psychology are more crucial than the role of frequency in learning and retention. Yet, ever since E. L. Thorndike repudiated the "law of frequency," the theoretical stance of educational psychology on this issue has tended to be confused, contradictory, and somewhat schizophrenic. On the one hand, in accordance with Thorndike's pronouncement, it is held that frequency is unnecessary for and really makes little difference in learning outcomes. This position finds much favor with progressivist educators, who are hostile to drill of any kind; with gestalt theorists, who conceive of all learning as insightful; and with "discontinuity" ("nonincremental") learning theorists, who maintain that learning invariably takes place in a single trial. Thus, educational theory frequently tends to minimize the role of drill, regarding it as rote, mechanical, passive, old-fashioned, psychologically unnecessary for the learning process, and actually harmful for active, meaningful learning.

On the other hand, educational psychologists implicitly accept the concept of a learning curve, in which gradual increments in learning are plotted against successive trials, and they place great stress on the importance of overlearning for long-term retention. This latter position is actually adopted by the vast majority of teachers, coaches, parents, and students, who follow the maxim "Practice makes perfect."

Quite obviously, both positions cannot be simultaneously valid. The upshot of this conflict in beliefs is that there is still considerable reliance on drill in actual classroom practice, but the drill is half-hearted, apologetic, and performed in ways which detract from its effectiveness.

EDUCATIONAL ISSUES VIS-À-VIS FREQUENCY

In actual classroom practice, the issue of frequency is expressed most saliently in the conflict between structured practice (drill) and "natural" learning settings, and between repetitive and diversified practice. Proponents of activity programs tend to favor task heterogeneity in practice; that is, they seek, in part, to escape the opprobrium associated with drill by stressing diversity both in the types of learning tasks and in the examples of each type that are presented to the learner. This approach undoubtedly has merit, in that, other factors being equal, the defining attributes of a new concept are learned most readily when the concept is encountered in many different contexts. Such experience obviously enhances the generalizability of abstract knowledge and the use of transferable skills. It also minimizes the possibility of boredom and of a rote, rigid approach to learning.

However, if diversity of learning-task content is provided at the expense of attaining mastery of the particular component tasks which comprise it, its over-all effect on learning is detrimental. Positive transfer from one learning task to another requires that particular examples of a given type of task as well as particular types of tasks first be consolidated (that is, mastered, overlearned) before new task content is introduced.

Many cases of disability in such academic skills as arithmetic, reading, spelling, and grammar can undoubtedly be attributed to over-emphasis on the importance of diversified experience in unstructured learning situations. Failure to provide sufficient repetitive practice (drill) in antecedent learning tasks does not allow for the adequate

A Cognitive-Structure Theory / AUSUBEL • 245

mastery of these tasks that is essential if sequentially related tasks are to be successfully handled in the acquisition of concepts, generalizations, and intellectual skills.

Activity-program enthusiasts also tend to insist that factual information and intellectual skills be acquired in the real-life, functional contexts in which they are customarily encountered, rather than through the medium of artificially contrived drills and exercises. It is true, of course (providing that all other factors are equal), that learning is enhanced when the conditions of practice closely resemble the conditions under which the skill or knowledge in question will eventually be used. Wholly natural settings, however, rarely provide the practice conditions that are either necessary or optimal for efficient learning. Generally, it is only during the latter stages of learning, *after* component aspects of the learning task have already been identified and mastered in structured practice sessions that naturalistic "dress rehearsals" become feasible.

This is so, in the first place, because unstructured learning settings typically fail to furnish examples that come along frequently, repetitively, and close enough together to make possible the learning of concepts and principles. Under these circumstances, there is also inadequate opportunity for differential practice of particularly difficult components. Second, unstructured practice does not receive the benefit either of skilled pedagogic selection, presentation, and organization of material or of careful sequencing, pacing, and gradation of difficulty.

FREQUENCY AND MEANINGFUL LEARNING

The role and significance of frequency are different for meaningful than for rote learning precisely because rote and meaningful learning processes themselves are so different from each other. Repeated encounters with the same array of stimulation presumably enhance rote learning and retention by increasing the strength of discrete, arbitrary, and verbatim associative linkages, that is, their resistance to the short-term interfering effects of prior and subsequent stimulation. The same repetitiveness presumably enhances meaningful learning and retention by increasing the dissociability strength of nonarbitrary, nonverbatim relationships that have been substantively incorporated within a more inclusive subsuming concept or principle in existing cognitive structure, that is, the emergence of clear and stable meanings and their resistance to irreversible subsumption.

It is reasonable to assume that sheer repetition would play a more significant role in the learning and short-term retention of discrete and arbitrary associations largely isolated from cognitive structure than it would in the learning and longer-term retention of materials that can be meaningfully incorporated within that structure. In meaningful as opposed to rote learning situations, such other factors as the availability of clear and stable subsumers, the discriminability between these subsumers and the learning task, and the internal logic and lucidity (the potential meaningfulness) of the learning task undoubtedly detract from the role played by repetition. Nevertheless, on theoretical grounds, there are many reasons for believing that repetition is typically required not only for the acquisition and retention of adequately clear, stable, and valid meanings, but also for that degree of consolidation of antecedent portions of sequentially organized subject matter that is necessary for efficient learning of subsequent portions.

THE EFFECTS OF FREQUENCY

The position is taken here that frequency affects learning and retention in two different and complementary ways. Directly, each successive trial cumulatively modifies existing cognitive structure in an organizational sense by summating the effects of such variables as contiguity and feedback, and hence enhancing the strength of meanings. Indirectly, the alterations in cognitive structure resulting from earlier trials affect learning and retention processes during subsequent trials.

The first and most direct consequence of repetition on learning is an increase in the dissociability strength of recently acquired meanings. This dissociability is reflected in an increment in the immediate and delayed availability of the material. An additional study trial provides another opportunity for the learner to interact with the material and to relate the potential meanings it embodies to his structure of knowledge, thereby enabling actual or experienced meanings to eventuate and/or be consolidated. In other words, he has another opportunity to acquire potential meanings that he partially or completely missed on the first trial, as well as to consolidate meanings initially established at that time.

A Cognitive-Structure Theory / AUSUBEL · 247

Another study trial also provides the learner with informational feedback, in the form of textual reference, for testing the correctness of the knowledge he retained from the first trial. This testing confirms correct meanings, clarifies ambiguities, corrects misconceptions, and indicates areas of weakness requiring differential concentrated study. The net effect is the consolidation of learning.

In addition to enhancing meaningful learning and retention in the two aforementioned direct ways, repetition also influences these processes in two indirect ways through modifications in cognitive structure wrought by earlier trials. These alterations in cognitive structure increase the learner's responsiveness to the learning task on subsequent trials and also enable him to cope better with decremental processes. Thus, I would hold that frequency has distinctive effects of its own on learning and retention that cannot be reduced simply to the opportunity which additional trials provide for *other* effective variables to influence, cumulatively, the processes and outcomes of learning and retention.

In the first place, not only do repeated presentations of the learning task determine and enhance cognitive content, but also the newly acquired cognitive content *reciprocally* induces changes in the *perceived* learning task which make it more learnable. In other words, initial contact with the material *sensitizes* the learner to the meanings it contains when he encounters it again. Since he had previously derived meanings from the learning material on the first trial—by incorporating potential meanings into his cognitive structure—now, on second reading, the ideas as a whole, not merely the component words, immediately convey actual rather than potential meaning to him. Hence, on the second trial, actual rather than potential meanings interact with the residue of those recently acquired meanings in his cognitive structure established as a consequence of his first encounter with the material. This type of interaction particularly enhances the consolidation of the previously established meanings, since this time the learner does not have to grasp meanings and can concentrate solely on trying to remember them. Furthermore, the establishment of gross meanings on the first trial sensitizes the learner to more refined meanings and subtle distinctions on the second trial.

Initial contact with the learning material also has an "immunizing" effect with respect to factors making for forgetting when the learner interacts with the material on subsequent occasions. It is postulated that previous obliterative experience with subsuming processes confers some degree of immunity to the recurrence of their detrimental effects on retention, and hence promotes a higher residual level of dissociability strength. As a result of prior experience both of trying to remember and of forgetting the material, the learner becomes aware of those negative elements in the learning situation that induce forgetting, that is, areas of instability, ambiguity, confusion, and nondiscriminability. Thus forearmed, he can take appropriate measures to counteract those factors that foster forgetting when he encounters the material again. For example, he can strengthen relevant subsuming concepts and particularly weak components of the learning task, and increase discriminability between established ideas and related new propositions. In this way, the experience of prior forgetting tends to prevent new forgetting when material is relearned.

Other Variables

A research void prevails with regard to the status of such other traditional practice variables as massed versus distributed practice, recitation, task homogeneity, part versus whole learning, prompting and guidance, type and overtness of response, and amount and kind of feedback. Most of the research either has involved rote learning in nontransfer situations or, if concerned with meaningful learning, has yielded equivocal findings as a result of being conducted almost exclusively in a context of small step size and low error rate.

Knowledge about significant task variables in relation to meaningful verbal learning is similarly negligible. There are no good reasons, either theoretical or empirical, for believing that task size, step size, and task difficulty affect the efficiency of rote and meaningful learning in similar ways. Yet, in favoring small step and task size and low task difficulty, almost all programers of instructional materials implicitly tend to assume that there is similarity. Also, practically nothing is known about intertask pacing (that is, about optimal time intervals between different segments of sequentially organized materials) and about the ways in which the internal logic of instructional material affects the extent to which it is endowed with potential meaning.

Motivational Variables in Meaningful Learning

Role and Kinds of Motivation

Motivation is probably less indispensable for reception learning than it is for any other kind of learning. Because such learning requires relatively little effort and, when successful, furnishes its own reward, less reliance need be placed on existing drives and motives within the learner, on incentive conditions, and on extrinsic rewards than is required in rote learning or problem solving. But to assert that meaningful learning (particularly of a fragmentary and short-term nature) can occur in the absence of motivation is not to deny the fact that motivation can significantly facilitate learning whenever it is present and operative.

The causal relationship between motivation and learning is also typically reciprocal in nature. Both for this reason and because motivation is not an indispensable condition of learning, it is unnecessary to postpone learning activities until appropriate interests and motivations have been developed. Frequently the best way of teaching an unmotivated student is to ignore his motivational state for the time being and to concentrate on teaching him as effectively as possible. Much to his surprise and his teacher's, he will learn despite his lack of motivation. From the satisfaction of learning, he will probably develop the motivation to learn more. Paradoxically, therefore, it may be discovered that the most effective method of developing intrinsic motivation to learn is to focus on the cognitive rather than on the motivational aspects of learning and to rely on the motivation that is developed retroactively from successful educational achievement.

Also because meaningful learning provides its own reward, cognitive drive (the desire for knowledge as an end in itself) is more important here than in rote or instrumental learning and is potentially the most important kind of motivation in meaningful reception learning. Cognitive drive is probably derived in a very general way from curiosity tendencies and from related predispositions to explore, manipulate, understand, and cope with the environment. However, these predispositions originally manifest potential rather than actual motivating properties and are obviously nonspecific in content and direction. Their potential motivating power is actualized in expression and particularized in direction by the developing individual, both as a result of successful exercise and the anticipation of future satisfying consequences from further exercise and as a result of the internalization of the values of those significant persons in the familial and cultural environments with whom he identifies. Far from being largely endogenous in origin, therefore, specific cognitive drives or interests are primarily acquired from and dependent upon particular experience. Hence, it is observed again that the relationship between cognitive drive and learning, like the relationship between motivation and learning generally, is a reciprocal one.

Despite the potential centrality of cognitive drive for the motivation of meaningful reception learning, it is nevertheless true that in this utilitarian, competitive, and achievement-oriented culture, such extrinsic considerations as career advancement, ego enhancement, and anxiety reduction become, with increasing age, progressively more significant sources of motivation for school learning. Even material rewards tend to become less ends in themselves than symbols of academic status, achievement, and competitive advantage, and hence subsidiary sources of self-esteem. Eventually, of course, the viability of the cognitive drive as an intrinsic, task-oriented type of motivation is impaired as a consequence of the almost exclusive prior association of intellectual interests and activities with motives toward ego enhancement and anxiety reduction. If the desire to learn and understand is almost invariably exercised in the context of competing for grades, obtaining degrees, preparing for a vocation, striving for advancement, and reducing the fear of academic and occupational failure, there is little reason for believing that much intellectual curiosity survives as an independent goal. This trend is reflected in the progressive decline in school interests and intellectual enthusiasm as children move up the academic ladder.

Hence, if it is desired to develop the cognitive drive so that it remains viable during the school years and in adult life, it is necessary to move still further away from the educational doctrine of gearing the curriculum to the spontaneously expressed interests, current concerns, and life-adjustment problems of pupils. Although it is undoubtedly unrealistic and even undesirable in this culture to eschew entirely the utilitarian, ego-enhancement, and anxiety-reduction motivations for learning, increasingly greater emphasis must be placed upon the value of knowing and understanding as goals in their own right, quite apart from any practical benefits they may confer. Instead of denigrating subject-matter knowledge, as so many allegedly progressive educators have done over the past fifty years, educators must discover more efficient methods of fostering the long-term acquisition of meaningful and usable bodies of knowledge and of developing appropriate intrinsic motivations for such learning.

Even though *particular* instances of learning may be largely unmotivated, it is undoubtedly true that the subject matter in question must be related to felt needs for significant, *long-term* meaningful learning to occur. The inability to see any need for a subject is the reason students mention most frequently for losing interest in high-school studies. Doing without being interested in what one is doing results in relatively little permanent learning, since it is reasonable to suppose that only that material which is relevant to areas of concern in the psychological field of the individual can be meaningfully incorporated and integrated into cognitive structure on a long-term basis. Learners who have little need to know and understand quite naturally expend relatively little learning effort; manifest an insufficiently meaningful learning set; fail to develop precise meanings, to reconcile new material with existing concepts, and to reformulate new propositions in their own terms; and do not devote enough time and effort to practice and review. Material is therefore never sufficiently consolidated to form an adequate foundation for sequential learning. Hence, it is unrealistic to expect that school subjects can be effectively learned and retained until pupils develop a felt need to acquire knowledge as an end in itself, since much school knowledge can never be rationalized as necessary for meeting the demands of daily living. Once such a need is developed, learning naturally becomes more meaningful; but it is difficult to stimulate the development of such a need until subject matter can be presented meaningfully in the first place.

Mediation of Motivational Influences

Cognitive variables are *directly* implicated in the cognitive interactional process during meaningful reception learning and retention and are therefore directly involved in the determination of dissociability strength. Their effects are also mediated through the same mechanisms in both learning and retention. Typically, however, motivational and attitudinal variables are *not directly* involved in the cognitive interactional process. They energize and expedite this process during learning by enhancing effort, attention, and immediate readiness for learning, and thereby facilitate dissociability strength catalytically and nonspecifically. Furthermore, the effects of motivational variables on learning and retention, respectively, unlike their cognitive counterparts, are not mediated through the *same* mechanisms. After learning is completed, these variables cannot independently affect dissociability strength (that is, apart from their effects on learning itself) and can only influence retention during the reproductive phase of memory by elevating thresholds of availability and by shaping the qualitative aspects of imaginative reconstruction.

Thus, motivational and attitudinal factors affect meaningful reception learning and retention in ways that are qualitatively different from the comparable effects of relevant cognitive variables. These variables directly and specifically influence the parameters of the cognitive interactional process underlying meaningful reception learning and retention, and are thus organically involved in the determination of dissociability strength. Motivational and attitudinal variables, on the other hand, are not organically involved in the cognitive interactional process or in the determination of dissociability strength. For the most part, they merely impinge on it in nonspecific facilitating fashion. For example, through such mechanisms as the mobilization of effort and the concentration of attention, more repetitions of the material are completed within the stipulated learning time, and each repetition is conducted more efficiently. The net result is an indirect, over-all increase in dissociability strength for the learning process so energized.

Motivation and Retention

It is also reasonable to assume that the effects of cognitive variables on meaningful reception learning continue along similar lines during retention and are mediated by the same mechanisms. Whatever these effects on the interactional process are, they are simply extended temporally from learning to retention. Thus, the rate at which dissociability strength declines during retention is always proportional to the initial dissociability strength influenced by these same variables during the course of learning. However, once the learning sessions have been completed and the cognitive interactional products have been formed, a channel of communication no longer remains open for the energizing and expediting aspects of motivation to influence dissociability strength, even in a catalytic or nonspecific way. Hence, whenever motivational factors appear to affect retention independently of learning, a new mechanism is required to mediate this influence. This mechanism is operative during the reproductive stage of memory rather than during the retention interval per se. The factors that determine the elicitability of memory are considered briefly below.

In order for subsumed materials to be available in memory, their dissociability strength must exceed the threshold of availability. The most important cause of the unavailability of meaningfully learned materials, therefore, is a fall in dissociability strength below the level required to reach this threshold. However, still another independent, although secondary, source of variability in the availability of subsumed materials inheres in fluctuations in the threshold of availability itself. Hence, a particular item of knowledge may manifest more than sufficient dissociability strength to exceed the typically prevailing threshold value, but may still be unavailable because of some temporary elevation of the threshold of availability. The most common reasons for such an elevation of threshold value are (1) initial learning shock, (2) the competition of alternative memories, and (3) negative attitudinal bias or motivation *not* to remember (repression). Removal of these threshold-raising or memory-inhibiting factors (that is, disinhibition) results in an apparent facilitation of memory. The most extreme example of disinhibition occurs during hypnosis, which both removes repression and, through restriction of the learner's field of awareness, reduces the competing effect of alternative memory systems to a bare minimum. More commonly, such inhibitory conditions as initial learning shock and the competition of alternative memories tend to dissipate spontaneously. The apparent increment in retention that results in the former instance is known as reminiscence.

Both theoretical considerations and the weight of the available evidence suggest that motivational factors influence meaningful retention selectively by inhibiting rather than facilitating particular thresholds of recognition and recall. Positive ego involvement and favorable attitudinal bias, in other words, do not increase retention by lowering thresholds of memorial elicitation; rather, strong motivation to forget and certain kinds of attitudinal bias (that is, in ego-threatening or anxiety-producing situations) may selectively promote forgetting by raising thresholds of availability (repression). Thus, unlike the situation in learning, not only is the selective influence of motivational variables on retention inhibitory rather than facilitating, but also the influence of these variables is mediated solely through a change in thresholds of memorial elicitation, without any change whatsoever in dissociability strength. Although the latter remains constant, recall or recognition is nevertheless rendered momentarily more difficult because of the selective elevation of particular thresholds of availability.

It appears likely, therefore, that motivational factors influence retention per se only in those relatively rare instances where retrieval of particular information would be ego-threatening or anxiety-producing. The more common facilitating effect of positive attitudinal bias on retention can be explained more parsimoniously in terms of the *cognitive* or nonaffective components of attitude structure. In regard to positive attitudinal bias, these elements tend to provide a highly clear and stable set of subsuming elements for the learning of controversial material (Fitzgerald and Ausubel, 1963).

As Bartlett (1932) pointed out, motivational variables are probably also involved in the reconstructive aspects of the reproductive phase of memory, that is, in making a selection from among the available remembered items and in organizing them into a coherent verbal response to meet the demands of a current situation. Strictly speaking, however, the framing of a response in which memories are reported is not part of the retention process.

Drive Reduction and Reinforcement

Whether drive reduction has a direct and selective strengthening (reinforcing) effect on the drive-reducing response *itself* (thereby increasing the probability of its recurrence) and how this effect is mediated are exceedingly complex and controversial topics, full discussion of which is obviously beyond the scope of this chapter. It suffices to take the position here that drive reduction directly and selectively reinforces instrumental responses only in the *rote* learning of discrete, arbitrary, and verbatim stimulus or stimulus-response connections and that it does so not by retroactively increasing habit or associative strength (as a consequence of the satisfying effects induced by the response), but by lowering thresholds of elicitability or availability.

In *meaningful* learning, on the other hand, no mechanisms exist through which the satisfying effects of drive reduction can lead directly to the reinforcement of successful (drive-reducing) meanings. Unlike the informational consequences of drive reduction, these effects cannot increase the dissociability strength of previously learned meanings. They can only energize meaningful learning catalytically on succeeding trials or related tasks. As previously pointed out, meaningfully learned ideas are psychologically and neurophysiologically much too complex for their thresholds of availability to be directly lowered by any kind of variable, motivational or otherwise.

This does not mean, however, that reward (or drive reduction) does not facilitate meaningful learning. Reward and reinforcement, after all, are not coextensive variables. Reinforcement is only one aspect of reward—that aspect which directly increases the elicitability of *rotely* learned responses by lowering their thresholds of availability. In meaningful learning, reward has two other more indirect kinds of facilitating effects.

In the first place, from a motivational standpoint, successful learning energizes subsequent learning efforts by enhancing the learner's self-confidence, encouraging him to persevere, and increasing the subjective attractiveness of the learning task. At the same time, it motivates the individual to practice, rehearse, and perform what he has already learned and encourages him to continue developing and exercising the motives that were satisfied or rewarded, namely, the desire for knowledge both as an end in itself and as a means of enhancing status and self-esteem.

Second, drive reduction, whether of cognitive or extrinsic drives, also has all of the cognitive or informational effects of feedback. These effects are probably more important for meaningful learning and retention than are the motivational and reinforcement consequences of drive reduction. By indicating areas of confusion, correcting errors, clarifying ambiguities and misconceptions, and confirming appropriately understood meanings, the cognitive aspects of drive reduction consolidate the stability and clarity of learned material, enhance the subject's confidence in the correctness of his understandings, and enable him to focus his learning efforts selectively on inadequately learned portions of the material. They have not only informational value for subsequent trials of the same learning task, but also transfer value for related new tasks.

CONCLUSION

Much disillusionment has arisen in recent years regarding the relevance and usefulness of learning theory for educational practice. It is the thesis of this chapter that the historical failure of learning theory to provide an adequate basis for pedagogy is not indicative of any inherent limitation in the applicability of such theory to problems of teaching. It is rather a reflection of the prevailing tendency for educational psychologists uncritically to extrapolate theory and evidence from rote, motor, animal, short-term, and stimulus-response learning to meaningful ideational learning in the classroom.

I still cling to the view that psychological processes are implicated in the acquisition of subject-matter knowledge and that it is important for teachers and curriculum specialists to understand the nature of these processes and how they are influenced by relevant and significant variables. Toward this end, I have presented a theory of school learning which proposes a cognitive-structure theory of meaning and a subsumption theory of meaningful learning and forgetting. I have also attempted to identify the major cognitive-structure variables that influence meaningful learning and retention and to indicate how these variables may be deliberately manipulated in actual teaching practice. Finally, I have tried to relate the role of certain traditional practice, task, and motivational variables to the proposed theory of school learning.

PART·IV·

INTEGRATIVE

FORMULATIONS

In designating the formulations in Part IV as "integrative," I do not mean to imply that they were written with the intention of somehow weaving together the contents of the preceding chapters. Instead, they are integrative in the sense that they give about equal emphasis to teacher behavior and learner behavior. Thus, they are set apart from the formulations in Part II, which emphasize teacher behavior, and those in Part III, which emphasize learner behavior.

The two chapters in Part IV approach theories of instruction from different directions. Siegel and Siegel enter through a methodological door by suggesting the potential fruitfulness of studying interactions as well as main effects and by regarding control-group comparison designs as relatively sterile for theoretical purposes. Gagné's entrance is gained by developing a taxonomy of learned performances and by inquiring into the conditions that are effective for stimulating each one.

In spite of this difference in approach, there are two important points of contact between these chapters. They concern essentially similar variables, and they take a similar position concerning the nature of "effective" instruction.

The Siegels distinguish four classes of interacting variables: those related to learners, instructors, environments, and courses. Although Gagné organizes the variables into two classes (learner and situational), the overlap between these conceptualizations is evident.

More importantly, both formulations emphasize interactions between the variables. Gagné writes: "Instruction may be thought of as the institution and arrangement of the *external* conditions of learning in ways which will optimally interact with the internal capabilities of the learner, so as to bring about a change in these capabilities." And the Siegels say: "The burden of investigation . . . is to discover combinations of learner, instructor, environmental, and course variables optimizing desired educational outcomes."

Despite this fundamental agreement about interactions, the formulations diverge in their applications. In the latter portion of his chapter, Gagné considers specific instructor behaviors in terms of their appropriateness or inappropriateness for particular learners and objectives. Siegel and Siegel end their chapter by formulating tentative generalizations about the interactions within and between variable classes.

9

The Instructional Gestalt

LAURENCE SIEGEL AND

LILA CORKLAND SIEGEL*

ℐ

THIS CHAPTER PROPOSES A PARADIGM FOR INVESTIGATING WHAT WE HAVE termed the "instructional gestalt." We anticipate that implementation of the paradigm increases the likelihood of making further progress toward developing a theory of instruction which integrates both teacher and student behavior. After making a case for the paradigm, we describe its application and cite some representative findings.

THE CASE FOR A MULTIVARIATE PARADIGM

This paradigm was developed largely to overcome certain methodological deficiencies described in Chapter 2 as impediments to theorizing about instruction. If it is true, as we believe, that the development of instructional theory has been impeded by a persistent emphasis upon experimental control-group comparisons, the solution is to alter the way in which instructional research is conducted and the kinds of questions toward which it is directed. The time is long overdue for investigators to stop inquiring whether one mode of presentation is as good as another and to undertake instead investigations of those conditions thought to optimize the realization of educational objectives

* The studies we describe in this chapter were conducted under grant from the Office of Education, U.S. Department of Health, Education, and Welfare while we were affiliated with Miami University (Oxford, Ohio).

under clearly specified and delimited conditions (Siegel, 1960; Deese, 1961).

The investigation of conditions requires increased precision in conceptualizing the purposes of education and the settings (or learning environments) that may be provided to accomplish these purposes. Although proportionately in the minority, several studies specifically focusing upon alternative *procedures* rather than existing products have been reported in the literature. Investigations of the relative effectiveness of presenting one versus both sides of an issue and of the advantage of audience participation (Hovland, Lumsdaine, and Sheffield, 1949) are noteworthy examples of this more precise and fertile approach.

The Purposes of Education

From a practical standpoint, disagreements about the relative importance of objectives within the cognitive and affective domains have significant implications for structuring learning environments. On the one hand, there is the traditional view of the classroom as an environment for transmitting knowledge. This is in sharp contrast to the view, reflecting a psychotherapeutic bias, that cognitive accomplishments without affective involvement have little or no significant influence on behavior (Rogers, 1961). The former position suggests that the learner is a manipulatable object to whom something is done by the teacher and his resources. The latter stresses the importance of "independent discovery" and leads to a view of teaching and learning wherein teacher and learner reverse roles frequently and comfortably. The distinction from the learner's point of view is between "being taught *to*" and "participating and being involved *in*."

As a rule, individual courses within a curriculum generally strike some sort of middle ground between these extremes. Large lecture or televised courses may tend to dispense more information; seminar courses at an advanced level may tend to encourage more student involvement and participation. But some students under some circumstances become vitally involved even in lecture courses, while certain students under some circumstances remain personally uninvolved even in seminar classes.

Learning Environments

The observation that students are differentially involved even when exposed to an apparently uniform instructional environment calls attention to the problem of heterogeneity within such grossly designated conditions as "lecture," "seminar," "televised," or "conventional" classes. These designations are predicated primarily upon a consideration of certain aspects of the physical environment in which the course is conducted, neglecting variations within each condition. Furthermore, gross comparisons between conditions so designated tend to neglect factors aside from the classroom environment that also bear upon teaching and learning.

Neither the *criterion-of-effectiveness* paradigm nor the *process* paradigm (for example, Stone and Leavitt, 1955; Mitzel, 1957; Runkel, 1958; Ryans, 1960; Smith, 1960) is intrinsically suited to overcoming the lack of homogeneity within each of the investigated conditions. Furthermore, both kinds of paradigm oversimplify the reality of classroom instruction in ways that may seriously interfere with the validity and generalizability of resultant findings.

What is required instead is a paradigm sufficiently broad in concept to embrace the full multiplicity and patterning of factors that enter into the teaching-learning configuration. This paradigm must include, but not be limited to, the variables comprising the classroom environment. In addition, it must allow for the likelihood that the factors comprising the instructional complex interact differently in different kinds of classroom environments.

Multivariate Analysis in Instructional Research

The two distinguishing features, multivariate analysis and provision for studying interactions among variables, suggested for such a paradigm have been discussed or implied by several other writers. Hovland, Lumsdaine, and Sheffield (1949) made a similar case for multivariable experimentation with particular reference to media research. They distinguished among "population," "film," and "external" variables and hypothesized that the impact of a single variable within any one of these clusters might be contingent upon the accompanying variables. In a broader context, Tiedeman and Cogan (1958) and

Stanley (1960) have cautioned against ignoring or only superficially considering the effects of possible interactions among instructional variables.

It is precisely these kinds of interactions that we suspect are partly responsible for producing cancellation effects in mean-performance comparisons between grossly described classroom groups. Thus, the thrust of the present chapter is to conceptualize the formal educational process in a broad framework giving appropriate recognition to the variety of instructional settings, teaching procedures, simultaneously exposed learners, and multiple criteria of effectiveness without sacrificing either the essential flavor of the instructional process or the specificity of its conditions. In order to convey the intended comprehensiveness of this framework, we have chosen to call it a paradigm of the *instructional gestalt*. Although this paradigm has undergone continual refinement (Siegel, 1960; Siegel and Siegel, 1963, 1964), we still regard it as rudimentary.

The Instructional-Gestalt Paradigm

Whereas the classroom or student station is a *site* of teaching, it does not constitute the entire context for learning. Students arrive at this site with a history; their activities while there are but a small fragment of their ongoing daily regimen; and their concerns during each fragmented learning session reflect the interaction of this history with other aspects of the immediate real world both in and out of the classroom. Although some instructors behave as though they are providing students with the one valid educational experience they will ever have in their entire lifetimes, theirs is a uniquely biased perception. The instructor's intellectual commitment to an academic discipline is the culmination for him of many educational and personal experiences. Most undergraduate students are not yet ready to make such a commitment.

Independent Variables

We were guided by four fundamental considerations in identifying specific variables for inclusion in the paradigm:

1. Each variable could legitimately be expected to have some bearing upon at least one criterion of instructional effectiveness. This expectation usually followed directly from previous research; for example, academic ability has been clearly identified as an important independent variable. Occasionally, the expectation was an inference about variables not previously explored in a comprehensive manner.

2. Each variable had to be either measurable or amenable to categorization and classification. Thus, the variables comprising the paradigm had to be defined with a certain amount of precision.

3. Each variable could be "manipulated" along some unidimensional continuum. Organismic variables are indirectly "manipulated" by identifying critical subjects from a subject pool on the basis of their test scores and assigning them to particular kinds of instruction. Nonorganismic variables, like features of the classroom environment or techniques of instructional presentation, may be directly manipulated and empirically controlled.

4. There is reason to believe that each variable underlies what takes place in the instructional gestalt in a "fundamental" or "causative" fashion. This is a highly subjective consideration, particularly when considering organismic variables. Because of the interrelationships among these variables, inferred cause-effect relationships are exceedingly tenuous. Nevertheless, without this requirement, the variables embodied in this paradigm would have proliferated to the detriment of the scheme's usefulness. Thus, we somewhat arbitrarily decided that a variable like "instructor's neatness of appearance" was not sufficiently important materially to affect the instructional gestalt.

Four major classes of independent variables are included in the conceptual scheme: those related to learning environments, instructors, learners, and courses.

LEARNING ENVIRONMENTS

The learning environment is defined by the physical setting and characteristics of the classroom or other instructional site and by certain events transpiring in the physical environment. The paradigm recognizes that classrooms constitute the primary but not the sole learning environment. Other kinds of environments include the library carrel (for independent-study courses), the student station in a language or other autoinstructional laboratory, the room at home where an off-campus telecourse is taken for credit, and so on.

Some of the specific variables entering into the composition of the environment include (1) class size; (2) physical characteristics of the classroom; (3) the physical presence or absence of an "authority figure" maintaining discipline, taking attendance, and the like; (4) the methods by and extent to which audiovisual devices of various kinds are utilized; and (5) the extent and level of participation by students in class activities.

It is readily apparent that gross classifications by environment, like "televised versus conventional classes," provide for variations with respect to such variables. However, it is important to note that different sections of any course designated by the same gross environmental classification (for example, "televised class") may really constitute different environments. A useful analogy here is that of siblings who experience different environments even though raised in the same home.

INSTRUCTOR VARIABLES

The teacher's behavior both in and out of class constitute the "strategies and tactics of teaching." Whereas learning environments describe the physical setting and structure provided for the course, the instructor variables describe the unique contribution to a given learning environment made by the teacher. The teacher's operations that have been selected as particularly pertinent to the general conceptual scheme for the instructional gestalt are described in the following paragraphs.

1. *The instructional objectives manifested to his students by his behavior in class and by his examining procedures.* Note that this variable is defined by classroom behavior rather than by the instructor's verbalizations to the investigator about his objectives. The teacher, for example, who maintains that he is attempting to stimulate critical thinking but who tests and grades only for rote recall actually reinforces rote memorization in at least two ways. First, the test itself implies to the students that rote recall is the most important instructional objective. From the student's perspective, a test reflects in its sampling of questions the importance attached by the teacher to the

various aspects of the course content. Second, since tests are graded, students are rewarded for learning whatever content the test samples.

In addition to test content, a teacher manifests his instructional objectives by his behavior both in and out of the classroom. Such manifestations may be obvious and deliberate, as when the teacher announces to his class that it is not necessary to learn a particular point, that the understanding of some issue must be deferred until a factual base has been acquired, or that a question raised by a student is more properly the subject matter of some other course. Manifestations of instructional objectives may also be less obvious, and possibly not even deliberate on the teacher's part. A gesture, facial expression, reply that is overly brief or lengthy, and so on may effectively cue students about the content deemed most important by the instructor.

2. *The amount and quality of personal contact between teacher and students.* Instructors differ considerably in the extent to which they display interest in students as persons and derive genuine satisfaction from developing personal relationships with them. Some teachers actively seek personal contact with students, occasionally extending their influence beyond the confines of the classroom. Their students are more likely than those of "avoidant" teachers to sense a rapport with the instructor and to feel that they are personally known to him. "Avoidant" teachers perceive their role as limited to dispensing information or conducting in-class discussion in a rather impersonal fashion. They may not even learn their students' names and generally are rather unavailable to their students either in or out of class.

3. *The intellectual climate developed by the instructor.* Provision or lack of provision for classroom participation by students has already been cited as one of the important variables in defining the structure of the learning environment. In an environment arranged to encourage student participation, the instructor may encourage either "intellectually divergent" or "intellectually convergent" participation as poles on a continuum of intellectual climates (terminology after Guilford, 1959).

In a convergent climate, subjects may ask questions closely related to the immediate situation (lecture presentation, laboratory task, demonstration, and the like) with some assurance that their questions will be answered. A convergent climate for interaction aids the student's comprehension of whatever tasks or knowledge is germane to the immediate learning environment.

In an intellectually divergent climate, the student is reinforced for stating ideas and making intellectual discoveries. The instructor implementing this climate is not threatened by questions to which he does not have facile answers and which may be only tangentially related to his planned sequence for the class period. This kind of climate rewards such student behaviors as application, synthesis, perception of relationships, and creative problem solving.

LEARNER VARIABLES

The students exposed to any combination of classroom environment and instructor variables are heterogeneous with respect to a large number of learner variables. The ones selected as particularly pertinent to the paradigm are the following:

1. A constellation of characteristics variously designated as intelligence, academic ability, scholastic aptitude, and the like.

2. Knowledge about the subject matter prior to enrollment in the course. Such prior knowledge may have been obtained from courses previously taken or from readings of a general nature.

3. Motivation with respect to the specific course content. Why is the student taking the course? What significance does it have for him in terms of his vocational or personal objectives?

4. The student's set toward education. The extreme poles on the continuum of set may involve a predisposition, on the one hand, to accumulate isolated or specific facts and, on the other, to attempt generalization by learning fact clusters, developing concepts, and discovering principles.

5. Creativity in organizing his perceptual field and in solving problems.

COURSE VARIABLES

Certain kinds of courses lend themselves more readily than others to particular kinds of structures (learning environments) and instructor behaviors. This is true because courses differ in the kinds of students attracted to them, the kinds of instructors desirous of teaching them, and the demands of the subject matter. Hence, at least three features of the course are important to the paradigm: (1) the subject-matter area, (2) the level of presentation (elementary or advanced), (3) whether the course is required or elected by the students.

Interactions among Independent Variables

In the foregoing paragraphs, we have provided a basis for comprehensive thought about the process of teaching and learning by identifying four clusters of independent variables and specifying certain critical variables within each cluster. Once the instructional gestalt is conceptualized in this fashion, the importance of interactions among the independent variables is immediately apparent. These interactions occur both among the variables within a given cluster and among variables across the four clusters.

By way of simple illustration, consider the learner variable "academic ability." The powerful main effects of this variable have been repeatedly demonstrated in scholastic settings. Other things being equal, bright students tend to learn more than do less capable students. However, at least for certain criteria, academic ability has been shown to interact with another learner variable: creativity (Getzels and Jackson, 1962). It is conceivable also that the interaction between ability and creativity could be further elaborated, under some circumstances, by such other learner characteristics as motivation, set, and prior knowledge of the task under consideration.

In addition to these interactions among organismic variables, academic ability undoubtedly interacts with selected environmental, instructor, and course variables. Whereas specific aspects of the instructional gestalt may stimulate bright students, these same elements may threaten or discourage students who are not so bright. Other aspects of the instructional gestalt that are encouraging to low-ability students may cause brighter ones to lose interest or to "coast."

As a generalization, the effects of various kinds of instruction within a given course can be conceptualized and empirically studied in relation to variations in learning environments, learner characteristics, and the relevant activities of the instructor. The burden of investigation proceeding from this view is to discover combinations of learner, instructor, environmental, and course variables optimizing desired educational outcomes.

The conceptual framework heretofore described does not in any way limit the range of potential dependent variables. The impact of particular configurations within the instructional gestalt can be assessed by both "effectiveness" and "process" criteria. The criteria might be derived from measures of student acquisition or retention, teacher satisfaction, quality of thinking evoked by presentations, and so on. The particular criteria selected for study must follow from the prior delineation of limited course objectives and broader educational or curricular objectives. Different interactions within the gestalt are to be expected for the various criteria.

One of the ultimate goals of effective education is to maximize each student's capacity for thinking critically and creatively (Ericksen, 1962). To implement this broad curricular objective, Bruner (1961) emphasizes the importance of teaching about relationships (that is, "structure"), and Rogers (1961) similarly emphasizes a "problem" orientation. The emphases are alike in that they maximize educational gain for the student by a process of independent discovery founded upon intrinsic involvement.

It is evident that some instructional configurations are more appropriate to this objective than others. It has been demonstrated, for example, that students think more relevantly in discussion classes than in lecture classes (Bloom, 1953). However, it is equally clear that practical exigencies often militate against utilization of the instructional configuration most appropriate to this objective. Hence, it is important to discover the limits of effectiveness of alternative instructional configurations in terms of a fairly broad range of criteria.

Four classes of student-oriented criteria have been selected as meaningful dependent variables for exploring the instructional gestalt: achievement, thought, attitude, and extraclass behavior.

Achievement

A hierarchy of potential achievements in subject-matter areas has been thoroughly described in the well-known *Taxonomy of Educational Objectives* edited by Bloom (1956). For initial explorations within the context of our paradigm, it seems sufficient to distinguish between two levels of achievement, designated *factual* and *conceptual*.

ACQUISITION AND RETENTION OF FACTS

We have already argued against continued reliance upon assessments of factual acquisition and retention as the sole or even a major criterion for educational research. Nevertheless, it is evident that virtually all educational experiences attempt to convey or illustrate a body of factual content as at least a partial objective. Thus, measures of factual acquisition and retention must be included in any attempt to list broadly applicable research criteria.

The importance placed upon this criterion must be proportional to the emphasis upon factual learning within the instructional gestalt under consideration. When factual learning occupies (as it *should*) a relatively low position in the hierarchy of instructional objectives for a particular gestalt, it ought to occupy a correspondingly minor position in the hierarchy of criteria for assessing the effectiveness of variable combinations within that gestalt.

ACQUISITION AND RETENTION OF CONCEPTS

We use "conceptual learning" as a broad classification embodying some of the higher levels of cognitive attainment outlined in the *Taxonomy of Educational Objectives*. Conceptual learning is really a criterion cluster that could, if desired, be differentiated into its more homogeneous and narrowly defined components. However, during the initial phases of exploration using the paradigm, we regarded it as sufficient to group together all cognitive attainments requiring more than mere factual acquisition. Thus we combine, for criterion purposes, those cognitive behaviors involving the application of facts for problem solution, and the interrelationship of previously discrete facts to form principles.

The key to our use of "conceptual acquisition" as a criterion is the cognitive operation performed by the learner. We can illustrate this with the developmental principle of progressive differentiation of animal behavior from mass to specific responses. Because of the treatment accorded this principle in the lectures and in the textbook, we might be compelled to classify knowledge of the principle merely as factual knowledge. This would be the case when the instructor or text has stated this developmental principle in a way that would make it possible for a student to have learned it by rote.

In order to be classed as "conceptual" learning for criterion purposes, the students must be required by the criterion measure either (1) to construct the principle from the facts at his disposal without having previously encountered a statement of the principle per se, or (2) to apply the principle, regardless of how it was acquired, to integrate or explain the relationship between what for him had previously been disparate facts.

Thought

Even when course examinations adequately reflect the instructional objectives, they are not entirely satisfactory as research criteria because examination performance may be contaminated by factors outside of the classroom (see discussion in Chapter 2, pp. 29–30).

An assessment of the quality of student thinking during the class period while the presentation is being made or the discussion is in progress is therefore useful as a supplemental criterion. Such an assessment provides a unique criterion since it is obtained *in situ* rather than as a postcourse measure. Reports of student thinking are systematically sampled at "critical points" in the presentation and are judged (that is, weighted) for relevance of thinking. The scoring continuum extends from irrelevant thinking at one extreme, through passive attention and simple comprehension, to highly relevant thinking including attempts to apply information and to synthesize. The procedure has been described elsewhere (Siegel *et al.*, 1963).

Attitude

In cross-sectional educational research, criteria in the affective domain are less frequently utilized than are those in the cognitive domain. This is so in spite of the fact that noncognitive outcomes involving attitudes and values are usually placed high in any ordering of educational objectives. In part, this neglect of affective criteria results from the brief time span encompassed by most cross-sectional studies. Since the educational experience under investigation occupies a relatively brief segment of the total life-span of the student, it may not be sufficiently powerful to produce significant noncognitive change. Furthermore, these objectives are particularly difficult to specify in terms permitting evaluative instrumentation. The time and effort needed for such specification are more likely to be expended in longitudinal than in cross-sectional studies.

Practical considerations aside, a generalized paradigm must provide adequately for the assessment of noncognitive as well as cognitive criteria. We have limited our listing of critical noncognitive dependent variables for exploring the instructional gestalt to two types of attitudinal measures: those related to a particular course or other instructional experience, and those pervading the entire curriculum.

COURSE-RELATED ATTITUDES

It should be possible to delineate specific desired affective outcomes for almost every course or other limited educational experience. For example, it might be expected that an elementary psychology course should encourage certain attitudes concerning the appropriateness of scientific method for the behavioral sciences, the sources of international tension, the status of psychology as a profession, and so on. If these are important instructional objectives, the gestalt for elementary psychology cannot be fully explored without using appropriate attitudinal measures as partial criteria of instructional effectiveness.

CURRICULUM-RELATED ATTITUDES

Certain kinds of affective development or change may be anticipated as a result of the total curriculum rather than of a single course. This development may involve changes in the student's self-perception and general approach to new or unfamiliar circumstances and problems.

Although this kind of development is most properly regarded as a pervasive curricular objective, it may be appropriate to define the "most effective" instructional gestalt for a given course as the one enabling that course to make a maximum contribution to the over-all objectives of the curriculum.

Extraclass Behavior

The question of the behavioral validity of attitudinal measures has been too frequently raised to merit repetition here. Even if a correspondence between expressed attitude and behavior is assumed, there would still remain the important schism between situationally expressed attitudes and extrasituational behavior. Experiences in industrial training programs, for example, often lead to certain attitudinal changes within the context of the program which do not generalize to the working environment.

This circumstance is by no means limited to noncognitive attainment. Elements of course content learned sufficiently well to meet the challenge of the final examination may subsequently be rapidly forgotten. And there is often a noteworthy discrepancy between the ability to state and apply principles on an examination and the ability to make applications in the world outside of the classroom.

Dissatisfaction with total reliance upon criteria of educational effectiveness obtained in the scholastic setting is expressed in many ways by all parties to the instructional endeavor. Parents, students, and teachers regard "life" as a broad practical test of the validity of educational experiences. The ways in which life provides this test are diverse. Some persons regard "vocational success" as the acid test; others, "self-realization" and "personal adjustment"; still others, "continued intellectual growth"; and so on. Each of these extraclass objectives can be specified and defined behaviorally. Once delineated, these behaviors provide yet another criterion of the effectiveness of particular instructional gestalts.

An Investigative Pattern following the Paradigm

We discuss next the particular analysis of variance underlying our current series of investigations. In making the transition from the generalized multivariate paradigm described above to our application of it, we discuss related methodological and statistical issues.

The generalized paradigm restricts the researcher's attention to four classes of independent variables: environmental, instructor, learner, and course. In view of the wide range of research possibilities suggested by the generalized paradigm, certain critical decisions were required to effect a transition between it and a manageable research strategy. Paramount among these was the decision to use an analysis of variance rather than a correlational approach.

Advantages of the Analysis of Variance

The point at issue is whether the combination of factorial design and analysis of variance is a better way of studying the instructional gestalt than correlational analysis using the full range of talent. The generalized paradigm includes a number of organismic (that is, learner) variables. To the extent that these individual-difference variables are intercorrelated, F-ratio interactions involving these variables may be spurious (Underwood, 1957).

This difficulty could be circumvented by electing a correlational strategy involving the usual multiple regression approach with multiplicative terms for the interactions. This strategy would generate a multiple correlation and associated weights using the learner variables to predict criterion performance *for each combination of instructor-environment conditions*. Since the latter are manipulated conditions (that is, the instructor manifests either a factual or a conceptual objective), they cannot be entered into the equations as predictors.

Thus, although the correlational approach would overcome one difficulty, that of possible intercorrelations between organismic variables, it would not provide information about interactions within the other independent variable clusters or between, say, learner and instructor variables.

An additional reason for rejecting the correlational strategy is that interactions may reflect nonlinearity. Correlational analysis would obscure the existence of such interactions.

In view of the patently exploratory nature of the series of investigations we were attempting, the factorial design using analysis of variance seemed clearly to be more promising than the correlational approach. Some of the interactions resulting from this analysis may be spurious although, as we indicate subsequently, this likelihood is not as great as might be imagined.

Having elected an analysis-of-variance design, we found it necessary to make two additional decisions in order to facilitate its implementation: to limit the number of variables used, and to dichotomize each variable. Although it is convenient to discuss these as separate issues, they stemmed from the same basic concern: to maximize the empirical yield from a limited number of available courses and potential subjects.

The Independent Variables

The generalized paradigm involves a complete factorial arrangement of 16 independent variables. On the assumption that each of these variables could somehow be dichotomized, thereby reducing the number of experimental conditions to a minimum, this paradigm generates 65,536 different combinations of environmental-instructor-learner-course circumstances. Obviously, this number is unmanageable. Even with one subject per matrix cell, the available pool of subjects would have to number in the hundreds of thousands in order to provide the required number of "critical" subjects. Therefore, it was necessary to simplify the multivariate paradigm for research purposes by arranging circumstances so that some of the variables could be treated as constants.

ENVIRONMENTAL VARIABLES

Control over the environmental variables was facilitated by conducting the explorations in televised courses. These courses were chosen as a starting place for research based upon the generalized paradigm for methodological reasons. First, it is possible simultaneously to transmit a lecture emanating from a single source to a number of different classrooms. Then by manipulating or otherwise arranging circumstances within each receiving room, it is feasible to explore various dimensions of the instructional gestalt under otherwise controlled conditions.

The virtues of this use of televised instruction in providing desired experimental controls over the learning environment are self-evident. Several receiving rooms simultaneously provide data for a given matrix. The physical characteristics of the several rooms are essentially similar with respect to capacity and physical arrangement. Students in all rooms receive the identical presentation at the identical moment in time. Since these courses are televised, the enrollments tend to be rather large, thereby providing a sizable pool of subjects. In advanced courses where enrollments are low in spite of the televised offering, replication of the course during subsequent semesters, permitting the desired experimental manipulations, is facilitated by using videotape.

Since most of the research is conducted in televised courses, two environmental variables particularly germane to televised instruction were systematically manipulated: the presence or absence of a room proctor; the extent and level of participation by students in classroom discussion.

The fact that the studies are, in the main, conducted in televised courses imposes certain limits upon the generality of our findings. It is not anticipated that findings derived from televised courses will necessarily be generalizable to the instructional gestalt in face-to-face settings. However, it would probably be erroneous to regard these findings as applicable *only* to televised courses. In terms of the variables comprising the paradigm, we regard the series of investigations conducted in televised courses as exploring those portions of the instructional gestalt pertinent to lecture-type instruction in a relatively convergent instructional climate. This type of instruction and environment is not restricted to televised courses. It is provided by many instructors in face-to-face settings even with relatively small classes.

COURSE VARIABLES

The three course variables (subject-matter area, level of presentation, required or elected by students) were eliminated from the analyses by the expedient of developing separate matrices for each course. Although this expedient prevented us from accumulating empirical data pertinent to the interactions between these three variables and the others that were systematically explored, certain inferences about their impact were possible because of the spread of courses investigated.

INSTRUCTOR VARIABLES

Each of the courses in which an investigation is conducted is taught by a single instructor throughout the period of the research. Therefore, we could also have elected to treat the instructor variables as constants, following the procedure indicated above for course variables.

We rejected this alternative because of our conviction a priori that instructor variables are sufficiently critical to the instructional gestalt to merit their empirical exploration. The importance we attached to these variables was congruent with both the lore of teaching and a sizable body of accumulated evidence that the teacher makes a difference in the effectiveness of instruction. The two instructor variables explored in depth were "manifest objectives" and "personal contact."

The instructor manifested his objectives by means of the hourly examinations he administered throughout the semester in his course. Three such examinations were given each semester, and two forms of each examination were developed. One of these forms, designed to manifest a *factual* objective, consisted solely of items judged to demand only rote recall for the factual content and principles presented in lectures and assigned readings. The other form manifested a *conceptual* objective by containing only items requiring students to apply factual information to a situation previously unencountered, or to synthesize and integrate factual information in some new way.

The content coverages of the two forms of each examination were parallel. The factual and conceptual forms of examinations were consistently administered throughout the semester to selected subjects in order to establish the "manifest factual" and "manifest conceptual" conditions.

Two conditions were also developed for the personal-contact variable. An "avoidant" condition was created for some of the receiving rooms by discouraging any personal contact with the televised instructor either in his office or after class. The personal-contact condition was established in various ways in different courses. In one course, following his appearance on television, the televised lecturer personally conducted thirty-minute discussion periods in sections containing the "contact" subjects. Parallel discussion periods for the "no-contact" group were conducted by graduate assistants. In another course, personal contact was effected for the selected subjects by having the televised lecturer himself teach the two-hour weekly laboratory into which these subjects were assigned. In a third course, the instructor attempted to visit the receiving rooms containing "contact" subjects following each televised presentation and to encourage them to visit him in his office.

LEARNER VARIABLES

All students enrolled in a course were pretested during the first class meeting. These data were used to classify students with respect to salient independent learner variables. The basic pretest battery consisted of the following instruments, the first three of which were developed for the series of investigations employing the multivariate paradigm.

Course-specific motivation was assessed by means of a Thurstone-type scale designed to measure initial attitudes toward the course. Representative statements near the "favorable" pole were:

57. I believe I will learn more from this course than any other I am taking this semester.
55. This course will help me realize my professional or vocational goal.

Two of the statements near the "unfavorable" pole were:

2. I wish I could have avoided taking this course.
5. I have no interest in this subject area.

A detailed discussion of the development of the *educational-set* scale has been presented elsewhere (Siegel and Siegel, 1965). This scale is a forced-choice inventory, yielding scores on a continuum characterized by a predisposition, on the one hand, to learn isolated facts and, on the other, to learn principles, relationships, fact clusters, and concepts.

The alternatives constituting each triad were paired on several different preference indices, including judgments about "how bright you have to be to learn this" and "the kind of impression knowing this would make on the naive person." One triad with its scoring weights will serve to illustrate the format of this inventory.

Items 70–72. Assume you are enrolled in a natural science course and must learn about the following. Which one will interest you most? Which one will interest you least?

Scoring

Most	Least	
−1	+1	70. The names of the elements included within the "halide" group.
0	0	71. Statement of Newton's Third Law of Motion.
+1	−1	72. The significance of a pH of 6.

Prior knowledge was measured in each course by a test consisting of about twenty multiple-choice items drawn from a previously administered final examination for the course. Its purpose was to distribute students along a continuum of initial knowledge of the course content.

The American College Testing Program battery is routinely administered to all incoming freshmen. The composite ACT score was taken as our measure of *academic ability*.

Two of the tests for *creativity* developed by Guilford and his associates were administered for the purpose of positioning subjects on a continuum of creative abilities. These were the *Consequences Test* (Christensen, Merrifield, and Guilford, 1958) and *Pertinent Questions* (Berger, Merrifield, and Guilford, 1960).

Dichotomizing the Independent Variables

As indicated above, our research thus far has been limited to 9 of the 16 variables specified by the generalized multivariate paradigm. Of these 9, 5 are learner variables, 2 are instructor variables, and 2 are environmental variables. Even this decision to limit the scope of the research before beginning the investigations would have left an unmanageable series of studies if further limitations had not been imposed.

In this regard, it is helpful to think of each of our 9 independent variables as being of two types: 5 were organismic variables, and 4 were instructor-environment conditions. Because of the requirements of a full factorial design, it was necessary to identify sets of "critical" subjects so that each set represented all possible combinations of the organismic variables and to assign these sets randomly to all possible combinations of instructor-environment conditions.

The number of critical subjects comprising a set depends upon the number of levels (or conditions) identified for each of the learner variables. Since each of these variables is continuously distributed, arguments could be made for differentiating four or more levels for each. Without belaboring a point, we should point out that even cutting the continuous distributions for the organismic variables at their quartiles would have required that each set of critical subjects providing all combinations of the 5 organismic variables contain 1,024 cases. Furthermore, it would have been necessary to identify as many of these sets of 1,024 critical cases as there were combinations of instructor-environment conditions. This obviously would have been impossible with total course enrollments (even accumulating data across years) of well under 1,000 students.

Therefore, all organismic variables were dichotomized even though they are continuously distributed. Students at or above the 70th percentile of a distribution were designated as "high" on that variable; those at or below the 30th percentile were designated "low" on that variable.

Partly because we excluded the middle 40 per cent of each organismic variable distribution, not all students enrolled in a course were available as potential subjects. To be a potential subject, the student had to be classifiable as either "high" or "low" on all organismic variables. Identifying a complete set of critical subjects (16 cases for 4 organismic variables; 32 cases for 5 organismic variables) further strained the subject pool because each of these subjects had to represent a particular pattern of high and low scores on the organismic variables under consideration. We found that typically only 20–25 per cent of the students registered in a course could actually be used as experimental subjects.

A Representative Design

Once parallel sets of critical subjects who fulfill the learner-variable requirements are identified, they are randomly placed in specific viewing sections providing the necessary instructor and environmental conditions. Since each viewing section is attended by at least 60 students, only 16 of whom are subjects, it is unlikely that anyone other than the experimenters knows the identity of the subjects.

After conditions are established for a given design, four analyses of variance are computed: one for each of four criteria. Two of these, factual and conceptual acquisition, are derived from subsets of items comprising the final examinations. The classification of items into these criterion categories mirrored the definitions of item content for manifesting factual and conceptual objectives.

The two remaining criteria, "relevance of thinking" and "attentiveness" *in situ* are obtained by sampling students' reports about their thoughts at various times during videotape playbacks of original lecture presentations. This procedure of "stimulated recall" has been described in detail elsewhere (Siegel *et al.*, 1963).

Statistical and Methodological Considerations

Both the general paradigm and the illustrative analysis of variance ensuing from it compel us to direct further attention to three methodological issues: (1) the choice of an error term for analyses of variance with one case per cell; (2) correlations between organismic variables; and (3) the dichotomization of organismic variables and consequent differential regression.

The Error Term

The choice of an error term in an analysis-of-variance design with a single replication creates certain problems because of the absence of any estimate of experimental error corresponding to the mean square within treatments. One solution to this problem discussed by Edwards (1960) is to combine higher-order interactions as an estimate of experimental error. Accordingly, the error term employed for all of our analyses has been a pooled-mean square based upon the interactions involving more than four variables. In a 2^7 design, this error term has 29 degrees of freedom: 21 associated with fourth-order interactions, 7 with fifth-order interactions, and 1 with the sixth-order interaction.

Since a number of the higher-order interactions comprising the error term may themselves be statistically significant, this procedure tends to underestimate the statistical significance of the lower-order interactions under consideration by an unknown amount. By regarding as statistically significant only those F-ratios with $p < .05$, we may tend to err on the side of undue caution and consequently to neglect significant relationships. On the other hand, by liberalizing the criterion of significance to, say, $p < .10$, we run the risk of interpreting nonsignificant findings.

The decision about whether to accept as statistically significant those F-ratios with $p < .05$ or $p < .10$ is made for each matrix as follows: We test the significance of each of the fourth-order interactions, using the mean square of the eight highest-order interactions as the error term. Similarly, we test the significance of each of the fifth- and sixth-order interactions, using the mean square of the 21 fourth-order interactions as the error term. If none or few of the error-term components tested in this fashion are themselves statistically significant, we require $p < .05$ before attempting to interpret an F-ratio. However if several—we arbitrarily use four or more—of these higher-order interactions are statistically significant by this test, we accept as significant those F-ratios with $p < .10$.

Correlations between Organismic Variables

Although, as Edwards (1960) indicates, organismic variables may be meaningfully entered into factorial designs, this use of organismic variables is open to a certain amount of criticism. Such criticism rests upon the likelihood that all individual-difference variables tend to be correlated in nature to some degree. Thus, a group scoring high on a test of academic ability, for example, tends to exhibit a somewhat uniform pattern of scores on other associated characteristics.

This fact generally has two important implications: First, cause-effect inferences concerning organismic variables are tenuous because of the possible effect of a more basic underlying variable correlated with the ones investigated, but not itself selected for study. This implication is not, of course, restricted to factorial designs. In any research with organismic variables, there is always the risk that the factors investigated may merely be associated with underlying causal conditions, and are not themselves causal.

The second implication *is* unique to factorial designs with organismic variables and therefore merits more careful consideration. To the extent that two or more organismic variables are correlated, interactions between them may be spurious because these interactions are based upon a systematic rather than a random assignment to "treatment conditions." With reference to the design we have suggested, this point is relevant only to interactions among the learner variables themselves. It is not germane to interactions involving one or more of these with at least one of the experimental treatments (instructor and environmental variables) because critical subject-sets are *randomly* assigned to these treatment conditions.

The validity of interpretations of interactions among organismic variables themselves rests upon (1) the magnitude of the correlations between these variables and (2) the reliability of the measures used for their assessment. The lower the intercorrelations (assuming high reliabilities), the safer the basis for interpretation.

Differential Regression

Earlier in this chapter we stated our reasons for electing to create just two conditions for each organismic variable: the "high" condition, containing subjects scoring in the upper 30 per cent of the distribution; the "low" condition, containing subjects scoring in the lower 30 per cent of the distribution. Even four levels or conditions for each organismic variable (that is, cutting at quartiles) would have required as many sets of 1,024 critical subjects as there were instructor-environment conditions within each course. Obviously, this would have been an unmanageable design.

By using only high and low groups for each organismic variable, we open the way for spurious interactions to occur by virtue of differential regression. To the extent that organismic variables are correlated, high-low groups will regress more on retest than either high-high or low-low groups. This differential regression occurs with correlated variables because there is greater capitalization upon chance in selecting high-low or low-high combinations than in selecting high-high or low-low combinations.

In practice, we have generally found the organismic variables with which we have been working to be relatively uncorrelated; therefore, we have not been unduly concerned about the effects of differential regression.

SOME REPRESENTATIVE FINDINGS

The foregoing pattern of investigation has been applied to a number of problems. The aim has been to develop fairly broad post-hoc generalizations meriting further empirical test and refinement.

Two Organizing Concepts

Proceeding from the interaction patterns uncovered by the research design, we have formulated two concepts that seem to impose order upon the data. These concepts relate to idiosyncratic drive pattern and instructional press.

This refers to the role of combinations of learner characteristics as partial determinants of the power and impact of specific instructional circumstances. Thus, a student characterized by a particular combination of motivation, academic ability, educational set, and so on displays a drive pattern characteristic of students with that particular combination and different from the pattern characteristic of students with other combinations of these same organismic variables.

As a generalization, educational performance is encouraged when the instructional setting and the learner's idiosyncratic drive pattern are congruent and is discouraged when they are dissonant.

This generalization is certainly not revolutionary. Idiosyncratic drive patterns probably control educational performance in two ways: First, they determine the appropriateness or inappropriateness *for particular students* of selected aspects of the instructional setting. Obviously, provision of considerable opportunity for personal contact with the instructor is more appropriate for a student who needs to experience a nurtural relationship than for one who does not need such a relationship.

Second, the idiosyncratic drive pattern helps shape the student's perceptions about and approach to the course. A student taking a course merely to fulfill some requirement, for example, responds quite differently from one who enrolls because of a genuine preprofessional commitment to the discipline.

The significance of the generalization, and hence its value once we probe it, is that it directs our attention to identifying (1) the components of idiosyncratic drive patterns, and (2) specific instructional circumstances that are congruent with or dissonant from these patterns.

INSTRUCTIONAL PRESS

In a way, instructional press is the obverse of idiosyncratic drive pattern. The latter generates predictions about the role of learner characteristics as determinants of the impact of instructional circumstances. Consideration of instructional press, on the other hand, generates predictions about the impact upon students as a group of specific aspects of instructional management.

We believe that the patterns of main effects obtained in particular courses enable us to differentiate between *extrinsic* and *intrinsic* presses. When performance is highly dependent upon instructor-environment conditions, we have evidence for an "extrinsic" instructional press. Conversely, when performance is particularly dependent upon learner characteristics, we have evidence for an "intrinsic" press.

We hypothesized the operation of instructional press as a differential power factor affecting educational performance. Whereas all instructional environments are potentially supportive and potentially threatening to some students, the former aspect is hypothesized as more powerful in the context of an intrinsic press and the latter as more powerful in the context of an extrinsic press.

In view of this expectation, we offer the following generalization as a second organizing concept: An extrinsic instructional press sensitizes students to the potentially punitive and threatening (that is, inhibiting) aspects of the instructional environment; an intrinsic instructional press sensitizes students to the potentially supportive (that is, facilitating) aspects of the instructional environment.

Toward a Theory of Instruction

In the light of the foregoing generalizations, our view of the instructional process is summarized in the following three statements which are consistent with the results we have obtained thus far:

1. There are identifiable patterns of idiosyncratic drive for academic attainment. These patterns are associated with interactions among learner characteristics.

2. Certain features of the instructional environment which are congruent with a particular idiosyncratic drive pattern have the power to facilitate performance. Other features of the instructional environment which are dissonant from an idiosyncratic drive pattern have the power to inhibit performance.

3. Whether or not these congruent and dissonant features of the instructional environment operate in fact as facilitators or inhibitors depends, in part, upon the instructional press. This press is a "wash" which accentuates or obliterates the facilitating and inhibiting effects resulting from the congruence or dissonance between environmental conditions and idiosyncratic drive patterns.

Viewed this way, research on teaching-learning must be directed toward discovering patterns of idiosyncratic drive and identifying the environmental conditions appropriate to each. Similarly, a theory of instruction would specify such unknowns as (1) the kinds of identifiable idiosyncratic drive patterns, (2) the salient features of the instructional environment, and (3) the dynamics of instructional press.

We have interpreted the data following our paradigm post hoc in this way. Note in the sections following that we speak of empirically derived *hypotheses* rather than theoretical propositions. The next step would be to conduct studies specifically designed to test these hypotheses. If the hypotheses are thereby supported, they can serve as propositions to be incorporated in a more comprehensive theory of instruction than those heretofore developed.

Because this section is intended merely to be illustrative, we have restricted it to two sets of hypotheses. One of these focuses upon a tried and true variable in educational research: academic ability. The other concerns one of the more unusual variables in the general paradigm: educational set.

HYPOTHESES ABOUT ACADEMIC ABILITY

When we consider academic ability as a partial determinant of educational performance, we tend to think in terms of correlations using ability as a predictor of some academic criterion. In contrast, the paradigm for exploring the instructional gestalt implicitly suggests that different patterns of instructor and environment conditions may optimize performance by students of different levels of ability. In terms of our earlier statements about idiosyncratic drive patterns, we can now make explicit our expectation that certain of these patterns are ability-linked. Furthermore, if the hypotheses suggested by our data are further substantiated, instructional circumstances could profitably be differently structured to facilitate academic performance by students at particular levels of ability.

Concretely, the interactions involving academic ability as a component have suggested the following two post-hoc hypotheses:

1. A facilitating learning environment for students of *low ability* reduces their perceptions of the likelihood of failure and/or directs their attention to the material to be learned. Conversely, their perfor-

mance is adversely affected by circumstances increasing their perception of the likelihood of failure and/or directing their attention away from the content to be learned.

2. A facilitating learning environment for students of *high ability* provides a perceived intellectual challenge appropriate to their level of ability. Again, the converse of these conditions (that is, a perception that the material is inappropriately easy) adversely affects performance by students of high ability.

These hypotheses suggest that features of the instructional environment ordinarily regarded as desirable, such as opportunities for personal contact with the instructor, may actually be desirable only for certain kinds of students and either undesirable or inconsequential for others. The critical factor is not the provision of personal contact, but the nature of the contact as perceived by the student. This perception, in turn, reflects both what transpires in the instructional setting and the student's previous history of reinforcements for educational attainment. Presumably, academic ability interacts with environmental circumstances as noted in the two hypotheses above because the student's history of reinforcement for educational attainment prior to coming to the university is partly dependent upon his level of ability.

These hypotheses are congruent with certain incidental findings derived from entirely different research designs. Macomber and Siegel (1960), for example, reported that students of low ability hold more favorable attitudes toward televised and lecture instruction than do students of high ability.

HYPOTHESES ABOUT EDUCATIONAL SET

The assumption underlying our use of educational set as an organismic variable is that certain students are predisposed to learn factual information; others, conceptual information; and still others, some mix of the two. Thus, educational set was presumed to reflect the learner's broad cognitive style as a "given" with which he enters the course and as a partial determinant of his idiosyncratic drive pattern.

Ausubel's (1963) notion of *subsumption* leads to the expectation that, other things being equal, conceptually set students are more likely than factually set students to learn both conceptually oriented content (that is, principles, generalizations, and applications) and factually oriented content. Although this expectation is concisely stated, it does not coincide with the spirit of the multivariate paradigm. By oversimplifying reality (namely, "other things being equal"), it increases the likelihood of obscuring important interactive relationships even though subsumption might still be a valid principle.

We have elsewhere reported our findings that a conceptual set is associated with superior acquisition as a main effect in certain courses but not in others. Furthermore, in those courses where the main effect favoring conceptual set is not obtained, there is an interaction between set and manifest objectives: conceptually set students performed best when reinforced throughout the semester for conceptual acquisition; factually set students performed best when consistently reinforced for factual acquisition.

We formulated the following two hypotheses post hoc:

1. As predicted from Ausubel's principle of subsumption, conceptual set predisposes more effective educational performance than factual set provided that the classroom affords an "intrinsic" motivational press.

2. When the classroom structure provides an "extrinsic" instructional press, educational set influences performance only when appropriately buttressed by specific features of the instructional environment (for example, the content emphasis of the course examinations administered during the semester).

CONCLUSION

We have proposed and illustrated the implementation of a multivariate paradigm for educational research. In our preferred implementation, we make use of a factorial design and analysis of variance in spite of certain methodological problems associated with this design and discussed in this chapter.

The primary value of the paradigm is that by focusing upon interactions in addition to main effects, it allows us to come closer to approximating what actually transpires in instructional settings. Patterns of interaction are used to generate post-hoc hypotheses with the understanding that (1) the implication of causality in formulating some of these hypotheses is nothing more than an inference, and (2) the particular hypotheses formulated are by no means the only ones that could have been generated from the same set of data. An advantage of these hypotheses over those developed in other ways is that they tend to reflect the complexities we perceive as existing in the instructional gestalt. Hence, they are potentially fertile for stimulating subsequent investigation pointed toward the ultimate goal of developing a theory of instruction.

10

Instruction and the Conditions
of Learning

ROBERT M. GAGNÉ
University of California, Berkeley

∽

INSTRUCTION OF THE YOUNG, AS WELL AS OF THE UNINFORMED OF ANY age, has been considered a worthy enterprise throughout history. It has usually been acknowledged to be a highly complex human activity. For the most part, it must be carefully planned and executed in order to accomplish its objective, which is to bring about learning in another individual. Typically, it requires an intricate web of communication with a learner, and this communication is calculated rather than casual.

The planning and design of instruction nowadays are done both in a long-range and a short-range fashion. Long-range design, for instruction that extends beyond about one day, is done by a number of different agents, including the curriculum designer, the faculty committee, and the textbook writer. Short-range instructional design is usually accomplished by a teacher in the development of a course outline, a lesson plan, or a set of notes.

A specific kind of instructional design, often thought of as the particular province of teacher activity, may be called *extemporaneous* design. It occurs when the teacher decides upon each new communication as a result of what has immediately gone before within the give and take of a classroom, seminar, or tutoring session.

In a broad sense, then, there are many possible agents who may be involved in the design of instruction. The teacher is not the only designer of instruction simply because he is also its practitioner. The principles of design must be highly similar, if not identical, whether instruction is short-range or long-range.

291

There are undoubtedly some other principles pertaining to the execution of instruction, different from those relating to its design. The activity of the teacher, naturally enough, tends to carry out extemporaneous design and also the execution of instruction in rapid succession, so that it is sometimes difficult to make a definite distinction between design and execution. In this chapter, I deal almost entirely with the *design* of instruction, and accordingly with only that part of the teacher's performance pertaining to such design. The main interest is in how instruction may be designed, whether on a short-term or a long-term basis and whether by teachers or by other agents.

CLASSES OF VARIABLES IN LEARNING

The purpose of instruction is to bring about a change within the learner, a change of the sort called *learning*. At time t, it may be observed that the learner is incapable of performing task X. A period of instruction is then instituted. Then, at time $t + 1$, it is noted that the learner is now able to perform task X and that he is also able to perform the same task after an additional interval, say, at time $t + 2$. Basically, these are the observations that lead to the inference that learning has occurred. A change in performance has occurred and is retained over a period of time. The inference is that some internal capability of the individual learner has been altered by the instruction which was given, and it is this change in capability that is called learning.

What are the variables that enter into the situation and affect the phenomenon of learning? There are a number of variables; some of them are appropriately a part of what is called instruction, while some are not. It will be useful at the outset to draw some distinctions among these variables.

Variables within the Learner

This category includes the learner variables *initial capabilities* and *motivation*. If the learner is to be instructed in task X, it is assumed for purposes of this example that this particular capability is not initially present. But there may be other capabilities which are also not present, and if they are not, instruction specifically designed to teach task X will not work. Certain innately determined capabilities may be absent, as in a mentally deficient individual; or certain capabilities ordinarily dependent upon previous learning may be missing. For example, instruction in the solution of problems involving vector resolution of forces may be impossible if representation of trigonometric ratios has not previously been learned. To take a simpler example, instruction in pronouncing printed letter combinations will not work if the child has not previously learned to distinguish the printed letters one from another. The learner's initial capabilities constitute some of the most important variables in the process of learning.

Motivation is another kind of state internal to the learner and prerequisite to effective instruction. Motivational states are usually considered to be alterable by different means than are initial capabilities. However established, it seems fairly clear that a certain kind of motivational state must be present as a precondition for learning (Gagné and Bolles, 1959). It is probably a mistake to think of the necessary state as "motivation for learning." Instead, the essential motivation is something more like "willingness to enter into the learning situation." Obviously, if an individual is determined not to respond to a learning situation, but to escape from it physically or otherwise, instruction cannot be effective. If a child turns his attention from the learning situation, instruction will not operate to bring about a change in his capabilities.

Another motivational state necessary for learning is called *alertness*. According to recent evidence (Lindsley, 1957), the receipt of stimulation by higher levels of the central nervous system is a specific brain function. If this alerting system is functioning in a particular way, environmental stimuli will reach the higher centers; if it is functioning in another way, they will not. Therefore, this system must also be operating properly in order for instruction to affect the individual.

Variables in the Learning Situation

The second broad class of variables affecting learning consists of those located outside the learner and within his immediate environment. Together these variables constitute what is usually called the learning situation. A number of different variables may be distinguished.

There are stimuli which direct the learner's *attention* and thus determine which aspects of the total stimulus situation will be received. Almost any form of stimulation is possible as a director of attention. Initially, any sudden change in stimulation commands attention. But the learner may also have acquired certain observational habits, and because of these his attention may be directed by moderate or even faint stimuli. The first-grade teacher may initially direct her pupils' attention by clapping her hands quite smartly; but the pupils rather quickly learn to pay the same attention to a much less intense handclap or even to a spoken word.

The stimuli which are to be involved in the *performance* being learned constitute another part of the total learning situation. These specific stimuli are of course only a portion of the total stimulation of the learning situation, but they are essential ones. For a science student learning the concept of vaporization, the specific stimulus is a liquid in the process of vaporizing. For a child learning to read, the essential stimuli are printed words. As the individual develops in language ability, it becomes increasingly feasible simply to represent the specific stimuli by means of printed or spoken words. To an adult who "knows the words," it is possible to represent the stimulus of a telephone pole in the verbally stated proposition "Telephone poles are at least one foot in diameter." Even for adults, however, many learning situations need to include the essential stimuli themselves.

Verbal communications which stimulate learner responses constitute a fairly large subclass of variables within the learning situation. In general, these are commands, suggestions, or other statements to which the learner is presumed able to respond correctly. For example, a statement beginning "We have already seen that . . ." suggests the action of recall on the part of the learner. "Now, we shall consider . . ." is another kind of verbal communication in this general class. "See if you can follow . . . ," "Now notice that . . . ," and "It should be possible to find out whether . . ." are still other examples. Very often, such verbal communications are made in the form of questions, like "Can you show that these two statements are equivalent?" In a later section, the attempt is made to classify the functions of verbal communications more precisely. For the moment, it is important to note the following two things about them: (1) They function to *direct the behavior* of the learner within the learning situation; perhaps they might be called "verbal directions" for this reason. (2) They actually *convey no content* to the learner pertaining to the capability to be learned; instead, they are independent of content.

The presentation of stimuli and verbal directions within a learning situation is subject to variation in *sequence*. Thus, the essential stimuli may be presented first, they may follow one or more verbal directions, or they may remain throughout the learning event. The sequence of questions constituting the verbal directions may also be varied. A question which generates recall of some previously learned capability may come first, or it may be preceded by a statement informing the learner about the objective of the learning. Other variations are possible. Sequence of verbal communication is likely to have some demonstrable importance in most kinds of learning situations, derived in large part from the effects of *contiguity* of certain events within the total act of learning (see Underwood, 1952).

Instruction and Learning

There are, then, two broad classes of variables that influence learning: those within the learner, and those in the learning situation. These sets of variables undoubtedly have interactive effects upon learning, as many writers have emphasized. The external variables cannot exert their effects without the presence in the learner of certain states derived from motivation and prior learning and development. Nor can the internal capabilities of themselves generate learning without the stimulation provided by external events. As a problem for research, the learning problem is one of finding the necessary relationships which must obtain among internal and external variables in order for a change in capability to take place.

What is instruction? Instruction may be thought of as the institution and arrangement of the *external* conditions of learning in ways which will optimally interact with the internal capabilities of the learner, so as to bring about a change in these capabilities. Instruction thus deals with the manipulation of the conditions of the learning situation—with commanding attention, with presenting essential stimuli, and with the nature and sequence of verbal directions given to the learner. *The function of instruction is the control of the external conditions of the learning situation.*

Varieties of Change Called Learning

The determination of the nature and sequence of the external conditions of learning is surely the purpose of the great bulk of learning research over a period of many years. Over much of this period of time, too, there has been a guiding assumption that the nature of the change called learning must be in some fundamental sense the same, regardless of what is being learned. Accordingly, for a great many years, theories about the optimal conditions for learning have been dominated by concern with the variables of *contiguity, reinforcement,* and *frequency.* Investigators have searched for certain *general laws* relating these obviously important variables to learning outcomes, independently of "what is being learned," that is, of the nature of the change in capability being studied.

Although the verification of general laws is surely a desirable objective, the assumption that the *kind of change* in capability being studied is always somehow "the same" may be unjustified. How much similarity is there, actually, between the kind of change represented by a child learning to say his first word and that represented by a more experienced child learning to read printed English sentences? Or between learning to distinguish triangles from rectangles and learning to demonstrate that the sum of the internal angles of a triangle is the same as a straight angle? How much similarity is there between the learning of new "facts" by a beginning chemistry student from a textbook and the learning of new "facts" by his chemistry professor from a technical journal? All of these are surely examples of learning; that is, they involve a change in capability which can be inferred from a before-and-after comparison of performance. But are they the same kind of change?

Despite the prevailing emphasis on fundamental similarities of process in various learning situations, investigators of learning have always recognized certain "types" of learning. There is "trial-and-error learning," "discrimination learning," "paired-associates learning," "concept learning," "conditioned-response learning," and so on (see, for example, Melton, 1964). But these varieties of learning have tended to be identified with certain kinds of stimulus situations generated by particular equipment or materials, like the bar-pressing apparatus, the memory drum with verbal syllables, or the maze with choice points. The tendency has *not* been for these types of learning to be distinguished in terms of the *kind of change in capability* they imply. The questions that have tended *not* to be answered are of this kind: What sort of capability does the learner have (that he didn't possess before) when he has completed learning a list of verbal paired associates? Or when he has acquired a distinction between responses appropriate to a white card and to a black card? Or when he has learned to identify "food words" and "flower words"?

Differences in Performance Outcomes

An examination of the performances which reflect the outcomes of learning has led me to the conclusion that there are a number of varieties of these activities (Gagné, 1964, 1965). These kinds of performances may be called:

1. Specific responding.
2. Chaining (motor and verbal).
3. Multiple discrimination.
4. Classifying.
5. Rule using.
6. Problem solving.

Each differs from the others, in the sense that it is possible to distinguish the kinds of things that the learner can and cannot do in each instance. The capabilities underlying these performances form a partially ordered set; the acquisition of a more complex capability requires the previous existence of a simpler one, whereas the possession of a simpler capability does not imply that the individual can exhibit a more complex one.

For example, the performance known as rule using (or principle using) implies that the individual can also classify the terms which make up the rule; otherwise, he would not have been able to learn the rule. On the contrary, the individual who can classify the terms contained in a rule does not necessarily know the rule; that is, he cannot necessarily show that he can use it. At one point in his education, a student may know what the concept "borine" means (as a member of a class of chemical elements), what "gas" means, and what "room temperature" means. Yet he may not have acquired the principle (rule) reflected in the statement, "Borine is a gas at room temperature." If he already knows how to classify these terms, learning the principle is easy; if he does not know the terms, acquiring the principle cannot take place until he does.

Differences in What Is Learned

The existence of differentiable performances as outcomes of learning naturally leads to the inference that different kinds of capabilities are established by learning. The neural mechanisms determining these capabilities are presumably different for each one, but this possibility can only be guessed at with present evidence. However, the capabilities inferred from the performances do have different names, more or less familiar to psychologists. It is important to the present discussion to draw a careful distinction between the *performances* made possible by learning and the *capabilities* inferred as underlying these performances.

Table 10–1 contains a list of distinguishable kinds of performance which may be observed as learning outcomes. The second column defines each of these performances in terms which imply the criteria of distinction. The third column contains an example of each performance. The final column provides the name most commonly used to identify the inferred capability corresponding to each performance. It may be noted that, in certain instances, the commonly used name for the type of performance is at least partially the same as that used for the capability. This is unfortunate, but changing language customs cannot be attempted within the scope of this chapter. Successive rows of the table, reading down, refer to increasingly complex kinds of performance; and the more complex performances are hypothesized to imply the preexistence of less complex capabilities (that is, classifying implies that discrimination capability already exists in the individual, and so on).

TABLE 10–1. TYPES OF PERFORMANCE WHICH ARE OUTCOMES OF LEARNING, WITH
DEFINITIONS, EXAMPLES, AND CORRESPONDING INFERRED CAPABILITIES.

Performance type	Definition	Example	Inferred capability
Specific responding [1]	Making a specific response to a specified stimulus	Child saying "doll" when mother says "doll"	Connection
Chaining:			
Motor	Exhibiting a chain of responses each member of which is linked to each subsequent member	Unlocking a door with a key	Chain
Verbal	Exhibiting a chain of verbal responses linked by implicit codes	Giving French equivalents of English words; saying "A stitch in time saves nine"	Verbal association; verbal sequence
Multiple discrimination	Making different (chained) responses to two or more physically different stimuli	Naming a specific set of object colors	Discrimination
Classifying	Assigning objects of different physical appearance to classes of like function	Distinguishing various objects as "plant" or "animal"	Concept
Rule using	Performing an action in conformity with a rule represented by a statement containing terms which are concepts	Placing *i* before *e* except after *c* in spelling various English words	Principle (or rule)
Problem solving	Solving a novel problem by combining rules	Raising an automobile without using a jack	Principles plus "problem-solving ability"

[1] In commonly accepted terminology, this is the *instrumental response.*

Conditions of Learning / GAGNÉ • 299

The account of various kinds of *performance* has been given because it seems highly probable that there are corresponding varieties of *performance change.* In other words, the identification of these different kinds of performance, together with the different kinds of capability they imply, suggests that there may be at least as many different kinds of learning. And if this is so, it may be supposed that there exist an equal number of *conditions of effective learning* to correspond with each variety. A theory of instruction, then, cannot be maximally useful if it concerns itself with only those conditions that are general to all classes of learning. Instead, such a theory must concern itself in an individual manner with each of the types of learning.

Kinds of Learning

The idea that there are as many as seven kinds of learning is not entirely a novel one. A number of writers (Woodworth, 1958; Tolman, 1949; Mowrer, 1960) have emphasized the importance of giving separate consideration to several learning varieties. Skinner (1938, 1957) also describes different conditions for establishing connections (operants), chains, discriminations, concepts, and several types of verbal sequences, without necessarily using these names for them. Actually, the kinds of performance listed in Table 10–1 are distinguished by most educational psychologists when they find themselves in the position of being required to survey the range of naturally occurring events called learning.

These seven varieties of learning may be established by different sorts of conditions for learning, that is, by different kinds of *instruction.* Although the requisite conditions for the simpler types are fairly well known, those for the more complex types are not well known and have not yet been thoroughly established by careful experimentation. It is possible, however, to describe what does appear to be known about the conditions for bringing about these varieties of performance, based upon existing experimental evidence liberally supplemented by ordinary observation. A summary of the learning conditions appropriate to each of these varieties is given in Table 10–2 (see Gagné, 1965). The table indicates, for each kind of performance learned, the internal

Performance established by learning	Internal (learner) conditions	External conditions
Specific responding	Certain learned and innate capabilities	Presentation of stimulus under conditions commanding *attention;* occurrence of a response *contiguous* in time; *reinforcement*
Chaining:		
Motor	Previously learned individual connections	Presenting a *sequence* of external cues, effecting a sequence of specific responses *contiguous* in time; repetition to achieve selection of response-produced stimuli
Verbal	Previously learned individual connections, including implicit "coding" connections	Presenting a *sequence* of external verbal cues, effecting a sequence of verbal responses *contiguous* in time
Multiple discrimination	Previously learned chains, motor or verbal	Practice providing *contrast of correct and incorrect stimuli*
Classifying	Previously learned multiple discriminations	Reinstating discriminated response chain contiguously with *a variety of stimuli* differing in appearance, but belonging to a single class
Rule using	Previously learned concepts	Using external cues (usually verbal), effecting the recall of previously learned concepts contiguously in a suitable sequence; specific applications of the rule
Problem solving	Previously learned rules	Self-arousal and selection of previously learned rules to effect a novel combination

conditions presumed to be necessary for learning and the external conditions which may be used to bring about the learning. It will be noted that each more complex performance is considered to require simpler capabilities as prerequisites. The external conditions, which should provide direct implications for instruction, vary considerably with the kind of performance the learning is expected to make possible in each case.

Some examples, which may be helpful in the interpretation of Table 10–2, are given in the following sections.

Example: Learning that the English words "the foot" are a translation of the printed French words *le pied*.

First, the internal conditions listed in the table tell us that some previously learned individual connections must be recalled. These are (1) saying "foot," a capability which can be assumed; (2) observing the printed word *pied*, which can be checked by asking the learner to pick it out or to say it; and (3) a coding connection such as *pedal*, which will form the sequence *pied–(pedal)–*"foot." This last connection may be supplied as part of the instructions, or the learner may be encouraged to supply his own. The internal conditions having been satisfied, the external ones are easy. The stimulus *pied* is presented; verbal cues such as the printed words *pedal* and *foot* are presented at the same time (that is, contiguously), and the learner says the word "foot." Assuming now that the learner knows that this is the kind of performance expected of him, it may be said that the verbal sequence *pied–*"foot" has been learned.

Example: Learning a number of different English words for a number of different French words.

Suppose now that the learner is expected to acquire not only *pied–*"foot" but also *main–*"hand," *doigt–*"finger," and perhaps several others as well. It is reasonable to think that each of them can be learned under the same kind of internal and external conditions as was the first. But another difficulty arises if he attempts to learn them all: there will be *interference* among these chains. Unless some additional set of conditions is added, the words will tend to be forgotten almost as fast as they are learned. The kind of condition used is practice. Again and again, these previously learned individual chains are recalled, using external verbal cues as before and differentiating the right from the wrong stimuli to be associated with each response by telling the learner when his response is right or wrong. Of course, the amount of practice necessary will depend on how many of these chains the learner attempts to acquire as a total set. But practice is the major emphasis of the external learning conditions when multiple discriminations are to be acquired.

Example: Learning the botanical classification *tuber* and the verbal classification "tuber."

The table indicates that previously learned discriminations must be recalled. In the example at hand, these discriminations pertain to the physical appearance of plant stems on the one hand and of roots on the other. Following this recall, a *variety of examples* is presented, illustrating the appearance of tubers as enlarged stems. In each case, there is reinstatement of a chain such as *potato* (or pictured potato)–*tuber*–"tuber." In order to emphasize the distinction, a similar set of examples may be presented for *root*.

RULE USING

Example: Learning the rule "Pronouns which are the subjects of sentences are in the nominative case."

According to the table, the first concern is with the recall of previously learned concepts. External conditions must be arranged to supply verbal cues to stimulate such recall. Verbal cues may be in the form of questions, such as "Which of the following are pronouns? Which of these words is the subject?" These concepts having been aroused, it is then a fairly simple matter to use their names as verbal cues for the rule to be learned; in other words, to state the rule: "Pronoun subjects are nominative." But it is also important at this point to insure that such a statement is not learned merely as a verbal sequence. The next step in arranging external conditions, then, is to require a number of specific applications of the rule, such as "Supply the first-person pronoun for the following sentence: '—— students like football games.'" A suitable variety of examples of rule application, of course, needs to be provided.

FUNCTIONS OF THE INSTRUCTOR

The viewpoint presented here is that the form taken by instruction needs to be tailored to the particular objective which represents the kind of performance change to be brought about. Instruction is used to establish the necessary conditions for learning, and instruction differs in accordance with what is to be learned. The kinds of communication required for establishing a verbal chain are quite different from those required for establishing a principle, and they are likewise different for all the other categories of performance change listed in Tables 10–1 and 10–2.

The major implication of this approach to the problem of instruction is surely that the instructor cannot be guided by a simple set of rules that apply to all cases. The important aspects of the instructor's behavior do not lie in the fact that he uses a *general principle* to control learning (such as reinforcement or contiguity), but rather in the fact that he employs *different techniques* for different kinds of learning.

The functions performed by an instructor in helping to bring about these various kinds of change are discussed in the following paragraphs. For convenience, these functions are classified under four headings: (1) functions performed early in the instructional sequence, (2) functions designed to evoke and guide learning, (3) functions encouraging generalization, and (4) functions permitting an evaluation of outcomes.

Performing Early Instructional Functions

PRESENTING THE STIMULUS

This important function for the instructor can be implemented by pictures and other audiovisual aids. Selecting the proper stimulus requires making some good decisions. For example, if motor chains are to be learned, a portion of the necessary stimuli ought to come from muscular movement; presenting these stimuli becomes a matter of permitting repetition of the motor acts. If a child is learning to name a specific object (a verbal chain), the object itself must be presented; it cannot be represented by a word, as may be done with an adult, who has already acquired such a link. If a classification is being learned, a sufficiently great variety of stimulus objects must be presented to represent the class; otherwise, the concept acquired will be inadequate. If a rule is being learned, the verbal statement of the rule is not always a sufficient stimulus, since it may merely lead to learning the verbalization itself. Instead, situations requiring application of the rule must be presented as stimuli.

Directing the learner's attention to essential aspects of the stimulus situation is another function the instructor performs in controlling the conditions of learning. This is done in various ways, perhaps by introducing extra stimuli into the situation (arrows, pointers) and often by verbal commands. It is obviously important to all forms of learning that the relevant stimuli be perceived. For example, the attainment of the biological concept *cell* may require that attention be paid to such characteristics as membrane, nucleus, and cytoplasm since these are the major identifications to be recalled.

INFORMING THE LEARNER OF OBJECTIVES

A requirement of instruction which may transcend the conditions of learning previously discussed is that the learner be informed about the nature of the performance expected when learning is finished. Presumably, this procedure establishes a continuing *set* which facilitates learning, perhaps by making possible reinforcement at several points in a rather lengthy sequence of activities (see Gagné, 1965, Chap. 9). Providing information about expected performance may also be justified as a way of establishing a conceptual structure under which ideas to be learned are subsumable (see Ausubel, 1963).

Suppose that a new rule is to be learned, such as "adding the numerators of fractions with identical denominators to obtain a sum." The instructor communicates to the learner what is meant by obtaining a sum and, particularly, what a sum may look like. He might do this, for instance, by saying, "Now you need to learn how to obtain the sum of two fractions having common denominators, such as $\frac{3}{5}$ and $\frac{4}{5}$. The sum of these, you will see, is $\frac{7}{5}$." It appears probable that a sequence of instruction which begins by communicating the objective of learning is more effective than one which does not begin this way. However, additional experimental evidence on this point is needed.

STIMULATING RECALL OF PREVIOUSLY LEARNED CAPABILITIES

I have already indicated that stimulation of recall is a very important part of instruction, applicable to all of the varieties of learning.

Accordingly, it is one of the essential functions of an instructor. As described in Table 10–2, the necessary internal conditions for learning always include some previously learned capability of a simpler sort. Recalling these capabilities is usually an early step in instruction.

Recall is often stimulated by means of verbal communication, although it need not be. A question may be "Do you remember that we learned to distinguish between a stem and a leaf?" In another form, a question of similar intent might be "What are the main parts of a plant above ground?" The first of these questions requires only a recognition response on the part of the learner, while the second requires him to reinstate a previously acquired performance. It is not possible to find a simple rule governing the relative effectiveness of these two forms of question; the important thing is that they both have the function of stimulating *recall*. The necessity for having these previously learned capabilities "lively" in memory provides still another example of the importance of *contiguity* in learning. Not only must external events be contiguous for effective learning; but also recalled memories must be contiguous with these events.

Evoking Performance

Presumably, the activities of presenting the essential stimuli, controlling attention, informing the learner of objectives, and stimulating recall constitute the early events of instruction and need to occur approximately in the order given. The next step, broadly speaking, is one of evoking the required performance that is being learned. Thus, the application of a particular sequence of events to stimulate the learner is another function which may be carried out by the instructor.

DETERMINING A SEQUENCE

There are probably effective and ineffective sequences depending upon the category of performance dealt with. For example, as is well known, a relatively short verbal sequence (such as *wollen Sie bitte*) may readily be learned by being presented all at once, whereas a long one (like the stanza of a poem) may well require a more elaborate sequence of presentation, as is implied by the "progressive-part method" (McGeoch and Irion, 1952). Similarly, 4 objects requiring multiple discrimination can often be effectively presented in a single "trial," whereas 20 objects typically imply the need for a series of interspersed learning and recall trials (Gagné, 1965, Chap. 5). Each of the varieties of learning requires a different decision about a proper sequence of presentation; moreover, the length and nature of the content to be learned are also likely to affect this decision.

PROMPTING AND GUIDING THE LEARNING

The need for prompting as a part of the learning situation is quite frequent for many types of performance change. For example, evoking the correct verbal chain which provides the French word for "horse" requires that the instructor supply not only the stimulus *horse* but also the printed or spoken word *cheval,* in order that the learner for the first time institute the performance of saying "cheval." An additional prompting word or phrase may also be used for the coding response, as when the presentation of *horse–(chevalier)–*"cheval" is made to the learner. External verbal cues (prompts), such as the verbal name for a concept, are commonly used in connection with learning of the classifying sort. Thus, the presentation of each of several varieties of cell is often accompanied by the prompting verbal sentence "This is a cell." (Note that the learner in this situation is not learning to say the word "cell"—he already knows that; prompting him to say it in this situation is simply a means to the end of learning the correct classification for several different stimuli.)

A somewhat more elaborate kind of prompting, which may be called *guiding learning,* may be employed by the instructor when relatively complex rules are being learned or when the learner is being encouraged to discover new rules for himself, as in problem solving. In such cases, a sequence of verbal statements or questions may be employed in order to aid the learner's progress through several steps of reasoning to the principle being acquired. Learning to employ a rule and discovering how to combine principles in novel ways are both examples of complex intellectual activity, most of which occurs internally. But the direction of such activity can be influenced by external stimulation, usually in question form, and the course of learning can accordingly be shortened and made more efficient. Guiding learning in this sense is generally considered an important and frequent instructor function.

Encouraging Generalization

An account of instructor functions would be quite incomplete without mention of the activities having the purpose of encouraging the generalization of what is learned. This function is particularly applicable to the learning of concepts and rules and to problem solving. Generalization of the concept is encouraged by the procedure of presenting a suitable variety of stimuli to be classified; if the variety is too constricted, the concept is likely to be inadequate. Similarly, the diversity of examples used in illustrating specific problems to which rules are to be applied can determine the amount of generalization to be expected as a result of the learning. Actually, a variety of specific techniques may be employed by the instructor to encourage generalization (or transfer of learning, as it is sometimes called). In general, these techniques stimulate the learner to apply his recently acquired capabilities within widely differing contexts.

Assessing Outcomes

Naturally enough, the instructor must be concerned with assessing the outcomes of learning. Regardless of the type of performance, there are differential criteria to indicate whether or not learning has actually taken place. These are suggested, although not specifically described, by the final column of Table 10–2. For example, if multiple discrimination of 15 stimuli has been learned, then the learner should be able to identify each of these stimuli without error when they are presented all together (or one by one, for that matter). If a concept has been acquired, the presentation of an example not previously encountered should result in its being correctly classified. If a principle has been learned, an assessment of the learning should be possible by requiring the learner to apply it to a problem or situation novel to him.

Assessing learning outcomes may readily be seen to be a very frequent requirement of the instructional process. Each new kind of learned performance ought to be assessed in some manner or other, and the results made known to the learner. Such testing is often done informally by the teacher. Other kinds of testing of a more formal sort may, of course, also be needed at periodic intervals.

It may readily be realized from the preceding discussion that instruction is not a simple task. It cannot be reduced to simple formulas, such as "applying reinforcement," "communicating with the learner," or "stimulating discovery." Although all of these functions may be involved in any given instance, they are not the sole requirements for learning.

Controlling attention, presenting the essential stimuli, guiding learning, encouraging generalization, assessing outcomes—any or all of these functions may constitute the task of the instructor for any given act of learning. In making decisions about each one of them, the instructor must be guided by three principles of primary importance: (1) What is sought is a change in capability, represented by a change in performance. (2) One of the major determinants of this change is the initial capability of the learner, originating in turn with previous learning (see Glaser, 1962). (3) Different kinds of change (learnings) have different instructional requirements.

Viewed as a whole, the task of instruction is a tremendously complex one and therefore likely to be quite difficult. The skilled practitioner of this art, who is able to select and manipulate the variables comprising the external conditions of learning, of whatever type, is surely worthy of admiration. There is reason to wonder whether there are very many people who can really do a good job of instruction, particularly if they have been able to practice it for only a few years. Might it be possible to raise the standards of achievement in this field by somehow reducing the complexity of the instructional task?

Certain practical measures can be taken to simplify the instructional task for a teacher. Audiovisual aids are perhaps a *partial* answer to this problem. They are, for example, excellent for such functions as controlling attention and presenting the essential stimuli (see Gagné, 1965, Chap. 10). A more comprehensive approach to the problem, however, is provided by the notion of *predesigning* instruction, so that the entire set of decisions which must be made by an instructor is reduced in number and simplified. Informing the learner of objectives, stimulating recall, determining a sequence of presentation, guiding and prompting, and assessing outcomes are all functions which can be predesigned in order to generate effective learning conditions. As they are currently constructed, textbooks make no real attempt to accomplish predesign, and neither do educational films and television programs. Teaching-machine programs do make an attempt at predesigning, and some of them are quite successful at it. If their purposes and potentialities can be viewed with sufficient breadth, perhaps these programs will show the way to the accomplishment of such a goal.

Instruction and the Control of Behavior

It is interesting to consider the question of just what instruction is doing, as far as the behavior of the learner is concerned. How can the effects of instruction be conceived, in a general sense? Does instruction stimulate, communicate, or restrict behavior (for example, in its prompting and guiding function)? Does it exert a direct control over the process of learning?

One relatively prevalent conception of how instruction works is that it creates a learning situation which in a sense "captures control" of the nervous system of the individual so that he inevitably learns. Provided the external conditions of learning are optimally chosen and provided they are made consistent with the individual's previously learned capabilities (that is, the internal conditions), the learning situation may be conceived as one which "takes hold" of the learner and brings about the desired learning as a consequence. Actually, this is not a bad way of conceiving of what should be true of the learning situation. In an experimental study of learning, when both internal and external conditions are independently measured and controlled, the experimenter may well gain the impression that he has an unusual degree of control over what is happening.

However, such a view of the effects of instruction on learning has another side to it, which may be at least equally illuminating of the process of instruction. Regardless of how much "control" is exerted by external conditions, the internal processes of the learner are likely to make a crucial contribution to the events of learning. Furthermore, this crucial internal process contributed by the learner's nervous system is, so far as is now known, highly idiosyncratic. At present, it cannot be predicted or even described adequately, and it can be "controlled" only in a probabilistic sense.

Even the simpler kinds of learning described in Table 10–1 are greatly affected by idiosyncratic internal events. Motor chains require practice, it has long been believed, because the learner must "discover" the proper kinesthetic stimuli which are controlling a smoothly organized response. The training of a motor skill, like driving a golf ball, is often frustrating to both learner and instructor because these crucial internal kinesthetic stimuli cannot be directly controlled; they must be courted during periods of practice. A number of studies of verbal associates have shown that the patterns of associations previously acquired by the individual enter into the establishment of verbal chains as crucial mediating links (Bousfield, 1961; Jenkins, 1963). A study of French-English word association (referred to by Gagné, 1965, p. 100) found that the most effective learning of such associates results from a condition in which learners were encouraged to supply their own "codes," rather than having codes suggested in pictures or words.

In a consideration of the more complex varieties of learning, the contribution of events internal to the learner becomes even more prominent. Seven-year-old children can learn to "choose the opposite" card of a black-white or large-small set very quickly and presumably by means of a mediating concept; whereas four-year-olds learn such a reversal task slowly, by "trial and error" (Kendler and Kendler, 1961). But whatever set of internal events is represented by "choosing the opposite," it is doubtful that it is a matter of using these words, and likely that the events are highly idiosyncratic. A number of studies of concept learning have verified Hull's (1920) finding that conceptually based performance can be exhibited at the same time that the learner cannot "name" the concept or otherwise describe it.

The individualistic nature of internal events is perhaps even more strongly apparent in rule using and problem solving. Katona (1940) found that a demonstration illustrating the effects of rule application was often more effective in solving matchstick problems than was the supplying of a verbalized "arithmetic rule." A study requiring learners to verbalize while learning to solve a problem (Gagné and Smith, 1962) was unsuccessful in turning up consistent patterns of verbalization; again the suggestion is that the processes contributed by the individual are highly idiosyncratic. Many students of problem-solving behavior would probably take this idea for granted, a judgment based in part upon outcomes of earlier studies which have attempted to get the learner to "think aloud" while solving a problem (Woodworth, 1938, pp. 768–800). In addition to the specific rules which may be involved in solving a problem, some writers, notably Bruner (1961), have emphasized the importance of approaches to problem solving, called *strategies*. Although such self-directed principles may perhaps be categorized (Bruner, Goodnow, and Austin, 1956), there seems little doubt that they too are unique to the individual.

From its simple to its complex forms, then, an act of learning appears to be characterized by some internal events which have so far resisted precise description and analysis. There are some uniquely individual processes contributed by the learner's nervous system. Furthermore, these internal events are not properly viewed as artifacts of the learning process, but instead must be considered as essential components, without which no learning can occur. It is noteworthy that even the learning of a connection (see Table 10–1) is considered by many modern theorists to require a contribution of internal "feedback stimulation" for its establishment (Mowrer, 1960, Chap. 7). (This discussion of learning types does not include the classical conditioned response, which may be even simpler than the connection, or instrumental response, with which Table 10–1 begins.)

It seems evident, then, that in controlling all of the aspects of external learning conditions described previously, instruction nevertheless can only make the occurrence of this crucial, internal, idiosyncratic event more probable. So far as is now known, instruction cannot directly control this internal event. The careful design of instruction can surely increase its probability and, by so doing, can make the entire process of learning more sure, more predictable, and more efficient. But the individual nervous system must still make its own individual contribution. The nature of that contribution is, of course, what defines the need for the study of individual differences.

Conclusion

The practical implications of this discussion suggest a goal for instruction which seems quite consistent with what is known of the educative process as a totality. One of the major goals of instruction might well be to bring about progressively the elimination of the need for instruction directed at the individual. Doesn't this suggest, after all, the major difference between a fourth-grader and a graduate student? The former needs all the help he can get from the external conditions established by properly designed instruction. The latter needs almost none of this help because he performs the various functions himself. In other words, to a very large extent he carries out self-instruction. What he does when he "studies" is first to analyze and organize the content to be learned in such a way that it can in fact be readily learned.

It may be that additional emphasis needs to be given, in a very broad and comprehensive sense, to the notion of *self-instruction*, not simply as an immediately applicable technique, but as a goal. This may be the direction of practical development which could best exploit the unique internal contribution of the individual learner.

PART·V·

SUMMATION

∽

I attempt to do two things in this conclusion: to summarize major points of agreement and disagreement among the theories sampled in this book; and to make some more personal comments about the present state of instructional theory and practice. The purpose is to identify what seem to me to be some (1) germinal concepts of instructional purpose and practice presented in this book, (2) unresolved questions requiring additional research, (3) issues meriting further theoretical concern, (4) needed changes in teacher training, curriculum structure, and instructional implementation.

11

Integration and Reactions

LAURENCE SIEGEL [*]

ᥬᥨ

THE PURPOSES OF INSTRUCTION

The purposes of instruction can be stated in terms of either the terminal behavior it should generate or inferences about the kinds of organismic development it should encourage. Since Hedegard's historical introduction in Chapter 1 makes the latter kind of statement, it is convenient to follow his direction in considering how contemporary instructional theorists view the purposes of instruction.

Hedegard's cluster analysis of early theories of instruction results in his identification of three central, historically important concerns relative to the purposes of instruction: moral development, ego development, and adaptability. He observes that while the first of these, moral development, can be broadly conceived as an implicit objective of many classroom activities, it received little systematic consideration by early theorists. It is still neglected. None of the present contributors refers specifically to moral development as an instructional objective.

Yet current educational practitioners seem committed to developing ethical-social morality. The school is a partner in this endeavor, supplementing the efforts of other social institutions. Recognition of the school's participation in this partnership is evident from the scrutiny given by boards of education and boards of trustees to library

* I am particularly indebted to Irwin A. Berg, Harold B. Pepinsky, and Lila C. Siegel for their careful critical reading of a draft of this chapter. Many of their suggestions have been incorporated in it.

317

contents, to assigned readings, and to teachers' activities both in and out of class. The tradition of academic freedom is tempered by society's investment in perpetuating its current values. Thus, to a large extent, schools in general, and particularly those that are publicly supported, tend to mirror rather than form societal views of social-political issues. If the contemporary formulations of this book are a representative sample, instructional theorists are not directly concerned with this problem.

All of the contributors who deal with instructional objectives either imply or state outright the value they put upon adaptive behavior rather than upon the acquisition of knowledge and skill. They emphasize creativity, synthesis, conceptualization, problem solving, and thinking; they regard facts merely as intellectual tools.

Ego development, too, is a recurring theme in these chapters. The educational experiences that underlie both independent learning and continued cognitive growth after formal education is terminated are succinctly described by Rogers. He writes that these experiences must have the qualities of (1) personal involvement, (2) self-initiated learning, (3) pervasiveness, (4) an internal locus of evaluation, and (5) personal meaning and relevance. This enumeration assumes that educational experiences must have an organismic impact upon the learner. Rogers's emphasis upon the student as an idiosyncratic learner is consistent with the beliefs expressed in Chapters 6, 8, 9, and 10.

Just as there is general agreement on ego development and adaptability as the most important educational objectives, so there is agreement on the fundamental purpose of instruction: to structure the conditions of education so that students may best attain these objectives.

For the most part, each of the contributors to this book focuses on a relatively limited aspect of instruction. Three broad organizing concepts have been selected for the purpose of integrating these contributions: processes, participants, and environments.

The instructional *processes* are learning, teaching, and miscellaneous interpersonal processes occurring among persons other than teachers and learners. The primary *participants* are students and teachers, although others, such as members of the student's family, the teacher's colleagues, school administrators, and society in general, may be regarded as at least secondary participants in the instructional process. Similarly, although the classroom or study carrel is the immediate *environment* for instruction, more remote environments that may affect instructional outcomes are the home, residence hall, and other extraclass settings.

THE PROCESSES OF INSTRUCTION

Since there can be no quarrel with the idea that instruction should be directed toward having certain of its participants learn something. the summary remarks about processes center first upon "learning." Then, because school learning is mediated by people (especially teachers) and resources of various kinds (for example, instructional devices), these are reviewed next as "primary mediational processes." Finally, certain "secondary mediational processes" are discussed: interactions between learners and persons other than the teacher or the teacher-substitute.

Learning

Stated theoretical issues relevant to classroom learning can be summarized as a simple question: "How do students come to modify their beliefs and their behavior?" Once phrased, this question must inevitably be elaborated by a specification of *what* is to be learned. Although the language of elaboration differs among the several formulations comprising this book, the contributors make essentially similar distinctions between the kinds of educational objectives and the processes appropriate to their attainment. Rogers, for example, differentiates between associational and experiential learning; Ericksen distinguishes between teaching students to roll the French *r* and teaching them to think; Ausubel writes of rote versus meaningful learning; and the Siegels speak of factual versus conceptual acquisition.

There are two striking features about these distinctions. First and most apparent, virtually all of the authors treat higher-order objectives, such as learning to think, to conceptualize, to synthesize, and to be receptive to experience, as primary. Second and perhaps less apparent, is the artificiality of the distinction between cognitive and noncognitive processes when these higher-order objectives are emphasized.

The attainment of these objectives is assumed to involve the intellect and the viscera. The learner's attitudes, drives, and emotions are believed to interact with his sensory impressions and intellectual endowment jointly to determine the over-all impact of instruction. In Chapter 1, Hedegard notes a historical progression from an earlier view that learning involves the acquisition and elaboration of relatively independent faculties and skills to a later view that learning is a unitary process which involves the total organism. The latter position is held more or less uniformly by all of the contributors to this book.

AN IDIOSYNCRATIC PROCESS

All of the chapters tend to emphasize the individual learner. Classes do not learn; students learn. Therefore, rather than speaking of "best" instructional arrangements, many of the contributors refer to optimal instructional arrangements *for particular learners.* This emphasis is especially central to Chapters 6 and 9. It is also made explicit by Rogers, however, when he discusses the nature of experiential learning, by Woodruff in his discussion of referential inputs as the sole sources of percepts, by Ausubel's frequent distinction between phenomenological and logical meaning, and by Gagné's view of instruction as the arrangement of situational variables to interact optimally with learner variables.

In one way or another, all of these writers regard instruction as an interaction between the "givens" brought to the instructional setting by the learner and the circumstances (including other persons) comprising that setting.

AN ACTIVE PROCESS

There is general agreement also that contemporary society requires active student involvement and participation in learning. All of the contributors reject the reactive-passive learner model, that is, the learner as a person to whom something is done.

The activity, participation, and involvement to which these writers refer is not to be confused with the simple, but often ineffective expedient of having students "take part" by doing something. Whereas, for example, a laboratory exercise requires activity by the student, it may or may not contribute effectively to his learning. The kind of activity to which these writers refer requires, in addition, that learners perceive what they are doing as personally relevant and that they take responsibility for assessing the quality of their own performances. Thus, participation and involvement cannot be inferred from the superficial appearance of the instructional setting. Some students listening to a lecture may be very active participants; others, despite their exposure to what have been called "discovery experiences," may be passive.

It is striking that these contributions make only oblique references to "classical" learning theories. The trend away from reliance on classical learning theories in formal education was noted also in the National Society for the Study of Education Yearbook, *Theories of Learning and Instruction*, edited by Hilgard (1964). In his postscript to the Yearbook, Hilgard notes that the era of the "great debate" among learning theorists is over. Instead of generalized theories of learning, attention is increasingly being given to theories of *particular kinds* of learning.

Gage, in the same Yearbook, observes that at least three "families" of learning theory seem compatible, in the sense that they were developed to account for different kinds of learning in different kinds of situations. The three to which Gage refers are conditioning theory, identification theory, and cognitive theory. And, as he indicates, all three may be valid for different kinds of persons learning different things in different situations. In the formulation of theories of instruction, it is appropriate to identify the goals, participants, and circumstances under which particular learning theories are appropriate, rather than to choose among systematic theoretical positions without regard for these specifications.

Although this view is held more or less by all contributors, it is perhaps best summarized by Gagné. He writes about *varieties* of learning rather than about learning as a unitary phenomenon. And he argues that if there are several kinds of learning, it is reasonable to suppose the existence of an equal number of conditions of effective learning.

Primary Mediational Processes

The meaning I have given to "primary" mediational processes restricts their occurrence to formal instructional settings. This designation is preferred to "classroom teaching" because the latter is a generic term, much like "learning." Just as it is possible to distinguish kinds of learning, so too is it possible to distinguish kinds of teaching. For convenience, I distinguish further between the teaching done by teachers and that done (or mediated) by devices and instructional materials.

TEACHING BY TEACHERS

Hedegard notes the long-standing concern of educational theorists about the extent to which teachers should personally engage their students. Should the teacher evoke responses from students by involving them in some form of personal interaction? Or should he instead dispense information and display his thought processes to students who assume passive roles as members of an audience?

The general agreement among contributors upon the active nature of the learning process should not be construed also to imply agreement upon the desirability of teacher-pupil interaction. The authors of Chapter 9, for example, suggest that whereas personal interaction may facilitate performance by certain kinds of students, insulation from such interaction may prove optimal for other kinds of students. In their view, the critical factor is congruence between the learner's idiosyncratic drive pattern and the instructional press generated, in large measure, by the teacher's behavior and expectations.

Insulation from the teacher might, perhaps, be unnecessary if teachers were able to hold the model attitudes suggested for them by Rogers. If the teacher were, in Rogers's sense, always "real," if he engaged his students in direct personal encounter as a person rather than a role player, if he prized each student and were empathically understanding, then he likely would not represent a potential source of threat to any student. If the teacher exemplified these attitudes, the primary teaching process might well be as Rogers suggests: that of serving the students as an additional resource upon which they may draw in order to facilitate their own learning. Rogers might well be correct if he went on to assert that, without these attitudes, the person designated "teacher" could not properly fulfill his obligations.

However much this teacher model may be valued, it conflicts with certain realities. There are, in fact, many teachers who could not integrate such a set of attitudes without psychotherapeutic assistance. In addition, teaching strategies rest, at least in part, upon such factors as class size, student motivation and ability, and so on.

In contrast with Rogers's strong emphasis upon what kind of person the teacher ought to be, Woodruff's analysis emphasizes what the teacher ought to *do*. Woodruff suggests a number of actions that are feasible in spite of relatively large classes and the heterogeneity of students in these classes. He asserts that teachers must affect learning at five points by (1) providing appropriate referential stimulation; (2) encouraging thinking, conceptualization, and storage; (3) facilitating decision making; (4) providing opportunities for trials; and (5) permitting and encouraging empirical feedback of trial results. Woodruff argues persuasively that the three latter points of impact are too often neglected in the normal course of instruction. The theme that effective teaching must provide opportunities for realistic simulation and feedback in addition to facilitating cognitive change is a recurrent one. In addition to Woodruff, it is sounded in particular by Rogers and Gagné.

Another recurrent theme, sounded with variations by all contributors, is that effective teaching implies the attainment of two related outcomes: that students develop the desire for self-instruction, and that students learn how to learn.

In asserting the primacy of these objectives, the contributors generally have neglected to make explicit two important points. First, from a practical standpoint, these objectives must pervade the curriculum before they can become objectives of individual teachers. The learner's life space includes more than his experiences with any one teacher or set of teachers. Second, these objectives and the teaching processes required for their attainment may be relatively inappropriate for a particular learner. Given his past history and his present living environment, there may be more pressing and realistic goals for *him*. This seems clearly to be true of youngsters for whom the most realistic efforts toward social acceptance in this generation requires the attainment of marketable skills. Although less obvious, it is also true of youngsters who have not been "culturally deprived" in the usual sense of minority-directed prejudices, but who nonetheless are educationally impoverished.

More than any other contributor, Ericksen emphasizes that the teacher is but one source of inputs in the teaching-learning system. Other input sources are books, programs, and laboratory exercises, to name a few. Although these are typically considered "instructional materials," they do encourage learning and, at least under certain conditions, can provide the student with feedback about his performance.

A limitation inherent in these materials is that they are relatively inflexible and therefore insensitive to individual differences. What flexibility can be built in, for example, by arranging branches in programed instructional materials, is relatively insignificant compared with the potential flexibility of human teachers.

Thus, there are at least two important determinants of the effectiveness of teaching materials and devices. First, they must be matched to the idiosyncratic needs and abilities of the learner. This is typically done, for example, in elementary-school classes when pupils differing in achievement are assigned different reading materials. Second, extreme care must be devoted to the internal organization of the materials. Once the student begins a laboratory exercise or textbook, there are narrow limits of internal adjustment to his erroneous learning or flagging interest.

The organization of teaching materials so that the learner can most effectively interact with them is one of Ausubel's particular concerns. He notes the essential similarities between the organizational principles underlying teaching, regardless of whether teaching is mediated by persons or devices. His distinction between logical and psychological organizers, in particular, is especially pertinent. Instructional materials tend to rely heavily upon the former, which can impede rather than facilitate the kind of cognitive integration generally held to be a highly important educational goal.

Secondary Mediational Processes

All of the chapters emphasize the dyadic interaction between learner and teacher. Most of them, with the exception of the one by Biddle and Adams, make scarce if any mention of interactions other than the one between pupil and teacher or teacher-substitute.

Biddle and Adams are uniquely concerned about the classroom as a social system. They regard teacher behavior and pupil behavior as components of, and responses to, this system. Their model suggests the relevance of social processes in the classroom to instructional strategies and outcomes. As these authors carry out the research design outlined in their chapter, they anticipate that their findings will add breadth to instructional theory because of their treatment of teaching and learning as social-psychological phenomena.

THE PARTICIPANTS IN INSTRUCTION

The foregoing discussion of processes suggests a parallel organization for considering the participants in instruction. Attention is given first to students, next to teachers, and last to other participants.

Students

I have already indicated the extent to which the contributors have affirmed the importance of individual differences and the consequent necessity of teaching *to*, rather than in spite of, these differences. Ericksen, in particular, builds his chapter upon learning as an idiographic process. In a related vein, Woodruff and Ausubel emphasize the idiosyncratic nature of meaning and the consequent centrality of cognitive theory to improving instruction. In Chapter 9, the authors write of "idiosyncratic drive patterns" and the necessity for effecting optimal matches between these patterns and instructional circumstances. Chapter 10 similarly discusses instruction as an interaction between variables within the learner and variables comprising the learning situation.

The importance of certain student characteristics is repeatedly emphasized by these writers in their assertion of the centrality to instructional theory of the differences between learners. In one way or another, most contributors refer to the student's past history and present capabilities. These are the "givens" with which he approaches a formal instructional experience. In large measure, such givens determine his motivation for performance and the phenomenological significance of the content to which he is exposed.

Granted the dependence of instructional effectiveness upon organismic variables, consequent instructional practices may follow two quite opposite directions. On the one hand, these organismic characteristics can be utilized in fact as givens, and the remainder of the instructional context structured to capitalize upon the student's strengths and to minimize the interfering effects of his weaknesses. The primary impact of this approach upon instruction would be to generate desired understanding, concepts, knowledge, and so on as efficiently as possible. An alternative approach is to structure the remainder of the instructional context in ways calculated to help students overcome their weaknesses and further develop their strengths. Rather than "feeding" the organismic characteristics, this approach would seek sometimes to alter them.

Teachers

Although considerable attention is given to teaching processes, these formulations contain relatively little in the way of a systematic consideration of teacher characteristics. With the few exceptions noted below, the emphasis is upon what the teacher *does,* and not upon what he *is* or *should be.*

In his chapter, Rogers gives a clear picture of at least one kind of teacher. In line with his view of instructional outcomes and the processes appropriate to their realization, Rogers emphasizes that the teacher must hold the attitudes he characterizes as realness, acceptance, and empathic understanding.

Although the other contributors would probably agree that these are desirable attitudes for people in general and teachers in particular, they might question the centrality of these attitudes to effective instruction. As I have already said, most of the other writers give more attention to teacher behavior than to teacher attitudes.

In Chapter 9, for example, the viewpoint is that the instructor's manifest objectives (that is, those objectives made evident to the students by his examinations, classroom behavior, and so on) are powerful shapers of instructional outcomes. The amount and type of personal contact between student and instructor and the quality of the intellectual climate developed in class are regarded as similarly important. Furthermore, it is argued that since students comprise heterogeneous groups, it is probably an oversimplification to postulate a single "best" type of teacher just as it is an oversimplification to postulate a single best type of student. This view is shared by Biddle and Adams.

Ancillary Participants

At least two types of ancillary participants (persons other than the teacher and student) affect the progress of instruction. One of these includes all persons who have contributed in some way to the student's and the teacher's history; the other includes the student's and the teacher's contemporaries at the particular moment in time when the instructional process is studied.

The authors in this book uniformly neglect consideration of those participants ancillary to the teacher's developmental history and present behavior. This neglect, which may be serious, is reflected in the ensuing discussion, which is restricted to those ancillary participants affecting student behavior.

THE STUDENT'S HISTORY

All of the chapters attach considerable importance to the student's history. In Chapters 4 and 8, preinstructional experiences are regarded as determinants of the student's present cognitive structure and hence of the meaningfulness of new material presented to him. The student's behavioral repertoire, as discussed in Chapters 7 and 10, similarly reflects his history. The individual-difference variables, central to Chapters 6 and 9, are heavily grounded in the student's previous experiences.

In view of the general agreement upon the importance of the student's history, it is somewhat surprising that these writers give so little attention to the significant elements comprising that history. In particular, the influence of parents, siblings, and previous school experiences are relatively neglected, with the exception of the discussion on this point by Biddle and Adams.

THE STUDENT'S CONTEMPORARIES

The model by Biddle and Adams stands alone also as the only one evidencing substantial concern for the here-and-now participants in instruction apart from the teacher and students. In contrast with the

Integration and Reactions / SIEGEL • 327

other chapters, theirs treats social characteristics of the classroom as central to understanding instruction.

Instructional Environments

A distinctive characteristic of contemporary theorizing is that it is relatively free from the traditional concerns about superficial features of the instructional environment. Instead of regarding variables like class size and physical arrangements as central to theories of instruction, the contributors consider these only as facilitators or inhibitors of the underlying instructional processes. Even the one formulation most concerned with the physical and social environment (Biddle and Adams) casts this concern in terms of the implications of the environment for social interaction. It appears that, at last, the relatively unprofitable era of assessing the relative effectiveness of such environmental variations as large and small classes, televised and conventional classes, and so on may have come to an end.

In structuring instructional environments, the authors urge consideration of the appropriateness of alternative environments for particular students and teachers and for the realization of predetermined, carefully delineated goals. Rather than advocating a search for uniformly better instructional environments, most of the authors urge the development of parallel environments, each designed to maximize the attainments for specified student subgroups.

Some Personal Reactions

In the remainder of this chapter, I wish to take stock of the various contributions in an entirely personal fashion. In exercising this editorial prerogative, I do not claim that these views are shared by the contributors or by other contemporary theorists who have considered instruction.

Taking the formulations that are here included as a sample of thinking in this field, I distinguish three levels of discourse by the contributors.

The most highly developed theoretical statements are presented in the chapters by Ausubel, Jahnke, and Rogers. Each of these writers assumes a particular posture which he maintains consistently in his attempt to organize and understand large bodies of empirical data about instruction.

The chapters by Ericksen and Gagné seem to me to be "pre-theoretical," although a distinction between theoretical and pretheoretical writings is clearly arbitrary. These two chapters present concepts which can subsequently be made central to more rigorous theoretical statements. This is not to be construed as an assessment implying that I attach less importance to these contributions than to those cited in the preceding paragraph. On the contrary, both present internally consistent views suggesting modifications of educational practice as well as future directions for theorizing.

A third type of focus appears in the remaining chapters: those by Biddle and Adams, Siegel and Siegel, and Woodruff. These authors seek to conceptualize the instructional process or selected aspects of it in new ways calculated to suggest fertile directions for empirical investigation and subsequent theorizing.

Particularized versus Generalized Theories of Instruction

The most exciting and far-reaching generalization emerging for me from this sample of contemporary formulations is that to be most effective, instruction must be tailored to the needs, capabilities, and histories of the individual learners. Virtually all of the contributors assert the desirability of multiplicity—both of educational goals and of the instructional means toward the attainment of these goals.

In one sense, there is certainly nothing revolutionary about this reassertion of the existence and importance of individual differences. Yet in another, it makes explicit a general dissatisfaction with prevalent educational practices which are class-directed rather than learner-directed and with those research patterns which compare the "effectiveness" of instructional procedures for groups of learners without regard for the interactions among pupils, teachers, goals, and procedures. It also makes explicit the infeasibility of a generalized theory of instruction appropriate to all objectives and learners. All contributors have envisioned a need for schools that are more complex than the ones in existence. This complexity extends beyond equipment and facilities to new concepts of educational purposes and of the appropriate means for attaining these.

Impediments to Change

Although each of the contributors has addressed himself to these new concepts, the implementation of these concepts is impeded by a number of factors aside from the obvious one of inertia. Among these impediments are (1) the fact that simple organizations are easier to manage than complex ones; (2) the essentially "unprofessional" attitudes often held by teachers; (3) the democratically derived ideal of providing identical educational experiences without regard for individual differences as preparation for equal life, leisure, and work opportunities; and (4) the traditional discontinuity between elementary and secondary education on the one hand, and higher education on the other.

SIMPLE VERSUS COMPLEX ORGANIZATIONS

With the class as an organizational unit, the teacher's job as manager is clearly simplified when all members are doing the same thing at the same time in an attempt to attain the same goal. Diversity of objectives implies a corresponding diversity of activity. The management task under such circumstances requires sensitivity and flexibility. The teacher must prize and encourage difference rather than uniformity and must be sufficiently skilled so that the absence of uniformity does not lead to mayhem. These management difficulties and corresponding requirements are, of course, compounded when the school or school system is considered as the organizational unit, but this discussion is restricted to classroom organizations.

Virtually all teachers do, in fact, recognize and make moderate provisions for individual differences between learners. However, they are seriously impeded in doing so by tradition-bound approaches to instruction encouraged by the society and reflected in the curricula of most teacher-training institutions. Increased acceptance of various kinds of learning resources and management aids (for example, team teaching) is a partial answer to providing for diversity. However, a danger associated with these devices and techniques is that they are too often regarded by teachers, school administrators, and parents as panaceas, and their use is perverted to quantitative ends.

The effective management of classroom learning, in the sense that contributors to this book conceive of it, requires teachers with advanced knowledges, skills, and attitudes with respect to human development and behavior as well as subject matter. In contrast with these requirements is the fact that a disturbing proportion of students elect to major in education in order to "have a job to fall back on" or to "have a job until they marry."

The situation at the college level differs from that at the elementary and secondary levels in that college teachers have had little, if any, preparation for managing learning. Whereas many college teachers are highly professional in their attitudes toward their scholarly disciplines, their responsibilities as catalysts for learning may be discharged superficially by assigning readings, meeting lectures, and administering some sort of examination for grading purposes.

Clearly, these unfortunate situations cannot be rectified without making the profession itself more attractive to the best college students. Although this is partly a matter of economics, it is more significantly a matter of selecting better teacher-trainees and providing them with more challenging and stimulating curricula.

It would be naïve to maintain that these factors alone would improve the general level of professional competence and personal involvement of teachers. Obviously, there also needs to be a further improvement in the perceived status of the profession and a consequent desire of the society to allow itself to be led by, rather than simply reflected in, its educational institutions.

DEMOCRACY AND EDUCATION

A democratic society implies by its very nature the availability of equal educational opportunities for all of its citizens so that they may realize their potentials. It does *not*, contrary to some applications of this fundamental principle, imply identical educational opportunity regardless of potential and motivation. To the extent that the latter course is pursued, schools are forced to provide a lockstep program something like a stretch sock—adaptable to everyone but not really fitting anyone.

In order for the formulations comprising the substantive chapters to be implemented most effectively, a high degree of continuity and articulation is required throughout the entire educational sequence. The recurring emphasis upon higher-order cognitive attainments, particularly at the college level, implies that, prior to coming to college, students have developed a sufficiently broad and integrated cognitive structure, a sense of responsibility for directing their own learning, and a set to synthesize and conceptualize.

The notion of an integrated instructional complex extending from elementary grades through higher education with opportunities for branching on the basis of student need and interest is being implemented in limited fashion. An ambitious experiment in articulated instruction of this sort is being undertaken, for example, at the South Florida Education Center (Fort Lauderdale), consisting of Nova elementary and secondary schools, Broward Junior College, and the projected Nova University of Advanced Technology. As the time nears when 50 per cent of high-school graduates will be pursuing some kind of higher education, it becomes increasingly imperative that this type of articulation become the norm rather than the exception.

Education of the Future

Theoreticians and educational administrators agree about the general shape of education in the future. In spite of enrollment pressures and the necessary increases in the number of learners assigned to each teacher, instruction increasingly will be custom-tailored to the needs and capabilities of the learner.

In accepting this as the direction for development, educators are admitting the feasibility and, indeed, the desirability of integrating relatively recent advances in teaching technology into the fabric of everyday instruction. Contrary to the view held in some quarters, that televised teaching and automated instruction are techniques for coping with education's quantitative problems, such devices and techniques will probably find their most significant applications in helping effect qualitative improvements.

Now that teachers' fears about "technological unemployment" are largely dispelled, the teacher can be envisioned as a learning-resources specialist. In this role, he will identify each student's level of attainment and cognitive development, establish legitimate goals for that student, and select from the full armamentarium of instructional aids (including books, seminars, televised lectures, programed courses, and the like) those that are best calculated to help *that* learner reach his goals.

Along with this change in the way teachers will function, corollary changes can be anticipated in the structure of formal education. The annual grade progression at precollege levels and credit accumulation in colleges will be supplanted by an ungraded system. Students may or may not still be required to devote eight years to elementary, four years to secondary, and four years to higher education, but their accomplishments within these time periods will more faithfully reflect their heterogeneities than they do now. Standardization of attainment supposedly represented by, say, the high-school diploma is largely a fiction. With an individually tailored instructional program, it will no longer be necessary to maintain this fiction.

Given this coming pattern of formal instruction, there are several problems and issues requiring consideration. Clearly, preservice and in-service teacher-training programs as now constituted are largely inadequate for the new roles teachers will be required to perform. As these programs are modified in the direction of increased intensity and breadth, they will become more intellectually demanding and, hopefully, will convey a greater sense of professional identification than is now cultivated. Along with this increased challenge, it may be anticipated that these programs will prove attractive to increasing numbers of the more capable undergraduate students.

Various modifications of teacher-preparation programs are suggested by the substantive formulations presented in earlier chapters. However, it is evident that considerably more needs to be discovered about the kinds of educational experiences optimally suited to learners with particular needs and capabilities. Given this information and the techniques for making reasonably sophisticated assessments of pertinent student characteristics, it should become possible to provide each learner with those particular instructional experiences calculated to maximize the educational gain *for him.*

For such individually tailored instructional guidance to be most successful, it is also necessary to discover more about the limits of behavioral change possible at various points in the instructional sequence. For example, is it efficacious to encourage and test for "conceptual" thinking at the college level if previous educational experiences have emphasized factual acquisition? Or, as another example, what are the optimal sequences for encouraging cognitive-structure development for learning mathematics, English composition, and other subject areas? Questions like these are central to curriculum reform as well as to the refinement of special instructional techniques and the improvement of teacher-training programs.

Another Glance at Educational Objectives

The search for greater "efficiency" in education is too often seduced by the model for increasing the efficiency of industrial organizations. For the latter, qualitative improvement at reduced cost represents a valid gain. For the former, even if output can be increased without a corresponding increase in expenditures, the question arises whether it is worthwhile doing more of whatever it is that is now done. Suppose a single teacher, with the aid of television, programed instruction, well-equipped laboratories, and the like, can "handle" twice as many students as effectively as he formerly did without these aids. Without belittling the press of numbers and the real need for quantitative improvement, it is not only legitimate, but imperative, to question the qualitative outcomes of instructional change. Merely holding the line on quality while increasing quantity is probably not enough when youngsters must be prepared for societal and technological changes the specific nature of which cannot be anticipated with certainty by either their teachers or their parents.

Thus, society and its educational institutions must make some decisions about the proper responsibility of formal instruction for effecting personal change. As noted above, to be most effective, instruction must be tailored to the needs, capabilities, and histories of individual learners. On the assumption that optimizing educational attainment by each learner is feasible, something more must be said about the kinds of educational attainments desired. It is imperative that priorities be established recognizing the existence of a hierarchy of attainments upon which formal education should focus.

Without such priorities, education can do no more than identify those needs the youngster carries into the schoolroom with him, and arrange circumstances accordingly to facilitate efficient learning. There are at least two dangers inherent in this limitation of educational responsibility:

1. Identification of intellectual needs with a consequent "fixing" of the curriculum may occur too early in the youngster's life. This may add to the number of youngsters designated "late bloomers" and "early wilters."

2. Relegation of formal education entirely to the service of society may result. In this role, education helps society get wherever it is going, but is relatively impotent in helping shape the destiny of mankind.

This brings us full circle to the issue with which I began this chapter and which, indeed, must precede all attempts to develop instructional theories and modify instructional practices: What are the purposes of instruction? Although all contributors emphasized increasing conceptualization, adaptability, and self-initiated learning, I liked best the statements by Ericksen and Rogers. They, in particular, resisted a tendency to objectify and depersonalize the learner.

If the implementation of such objectives as adaptability and conceptualization is probed, it becomes evident that these constructs must be reduced to intensely personal and concrete goals suggesting appropriately personal and concrete curricula and instructional methods. At least three very specific areas of knowledge, understanding, and appreciation underlie the attainment of these goals: the past, the present, and oneself.

Understanding and appreciation of the past (communicated particularly through history and literature respectively) serve at least two ends: they provide vicarious experiences and they provide perspective.

The vicarious experiences in part compensate for the severe limitations on the direct experiences that a person can have in his single lifetime. Moreover, history and literature telescope even these vicarious experiences. Again, the vicarious experiences of history and literature enable a person to grow without risking injury and to think without having himself to work out of each dead end encountered by his predecessors.

The perspectives provided through history and literature establish continuity between past and present, between man's present efforts and previous attempts to impose order upon the unknown. And this perspective facilitates conceptualization.

But knowledge of the past and of the continuity of past, present, and future is not enough. People must understand themselves and others if they are most effectively to contribute to and function in society. The need for such understanding is by no means reduced in an era of rapid scientific and technological advancement. Because of their specialized knowledge, scientists must assume greater rather than lesser social responsibility than ever before for the impact of their discoveries and innovations. And nonscientists must be prepared by the schools to be effective actors rather than passive reactors to the world in which they live.

The schools can contribute to the realization of these goals in several ways. First, the curriculum must be freed from the artificial compartmentalization of knowledge as represented by discrete courses and textbooks. Each discipline is simply a way of looking at the world, emphasizing certain of its attributes and deemphasizing others. To counteract the inevitable distortions produced by these distinctions of convenience, students at all levels must be given a feel for the interrelatedness of knowledge.

Second, the behavioral sciences (particularly psychology, sociology, and anthropology) must be made more central to curriculum planning and implementation. By this I mean not only that principles from the behavioral sciences ought to determine the arrangement of the curriculum and instructional experiences, but also that these disciplines be accorded more central status as components of that curriculum. The world is populated by people; in learning about the world and in developing a personal relationship to it, students need to know as much as possible about human behavior. The development of sensitivity, empathy, and self-knowledge is too critical to be left to chance.

Third, teachers themselves must have a better understanding of human behavior. It seems to me remarkable that society so often entrusts such great responsibility for shaping the values and destinies of coming generations to persons who lack such understanding both of themselves and of the students they instruct.

In conclusion, then, the teacher's role in dispensing facts has diminished in importance. There is general agreement that factual content can be communicated much more efficiently in other ways. This opens the way for teachers to function as learning directors and catalysts. By knowing each student, they can tailor instructional opportunities to him in an effort to help him progress ever further toward the ultimate goals of self-initiated critical evaluation and interpretation of the world around him.

However, the real significance of the possibilities for minimizing the teacher's role as dispenser of facts will be lost unless teacher-training institutions come to grips with what teachers ought instead to be doing and unless the schools themselves make appropriate curricular revisions. The contributors to this book have suggested that although there are many things about teaching and learning yet to be discovered, applications of principles and theories from the behavioral sciences can significantly improve the quality of current instruction.

References

✍

THE FOLLOWING ABBREVIATIONS
ARE USED THROUGHOUT THE REFERENCES:

A.A.C.T.E.	American Association of Colleges for Teacher Education
Amer. Educ. Res. Assn.	American Educational Research Association
Amer. Educ. Res. J.	*American Educational Research Journal*
Amer. J. Orthopsychiat.	*American Journal of Orthopsychiatry*
Amer. J. Psychiat.	*American Journal of Psychiatry*
Amer. J. Psychol.	*American Journal of Psychology*
Amer. Psychol.	*American Psychologist*
Annu. Rev. Psychol.	*Annual Review of Psychology*
Appl. Psychol. Monogr.	*Applied Psychology Monographs*
Arch. Gen. Psychiat.	*Archives of General Psychiatry*
A.S.C.D.	Association for Supervision and Curriculum Development
AV Commun. Rev.	*Audio-Visual Communication Review*
AV Instruction	*Audio-Visual Instruction*
Bur. of Publ., Tchrs. Coll.	Bureau of Publications, Teachers College
Child Developm.	*Child Development*
Coll. and Univer.	*College and University*
Contemp. Psychol.	*Contemporary Psychology*
Current Anthrop.	*Current Anthropology*
Dig. Neurol. Psychiat.	*Digest of Neurology and Psychiatry*
Educ. Comment	*Educational Comment*
Educ. Leadership	*Educational Leadership*
Elem. Sch. J.	*Elementary School Journal*

339

Harv. Educ. Rev.	*Harvard Educational Review*
Human Developm. Inst.	Human Development Institute
Human Relat.	*Human Relations*
Inst. Industr. Relat.	Institute of Industrial Relations
J. Abnorm. Soc. Psychol.	*Journal of Abnormal and Social Psychology*
J. Appl. Psychol.	*Journal of Applied Psychology*
J. Comp. Physiol. Psychol.	*Journal of Comparative and Physiological Psychology*
J. Consult. Psychol.	*Journal of Consulting Psychology*
J. Educ. Psychol.	*Journal of Educational Psychology*
J. Educ. Res.	*Journal of Educational Research*
J. Educ. Sociol.	*Journal of Educational Sociology*
J. Exp. Educ.	*Journal of Experimental Education*
J. Exp. Psychol.	*Journal of Experimental Psychology*
J. Gen. Educ.	*Journal of General Education*
J. Gen. Psychol.	*Journal of General Psychology*
J. Higher Educ.	*Journal of Higher Education*
J. Med. Educ.	*Journal of Medical Education*
J. Soc. Issues	*Journal of Social Issues*
J. Soc. Psychol.	*Journal of Social Psychology*
J. Tchr. Educ.	*Journal of Teacher Education*
Merrill-Palmer Quart. Behav. Developm.	*Merrill-Palmer Quarterly of Behavior and Development*
NEA J.	*National Education Association Journal*
Nat. Acad. Sci.	National Academy of Sciences
Nat. Soc. Stud. Educ.	National Society for the Study of Education
Phil. Phenom. Res.	*Philosophy and Phenomenological Research*
Psychol. Bull.	*Psychological Bulletin*
Psychol. Monogr.	*Psychological Monographs: General and Applied*
Psychol. Rep.	*Psychological Reports*
Psychol. Rev.	*Psychological Review*
Rev. Educ. Res.	*Review of Educational Research*
Sch. and Soc.	*School and Society*
Sch. Rev.	*School Review*
Sci. Amer.	*Scientific American*
Tchrs. Coll. Rec.	*Teachers College Record*
War/Peace Rep.	*War/Peace Reports*

CHAPTER 1

An Overview of Historical Formulations

✒

Adamson, J. W. *The educational writings of John Locke.* New York: Longmans, Green, 1912. Works excerpted were first published 1693–1706.

Anderson, L. F. *Pestalozzi.* New York: McGraw-Hill, 1931. Works excerpted were first published 1780–1826.

Ashton-Warner, S. *Teacher.* New York: Simon and Schuster, 1963.

Child, I. L., E. H. Potter, and E. M. Levine. Children's textbooks and personality development: An exploration in the social psychology of education. *Psychol. Monogr.,* 1946, *60,* No. 3 (Whole No. 279).

Comenius, J. A. *Selections.* Paris: Unesco, 1957. Works excerpted were first published 1623–1657.

Dewey, J. *Art as experience.* New York: Putnam, 1958. First published 1934.

———. *Democracy and education.* New York: Macmillan, 1916.

Firth, R. Ethical absolutism and the ideal observer. *Phil. Phenom. Res.,* 1952, *12,* 317–345.

Fitch, Sir J., ed. *Thomas and Matthew Arnold and their influence on English education.* New York: Scribner, 1897. Works excerpted were first published 1810–1888.

Fitzpatrick, E. A., ed. *St. Ignatius and the Ratio Studiorum.* New York: McGraw-Hill, 1933. Excerpted works of Ignatius Loyola were first published 1547–1599.

Froebel, F. *The education of man*. New York: Appleton, 1903. First published 1826.

Herbart, J. F. *The application of psychology to the science of education*. New York: Scribner, 1898. Consists of letters written about 1830–1833.

James, W. *Talks to teachers*. New York: Holt, 1922. First published 1899 as *Talks to teachers on psychology and to students on some of life's ideals*.

Marrou, H. I. *A history of education in antiquity*. New York: Sheed and Ward, 1956.

Montessori, M. *The discovery of the child*. Madras: Kalakshetra Publications, 1948. Revised and enlarged edition of *The Montessori Method*, originally published in Italian in 1909.

Neill, A. S. *Summerhill*. New York: Hart, 1960.

Sanford, N. The dynamics of identification. *Psychol. Rev.*, 1955, *62*, 106–108.

Schwickerath, R., S.J. *Jesuit education: Its history and principles*. St. Louis: Herder, 1903.

CHAPTER 2

An Overview of Contemporary Formulations

✑

Amer. Educ. Res. Assn., Comm. on the Criterion of Teacher Effectiveness. Second report. *J. Educ. Res.*, 1953, *46*, 641–658.

Bloom, B. S. Thought processes in lectures and discussions. *J. Gen. Educ.*, 1953, 7, 160–169.

———, ed. *Taxonomy of educational objectives*. New York: Longmans, Green, 1956.

Campbell, D. T., and J. C. Stanley. Experimental and quasi-experimental designs for research on teaching. In N. L. Gage, ed. *Handbook of research on teaching*. Amer. Educ. Res. Assn. Chicago: Rand McNally, 1963, pp. 171–246.

Carpenter, C. R., and L. P. Greenhill. An investigation of closed-circuit television for teaching university courses. *Instruction. Television Res.*, Proj. No. 2. University Park: Penn. State University, 1958.

Domas, S. J., and D. V. Tiedeman. Teacher competence: An annotated bibliography. *J. Exp. Educ.*, 1950, *19*, 101–218.

Gage, N. L. Paradigms for research on teaching. In N. L. Gage, ed. *Hand-*

book of research on teaching. Amer. Educ. Res. Assn. Chicago: Rand McNally, 1963, Chap. 3.

Hovland, C. I., A. A. Lumsdaine, and F. D. Sheffield. *Experiments in mass communication.* Princeton, N.J.: Princeton University Press, 1949.

Lumsdaine, A. A. Audio-visual research in the U.S. Air Force. *AV Commun. Rev.,* 1953, *1,* 76–90.

————. Graphic aids, models, and mockups as tools for individual and classroom instruction. In G. Finch, ed. *Educational and training media: A symposium.* Publ. No. 789. Washington, D.C.: Nat. Acad. Sci., Nat. Res. Council, 1960, pp. 69–113.

————. Instruments and media of instruction. In N. L. Gage, ed. *Handbook of research on teaching.* Amer. Educ. Res. Assn. Chicago: Rand McNally, 1963, pp. 583–682.

Maccia, E. S. The conceptions of model in educational theorizing. Paper 62–114. Columbus: Bur. Educ. Res. and Serv., Ohio State University, 1962.

Macomber, F. G., and L. Siegel. *Final report.* Exp. Stud. in Instructional Procedures. Oxford, Ohio: Miami University, 1960.

Siegel, L., F. G. Macomber, and J. F. Adams. The effectiveness of large group instruction at the university level. *Harv. Educ. Rev.,* 1959, *29,* 216–226.

Siegel, L., *et al.* Students' thoughts during class: A criterion for educational research. *J. Educ. Psychol.,* 1963, *54,* 45–51.

Smith, B. O. A concept of teaching. *Tchrs. Coll. Rec.,* 1960, *61,* 229–241.

CHAPTER 3

The Facilitation of Significant Learning

༄

Barrett-Lennard, G. Dimensions of therapist response as causal factors in therapeutic change. *Psychol. Monogr.,* 1962, *76,* No. 43 (Whole No. 562).

————. Personal communication, 1960.

Berlin, J. I., and L. B. Wyckoff. *Relationship improvement programs.* Atlanta, Ga.: Human Developm. Inst., 1963.

Bradford, L., J. Gibb, and K. Benne, eds. *T-Group theory and laboratory method.* New York: Wiley, 1964.

Buber, M. *Between man and man.* New York: Beacon Press, 1955. Works included were first published 1926–1939.

Fry, E. *Teaching machines and programmed instruction.* New York: Mc-GrawHill, 1963.

Gage, N. L. The educational psychology of American teachers. Paper presented to the advisory council of the Assn. of Organizations for Tchr. Educ., Washington, D.C., Oct. 1963.

Guetzkow, H., et al. *Simulation in international relations: Developments for research and teaching.* Englewood Cliffs, N.J.: Prentice-Hall, 1963.

Lippitt, R. *Teaching behavioral science in the elementary school.* Mimeo report. Ann Arbor: University of Michigan, 1962.

Pressey, S. Teaching machine (and learning theory) crisis. *J. Appl. Psychol.,* 1963, *47,* 1–6.

Rogers, C. R. The necessary and sufficient conditions of therapeutic personality change. *J. Consult. Psychol.,* 1957, *21,* 95–103.

——, ed. *The therapeutic relationship and its impact: A study of psychotherapy with schizophrenics.* Madison: University of Wisconsin Press, 1967.

Schwab, J. J. Inquiry, the science teacher and the educator. *Sch. Rev.,* 1960, *68,* 176–195.

Skinner, B. F. Why we need teaching machines. *Harv. Educ. Rev.,* 1961, *31,* 377–398.

Solomon, L. N. Reducing tensions in a test-tube world. *War/Peace Rep.,* July 1963, *3,* No. 7, 10–12.

Suchman, J. R. *The elementary school training program in scientific inquiry.* Urbana: University of Illinois, 1962.

——. Inquiry training: Building skills for autonomous discovery. *Merrill-Palmer Quart. Behav. Developm.,* 1961, 7, 147–169.

Wechsler, I. R., and J. Reisel. *Inside a sensitivity training group.* Los Angeles: Inst. of Industr. Relat., UCLA, 1959.

CHAPTER 4

Cognitive Models of Learning and Instruction

∾

Alexander, F. The dynamics of psychotherapy in the light of learning theory. *Amer. J. Psychiat.*, 1963, *120*, 441–448. See also abstract in *Dig. Neurol. Psychiat.*, Ser. 31, Dec. 1963, 438.

Allison, J. Cognitive structure and receptivity to low intensity stimulation. *J. Abnorm. Soc. Psychol.*, 1963, *67*, 132–138.

Archer, E. J. Concept identification as a function of obviousness of relevant and irrelevant information. *J. Exp. Psychol.*, 1962, *63*, 616–620.

Arieti, S. The microgeny of thought and perception. *Arch. Gen. Psychiat.*, 1962, *6*, 454–468. See also abstract in *Dig. Neurol. Psychiat.*, Ser. 30, June–July 1962, 244.

Aschner, M. J. M. The analysis of verbal interaction in the classroom. In A. A. Bellack, ed. *Theory and research in teaching.* New York: Bur. of Publ., Tchrs. Coll., Columbia University, 1963.

Battig, W. F., and L. E. Bourne, Jr. Concept identification as a function of intra- and interdimensional variability. *J. Exp. Psychol.*, 1961, *61*, 329–333.

Beberman, M. Improving high school mathematics teaching. *Educ. Leadership*, 1959, *17*, 162–166.

Bellack, A. A. Conceptions of knowledge: Their significance for the curriculum. In W. A. Jenkins, ed. *The nature of knowledge.* Milwaukee: Sch. of Educ., University of Wisconsin, 1961.

———. Selection and organization of curriculum content: An analysis. In A.S.C.D. *What shall the high schools teach?* Yearb. Washington, D.C.: N.E.A., 1956, Chap. 4.

———, ed. *Theory and research in teaching.* New York: Bur. of Publ., Tchrs. Coll., Columbia University, 1963.

———, and J. R. Davitz. *The language of the classroom.* New York: Inst. of Psychol. Res., Tchrs. Coll., Columbia University, 1963.

Bloom, B. S., ed. *Taxonomy of educational objectives.* Handbook I: Cognitive domain. New York: Longmans, Green, 1956.

Bourne, L. E., Jr. Long-term effects of misinformative feedback upon concept identification. *J. Exp. Psychol.*, 1963, *65*, 139–147.

Bristow, W. H. What knowledge is of most worth? *Educ. Leadership*, 1958, *15*, 447–449.

Broadbent, D. E. *Perception and communication.* New York: Pergamon Press, 1958.

Broudy, H. S. *Building a philosophy of education.* New York: Prentice-Hall, 1954.

Bruner, J. S. The conditions of creativity. In H. E. Gruber, G. Terrell, and M. Wertheimer, eds. *Contemporary approaches to creative thinking.* New York: Atherton Press, 1962, Chap. 1.

———. The course of cognitive growth. *Amer. Psychol.*, 1964, *19*, 1–15.

———. *The process of education.* Cambridge, Mass.: Harvard University Press, 1960.

Burlingame, M. Some determinants of concept formation. *Coll. of Educ. Rec.*, 1963, *11*, 14–19. (Moscow: University of Idaho)

Burton, W. H., R. B. Kimball, and R. L. Wing. *Education for effective thinking.* New York: Appleton, 1960.

Buswell, G. T. Helping children learn how to learn. In A.S.C.D. *Learning and the teacher.* Yearb. Washington, D.C.: N.E.A., 1959, Chap. 8.

———. Patterns of thinking in solving problems. *Univer. of Calif. Publ. in Educ.*, 1956, *12*, 63–148. (Berkeley: University of California Press)

Cornwell, H. G. Prior experience as a determinant of figure-ground organization. *J. Exp. Psychol.*, 1963, *65*, 156–162.

Cowley, W. H. The educated-man concept in the twentieth century. *Sch. and Soc.*, 1940, *52*, 345–350.

Cronbach, L. J. *Educational psychology.* New York: Harcourt, 1954.

Dale, E. Teachers and reading. *The News Letter*, 1962, *28*, 1–4. (Columbus: Ohio State University)

Davis, K. G., and H. F. Hess. The effectiveness of concepts at various levels of awareness. *J. Exp. Psychol.*, 1962, *63*, 62–67.

Davis, O. L., Jr. Children can learn complex concepts. *Educ. Leadership*, 1959, *17*, 170–175.

Dewey, J. *Experience and education.* New York: Macmillan, 1938.

Di Vesta, F. J. *Process concepts and values in the social and personal adjustment of adolescents.* Memoir 287. Ithaca, N.Y.: Agricultural Experiment Station, Cornell University, 1949.

Fiske, D. W., and S. R. Maddi, eds. *Functions of varied experience.* Homewood, Ill.: Dorsey Press, 1961.

Flanders, N. A. Teacher and classroom influences on individual learning. Paper presented to Seventh Annual Curriculum Res. Inst., Eastern Section, A.S.C.D., 1963.

Foshay, A. W. Knowledge and the structure of the disciplines. In W. A. Jenkins, ed. *The nature of knowledge.* Milwaukee: Sch. of Educ., University of Wisconsin, 1961.

Frank, L. K. *The school as agent for cultural renewal*. The Burton Lecture, 1958. Cambridge, Mass.: Harvard University Press, 1959.

Furth, H. G. Conceptual discovery and control on a pictorial part-whole task as a function of age, intelligence, and language. *J. Educ. Psychol.*, 1963, *54*, 191–196.

Gagné, R. M. Military training and principles of learning. *Amer. Psychol.*, 1962, *17*, 83–91.

——, *et al.* Factors in acquiring knowledge of a mathematical task. *Psychol. Monogr.*, 1962, *76*, No. 7 (Whole No. 526).

Gagné, R. M., and R. C. Bolles. A review of factors in learning efficiency. In E. Galanter, ed. *Automatic teaching: The state of the art*. New York: Wiley, 1959, Chap. 2.

Gagné, R. M., and N. E. Paradise. Abilities and learning sets in knowledge acquisition. *Psychol. Monogr.*, 1961, *75*, No. 14 (Whole No. 518).

Gagné, R. M., and E. C. Smith, Jr. A study of the effects of verbalization on problem solving. *J. Exp. Psychol.*, 1962, *63*, 12–18.

Geiger, G. Values and social science. *J. Soc. Issues*, 1950, *6*, 8–16.

Gell, H. D. Creativity in the field of music, in little children. *Educ. Comment*, Spring 1963, Coll. of Educ., University of Toledo.

Gibson, E. J., *et al.* Comparison of meaningfulness and pronunciability as grouping principles in the perception and retention of verbal material. *J. Exp. Psychol.*, 1964, *67*, 173–182.

Goodlad, J. I. The teacher selects, plans, organizes. In A.S.C.D. *Learning and the teacher*. Yearb. Washington, D.C.: N.E.A., 1959, Chap. 3.

Guilford, J. P., and P. R. Merrifield. *The structure of intellect model: Its use and implication*. Rep. No. 24 from the Psychol. Lab. of the University of Southern California, April 1960.

Hamalainen, A. E. Some current proposals and their meaning. *Educ. Leadership*, 1959, *26*, 271–274, 328.

Hambidge, J. *The elements of dynamic symmetry*. New York: Wittenborn, 1959.

Hanna, P. R. Education for survival and progress. Address, upon his installation as Lee L. Jacks Professor of Child Education, Stanford University, April 30, 1954.

Hardin, G. The threat of clarity. *ETC.*, 1960, *17*, 269–278. See also *Amer. J. Psychiat.*, 1957, *114*, 392–396.

Harlow, H. F. The formation of learning sets. *Psychol. Rev.*, 1949, *56*, 51–65.

——, and J. M. Warren. Formation and transfer of discrimination learning sets. *J. Comp. Physiol. Psychol.*, 1952, *45*, 482–489.

Harris, C. S., and R. N. Haber. Selective attention and coding in visual perception. *J. Exp. Psychol.*, 1963, *65*, 328–333.

Harvey, O. J., D. E. Hunt, and H. M. Schroder. *Conceptual systems and personality organization.* New York: Wiley, 1961.

Hebb, D. O. *The organization of behavior.* New York: Wiley, 1949.

———. *A textbook of psychology.* Phila.: Saunders, 1958.

Heidbreder, E. Language and concepts. *Psychol. Bull.*, 1936, *33*, 724.

Henry, G. H. Foundations of general education in the high school. In A.S.C.D. *What shall the high schools teach?* Yearb. Washington, D.C.: N.E.A., 1956, Chap. 5.

Henry, J. A cross-cultural outline of education. *Current Anthrop.*, 1960, *1*, 267–305.

Hoban, C. F., Jr. Research in new media in education. Working Paper in Nat. Conf. on Tchr. Educ. and New Media, A.A.C.T.E., Ann Arbor, Mich., Jan. 8–11, 1961.

Horowitz, M. M. The teacher utilizes group forces. In A.S.C.D. *Learning and the teacher.* Yearb. Washington, D.C.: N.E.A., 1959, Chap. 7.

Houston, J. P., and S. A. Mednick. Creativity and the need for novelty. *J. Abnorm. Soc. Psychol.*, 1963, *66*, 137–141.

Hyden, H. Biochemical aspects of brain activity. In S. Farber and R. H. L. Wilson, eds. *Control of the mind.* New York: McGraw-Hill, 1961, pp. 18–41.

Johannsen, W. Concept identification under misinformative and subsequent informative feedback conditions. *J. Exp. Psychol.*, 1962, *64*, 631–635.

Johnson, E. S. Ways of knowledge. In W. A. Jenkins, ed. *The nature of knowledge.* Milwaukee: Sch. of Educ., University of Wisconsin, 1961.

Johnson, R. C. Linguistic structure as related to concept formation and to concept content. *Psychol. Bull.*, 1962, *59*, 468–476.

Johnson, W. *People in quandaries.* New York: Harper, 1946.

Keedy, M. L. Mathematics in junior high school. *Educ. Leadership*, 1959, *17*, 157–161.

Kersh, B. Y. The adequacy of "meaning" as an explanation for the superiority of learning by independent discovery. *J. Educ. Psychol.*, 1958, *49*, 282–292.

———. The motivating effect of learning by directed discovery. *J. Educ. Psychol.*, 1962, *53*, 65–71.

Kety, S. S. Chemical boundaries of psychopharmacology. In S. Farber and R. H. L. Wilson, eds. *Control of the mind.* New York: McGraw-Hill, 1961, pp. 79–91.

Klotsche, J. M. The need for knowing. In W. A. Jenkins, ed. *The nature of knowledge*. Milwaukee: Sch. of Educ., University of Wisconsin, 1961.

Krumboltz, J. D., and R. G. Weisman. The effect of intermittent confirmation in programed instruction. *J. Educ. Psychol.*, 1962, *53*, 250–253.

Kubie, L. S. Are we educating for maturity? *NEA J.*, 1959, *48*, 58–63.

Lake, R. A. Toward a theory of interactive behavior. *Provo Papers*, 1959, *3*, 44–52. (Provo: Utah State Hospital)

Levine, M. Mediating processes in humans at the outset of discrimination learning. *Psychol. Rev.*, 1963, *70*, 254–276.

———. A model of hypothesis behavior in discrimination learning set. *Psychol. Rev.*, 1959, *66*, 353–366.

Lindgren, H. C. The teacher helps the learner interpret his experiences. In A.S.C.D. *Learning and the teacher*. Yearb. Washington, D.C.: N.E.A., 1959, Chap. 5.

Little, E. P. PSSC: A physics program. *Educ. Leadership*, 1959, *17*, 167–169, 192.

MacKinnon, D. W. The nature and nurture of creative talent. *Amer. Psychol.*, 1962, *17*, 484–495.

Mayzner, M. S. Verbal concept attainment: A function of the number of positive and negative instances presented. *J. Exp. Psychol.*, 1962, *63*, 314–319.

McDonald, F. J. *Educational psychology*. San Francisco: Wadsworth, 1959.

Medley, D. M., and H. E. Mitzel. Measuring classroom behavior by systematic observation. In N. L. Gage, ed. *Handbook of research on teaching*. Amer. Educ. Res. Assn. Chicago: Rand McNally, 1963, pp. 247–328.

Mednick, S. A. The associative basis of the creative process. *Psychol. Rev.*, 1962, *69*, 220–232.

Meyer, D. R. Intraproblem-interproblem relationships in learning by monkeys. *J. Comp. Physiol. Psychol.*, 1951, *44*, 162–167.

Morin, R. E. Factors influencing rate and extent of learning in the presence of misinformative feedback. *J. Exp. Psychol.*, 1955, *49*, 343–351.

Neisser, U., and P. Weene. Hierarchies in concept attainment. *J. Exp. Psychol.*, 1962, *64*, 640–645.

Nies, R. C. Effects of probable outcome information on two-choice learning. *J. Exp. Psychol.*, 1962, *64*, 430–433.

Northrop, F. S. C., and H. Morgenau, co-chairmen. *The nature of concepts and their inter-relation and role in social structure*. Proc. of the Stillwater Conf., sponsored jointly by the Found. for Integrated Educ., Inc., and Okla. A. & M. Coll., 1950.

Osler, S. F., and S. L. Weiss. Studies in concept attainment: III. Effect of instructions at two levels of intelligence. *J. Exp. Psychol.*, 1962, *63*, 528–533.

Peak, H. The effect of aroused motivation of attitudes. *J. Abnorm. Soc. Psychol.*, 1960, *61*, 463–468.

Penfield, W. The physiological basis of the mind. In S. Farber and R. H. L. Wilson, eds. *Control of the mind.* New York: McGraw-Hill, 1961, pp. 3–17.

Pishkin, V. Effects of probability of misinformation and number of irrelevant dimensions upon concept identification. *J. Exp. Psychol.*, 1960, *59*, 371–378.

Platt, J. R. Beauty: Pattern and change. In D. W. Fiske and S. R. Maddi, eds. *Functions of varied experience.* Homewood, Ill.: Dorsey Press, 1961, Chap. 14.

Pubols, B. H., Jr. An application of Levine's model for hypothesis behavior to serial reversal learning. *Psychol. Rev.*, 1962, *69*, 241–245.

Rapp, A. The experimental background of the problems of learning. *The Classical J.*, 1945, *40*, 467–480.

Resnick, L. B. Programmed instruction and the teaching of complex intellectual skills: Problems and prospects. *Harv. Educ. Rev.*, 1963, *33*, 439–471.

Restle, F. Toward a quantitative description of learning set data. *Psychol. Rev.*, 1958, *65*, 77–91.

Rhine, R. J. A concept-formation approach to attitude acquisition. *Psychol. Rev.*, 1958, *65*, 362–370.

Richardson, S. K., and F. W. Smitter. The learner. In A.S.C.D. *Learning and the teacher.* Yearb. Washington, D.C.: N.E.A., 1959, Chap. 2.

Riopelle, A. J. Learning sets from minimal stimuli. *J. Exp. Psychol.*, 1955a, *49*, 16–22.

———. Rewards, preferences, and learning sets. *Psychol. Rep.*, 1955b, *1*, 167–173.

———. Transfer suppression and learning sets. *J. Comp. Physiol. Psychol.*, 1953, *46*, 108–114.

Robinson, D. W. Democracy is not for children. *Phi Delta Kappan*, 1961, *42*, 361–362.

Roe, K. V., H. W. Case, and A. Roe. Scrambled versus ordered sequence in autoinstructional programs. *J. Educ. Psychol.*, 1962, *53*, 101–104.

Schwab, J. J. *The concept of structure in the subject fields.* Twentieth Annual Meeting, Council on Cooperation in Tchr. Educ., Washington, D.C., Oct. 20–21, 1961.

Sherif, M. Formation and structure of concepts. In F. S. C. Northrop and H. Morgenau, co-chairmen. *The nature of concepts and their inter-*

relation and role in social structure. Proc. of the Stillwater Conf., sponsored jointly by the Found. for Integrated Educ., Inc., and Okla. A. & M. Coll., 1950.

Sinnott, E. W. The creativeness of life. In H. H. Anderson, ed. *Creativity and its cultivation.* New York: Harper, 1959, Paper No. 2.

Smallenburg, C., and L. Newcomber. The teacher responds to evidences about learning. In A.S.C.D. *Learning and the teacher.* Yearb. Washington, D.C.: N.E.A., 1959, Chap. 6.

Smith, B. O., and M. O. Meux. *A study of the logic of teaching.* 3rd ed. of trial ed. Urbana: Bur. of Educ. Res., University of Illinois, undated. (U.S. Off. of Educ. Proj. No. 258 [7257])

Staats, A. W. Verbal habit-families, concepts, and the operant conditioning of word classes. *Psychol. Rev.,* 1961, *68,* 190–204.

Stratemeyer, F. The expanding role of direct experience in professional education. In Assn. for Student Teaching. *Student teaching.* 30th Yearb., 1951.

Taylor, H. *Art and the intellect.* New York: Doubleday, 1960.

Thomas, R. M. The teacher introduces learning tasks. In A.S.C.D. *Learning and the teacher.* Yearb. Washington, D.C.: N.E.A., 1959, Chap. 4.

Tolman, E. C. *Purposive behavior in animals and men.* Berkeley: University of California Press, 1932. Reprinted 1949.

Trabasso, T. R. Stimulus emphasis and all-or-none learning in concept identification. *J. Exp. Psychol.,* 1963, *65,* 398–406.

Tyler, V. O., Jr. Sensory integration with and without reinforcement. *J. Exp. Psychol.,* 1962, *63,* 381–386.

Walker, E. L., and R. W. Heyns. *An anatomy for conformity.* Englewood Cliffs, N.J.: Prentice-Hall, 1962.

Warren, J. M. Additivity of cues in visual pattern discrimination by monkeys. *J. Comp. Physiol. Psychol.,* 1954, *47,* 290–292.

Wegener, F. C. *The organic philosophy of education.* Dubuque, Iowa: W. C. Brown, 1957.

Wittrock, M. C. Verbal stimuli in concept formation: Learning by discovery. *J. Educ. Psychol.,* 1963, *54,* 183–190.

Woodring, P. *A fourth of a nation.* New York: McGraw-Hill, 1957.

Woodruff, A. D. *Basic concepts of teaching.* San Francisco: Chandler Pub. Co., 1961.

———. The roles of value in human behavior. *J. Soc. Psychol.,* 1952, *36,* 97–107.

———. The use of concepts in teaching and learning. *J. Tchr. Educ.,* 1964, *15,* 81–99.

CHAPTER 5

Teacher Behavior in the Classroom Context

ꜱ

Adams, R. S. The classroom as a communication system. In B. J. Biddle *et al. The social systems of the school*. Columbia: University of Missouri, 1965. (U.S. Off. of Educ. Contract 3–20–002)

Alden, E. The effects on non-target classmates of the teacher's use of expert power and liking power in controlling deviant behavior. Unpublished doctoral dissertation, Wayne State University, 1959.

Anderson, H. H., and H. M. Brewer. Studies of teachers' classroom personalities: I. Dominative and socially integrative behavior of kindergarten teachers. *Appl. Psychol. Monogr.*, 1945, No. 6, entire issue.

Anderson, H. H., and J. E. Brewer. Studies of teachers' classroom personalities: II. Effects of teachers' dominative and integrative contacts on children's classroom behavior. *Appl. Psychol. Monogr.*, 1946, No. 8, entire issue.

————, and M. F. Reed. Studies of teachers' classroom personalities: III. Follow-up studies of the effects of dominative and integrative contacts on children's behavior. *Appl. Psychol. Monogr.*, 1946, No. 11.

Aschner, M. J. The analysis of classroom discourse: A method and its uses. Unpublished doctoral dissertation, University of Illinois, 1958.

Barker, R. G., and H. F. Wright. *Midwest and its children*. New York: Harper, 1955.

Barr, A. S. *Characteristic differences in the teacher performance of good and poor teachers of the social studies*. Bloomington, Ill.: Public School Pub. Co., 1929.

Biddle, B. J. The integration of teacher effectiveness research. In B. J. Biddle and W. J. Ellena, eds. *Contemporary research on teacher effectiveness*. New York: Holt, 1964, Chap. 1.

————. Teacher role: Concepts and behavior. In B. J. Biddle *et al. The social systems of the school*. Columbia: University of Missouri, 1965. (U.S. Off. of Educ. Contract 3–20–002)

————, and T. E. Johns. Videotape records of classroom interaction. Columbia: University of Missouri, unpublished.

Biddle, B. J., H. A. Rosencranz, and E. F. Rankin, Jr. *General charac-*

teristics of the school teacher's role. II: Studies in the role of the public school teacher. Columbia: University of Missouri Press, 1961.

Bonney, M. E., and J. Powell. Differences in social behavior between sociometrically high and sociometrically low children. *J. Educ. Res.*, 1953, *46*, 481–495.

Borg, W. R. Prediction of small group role behavior from personality variables. *J. Abnorm. Soc. Psychol.*, 1960, *60*, 112–116.

Bowers, M. B., and R. S. Soar. Studies of human relations in the teaching-learning process. Final report: Evaluation of laboratory human relations training for classroom teachers. Chapel Hill: University of North Carolina, 1961. (U.S. Off. of Educ. Cooperative Res. Proj. No. 469)

Calvin, A. D., F. K. Hoffman, and E. L. Harden. The effect of intelligence and social atmosphere on group problem solving behavior. *J. Soc. Psychol.*, 1957, *45*, 61–74.

Cogan, M. L. The behavior of teachers and the productive behavior of their pupils: I. Perception analysis. *J. Exp. Educ.*, 1958, 27, 107–123.

————. Theory and design of a study of teacher-pupil interaction. *Harv. Educ. Rev.*, 1956, *26*, 315–342.

Cornell, F. G., C. M. Lindvall, and J. L. Saupe. *An exploratory measurement of individualities of schools and classrooms*. Urbana: Bur. of Educ. Res., University of Illinois, 1952.

Damrin, D. E. The Russell Sage social relations test: A technique for measuring group problem-solving skills in elementary school children. *J. Exp. Educ.*, 1959, *28*, 85–99.

Flanders, N. A. Diagnosing and utilizing social structures in classroom learning. In Gale E. Jensen, ed. *The dynamics of instructional groups*. Nat. Soc. Stud. Educ., 59th Yearb., Part II. Chicago: University of Chicago Press, 1960a.

————. Teacher-pupil contacts and mental hygiene. *J. Soc. Issues*, 1959, *15*, No. 1, 30–39.

————. Some relationships among teacher influence, pupil attitudes, and achievement. In B. J. Biddle and W. J. Ellena, eds. *Contemporary research on teacher effectiveness*. New York: Holt, 1964, Chap. 7.

————. *Teacher influence, pupil attitudes and achievement: Studies in interaction analysis*. Minneapolis: University of Minnesota, 1960b. (U.S. Off. of Educ. Cooperative Res. Proj. No. 397)

Gallagher, J. J., and M. J. Aschner. A preliminary report on analysis of classroom interaction. *Merrill-Palmer Quart. Behav. Developm.*, 1963, *9*.

Gordon, C. W. *The social system of the high school*. Glencoe, Ill.: Free Press, 1957.

Gump, P. B. Environmental guidance of classroom behavioral system. In B. J. Biddle and W. J. Ellena, eds. *Contemporary research on teacher effectiveness*. New York: Holt, 1964, Chap. 6.

Harrington, G. M. Smiling as a measure of teacher effectiveness. *J. Educ. Res.*, 1955, *48*, 715–717.

Horn, E. Distribution of opportunity for participation among the various pupils in classroom recitation. *Contribution to Educ.* No. 67. New York: Bur. of Publ., Tchrs. Coll., Columbia University, 1914.

Hughes, M. *Development of the means for the assessment of the quality of teaching in elementary schools.* Salt Lake City: University of Utah Press, 1959.

Jersild, A. T., *et al.* An evaluation of aspects of the activity program in the New York City public elementary school. *J. Exp. Educ.*, 1939, *8*, 166–207.

Johnson, M. W. The influence of verbal direction on behavior. *Child Developm.*, 1935, *6*, 196–204.

Kounin, J. S. Managing emotionally disturbed children in regular classrooms. Detroit: Wayne State University, unpublished.

———, and P. B. Gump. The ripple effect in discipline. *Elem. Sch. J.*, 1958, *59*, 158–162.

———, and J. J. Ryan. Explorations in classroom management. *J. Tchr. Educ.*, 1961, *12*, 235–246.

Kowatrakul, S. Some behaviors of elementary school children related to classroom activities in subject areas. *J. Educ. Psychol.*, 1959, *50*, 121–128.

Lewin, K., R. Lippitt, and R. K. White. Patterns of aggressive behavior in experimentally created social climates. *J. Soc. Psychol.*, 1939, *10*, 271–299.

Lippitt, R., N. Polansky, and S. Rosen. The dynamics of power: A field study of social influence in groups of children. *Human Relat.*, 1952, *5*, 37–64.

Mann, R. D. A review of the relationships between personality and performance in small groups. *Psychol. Bull.*, 1959, *56*, 241–270.

Measure of a good teacher. Burlingame: Calif. Tchrs. Assn., 1952.

Medley, D. M., and H. E. Mitzel. Measuring classroom behavior by systematic observation. In N. L. Gage, ed. *Handbook of research on teaching*. Amer. Educ. Res. Assn., Chicago: Rand McNally, 1963, pp. 247–328.

———. Some behavioral correlates of teacher effectiveness. *J. Educ. Psychol.*, 1959, *50*, 239–246.

————. *Studies of research behavior: Refinement of two techniques for assessing teachers' classroom behaviors*. Res. Ser. No. 28. New York: Board of Higher Educ., City of New York, Div. of Tchr. Educ., Off. of Res. and Evaluation, 1955.

————. A technique for measuring classroom behavior. *J. Educ. Psychol.*, 1958, *49*, 86–92.

Meux, M., and B. O. Smith. Logical dimensions of teaching behavior. In B. J. Biddle and W. J. Ellena, eds. *Contemporary research on teacher effectiveness*. New York: Holt, 1964, Chap. 5.

Mitzel, H. E., and W. Rabinowitz. Assessing social-emotional climate in the classroom by Withall's technique. *Psychol. Monogr.*, 1953, *67*, No. 18 (Entire No. 368).

Morrison, V. B. The relationship of student teacher performance and pupil performance to supervisory and pupil merit rating. Unpublished doctoral dissertation, University of Michigan, 1961.

Morsh, J. E. *Development report: Systematic observation of instructor behavior*. U.S.A.F. Personnel Training Res. Center. Developm. Rep. No. AFPTRC-TM-56–52, 1956.

Olson, W. T. A study of classroom behavior. *J. Educ. Psychol.*, 1931, *22*, 449–454.

Petrullo, L., and B. M. Bass, eds. *Leadership and interpersonal behavior*. New York: Holt, 1961.

Polansky, L. Group social climate and the teacher's supportiveness of group status systems. *J. Educ. Sociol.*, 1954, *28*, 115–123.

Puckett, R. C. Making supervision objective. *Sch. Rev.*, 1928, *36*, 209–212.

Ryans, D. G. *Characteristics of teachers*. Washington, D.C.: Amer. Council on Educ., 1960.

Smith, B. O. A concept of teaching. *Tchrs. Coll. Rec.*, 1960, *61*, 229–241.

Soar, R. S. *Multivariate statistical procedures in predicting teacher-pupil classroom behavior*. Columbia: University of South Carolina, 1962. (U.S. Off. of Educ., Cooperative Res. Proj. No. 1170)

Solomon, D. Teaching styles and student achievement. Paper delivered to Amer. Educ. Res. Assn., Atlantic City, N.J., 1962.

Spaulding, R. L. Achievement, creativity, and self-conflict correlates of teacher-pupil transactions in elementary schools. Urbana: University of Illinois, 1963. (U.S. Off. of Educ., Cooperative Res. Proj. No. 1352)

Thomas, D. S., *et al.* Some new techniques for studying social behavior. *Child Developm. Monogr.*, No. 1, 1929.

Thomas, E. J., and B. J. Biddle. Basic concepts for the properties of role phenomena. In B. J. Biddle and E. J. Thomas, eds. *Role theory: Concepts and research.* New York: Wiley, 1966.

Thorndike, R. L., J. J. Loftus, and B. Goldman. Observations of the behavior of children in activity and control schools. *J. Exp. Educ.,* 1941, *10,* 138–145.

Urban, J. *Behavioral changes resulting from a study of communicable diseases.* New York: Bur. of Publ., Tchrs. Coll., Columbia University, 1943.

Wilk, R. E., *et al. Student teacher activities and pupil responses: A report to participants.* Minneapolis: Bur. of Educ. Res., University of Minnesota, 1960.

Wispé, L. G. Evaluating section teaching methods in the introductory course. *J. Educ. Res.,* 1951, *45,* 161–186.

Withall, J. The development of a climate index. *J. Educ. Res.,* 1951, *45,* 93–99.

———. Development of a technique for the measurement of socio-emotional climate in classrooms. *J. Exp. Educ.,* 1949, *17,* 347–361.

———. An objective measurement of a teacher's classroom interaction. *J. Educ. Psychol.,* 1956, *47,* 203–212.

Wright, E. M. J. Development of an instrument for studying verbal behaviors in a secondary school mathematics classroom. *J. Exp. Educ.,* 1959, *28,* 103–121.

———, and V. H. Proctor. *Systematic observation of verbal interaction as a method of comparing mathematics lessons.* St. Louis: Washington University, 1961. (U.S. Off. Educ. Cooperative Res. Proj. No. 816)

Wrightstone, J. W. Measuring teacher conduct of class discussion. *Elem. Sch. J.,* 1934, *34,* 454–460.

Zander, A., and E. van Egmond. Relationship of intelligence and interpersonal relationship of children. *J. Educ. Psychol.,* 1958, *39,* 257–268.

CHAPTER 6

The Zigzag Curve of Learning

∽

Amsel, A. Review of O. H. Mowrer, *Learning theory and behavior. Contemp. Psychol.*, 1961, *6*, 33–36.

Ashby, Sir E. Investment in man. *The Advancement of Science*, 1963, *20*, 203–213.

Atkinson, R. C. A variable sensitivity theory of signal detection. *Psychol. Rev.*, 1963, *70*, 62–77.

Beach, F. A. Experimental investigations of species-specific behavior. *Amer. Psychol.*, 1960, *15*, 1–8.

Berlyne, D. E. *Conflict arousal and curiosity*. New York: McGraw-Hill, 1960.

Bigge, M. L. *Learning theories for teachers*. New York: Harper, 1964.

Briggs, L. J. The teacher and programmed instruction: Roles and role potentials. *AV Instruction*, 1964, *9*, 273–276.

Brown, D. R. Personality, college environments, and academic productivity. In N. Sanford, ed. *The American college*. New York: Wiley, 1962, pp. 536–562.

Brozek, J. Current status of psychology in the USSR. *Annu. Rev. Psychol.*, 1962, *13*, 515–566.

Bruner, S. *On knowing: Essays for the left hand*. Cambridge, Mass.: Harvard University Press, 1962.

Bugelski, B. R. *The psychology of learning applied to teaching*. Indianapolis: Bobbs-Merrill, 1964.

Callahan, R. E. *Education and the cult of efficiency*. Chicago: University of Chicago Press, 1962.

Carroll, J. B. Words, meanings, and concepts. *Harv. Educ. Rev.*, 1964, *34*, 178–202.

Cartwright, D., and A. Zander. *Group dynamics: Research and theory*. Evanston, Ind.: Row, Peterson, 1953.

Coleman, J. S. *The adolescent society*. Glencoe, Ill.: Free Press, 1961.

Diekhoff, J. S. The university as leader and laggard. *J. Higher Educ.*, 1964, *35*, 181–188.

Edwards, W. D. Dynamic decision theory and probabilistic information processing. *Human Factors,* 1962, *4,* 59–73.

Entwisle, D. R., and W. H. Huggins. Interference in meaningful learning. *J. Educ. Psychol.,* 1964, *55,* 75–78.

Ericksen, S. C. Pitfalls and bridges between learning theory and the teaching technologies. *J. Med. Educ.,* 1964, *39,* 298–303.

———. Studies in the abstraction process. *Psychol. Monogr.,* 1962, *76,* No. 18 (Whole No. 537).

———, and L. E. Thune. *Studies in abstraction learning: V. A pilot study of rote and concept teaching in the classroom.* Tech. Rep. No. 7. Nashville, Tenn.: Vanderbilt University, 1961.

Feigenbaum, E. A., and J. Feldman, eds. *Computers and thought.* New York: McGraw-Hill, 1963.

Festinger, L. *A theory of cognitive dissonance.* Evanston, Ind.: Row, Peterson, 1957.

Fitts, P. M., J. R. Peterson, and G. Wolpe. Cognitive aspects of information processing: II. Adjustments to stimulus redundancy. *J. Exp. Psychol.,* 1963, *65,* 423–432.

Fitts, P. M., and G. Switzer. Cognitive aspects of information processing: I. The familiarity of S-R sets and subsets. *J. Exp. Psychol.,* 1962, *63,* 321–329.

Fox, R. S., and R. Lippitt. The innovation of classroom mental health practices. In M. B. Miles, ed. *Innovation in education.* New York: Bur. of Publ., Tchrs. Coll., Columbia University, 1964, pp. 271–297.

Fricke, B. G. *Opinion, attitude and interest survey handbook.* Ann Arbor: Evaluation and Examinations Div., University of Michigan, 1963.

Gage, N. L. Paradigms for research on teaching. In N. L. Gage, ed. *Handbook of research on teaching.* Amer. Educ. Res. Assn., Chicago: Rand McNally, 1963, pp. 94–141.

Gagné, R. M. The acquisition of knowledge. *Psychol. Rev.,* 1962a, *69,* 355–365.

———. Military training and the principles of learning. *Amer. Psychol.,* 1962b, *17,* 83–91.

———, ed. *Psychological principles in system development.* New York: Holt, 1962c.

Gardner, J. W. *Self renewal: The individual and the innovative society.* New York: Harper, 1963.

Gardner, R. W. The development of cognitive structures. In C. Scheerer, ed. *Cognition: Theory, research, promise.* New York: Harper, 1964, pp. 147–171.

Getzels, J. W., and P. W. Jackson. *Creativity and intelligence: Exploration with gifted children.* New York: Wiley, 1962.

Glaser, R., ed. *Training research and education.* Pittsburgh: University of Pittsburgh Press, 1962.

Guilford, J. P. Three faces of the intellect. *Amer. Psychol.,* 1959, *14,* 469–479.

Hebb, D. O. The American revolution. *Amer. Psychol.,* 1960, *15,* 735–745.

Henry, N. B., ed. *The psychology of learning.* Nat. Soc. Stud. Educ., 41st Yearb., Part II. Chicago: University of Chicago Press, 1942.

Hilgard, E. R. Motivation in learning theory. In S. Koch, ed. *Psychology: A study of a science.* Study II, Vol. 5. New York: McGraw-Hill, 1963, pp. 253–283.

———. Theories of human learning and problems of training. In *Symposium on psychology of learning basic to military training problems.* U.S. Res. and Developm. Board, Joint Panel on Training and Training Devices, Committee on Human Resources. HR-HTD 201/1, May 1953, pp. 3–13.

———, ed. *Theories of learning.* Nat. Soc. Stud. Educ., 63rd Yearb., Part I. Chicago: University of Chicago Press, 1964.

Holland, J. L. Creative and academic performance among talented adolescents. *J. Educ. Psychol.,* 1961, *52,* 136–147.

Holtzman, W., *et al. Inkblot perception and personality: Holtzman inkblot technique.* Austin: University of Texas Press, 1961.

Hunt, E. B. *Concept learning: An information processing problem.* New York: Wiley, 1962.

Hunt, J. McV. *Intelligence and experience.* New York: Ronald, 1961.

Jensen, B. T. A comparison of student achievement under conditions of class attendance and non-attendance. *Coll. and Univer.,* 1951, *26,* 399–403.

Jones, A. Supplementary report: Information deprivation and irrelevant drive as determiners of an instrumental response. *J. Exp. Psychol.,* 1961, *62,* 310–311.

———, H. J. Wilkinson, and I. Braden. Information deprivation as a motivational variable. *J. Exp. Psychol.,* 1961, *62,* 126–137.

Katona, G. *Organizing and memorizing.* New York: Columbia University Press, 1940.

Kimble, G. A. Comments on "Theories of human learning and problems of training." In *Symposium on psychology of learning basic to military training problems*. U.S. Res. and Developm. Board, Joint Panel on Training and Training Devices, Committee on Human Resources. HR-HTD 201/1, May 1953, pp. 15–19.

Klein, G. S. Cognitive control and motivation. In G. Lindzey, ed. *Assessment of human motives*. New York: Rinehart, 1958, pp. 87–118.

Koch, S. Psychological science versus the science-humanism antinomy: Intimations of a significant science of man. *Amer. Psychol.*, 1961, *16*, 629–639.

Lindzey, G., ed. *Assessment of human motives*. New York: Rinehart, 1958, pp. 3–32.

McKeachie, W. J. Motivation, teaching methods, and college learning. In M. R. Jones, ed. *Nebraska symposium on motivation*. Lincoln: University of Nebraska Press, 1961, pp. 111–142.

———. Procedures and techniques of teaching: A survey of experimental studies. In N. Sanford, ed. *The American college*. New York: Wiley, 1962, pp. 312–364.

McNemar, Q. Lost: Our intelligence? Why? *Amer. Psychol.*, 1964, *39*, 871–882.

Marx, M. H., and W. A. Hillix. *Systems and theories in psychology*. New York: McGraw-Hill, 1963.

Meehl, P. E. The cognitive activity of the clinician. *Psychol. Rev.*, 1960, *67*, 229–242.

Meierhenry, W. C., ed. Learning theory and audiovisual utilization. *AV Commun. Rev.*, 1961, *9*, 1–87.

Miller, G. A., E. Galanter, and K. H. Pribram. *Plans and the structure of behavior*. New York: Holt, 1960.

Miller, J. G. *Living systems*. Reprint No. 69, Mental Health Res. Inst., University of Michigan, Oct. 1961, Chap. 4.

Miller, N. E. Graphic communication and the crisis in education. *AV Commun. Rev.*, 1957, *5*, 61–62.

Milton, O. Two year follow-up: Objective data after learning without class attendance. *Psychol. Rep.*, 1962, *11*, 833–836.

Mosel, J. N. The learning process. *J. Med. Educ.*, 1964, *39*, 485–496.

Murphy, G. *Personality, a biosocial approach to origins and structure*. New York: Harper, 1947.

Murray, H. A. Foreword. In G. G. Stern, M. I. Stein, and B. S. Bloom. *Methods in personality assessment*. Glencoe, Ill.: Free Press, 1956, pp. 9–20.

Newcomb, T. M. Student peer group influence and intellectual outcomes of college experience. In R. L. Sutherland *et al.*, eds. *Personality factors on the college campus: Review of a symposium.* Austin, Tex.: Hogg Found. for Mental Health, 1962, pp. 69–91.

Noble, C. E. The meaning-familiarity relationship. *Psychol. Rev.*, 1953, *60*, 89–98.

Peterson, J. Experiments in rational learning. *Psychol. Rev.*, 1918, *25*, 443–467.

Research and Development Board, U.S. Dep. of Defense, Committee on Human Resources, Panel on Training and Training Devices. *Symposium on psychology of learning basic to military training problems.* HR-HTD 201/1, May 1953.

Rokeach, M. *The open and closed mind.* New York: Basic Books, 1960.

Sherif, M., and C. I. Hovland. *Yale studies in attitude and communication: IV. Social judgment: An assimilation-contrast approach to attitudes and the effects of communication.* New Haven, Conn.: Yale University Press, 1962.

Spence, K. W., A. W. Melton, and B. J. Underwood. A symposium: Can the laws of learning be applied to the classroom? *Harv. Educ. Rev.*, 1959, *29*, 83–117.

Stewart, C. The place of higher education in a changing society. In N. Sanford, ed. *The American college.* New York: Wiley, 1962, pp. 894–939.

Suppes, P. Modern learning theory and the elementary school curriculum. *Amer. Educ. Res. J.*, 1964, *1*, 79–93.

Taylor, C. W., and J. L. Holland. Development and application of tests of creativity. *Rev. Educ. Res.*, 1962, *32*, 91–102.

Taylor, D. W. Creative thinking among scientists. In E. D. McDaniel, ed. *Creativity and college teaching.* Bull. of the Bur. of Sch. Serv., Vol. 35. Lexington: Coll. of Educ., University of Kentucky, 1963, pp. 27–44.

Thune, L. E., and S. C. Ericksen. *Studies in abstraction learning: IV. The transfer effects of conceptual vs. rote instruction in a simulated classroom situation.* Tech. Rep. No. 6. Nashville, Tenn.: Vanderbilt University, 1960.

Travers, R. M. *Essentials of learning.* New York: Macmillan, 1963.

Underwood, B. J., and L. J. Postman. Extra-experimental sources of interference in forgetting. *Psychol. Rev.*, 1960, *67*, 73–95.

Underwood, B. J., and R. W. Shulz. *Meaningfulness and verbal learning.* Chicago: Lippincott, 1960.

Walker, E. L. Psychological complexity as a basis for a theory of motivation and choice. In D. Levine, ed. *Nebraska symposium on motivation.* Lincoln: University of Nebraska Press, 1964, pp. 47–95.

Wertheimer, M. *Productive thinking.* New York: Harper, 1945.

White, R. W. Motivation reconsidered: The concept of competence. *Psychol. Rev.,* 1959, *66,* 297–333.

Witkin, Herman A. Origins of cognitive style. In C. Scheerer, ed. *Cognition: Theory, research, promise.* New York: Harper, 1964, pp. 172–205.

Xhignesse, L. V., and C. E. Osgood. *Bibliographical citation characteristics of the psychological journal network in 1950 and in 1960.* A preprint of research conducted as part of the American Psychological Association's Project on Scientific Information Exchange in Psychology. Nov. 1963.

CHAPTER 7

A Behavioristic Analysis of Instruction

Beck, E. C., and R. W. Doty. Conditioned flexion reflexes acquired during combined catalepsy and de-efferentation. *J. Comp. Physiol. Psychol.,* 1957, *50,* 211–216.

Bugelski, B. R. *The psychology of learning applied to teaching.* Indianapolis: Bobbs-Merrill, 1964.

Carroll, J. B. Language development in children. In *Encyclopedia of educational research.* New York: Macmillan, 1960, pp. 744–750.

Deese, J. *The psychology of learning.* New York: McGraw-Hill, 1958.

Ferster, C. B., and M. K. DeMyer. A method for the experimental analysis of the behavior of autistic children. *Amer. J. Orthopsychiat.,* 1962, *32,* 89–98.

Fiske, D. W., and S. R. Maddi, eds. *Functions of varied experience.* Homewood, Ill.: Dorsey Press, 1961.

Fowler, W. Cognitive learning in infancy and early childhood. *Psychol. Bull.,* 1962, *59,* 116–152.

Garner, W. R. *Uncertainty and structure as psychological concepts.* New York: Wiley, 1962.

Hebb, D. O. *A textbook of psychology.* Phila.: Saunders, 1958.

Kellogg, W. N., *et al.* Is movement necessary for learning? *J. Comp. Psychol.,* 1940, *29,* 43–74.

Kimble, G. A. *Hilgard and Marquis' conditioning and learning.* 2nd ed. New York: Appleton, 1961.

Light, J. S., and W. H. Gantt. Essential part of reflex arc for establishment of conditioned reflex. Formation of conditioned reflex after exclusion of motor peripheral end. *J. Comp. Psychol.,* 1936, *21,* 19–36.

Lindahl, L. G. Movement analysis as an industrial training method. *J. Appl. Psychol.,* 1945, *29,* 424.

Lundin, R. W. *Personality: An experimental approach.* New York: Macmillan, 1961.

Melton, A. W. The science of learning and the technology of educational methods. *Harv. Educ. Rev.,* 1959, *29,* 96–106.

Mowrer, O. H. *Learning theory and behavior.* New York: Wiley, 1960.

Pavlov, I. P. *Conditioned reflexes.* London: Oxford University Press, 1927. Consists of writings over a twenty-five-year period.

Pfaffman, C. The pleasures of sensation. *Psychol. Rev.,* 1959, *67,* 253–268.

Pierrel, R., and G. Sherman. *Barnabus, the Barnard rat demonstration.* New York: Barnard College, 1958.

Razran, G. The observable unconscious and the inferable conscious in current Soviet psychophysiology: Interoceptive conditioning, semantic conditioning, and the orienting reflex. *Psychol. Rev.,* 1961, *68,* 81–147.

Skinner, B. F. *Science and human behavior.* New York: Macmillan, 1953.

———. The science of learning and the art of teaching. *Harv. Educ. Rev.,* 1954, *24,* 86–97.

———. Teaching machines. *Science,* 1958, *128,* 969–977.

———. Teaching machines. *Sci. Amer.,* 1961, *205,* 90–102.

———. *Walden Two.* New York: Macmillan, 1948.

———, and J. G. Holland. The use of teaching machines in college instruction. In A. A. Lumsdaine and R. Glaser, eds. *Teaching machines and programmed learning.* Washington, D.C.: Dep. of AV Instruction, N.E.A., 1960, pp. 159–173.

Underwood, B. J. *Experimental psychology.* New York: Appleton, 1949.

Watson, J. B., and R. Raynor. Conditioned emotional reactions. *J. Exp. Psychol.,* 1920, *3,* 1–4.

White, R. W. Motivation reconsidered: The concept of competence. *Psychol. Rev.,* 1959, *66,* 297–333.

Woodworth, R. S., and H. Schlosberg. *Experimental psychology.* 2nd ed. New York: Holt, 1954.

CHAPTER 8

A Cognitive-Structure Theory of School Learning

ᔥ

Ausubel, D. P. The use of advance organizers in the learning and retention of meaningful verbal material. *J. Educ. Psychol.*, 1960, *51*, 267–272.

————, and D. Fitzgerald. Organizer, general background, and antecedent learning conditions in sequential verbal learning. *J. Educ. Psychol.*, 1962, *53*, 243–249.

————. The role of discriminability in meaningful verbal learning and retention. *J. Educ. Psychol.*, 1961, *52*, 266–274.

Ausubel, D. P., and M. Youssef. The effect of spaced repetition on meaningful retention. *J. Gen. Psychol.*, 1965, *73*, 147–150.

————. The role of discriminability in meaningful parallel learning. *J. Educ. Psychol.*, 1963, *54*, 331–336.

Bartlett, F. C. *Remembering*. London: Cambridge University Press, 1932.

Bruner, J. S. Going beyond the information given. In J. S. Bruner *et al. Contemporary approaches to cognition*. Cambridge, Mass.: Harvard University Press, 1957.

————. Learning and thinking. *Harv. Educ. Rev.*, 1959, *29*, 84–92.

————. *The process of education*. Cambridge, Mass.: Harvard University Press, 1960.

Duncan, C. P. Transfer after training with single versus multiple tasks. *J. Exp. Psychol.*, 1959, *55*, 63–72.

Fitzgerald, D., and D. P. Ausubel. Cognitive versus affective factors in the learning and retention of controversial material. *J. Educ. Psychol.*, 1963, *54*, 73–84.

Gage, N. L. Theories of teaching. In E. R. Hilgard, ed. *Theories of learning and instruction*. Nat. Soc. Stud. Educ., 63rd Yearb., Part I. Chicago: University of Chicago Press, 1964, pp. 268–285.

Haselrud, G. M. Transfer from context by sub-threshold summation. *J. Educ. Psychol.*, 1959, *50*, 254–258.

Inhelder, B., and J. Piaget. *The growth of logical thinking from childhood to adolescence*. New York: Basic Books, 1958.

Jones, E. E., and R. de Charms. The organizing function of interaction roles in person perception. *J. Abnorm. Soc. Psychol.*, 1958, *57*, 155–164.

McKillop, A. S. *The relationship between the reader's attitude and certain types of reading response.* New York: Bur. of Publ., Tchrs. Coll., Columbia University, 1952.

Morrisett, L., and C. I. Hovland. A comparison of three varieties of training in human problem solving. *J. Exp. Psychol.,* 1959, *58,* 52–55.

Postman, L., W. C. Bronson, and G. L. Gropper. Is there a mechanism of perceptual defense? *J. Abnorm. Soc. Psychol.,* 1953, *48,* 215–224.

Smith, B. O. Critical thinking. In *Recent research and developments and their implications for teacher education,* 30th Yearb. Washington, D.C.: A.A.C.T.E., 1960, pp. 84–96.

CHAPTER 9

The Instructional Gestalt

✍

Ausubel, D. P. *The psychology of meaningful verbal learning.* New York: Grune and Stratton, 1963.

Berger, R. M., P. R. Merrifield, and J. P. Guilford. *Pertinent questions.* Beverly Hills: Sheridan Supply Co., 1960.

Bloom, B. S. Thought processes in lectures and discussions. *J. Gen. Educ.,* 1953, 7, 160–169.

———, ed. *Taxonomy of educational objectives.* New York: Longmans, Green, 1956.

Bruner, J. S. *The process of education.* Cambridge, Mass.: Harvard University Press, 1961.

Christensen, P. R., P. R. Merrifield, and J. P. Guilford. *Consequences test.* Beverly Hills: Sheridan Supply Co., 1958.

Deese, J. Comment and summary: Learning theory and a-v utilization. *AV Commun. Rev.,* 1961, Supp. 4, 79–87.

Edwards, A. L. *Experimental design in psychological research.* New York: Holt, 1960.

Ericksen, S. C. The place of thinking in an ideal university. *Amer. Psychol.,* 1962, *17,* 763–771.

Getzels, J. W., and P. W. Jackson. *Creativity and intelligence.* New York: Wiley, 1962.

Guilford, J. P. Three faces of the intellect. *Amer. Psychol.,* 1959, *14,* 469–479.

Hovland, C. I., A. A. Lumsdaine, and F. D. Sheffield. *Experiments in mass communication*. Princeton, N.J.: Princeton University Press, 1949.

Macomber, F. G., and L. Siegel. *Final report*. Exp. Stud. in Instructional Procedures. Oxford, Ohio: Miami University, 1960.

Mitzel, H. E. *A behavioral approach to the assessment of teacher effectiveness*. New York: City College of New York, Div. of Tchr. Ed., 1957 (mimeo).

Rogers, C. R. *On becoming a person*. Boston: Houghton Mifflin, 1961.

Runkel, P. J. A brief model for pupil-teacher interaction. Personal communication, 1958. Cited in N. L. Gage, ed. *Handbook of research on teaching*. Amer. Educ. Res. Assn. Chicago: Rand McNally, 1963, p. 126.

Ryans, D. G. *Characteristics of teachers*. Washington, D.C.: Amer. Council on Educ., 1960.

Siegel, L. The instructional gestalt: A conceptual framework. *Tchrs. Coll. Rec.*, 1960, *62*, 202–213.

———, and L. C. Siegel. Educational set: A determinant of acquisition. *J. Educ. Psychol.*, 1965, *56*, 1–12.

———. The instructional gestalt: A conceptual framework and design for educational research. *AV Commun. Rev.*, 1964, *12*, 16–45.

———. *The instructional gestalt: Interim report*. Oxford, Ohio: Miami University, 1963 (mimeo).

———, et al. Students' thoughts during class: A criterion for educational research. *J. Educ. Psychol.*, 1963, *54*, 45–51.

Smith, B. O. A concept of teaching. *Tchrs. Coll. Rec.*, 1960, *61*, 229–241.

Stanley, J. C. Interactions of organisms with experimental variables as a key to the integration of organismic and variable-manipulating research. In Edith M. Huddleston, ed. *Yearb*. Ames, Iowa: Nat. Council on Measurement in Educ., 1960, pp. 7–14.

Stone, G. C., and G. S. Leavitt. A schematic analysis of teacher-pupil interaction. Personal communication, 1955. Cited in N. L. Gage, ed. *Handbook of research on teaching*. Amer. Educ. Res. Assn. Chicago: Rand McNally, 1963, p. 125.

Tiedeman, D. V., and M. Cogan. New horizons in educational research. *Phi Delta Kappan*, 1958, *39*, 286–291.

Underwood, B. J. *Psychological research*. New York: Appleton, 1957.

CHAPTER 10

Instruction and the Conditions of Learning

~

Ausubel, D. P. *The psychology of meaningful verbal learning.* New York: Grune and Stratton, 1963.

Bousfield, W. A. The problem of meaning in verbal learning. In C. N. Cofer, ed. *Verbal learning and verbal behavior.* New York: McGraw-Hill, 1961, pp. 81–91.

Bruner, J. S. The act of discovery. *Harv. Educ. Rev.,* 1961, *31,* 21–32.

————, J. J. Goodnow, and G. A. Austin. *A study of thinking.* New York: Wiley, 1956.

Gagné, R. M. *Conditions of learning.* New York: Holt, 1965.

————. Problem solving. In A. W. Melton, ed. *Categories of human learning.* New York: Academic Press, 1964, pp. 293–317.

————, and R. C. Bolles. A review of factors in learning efficiency. In E. Galanter, ed. *Automatic teaching: The state of the art.* New York: Wiley, 1959, Chap. 2.

Gagné, R. M., and E. C. Smith, Jr. A study of the effects of verbalization on problem solving. *J. Exp. Psychol.,* 1962, *63,* 12–18.

Glaser, R. Psychology and instructional technology. In R. Glaser, ed. *Training research and education.* Pittsburgh, Pa.: University of Pittsburgh Press, 1962, Chap. 1.

Hull, C. L. Quantitative aspects of the evolution of concepts. *Psychol. Monogr.,* 1920, *28* (Whole No. 123).

Jenkins, J. J. Mediated associations: Paradigms and situations. In C. N. Cofer and B. S. Musgrave, eds. *Verbal behavior and learning.* New York: McGraw-Hill, 1963, Chap. 6.

Katona, G. *Organizing and memorizing.* New York: Columbia University Press, 1940.

Kendler, H. H., and T. S. Kendler. Effect of verbalization on reversal shifts in children. *Science,* 1961, No. 141, 1619–1620.

Lindsley, D. B. Psychophysiology and motivation. In M. R. Jones, ed. *Nebraska symposium on motivation.* Lincoln: University of Nebraska Press, 1957, pp. 44–105.

McGeoch, J. A., and A. L. Irion. *The psychology of human learning.* New York: Longmans, Green, 1952.

Melton, A. W., ed. *Categories of human learning.* New York: Academic Press, 1964.

Mowrer, O. H. *Learning theory and behavior.* New York: Wiley, 1960.

Skinner, B. F. *The behavior of organisms; an experimental analysis.* New York: Appleton, 1938.

———. *Verbal behavior.* New York: Appleton, 1957.

Tolman, E. C. There is more than one kind of learning. *Psychol. Rev.,* 1949, *56,* 144–155.

Underwood, B. J. An orientation for research on thinking. *Psychol. Rev.,* 1949, *56,* 209–220.

Woodworth, R. S. *Dynamics of behavior.* New York: Holt, 1958.

———. *Experimental psychology.* New York: Holt, 1938.

Index

~

HESS, H. F., 346
HEYNS, R. W., 351
HILGARD, E. R., 1, 143, 153, 154, 158, 321, 359, 364
HILLIX, W. A., 150, 360
HOBAN, C. F., 58, 348
HOFFMAN, F. K., 117, 353
HOLLAND, J. G., 363
HOLLAND, J. L., 163, 359, 361
HOLTZMAN, W., 163, 359
HORN, E., 121, 354
HOROWITZ, M. M., 55, 348
HOUSTON, J. P., 78, 348
HOVLAND, C. I., 28, 164, 239, 262, 263, 343, 361, 365, 366
HUDDLESTON, E. M., 366
HUGGINS, W. H., 158, 358
HUGHES, M., 117, 119, 122, 354
HULL, C. L., 149, 311, 367
HUNT, D. E., 56, 348
HUNT, E. B., 159, 165, 359
HUNT, J. McV., 159, 359
HYDEN, H., 348

Identification, 7–9, 15
Idiosyncratic drive pattern:
  and academic ability, 287–288
  defined, 284
  and educational set, 288–289
INHELDER, B., 229, 364
Instruction:
  and cognitive theory, 56–59
  definitions of, 34, 143–145, 181–183
  formal and informal, 183–185
  and learning, 295–296
  requirements for, 300–303, 309–310
  See also Teaching
Instructional gestalt:
  illustrative design for, 281–284
  paradigm for, 264–274
Instructional innovation, 330–332
Instructional objectives, 145–148, 203–206, 262, 278, 317–319, 334–337
  See also Criteria and Output
Instructional press, 285–286
Instructional techniques: See Teaching techniques

Instructional theories, early:
  dimensions of, 6
  identification in, 7–9, 15
  learner behavior in, 9–10
  moral development in, 12–14
  motivation in, 14–15
  presuppositions underlying, 4–5
  reinforcement in, 11–12
  relevance of, 19–23
  school versus home in, 15–17
Instructional theories, particularized versus generalized, 329–330
Instructional theory and learning theory: See Learning theory
Instructor: See Teacher
Integrative reconciliation, 240–243
Internal manipulation:
  concept formation and, 72
  dimensions of, 60–61
  symbolization and, 61
  See also Concept formation
IRION, A. L., 306, 368

JACKSON, P. W., 163, 269, 359, 365
JAHNKE, J. C., 33, 137, 138, 139, 329
JAMES, W., 7, 13, 17, 18, 150, 342
JENKINS, J. J., 311, 367
JENKINS, W. A., 345, 346, 348, 349
JENSEN, B. T., 174, 359
JENSEN, G. E., 353
JERSILD, A. T., 113, 121, 354
JOHANNSEN, W., 84, 348
JOHNS, T. E., 125, 352
JOHNSON, E. S., 77, 348
JOHNSON, M. W., 117, 119, 354
JOHNSON, R. C., 348
JOHNSON, W., 72, 348
JONES, A., 159, 359
JONES, E. E., 221, 364
JONES, M. R., 360, 367

KATONA, G., 158, 311, 359, 367
KEEDY, M. L., 58, 348
KELLOGG, W. N., 195, 362
KENDLER, H. H., 311, 367
KENDLER, T. S., 311, 367
KENNEDY, J. L., 153
KERSH, B. Y., 66, 348

Research methodology:
  control-group comparisons, 27–29
  critique of, 26–30, 261–264
  multivariate analysis in, 263–264
  observation as, 113–136
RESNICK, L. B., 56, 57, 79, 350
RESTLE, F., 94, 350
Retention, 223–224, 233–235, 253–255
RHINE, R. J., 61, 80, 350
RICHARDSON, S. K., 55, 350
RIOPELLE, A. J., 94, 350
ROBINSON, D. W., 55, 350
ROE, A., 84, 350
ROE, K. V., 84, 350
ROGERS, C. R., 33, 35, 36, 46, 163, 262,
  270, 318, 319, 320, 322, 323, 326, 329,
  335, 344, 366
ROKEACH, M., 164, 361
ROSEN, S., 105, 354
ROSENCRANZ, H. A., 124, 352
Rote learning, 38, 171–174, 319
RUNKEL, P. J., 263, 366
RYAN, J. J., 117, 354
RYANS, D. G., 113, 263, 355, 366

SANFORD, N., 15, 342, 357, 360, 361
SAUPE, J. L., 113, 118, 121, 122, 123, 353
SCHEERER, C., 358, 362
SCHLOSBERG, H., 187, 363
SCHRODER, H. M., 56, 348
SCHULZ, R. W., 158, 361
SCHWAB, J. J., 48, 57, 344, 350
SCHWICKERATH, R., 8, 17, 342
Sensitivity training, 51–53
Set: See Educational set and Learning
  set
Shaping up: See Conceptualization,
  validation of
SHEFFIELD, F. O., 28, 262, 263, 343, 366
SHERIF, M., 56, 164, 350, 361
SHERMAN, G., 200, 363
SIEGEL, L., 27, 30, 32, 259, 260, 262, 264,
  272, 279, 281, 288, 329, 343, 366
SIEGEL, L. C., 32, 259, 260, 264, 279, 329,
  366
Simulation, 49–50
SINNOTT, E. W., 77, 351

SKINNER, B. F., 50, 184, 186, 196, 206,
  300, 344, 363, 368
SMALLENBURG, C., 55, 341
SMITH, B. O., 33, 86, 89, 93, 113, 114,
  117, 118, 119, 122, 134, 211, 213, 214,
  263, 311, 343, 351, 355, 365, 366
SMITH, E. C., JR., 347, 367
SMITTER, F. W., 55, 350
SOAR, R. S., 118, 353, 355
SOLOMON, D., 118, 119, 121, 355
SOLOMON, L. N., 49, 344
SOLOMON, R. L., 153
SPAULDING, R. L., 118, 119, 355
SPENCE, K. W., 149, 361
STAATS, A. W., 66, 351
STANLEY, J. C., 26, 27, 264, 342, 366
STEIN, M. I., 360
STERN, G. G., 360
STEWART, C., 162, 361
STONE, G. C., 263, 366
STRATEMEYER, F., 351
Student:
  behavior of, 107–108, 120–121
  characteristics of, 325–326
  See also Learning
Student-teacher interaction: See Teach-
  ing techniques
Subsumption:
  and educational set, 288–289
  implementation of, in teaching, 237–
  244
  kinds of, 225–226
  principle of, 222
  role of, in forgetting, 223–224
  role of, in learning, 222–223
SUCHMAN, J. R., 48, 344
SUPPES, P., 157, 165, 361
SUTHERLAND, R. L., 361

TAYLOR, C. W., 163, 361
TAYLOR, D. W., 153, 163, 361
TAYLOR, H., 351
Teacher:
  attitudes of, 45–46
  characteristics of, 326
  functions of, 303–308
Teaching, 118–120, 322–324
  behavioral theory and, 186–187